BISHOP IN THE DOCK

THE IRISH ABROAD

General Editor: Ruan O'Donnell, University of Limerick

This new series aims to publish short biographies of Irish men and women who made their mark outside their native country. Accounts of those who settled permanently overseas will be published along with the life stories of temporary residents and involuntary emigrants. Expatriates of all types will be considered whether explorers, travellers, military personnel, colonial pioneers, members of religious orders, professionals, politicians, revolutionaries, exiles or convicts. While it is envisaged that the majority of the subjects would have gone overseas during the early modern and modern period, persons from different times may also be deemed appropriate for inclusion. Most titles will concern the Irish in North America, the former territories of the British Empire (including Australasia) and Great Britain, although it is intended that biographies of those who journeyed to Spanish America, the West Indies, Africa, Continental Europe and other non-English speaking sectors will form part of the series. Men and women of Irish extraction will also merit inclusion if it is evident that their perceived ethnicity and family origins played a significant part in their careers. A number of autobiographies will be selected for republication with critical introductions by leading scholars.

Also in the Irish Abroad series from Irish Academic Press:

Thomas Francis Meagher
The Making of an Irish American
John M. Hearne and Rory T. Cornish (eds)

Through American and Irish Wars
The Life and Times of General Thomas W. Sweeny
Jack Morgan

Bishop in the Dock
The Sedition Trial of James Liston in New Zealand
Rory Sweetman

Bishop Liston (wearing mitre, fourth from right) at the opening of St Mary of the Angels, Wellington, 26 March 1922. New Zealand Freelance

Bishop in the Dock

The Sedition Trial of James Liston in New Zealand

RORY SWEETMAN

University of Otago

IRISH ACADEMIC PRESS

DUBLIN • PORTLAND, OR

First published 1997
Auckland University Press
University of Auckland

This edition published in 2007 by
IRISH ACADEMIC PRESS
44, Northumberland Road, Dublin 4, Ireland

and in the United States of America by
IRISH ACADEMIC PRESS
c/o ISBS, Suite 300, 920 NE 58th Avenue
Portland, Oregon 97213-3786

WEBSITE: **www.iap.ie**

British Library Cataloguing in Publication Data
An entry can be found on request

ISBN 0 7165 3396 0 (cloth)
ISBN 978 0 7165 3396 2
ISBN 0 7165 3397 9 (paper)
ISBN 978 0 7165 3397 9

Library of Congress Cataloging-in-Publication Data
An entry can be found on request

Typeset by FiSH Books, Enfield, Middx.
Printed by Biddles Ltd., Kings Lynn, Norfolk.

To E. R. S. (1922–1992)

Contents

Abbreviations

Archives

ACDA	Auckland Catholic Diocesan Archives
APF	Archives of Propaganda Fide, Rome
APL	Auckland Public Library
ATL	Alexander Turnbull Library, Wellington
CCDA	Christchurch Catholic Diocesan Archives
CLO	Crown Law Office
CO	Colonial Office, Public Records Office, London
DCDA	Dunedin Catholic Diocesan Archives
ICR	Irish College, Rome
MCDA	Maitland Catholic Diocesan Archives
NA	National Archives, Wellington
NLI	National Library of Ireland
PRO	Public Records Office, London
TCD	Trinity College, Dublin
WCAA	Wellington Catholic Archdiocesan Archives

Series and Periodicals

AS	*Auckland Star*
AWN	*Auckland Weekly News*
EP	*Evening Post*, Wellington
ES	*Evening Star*, Dunedin
LT	*Lyttelton Times*
MDT	*Manawatu Daily Times*
NZFL	*New Zealand Free Lance*
NZH	*New Zealand Herald*
NZO	*New Zealand Observer*
NZPD	*New Zealand Parliamentary Debates*
NZS	*New Zealand Sentinel*
NZT	*New Zealand Times*
SDN	*Southland Daily News*
WC	*Wanganui Chronicle*
WT	*Waikato Times*

Acknowledgements

It is a great pleasure to me to see Bishop in the Dock once again in print, for which I feel a lively gratitude to Ruan O'Donnell, Lisa Hyde and all at Irish Academic Press. Apart from a few minor corrections the text is as it first appeared. It will take this opportunity to pay a few debts of honour, first and foremost to Jacques and Anne Straetmans, and their children Thomas, Margaux and Philippe, whose hospitality and friendship in both London and Belgium has become legendary in the Southern Hemisphere. During my research visits to Ireland I was given a warm welcome by Francis and Patricia Bailey (Killiney), Fr Mark Noonan (All Hallows College), and the Christian Brothers community at Synge Street, Dublin. The Kelly clan of Kellys' Wood, New Ross, also coped splendidly with my regular visits, and helped me greatly towards a better understanding of Wexford life in all its exhausting complexity.

Rory Sweetman
July 2006

Series Editor Preface

Bishop James Liston secured an unusual place in British Empire and Irish history in May 1922 when he was tried for sedition in an Auckland court. Although frequently criticized and openly resented by Empire Loyalists, it was a sensation for a Catholic bishop to face prosecution for his public statements and activities. Liston, a New Zealander-born, had raised the ire of the Dominion's pro-British community by making inflammatory comments in the Town Hall of Auckland on St. Patrick's Day, 1922. New Zealand's Irish community and Liston's narrower Catholic constituency was a substantial element in the population, even if collectively overshadowed by the major Hibernian presence in Australia. Clearly, a coadjutor bishop's views carried much weight in New Zealand political circles, as well as on the Imperial stage where the colonial administration was anxious to be represented in the aftermath of the Great War.

Using emotive but factually correct information, Liston moved quickly from a vehement denunciation of the 'artificial' Great Famine to remind his audience of persons recently 'murdered by foreign troops' in Ireland. The use of the term 'foreign' in reference to British military forces in Ireland understandably irritated many New Zealanders. This was the same army which had fought alongside the ANZACs during the First World War and ostensibly stood ready to safeguard the security of the antipodean colonies. While it is unlikely that many understood that the word 'foreign' had been lifted from the 1916 Proclamation of the Irish Republic, most readily grasped the allusion to the notorious atrocities perpetrated by the 'Black and Tans' during the Anglo-Irish War of 1919-21. The catalogue of British wrongs condemned by Liston included the execution of the rebel 'martyrs' during the 1916 Rising and the death on hunger strike of Terence MacSwiney. The unmentioned but implied brutality of 'Bloody Sunday' cast the British Army in a very different light to that preferred by its champions.

As the speech continued it was evident that Liston broadly sympathized with the viewpoint of Eamon de Valera, the bete noir of the conservative press owing to his opposition to some of the terms negotiated by his associates in London. For reasons explained in detail by Rory Sweetman, Liston's comment could and were construed as a critique of the Anglo-Irish Treaty. His acknowledgement that 'Ireland has not got all she asked for ... and is determined to have the whole of it' clearly permitted subversive interpretation. This was far from the official line of the Catholic hierarchy in the Empire, even if its Irish contingent had moved much closer to the nationalist position following the Conscription Crisis of 1918. Partition, Liston implied, was a temporary condition that would be rectified in due course.

The Town Hall speech ignited a furore in New Zealand where social, cultural and political fault lines all but guaranteed a divisive debate. Sweetman's nuanced exposition of the background to the Liston trial illuminates important aspects of the lives of Irish migrants and their second generation in 1920s New Zealand. The fact that a man of Clare parentage could excite such fervour in the furthest reaches of the British Empire serves to remind that 'Irishness' had a much broader meaning in the early Twentieth century than generally entertained.

Dr Ruan O'Donnell
University of Limerick
August 2006

Preface

This book stems from the last chapter of my doctoral thesis, but has grown almost out of recognition. So rich were the sources, and so intriguing the tale they told, that what began as a brief essay has assumed its present size. Bishop Liston's papers, his lawyer's diaries, and the case files built up by both the Police Department and the Crown Law Office were all made available to me. Other pieces of the jigsaw were located in London, Dublin and Rome. Only Mr Justice Stringer's notebooks appear not to have survived the seventy-five years since the dramatic events of early 1922.

Readers should not expect to find a biography of James Liston in these pages. Nor does the book attempt to dissect New Zealand's turbulent ethnic and religious history in the first few decades of this century. Rather, my aim has been to tell the story of an unprecedented incident in our past, now almost completely forgotten.

Many debts of honour were incurred during the several years of research and writing, and it is my pleasure to acknowledge them now. Pride of place must go to Professor David Fieldhouse of Jesus College, Cambridge, my ever patient and supportive doctoral supervisor. Also in Cambridge, Katherine Chubb spent many a long evening deciphering tales of the misdeeds of 'the priest Kelly'. Memories of Dr James Kelly were also supplied by the late Dan and Winnie Davin, along with a warm welcome whenever I was in Oxford. Hospitality in London was generously supplied by Doug and Reiko Howland, and in Sydney by John Plater. In Rome, the Society of Mary and the Irish College were most supportive.

Thanks for access to the various Catholic archives go to the hierarchy, and especially to Bishop Denis Browne. Among the diocesan archivists who put up with my persistent demands were Sr Margaret D'Ath and Miss Patricia O'Connor (Wellington), Fr Kevin Clark (Christchurch), Fr Bruce Bolland (Auckland) and Monsignor Peter Mee (Dunedin). Brother Gerard Hogg SM gave me full access to the Society of Mary's archives in both Greenmeadows and Wellington.

I would like to thank Judith Hayward, the librarian of the Crown

Law Office, for her consideration, also the late Rolland O'Regan for permission to consult his father's papers. The National Library gave me its inaugural research fellowship, during which year the Alexander Turnbull Library provided a welcoming workplace. I am grateful to the judges of the Sir Keith Sinclair History Prize for 1995 who chose my manuscript for the award.

Those who had early drafts inflicted upon them were Brian Healy, Professor Don Akenson, Philip Lanigan, Fr Michael O'Meeghan SM, Dr Hugh Laracy, Frank Rogers (who also compiled the index), Dr Allan Davidson, John Stacpoole, Fr Kevin Roach SM, and Louis Campbell. The faults that remain are mine alone. For encouragement when the going got tough, Richard Hill, Jane Tucker, Helen Milne, Peter Haynes, Patrick Stokes, Elizabeth and the late Michael O'Flaherty, Vivien Kirk, Dr Clarence Beeby, Dr Chris Pugsley, Samuel Montgomery, Dr Helen Reynolds, Jacques Straetmans, Fr Dennis Lennon, Fr Séamus de Vál, Sally Wallis and Julia Millen all deserve a mention in despatches. My final thanks go to Anne, who sent me off to Ireland twenty years ago, and to Biddy who helped me to survive there. This book could not have been written without the inspiration of the late Fr Ernest Simmons, the doyen of religious archivists in New Zealand.

Rory Sweetman
May 1997

1

That Fatal Occasion of Temptation

Ireland, my Ireland, it's Oh! but the heart of me
Bounds at thy name and burns at thy wrong;
Ireland, my Ireland, it's proud every part of me
Thrills at thy spirits of beauty and song.

St Patrick's Night concert programme,
New Zealand Herald, 17 March 1922

In the gathering gloom of Friday evening, 17 March 1922, streams of people, eager, expectant, good humoured, flowed towards the Auckland Town Hall. The weather had finally cleared after a day of squally showers. There was a hum of anticipation among the largely Irish Catholic throng. On the first St Patrick's Day since a form of Irish independence had been achieved, the pent-up emotion of the last few years could finally be released. The old people rejoiced at having lived to see this day; the young were swept along on the tide of enthusiasm. Raised to consider Ireland as 'Home', they had inherited a passionate feeling for the land of their fathers and mothers. Over the coming weekend many of them would celebrate their Celtic heritage by marching, dancing and singing in honour of Ireland's national saint.

After six years of increasingly bloody conflict, and to almost everyone's surprise, peace had recently broken out in Ireland. Britain's Prime Minister, David Lloyd George, had at last come to terms with the Sinn Feiners, those Irish nationalists whom he had formerly denounced as a 'murder gang'.[1] The signing of the Anglo–Irish Treaty some three months previously ended more than seven centuries of British rule. The Union Jack was hauled down from the flagpole above Dublin Castle. British troops handed over their barracks to the soldiers of the newly created Irish Free State. While the Six Counties of Northern Ireland remained outside the settlement (temporarily, it was hoped), the historic fight for Irish national freedom seemed to be over at last.

However, in the early months of 1922 the cables brought contradictory and confusing news to trouble the Irish overseas.[2] A section of the Sinn Fein leadership under Eamon de Valera had rejected the treaty, and several Irish Republican Army units shared his hostility to the terms agreed in London. Would the growing division in Irish ranks end in renewed violence? Dail Eireann (the Irish parliament) had accepted the accord and all seemed set for its popular endorsement in the forthcoming elections. De Valera was reported as promising not to oppose the emergent Irish Free State, while Sir James Craig and Michael Collins (the rival leaders of North and South) had agreed to co-operate in preserving peace in their respective regions.

Despite these uncertainties, the keynote of the Auckland celebrations was relief and joy. Similar gatherings were taking place all over New Zealand and in every other country of the Irish diaspora. (A bishop in Australia boasted that the Irish formed a cordon around the globe with a wider sphere than the British Empire itself.)[3] For Irish colonials it was a day to celebrate their difference from other citizens, to remember and to romanticise the land that retained such a powerful grip on their emotions and identity.

Australian historians have traced how from the 1890s the largely secular and occasionally anarchic celebration of St Patrick's Day was taken over, tamed, and turned respectable by the Catholic clergy.[4] The focus was gradually shifted to a mythic era when Ireland had earned its reputation as the island of saints and scholars; the new heroes were figures from the dim and distant past, rather than the bloody and controversial present.

A similar phenomenon occurred in New Zealand. From the late 1860s Auckland's Irish community had marked the sacred day with a huge picnic in the Domain. In 1879 the Hibernian Society added a sports meeting and an evening ball to the festivities. Episcopal disapproval of dancing in Lent soon led to the replacement of the ball by a national concert, with the profits devoted to reducing church debts. A desire to avoid antagonising the wider community was evident. The resultant inoffensive blend of Celtic pathos and sentiment was reflected in a medley of saccharine songs and speeches.

The Auckland Town Hall as it was in 1922. The Grey statue was later deemed to be an obstruction to traffic and was removed to Albert Park. APL

Many of the pieces and performers could scarcely be called Irish. Such offerings revealed how remote and insubstantial Irish realities were becoming for the colonial children of Erin.[5]

From the turn of the century, a new generation of Irish nationalists, many immigrant clergy among them, came to prefer the shillelagh to the shamrock – and not merely for symbolic purposes. By 1914 the constitutional campaign for Irish home rule had ended in stalemate and frustration. Sectarian and ethnic conflict spread throughout the British Empire as the Great War dragged out its bloody length. Even after the guns fell silent on the Western Front, domestic battle continued to rage both in Ireland and in the Antipodes. Following the suppression of Dail Eireann in September 1919, guerrilla warfare by the IRA provoked an increasingly repressive response by the British Government. While colonial opinion was divided over Ireland's right to self-determination (and the threat this posed to imperial unity and security), the deepening Irish crisis to 1921 exercised a horrified fascination.[6]

In this peculiar post-war climate, the songs and speeches of St Patrick's Day received extra scrutiny. Clerical control of the celebrations turned out to be a mixed blessing. Marches and concerts in Australia became annual gestures of defiance towards an Anglo-

Bishop Cleary (right) resplendent in military chaplain's uniform. His fellow chaplain is Patrick Clune, Catholic Archbishop of Perth. ACDA

phile, Protestant establishment, with almost every city witnessing a set-piece battle between the critics and the supporters of Sinn Fein. Events in Melbourne, the cockpit of much of this conflict, generated a bitterness that poisoned community relations long after the Irish issue faded from the political foreground.[7]

Despite a sizeable Irish Catholic component, Auckland was largely to escape contagion from the sectarian disease across the Tasman. Its Catholic bishop from 1910 to 1929, the Irish-born Henry Cleary, was able to insulate his diocese from much of the divisiveness experienced elsewhere. Cleary had impeccable credentials as a loyal citizen, having backed up his frequent jingoistic utterances with service on the Western Front as a chaplain. (A prominent member of the Returned Soldiers' Association, Cleary was made an OBE in 1919.) From 1918 he opposed any advocacy of Sinn Fein in his diocese, blocked the raising of funds for Irish political purposes, and banned the use of provocative symbols and flags during Catholic ceremonies and marches.[8]

Accordingly, Catholic and Irish functions in Auckland gave little grounds for loyalist complaint. No fiery Irish speeches or resolutions were permitted to disturb the peace, while Cleary insisted on the national anthem being played on every possible occasion. In 1921, at the height of the Anglo–Irish war, Bishops Cleary and Liston (his new coadjutor) sat silent through the entire St Patrick's Night proceedings. By contrast, almost every other large centre produced a strongly worded resolution condemning British policy in Ireland, while in Dunedin the new Catholic bishop, James Whyte, got into trouble for a speech strongly critical of Lloyd George and his administration.[9]

What did Auckland Catholics think of their spiritual leader's non-provocation policy? While they accepted his refusal to allow the flaunting of Sinn Fein emblems during celebrations that were by now more Catholic than Irish in content anyway, there was much suppressed feeling.[10] Was it a coincidence that, with Cleary away in Ireland, the St Patrick's Day festivities of 1922 were to be celebrated in a way that provoked a head-on collision with the establishment he had courted so assiduously?

The achievement of Irish national freedom was expected to result in a flourishing of Gaelic culture which, its champions believed, would provide a healthy contrast to sordid British materialism. Patrick Power, the Catholic Dean of Hawera, boldly predicted that his country, once free, 'would show the English people what civilisation meant'.[11] There was little sign of this renaissance in the Auckland concert programme; rather, it offered a predictable mixture of song, dance and recitation. The only novel item was to be an address from the new coadjutor bishop, James Michael Liston.[12]

By eight o'clock the Auckland Town Hall was overflowing. Almost 3000 people packed the stalls and filled the galleries. Many others went home disappointed, unable to get in. When proceedings began, the expected note of Irish triumphalism was struck at once. Instead of the customary opening verse of 'God Save the King' from the orchestra, a choir of 400 children delivered a rousing version of 'A Nation Once Again'.

When boyhood's fire was in my blood,
I read of ancient freemen,
For Greece and Rome who bravely stood,
Three hundred men and three men.
And then I prayed I yet might see
Our fetters rent in twain,

James Liston on his first day as a bishop. ACDA

And Ireland, long a province, be
A nation once again.

Loud applause greeted this item, which enjoyed the status of an unofficial Irish national anthem. 'Sing it again. And sing it again', begged a woman in the gallery (with tears and pleading in her voice, according to one reporter). The children obliged with another chorus.[13] Soloist James Lonergan then treated the audience to 'O'Donnell Aboo', a stirring ballad celebrating one of the rare victories of Celt over Saxon.

Sacred the cause that Clanconnell's defending
The altars we kneel at, the homes of our sires;
Ruthless the ruin the foe is extending
Midnight is red with the plunderer's fires!

On with O'Donnell then,
Fight the old fight again;
Sons of Tirconnell all valiant and true!
Make that false Saxon feel
Erin's avenging steel!
Strike for your country now – O'Donnell aboo![14]

Miss Mary Higgins followed with the gentler ballad, 'Dublin Bay'. The sentimental nature of such items had a deep meaning for many in the audience, for whom Dublin Bay was the last glimpse of their native land. Over the previous century emigration had become painfully familiar to the Irish. Unemployment, famine, land hunger, eviction, political and religious oppression – all had contributed to the outpouring of humanity which halved the Irish population inside fifty years and scattered expatriate communities across the globe. In some parts of the province of Munster, two out of every three young people could expect to grow to maturity in a foreign land. Bishop Liston's parents, both born in famine-stricken Munster, were among those who had left Ireland in the mid-1860s.[15]

The sombre mood continued as Thomas Harris stood to recite 'The Little Irish Mother'. When he sat down there were few dry eyes in the house. Despite its maudlin sentiments, the poem touched the hearts of many listeners.

There's a Little Irish Mother – and her head is bowed and gray,
And she's lonesome when the evening shadows fall;
Near the fire she 'do be thinkin'', all the 'childer' are away,
And their silent pictures watch her from the wall.[16]

A quartet of songs by Thomas Moore and a lively Irish jig were more joyfully received by the audience, which loudly demanded and obtained encores from every contributor. One old woman, lost in her enthusiasm, stood at the end of every item and waved her handkerchief at the performers. The jig immediately brought her to her feet, and her interpretation of the dance received almost as much attention as the performers.[17]

Just before the interval Bishop Liston rose to speak. For most of those present it was the first opportunity to hear their new spiritual leader, who had arrived in Auckland from Otago barely fifteen months earlier. Before them stood a vigorous, wiry man of medium height, forty years of age, black-haired, eagle-eyed, sharp of nose and chin. His grave demeanour and formal manner commanded immediate respect. Shy and retiring by nature, Liston had been far from eager for the honour, allowing a fortnight to pass before accepting the organising committee's invitation. He finally agreed to speak at the last possible minute, on the very day the programme was to be printed. As he explained later, 'I was not out for the limelight'.[18]

Liston overcame his reluctance for several reasons. As president of the St Patrick's Day celebrations committee, he probably felt obliged to assist with the evening's entertainment. While an episcopal address on St Patrick's Night was not an Auckland tradition (at least not during Cleary's reign), Liston's friend and colleague, Bishop Whyte, was shocking Dunedin loyalists with his forthright views on Irish matters. Concerned at the press reports coming out of Ireland, Liston saw it as his duty to interpret Irish events in as reassuring a way as possible. He later claimed to have spoken 'so that the audience might realise the position of affairs in Ireland and that those who have nothing to guide them might know that there was another side to the story'.[19]

Liston may also have relished the chance to remind Auckland Catholics of all that they owed to Ireland, to stiffen their backbones against the enemies of their race and faith. It was widely held by southern Catholics that their fellows in the north needed corrective training in this regard. Liston described the Auckland malady as 'that wretched critical spirit that we all deplore up here'.[20]

Did Liston's late decision to speak influence the content of his address? There was little time to consult those more closely attuned to the likely reactions of his audience, both within and beyond the Town Hall. Liston believed that he had 'weighed his words carefully', and his detailed notes for the speech were exhibited in the subsequent court case. As it emerged, his principal preparation for the address consisted of a quick hunt for serviceable phrases through old issues of the *New Zealand Tablet*.[21]

Liston spoke calmly and deliberately to a hushed audience. The acoustics of the Town Hall were excellent,[22] and witnesses later agreed on his subdued, even-toned, unemotional delivery. His peculiar style of speech, a drawl which had withstood both elocution lessons and a recent nasal operation, gave his words an added intensity.[23]

Liston began by drawing a parallel between himself and St Patrick, the bishop who had brought Christianity to Ireland. He cited his Irish descent and episcopal office as giving him the right to speak that evening. When describing how his Irish parents had come to emigrate to New Zealand, Liston sounded a bitter note. Were the pathetic lines of 'The Little Irish Mother' still echoing in his mind?

> My parents were driven from the land in which they were born and in which they would have been content to live. Why were they driven out? Because their foreign masters did not want Irish men and women peopling their own land, but wanted to use it as a cattle ranch for snobs of the Empire.
>
> So my father and my little Irish mother, and thousands of others, had to go. They came to this country with the memory kept sacred of their privations and wrongs. They have left to us the sacred traditions of their sorrow.[24]

Liston next proudly declared his dual allegiance to Ireland and New Zealand, voicing the satisfaction felt by his audience at the recent happy turn of Irish events.

> I am a native of New Zealand and I love my country very well. In every land the children of Ireland this day are gathered by some common and holy impulse to rejoice that at long last they have won some measure of freedom and to hope for a complete deliverance from the house of bondage.

Exactly how he expected this deliverance to be completed was left in doubt. In December 1921, the Catholic Archbishop of Wellington, Francis Redwood, had greeted the signing of the Anglo–Irish Treaty with the claim that England had made peace only because it did not have sufficient economic strength to continue the fight.[25] While this sneer drew public protest at the time, Redwood had at least conceded that the treaty granted all that Ireland wanted. By his oblique reference to the continued partition of the

Archbishop Redwood of Wellington, known for his advocacy of Irish nationalism. NZFL

country, Liston now appeared to devalue the settlement, issuing what seemed like a call to arms – with divine sanction – to achieve that measure of freedom still denied to Ireland.

> I do not say for one moment that Ireland has got all she asked for, and all that her sons died for, but she has got the first instalment of her freedom, and is determined to have the whole of it. I say that because the omnipotent hand of God made Ireland a nation, and while grass grows and water flows there will be men in Ireland and women too to fight, and even die, that God's desires may be realised.

He then dwelt at length on the role played by the Irish in world history. They had brought their talents and spirituality to every country that received them. 'Above all Ireland has been a builder of Empire, not for self, but for others; not for filthy lucre, but for God's cause, honour and freedom.' This offensive allusion to the Empire most New Zealanders held dear was followed by another unflattering comparison in verse (which no press reporter seems to have noted).

> *We have robbed no race,*
> *We have wronged no land.*
> *We have never oppressed the weak.*
> *And this in the face of Heaven*
> *Is the nobler thing to speak.*[26]

While predicting a happy ending to the Irish Free State's troubles, Liston contrasted these with the complex problems facing the mighty British Empire, 'which still claims to be the greatest one'. A couple of his listeners swore later that the bishop boasted of the Irish having 'beaten' the British Empire.

Subsequent critics of his speech dwelt as much on what Liston left unsaid as on his controversial utterances. In particular, his attitude to the Anglo–Irish Treaty remained unclear. The Irish Catholic community's muted welcome of the London accord had drawn earlier press criticism in Auckland. This apparent equivocation was due partly to Liston's decision (on the advice of the Australian Catholic bishops) to defer celebrations until the treaty had been formally endorsed by the Irish electorate.[27]

Over the previous three months the New Zealand daily newspapers had competed with each other in heaping abuse on Eamon de Valera. He was portrayed as a wrecker, an irreconcilable, an ideologue who was dragging Ireland towards civil war.[28] In now praising the dissident leader, although not by name, Liston seemed to endorse

Contemporary cartoons portrayed Eamon de Valera as the principal threat to Irish peace. NZH

those bent on disturbing the fragile Anglo–Irish peace. The bishop's confidence in de Valera contrasted sharply with his evident distrust of British politicians.

> It seems to me providential that when Ireland is faced with difficulties the man who has carried us so far and enabled us to win is there to see that the rulers are not duped by England.

The real sting of Liston's address came in its tail. All his previous comments, apart from the bitter aside on the 'snobs of Empire', had been prepared in advance. Not so his final remarks. On that very afternoon he had received a printed memorial card from Ireland listing the names of those who had died in the recent national struggle. Liston made a late decision to incorporate it into his speech. In what sounded like a closing prayer, he continued:

> We must not forget the martyrs who died in the fighting in 1916, that glorious Easter. I have here a list of 155 men who during and since 1916 have died for Ireland. 16 were executed by shooting in 1916, 52 were killed while fighting during the Easter week in 1916, 7 died on hunger strike – including Terence MacSwiney the Lord Mayor of Cork – 8 were executed by hanging, 12 by shooting, and 57, including three priests, were murdered by foreign troops.

Liston's audience would have had no difficulty in recognising the notorious 'Black and Tans' in that last explosive sentence. Recruited from the pool of demobilised soldiers in post-war England, the 'Black and Tans' were sent to the Irish trouble spots during 1920–21 to strengthen the ranks of the Royal Irish Constabulary.

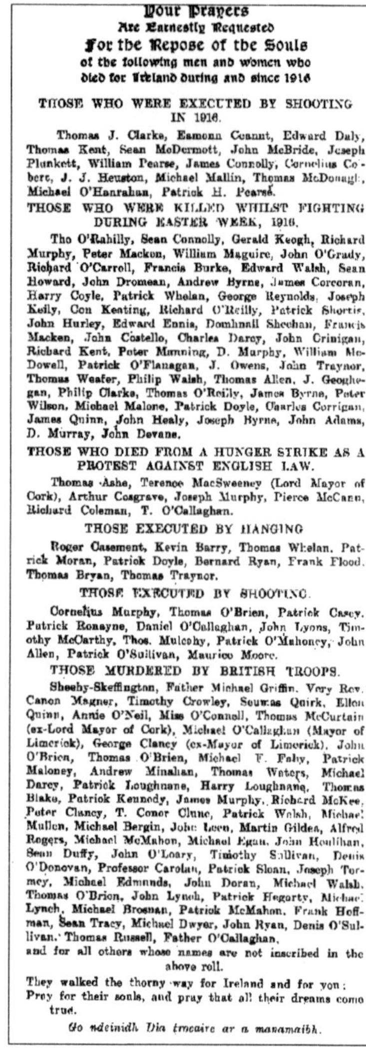

Your Prayers
Are Earnestly Requested
For the Repose of the Souls
of the following men and women who
died for Ireland during and since 1916

THOSE WHO WERE EXECUTED BY SHOOTING IN 1916.

Thomas J. Clarke, Eamonn Ceannt, Edward Daly, Thomas Kent, Sean McDermott, John McBride, Joseph Plunkett, William Pearse, James Connolly, Cornelius Colbert, J. J. Heuston, Michael Mallin, Thomas McDonagh, Michael O'Hanrahan, Patrick H. Pearse.

THOSE WHO WERE KILLED WHILST FIGHTING DURING EASTER WEEK, 1916.

The O'Rahilly, Sean Connolly, Gerald Keogh, Richard Murphy, Peter Macken, William Maguire, John O'Grady, Richard O'Carroll, Francis Burke, Edward Walsh, Sean Howard, John Dromean, Andrew Byrne, James Corcoran, Harry Coyle, Patrick Whelan, George Reynolds, Joseph Keily, Con Keating, Richard O'Reilly, Patrick Shortis, John Hurley, Edward Ennis, Domhnall Sheehan, Francis Macken, John Costello, Charles Darcy, John Crinigan, Richard Kent, Peter Manning, D. Murphy, William McDowell, Patrick O'Flanagan, J. Owens, John Traynor, Thomas Weafer, Philip Walsh, Thomas Allen, J. Geoghegan, Philip Clarke, Thomas O'Reilly, James Byrne, Peter Wilson, Michael Malone, Patrick Doyle, Charles Corrigan, James Quinn, John Healy, Joseph Byrne, John Adams, D. Murray, John Devane.

THOSE WHO DIED FROM A HUNGER STRIKE AS A PROTEST AGAINST ENGLISH LAW.

Thomas Ashe, Terence MacSweeney (Lord Mayor of Cork), Arthur Cosgrave, Joseph Murphy, Pierce McCann, Richard Coleman, T. O'Callaghan.

THOSE EXECUTED BY HANGING

Roger Casement, Kevin Barry, Thomas Whelan, Patrick Moran, Patrick Doyle, Bernard Ryan, Frank Flood, Thomas Bryan, Thomas Traynor.

THOSE EXECUTED BY SHOOTING.

Cornelius Murphy, Thomas O'Brien, Patrick Casey, Patrick Ronayne, Daniel O'Callaghan, John Lyons, Timothy McCarthy, Thos. Mulcahy, Patrick O'Mahoney, John Allen, Patrick O'Sullivan, Maurice Moore.

THOSE MURDERED BY BRITISH TROOPS.

Sheehy-Skeffington, Father Michael Griffin, Very Rev. Canon Magner, Timothy Crowley, Seumas Quirk, Ellen Quinn, Annie O'Neil, Miss O'Connell, Thomas McCurtain (ex-Lord Mayor of Cork), Michael O'Callaghan (Mayor of Limerick), George Clancy (ex-Mayor of Limerick), John O'Brien, Thomas O'Brien, Michael F. Fahy, Patrick Maloney, Andrew Minahan, Thomas Waters, Michael Darcy, Patrick Loughnane, Harry Loughnane, Thomas Blake, Patrick Kennedy, James Murphy, Richard McKee, Peter Clancy, T. Conor Clune, Patrick Walsh, Michael Mullen, Michael Bergin, John Leen, Martin Gildea, Alfred Rogers, Michael McMahon, Michael Egan, John Houlihan, Sean Duffy, John O'Leary, Timothy Sullivan, Denis O'Donovan, Professor Carolan, Patrick Sloan, Joseph Tormey, Michael Edmunds, John Doran, Michael Walsh, Thomas O'Brien, John Lynch, Patrick Hegarty, Michael Lynch, Michael Brosnan, Patrick McMahon, Frank Hoffman, Sean Tracy, Michael Dwyer, John Ryan, Denis O'Sullivan, Thomas Russell, Father O'Callaghan,

and for all others whose names are not inscribed in the above roll.

They walked the thorny way for Ireland and for you;
Pray for their souls, and pray that all their dreams come true.

Go ndeinidh Dia trocaire ar a manamaibh.

The New Zealand Tablet *published this list of Irish dead after the conclusion of the Anglo–Irish Truce in July 1921. No one seems to have remembered it ten months later when Liston was on trial.*

Their counter-terrorist tactics and bloody reprisals, against both IRA and civilian targets, earned them a hated reputation which endures to this day.

The press reporters were still frantically scribbling down Liston's last comment when he concluded with a note of qualified forgiveness: 'We cannot forget these men and women but in order that our dream about Ireland can come true, and while we cannot forget, we can forgive.' He had originally intended to elaborate on the theme of forgiveness, but changed his mind. The speech had taken longer than expected and the interval was approaching. He blessed his audience and resumed his seat, to thunderous applause.

As Liston left the stage, a customs officer named Robert Beswick stalked angrily out of the hall. He had leapt to his feet when the bishop mentioned his parents being driven from their native land, and despite the angry mutterings of those around him, remained standing in mute protest for the rest of the address. One of the ushers, Stanley Greenough, also yielded to irritation at Liston's remarks, walking out half-way through the speech. Several members of the orchestra were equally unhappy but decided to suppress their feelings. Apart from the obvious dangers of making so visible a protest, their future employment in the orchestra (led by a Catholic) would be placed in serious jeopardy; the post-war depression made sudden unemployment an unattractive prospect.[29]

Several items in the second half of the programme compounded the apparent mood of Irish republican defiance. Thomas Harris delivered a spirited rendition of 'The Irish Free State', a recitation mocking the worth of the new political creation in Ireland.

I went to see David, to London and David,
I went to see David and what did he do?
He gave me a Free State, a nice little Free State,
A Free State that's tied up with Red, White and Blue.

I brought it to Dublin to show to Dail Eireann,
I brought it to Dublin and what did they do?
They asked me what kind of a thing was a Free State,
A Free State that's tied up with Red, White and Blue.

Three-quarters of Ireland a nation – I told them,
Tied on to the Empire with Red, White and Blue;
And an oath they must swear to King George and Queen Mary,
An oath they must swear to the son-in-law new.

I'm teaching them Irish and painting their boxes
All over with green, sure what more can I do?
Yet they tell me they want just an Irish Republic
Without any trimmings of Red, White and Blue!

The audience was then treated to that tireless favourite 'The Wearing of the Green', a song the *Tablet* felt should be heard at every Catholic gathering: 'It is vibrant with the hopeless anger of a weak nation oppressed by a strong. Every line of it swims in tears and is saturated with blood.'[30] As a finale, almost all those present rose to sing 'God Save Ireland'. The choice of the concert-goers to entreat the Almighty to save Ireland rather than the King was not lost on subsequent critics.

Everyone dispersed, exhilarated and happy, looking forward to tomorrow's march through the city and the traditional sports meeting at the Domain. Liston returned home to St Benedict's, Newton, unaware of the impact his speech had had on two reporters among his audience. Gordon Stanbrook, staff reporter on the *New Zealand Herald*, hurried down Queen Street to write up the concert for the next morning's edition. The bishop's address had captured his attention rather than the musical items, but Stanbrook's shorthand skills proved inadequate and he was forced to work late into the evening deciphering his own longhand scrawl.[31]

The second reporter, Laurence O'Brien of the *Auckland Star*, faced different problems. Although he had taken a full shorthand note of the speech, O'Brien had apparently been celebrating St Patrick's Day not wisely but too well. If so, his hangover the next morning would not have helped in the transcription of what was clearly a sensational address.[32]

2

Murdered by Foreign Troops

IRELAND IN BONDAGE

CATHOLIC BISHOP'S VIEW
SUSPICIONS OF ENGLAND
'GLORIOUS MARTYRS' OF 1916

Speaking at the Irish concert in the Town Hall last evening, Bishop Liston said his Irish descent and the position he held in the Church gave him the right to speak to the audience on a subject which interested them all. He said his parents were driven from the country in which they were born and in which they would have been content to live, because their foreign masters did not want Irish men and women peopling their own land, but wished to use it as a cattle ranch for the snobs of the Empire.

He was a native of New Zealand, and loved his country. On this St. Patrick's Day the children of Ireland in every land were gathered by some common impulse to rejoice that at long last they had won some measure of freedom and to hope for a complete deliverance from the house of bondage. A year ago they lived in hope only. They could not say that Ireland had got all she asked for and all that her sons had died for, but she had got the first instalment of her freedom, and was determined to have the whole of it. (Applause) The omnipotent hand of God had made Ireland a nation, and while grass grew and water flowed there would be many to fight and even die in order that God's desires might be realised.

After speaking of Ireland's place in the world of art and letters followed by centuries of oppression, during which she had been unconquered and unconquerable, Bishop Liston said that many were thinking that the difficulties in the face of the Irish Free State were almost insuperable, but he thought that well wishers should not be dismayed. They had gone through the worst trials, and despite the many claims in the past that Ireland as a nation was dead she was still there. There was a mighty Empire, still claiming to be the greatest in the world, which also had its difficulties, and if they hoped to do this why should not the rulers of their little nation expect to be able to meet their difficulties. It seemed to him providential that the man who had faced the difficulties and carried them so far was there to see that the rulers of Ireland were not duped by England. He referred to the men and women who in the glorious Easter of 1916 were proud to die for their country – murdered by foreign troops. They could not forget these men and women, but in order that their dream about Ireland might come true they could forgive.

Neither at the beginning nor at the close of the concert was the National Anthem played or sung. Instead, at the end of the programme, the whole audience rose and sang 'God Save Ireland.'[1]

This page and opposite: Dublin in ruins after the six-day Irish rising, in which some 20,000 British troops fought a rebel force of under 2000. In early May 1916 fifteen rebel leaders were executed for their part in the revolt. Camera Press

New Zealand Herald subscribers must have choked over their breakfasts on Saturday morning when reading the column reproduced above. The report of Bishop Liston's speech occupied more than twice the space devoted to the St Patrick's Night concert. Its impact was not diminished by the colourful headlines 'Ireland in Bondage – Suspicions of England – "Glorious Martyrs" of 1916'. Few readers would have noticed that these headings mildly distorted what actually appeared beneath.

Stanbrook had scribbled down all of Liston's most sensational phrases. His brief summary of the twenty-five-minute speech could

be read in less than three minutes. The bishop's comments on his parents' eviction and the Irish rising of 1916 stood out most starkly. While these asides were faithfully reproduced, the summary of Liston's closing remarks on those who had died for Ireland was badly bungled. In place of his detailed list of martyrs was the bald sentence: 'He referred to the men and women who in the glorious Easter of 1916 were proud to die for their country – murdered by foreign troops.'

The distortion of recent events offered by this last phrase was clear to most readers. Moreover, the speech as reported seemed to contain a consistently outrageous interpretation of Irish history, past and present. Considering the context of the sentence, the bishop's critics could easily conclude that he had been correctly reported when describing the troops who quelled the rising as 'foreign murderers', while to Liston's supporters the misrepresentation of his true remarks was equally blatant and infuriating.

Faulty shorthand and a woeful ignorance of recent Irish history had led Stanbrook to produce his controversial sentence. The reporter had some excuses to offer. During the terrible influenza epidemic of 1918–19, he had run the *Herald* office almost single-handedly. Afterwards he recuperated by travelling widely in America and around

the Pacific. Evidently, reading the latest Irish news had not figured greatly in his holiday plans.[2]

One wonders how convinced was the *New Zealand Herald* editor about the accuracy of the report. A trusted employee of twelve years' standing, Stanbrook was willing to swear to the correctness of his version before a justice of the peace. Nevertheless, it may be that lingering doubts contributed to the relatively mild sub-leader devoted to the speech in the same issue. Headed 'The Irishman's Coat Tail', it complained that such utterances stirred up religious and racial antagonism in New Zealand. While pardoning Liston's reference to his parents, editor R. M. Hackett was not prepared to overlook his glorification of the Dublin insurrection, or 'his sneering allusions to the country and Empire to which the great majority of his fellow-citizens are proud to owe allegiance'.[3]

> Irish patriotism may be a beautiful thing, but when prominent and high-placed Irishmen go out of their way to make their expression of it an offence to other people they must expect protests and occasional retaliation. . . . That Dr. Liston acknowledged New Zealand as his birthplace with pride will not, to most of us, soften the harshness and disloyalty of the remainder of his speech. On the contrary it will arouse in many New Zealanders the feeling that they are not proud of him.

While most New Zealanders were hoping for 'something less bitter and provocative', the bishop had missed his cue. In Hackett's opinion, he had betrayed his high office and deserved everything that was coming to him. The *Herald*, however, should have been the last one to start throwing stones on the Irish issue. A long-standing enemy of Irish nationalism, it had vehemently opposed home rule for Ireland at a time when most other dailies supported it. In 1907, when the Irish MP Joseph Devlin toured the country promoting home rule, the *Herald* labelled him a 'peregrinating mendicant' and dismissed colonial enthusiasm for the reform as worthless. It was especially vitriolic when condemning the 1916 rising. While sharing its opposition to Sinn Fein, few newspapers were as bitter and unrelenting in their antagonism as the *New Zealand Herald*.[4]

From 1916 onwards, Irish Catholics in New Zealand had to endure general press hostility to advanced Irish nationalism. Malevolence rather than ignorance seemed to explain it. The cable news service was thought to be rigged by anti-Irish and anti-Catholic agencies. Dr James Kelly, editor of the *New Zealand Tablet*, detected a conspiracy against the Irish 'which extends to every daily paper published in this Dominion.'[5] This conspiracy explained the wave of anti-Catholic

Left: Robert Hackett, New Zealand Herald *editor from 1917 to 1942.* NZO
Right: Dr James Kelly, Catholic priest and passionate Irish nationalist, editor of the New Zealand Tablet *from 1917 to 1931.* NZ Tablet

feeling sweeping across the English-speaking world. Kelly referred to the daily papers as the 'Day Lies' and complained that 'never was a press as vile and despicable as the suborned hireling press of Britain and the colonies'.[6]

Of most concern to Kelly and his friends was the distorted picture New Zealanders were receiving of current Irish politics. 'Press lies and propaganda have kept the truth about Ireland from us for four years', he lamented in mid-1919.[7] Bishop Whyte also denounced what he regarded as 'the scientific system of misrepresentation of the Irish people' carried out across the British Empire in the post-war years.[8] One of Liston's reasons for speaking at the Auckland concert was his desire to challenge the current press reports on the degree of disunity among Irish nationalists.

Was the *Herald* really guilty of hostility to 'our religion and our race', as Kelly charged?[9] From 1917 it lent its columns to a virulently anti-Catholic organisation, the Protestant Political Association, which grew out of wartime frustration to play a noisy if obscure role in post-war New Zealand politics.[10] The *Herald* also drew its Irish news from British sources most antagonistic towards Sinn Fein, frequently reproducing clearly propagandistic material.[11] This said, the conclusion of peace in Ireland seemed to draw the sting from Hackett's editorial pen. In February 1922, the *Herald*'s professed sympathy with the Catholic community over the death of Pope Benedict XV, followed by its praise of his successor, Pius XI, impressed the *Tablet*'s Auckland correspondent:

> It is a very welcome change from the tone adopted in recent years towards most persons and things Catholic. Perhaps the solidarity of the Empire having been secured by the establishment of the Irish Free State, our local editors are becoming quite normal again.[12]

The *Herald*'s initial comment on Liston's speech was surprisingly moderate in tone. The speech was not denounced as seditious, nor was it subjected to scathing analysis phrase by offensive phrase. Even so, while not spelling out the 'retaliation' that the bishop might expect to receive, Hackett's charge of disturbing the peace and encouraging religious and racial antagonisms recalled the rubric of the law against sedition.[13]

Being chided rather than denounced was of little comfort to James Liston. On his busiest day of the year, the bishop had no time to dwell on the injustice done him, still less to remonstrate with the *Herald* management. In Cleary's absence he had a major part to play in the celebrations of Ireland's national saint. There had been some talk earlier among the organisers of the St Patrick's Day festivities of curtailing the procession, altering the route or even calling the whole thing off. This was possibly a response to the precariously balanced Anglo–Irish peace talks or a genuflection towards the recent truce in domestic sectarian conflict – at least until the Irish dust had settled. In the event, the celebrations were as vigorous as ever, with the new bishop in the thick of things.[14]

At 10 a.m. on Saturday, 18 March a procession of over 3000 school children left St Patrick's Cathedral in Wyndham Street, followed by a colourful stream of lorries and floats festooned in bunting, ribbons and banners. The children marched along Wyndham Street, down Albert Street to Customs Street, then up Queen Street and on to the Domain by way of Karangahape Road and Grafton Bridge. Before joining the convoy of vehicles behind the marchers, Bishop Liston probably discussed the *Herald*'s 'gross misrepresentation' and severe comments on his speech with several of his clergy and other friends. Was the Sinn Fein flag on his car a riposte to the *Herald*'s reproof?[15]

Despite threatening weather and a one-shilling admission fee, a large crowd had gathered at the Domain by midday. The festivities began with a medley of games, races and dancing competitions involving the children. Irish jigs, reels and hornpipes were enthusiastically performed. Athletics and cycling events (both amateur and professional) competed for the attention of the adults, many of whom hoped to profit from side bets on the results. The heavy ground did not lessen the excitement of several close contests, while no fewer than

The St Patrick's Day procession passes the Grey statue in Auckland's Queen Street. AWN

three bands added their noise to the general din. The afternoon's highlight came at 4 p.m. when hordes of school children marched across the ground and formed a living shamrock; the precision of their flag drill drew much praise, as did the music composed especially for the occasion.[16]

Bishop Liston was present throughout the proceedings, watching intently from the official enclosure and taking tea in the refreshment tent along with scores of thirsty spectators. His relaxed participation earned an admiring comment from the *New Zealand Observer* reporter:

> From the manner he handled the events in the Domain he is a keen sport and knows what he is doing and demands attention. A keen penetrating glance, almost a frown, changes into a broad Irish smile that cracks his cheeks into long lashes and his eyes twinkle with fun and he drinks his tea like a matron.[17]

One small cloud remained for Liston after an almost perfect day. His anger at the *Herald* misreport had not moved him to publish a correction in the *Auckland Star*, due to appear in the afternoon. It would have required a carefully worded response, and possibly the demands of his official duties at the Domain left him insufficient time. On returning home to St Benedict's presbytery, he discovered

The Catholic schoolchildren display their drill moves at the Auckland Domain. AWN

that the *Star* had printed exactly the same report of his speech as the *Herald*. For Liston, the whole business began to assume the dimensions of a monstrous plot – a deliberate distortion of his Town Hall remarks by men opposed to both his church and his race.[18] The real explanation for the identical reports was much less dramatic: human failing, and by a Catholic at that.

Laurence O'Brien's presumed hangover had not helped him when composing his account of events the night before. Despite possessing a complete shorthand note of the bishop's address, he managed to draft only a very abbreviated report. Did O'Brien, in the sober light of morning, realise the trouble Liston would find himself in should his remarks be fully reported? Feeling the speech to be 'over the edge', O'Brien wrote two summary paragraphs and then destroyed his original notes.[19]

Naturally, the *Star* editor, T. W. Leys, expected something better, especially after the fuss made by his morning rival.[20] The report disappointed in more than its brevity. Despite his closeness to the Town Hall stage, O'Brien had failed to hear the bishop say that his parents were 'driven' from Ireland, or that anybody at all had been 'murdered by foreign troops'. Stronger meat was required. His initial effort rejected, the hapless reporter was reduced to clipping out Stanbrook's column, and this had to satisfy his impatient boss. To no one's great surprise, the *Star* sacked O'Brien shortly after.[21]

O'Brien may have felt that he did Liston a great favour by destroying his shorthand note of the speech. In sedition trials over the previous decade, the existence of a verbatim report of the allegedly seditious statement was often crucial to the success of the prosecution case.[22] If O'Brien decided to censor his own report in this manner, it was surely due to muddled thinking. Had he produced a fuller ver-

Thomson Wison Leys, Auckland Star *editor.* NZO

sion of Liston's remarks to trump the *Herald*'s brief account, events might have taken a completely different course. This is also suggested by his belief that Liston 'toned down his earlier remarks' when speaking later of friendship between Ireland and England.[23]

A comprehensive and less abrasive report could have defused the explosive impact of Stanbrook's version. Would the editor of the *Auckland Star* then have written such a scathing denunciation of Liston's 'rasping and bitter' address? It was almost as though copying the *Herald* report obliged Leys to outdo his rival in the strength of his condemnation. The *Star* also spoke with the authority of a firm friend of Irish nationalism – something the *Herald* could never do – proclaiming itself as 'a newspaper that has fought Ireland's battles for a much longer period than Bishop Liston'.[24] In its enthusiasm for Irish freedom, however, the *Star* drew the line at separatism and violence, having only hard words for Sinn Fein and its local apologists.

The *Star* bemoaned Liston's terrible timing. 'What is required of Ireland is forgiveness and of England repentance. England is doing her part, will Irishmen not do theirs?' The bishop had used the word, 'but there was little spirit of forgiveness in his address'. Leys seemed to believe that the speech could even affect the political situation in Ireland. Recalling Archbishop Redwood's claim that English bankruptcy alone had brought about the Anglo–Irish accord ('an attitude that lacked both wisdom and charity'), the *Star* editor felt that Liston had now outdone his chief.[25]

The editorial continued with a careful dissection of the address. Leys was particularly offended by Liston's praise of de Valera, 'who is now striving with all his might to destroy the agreement and declaring that independence is "securable only by Irish bloodshed"'. (Across the page was a cable report of de Valera using those very words in an address at Carrick.) The reference to Easter 1916 was especially deplored:

> While Britain and the Empire were fighting for their lives, a section of the Irish people stabbed them in the back. Seeing the rebels started the fighting, the word 'murdered' has a stark humour about it. Has Dr Liston forgotten that at that very moment New Zealand soldiers, including men of his own church, were giving up their lives in company with other units of this so-called foreign army?[26]

The absurdity of what Liston was supposed to have said was apparent to Leys. Rather than question its accuracy, however, he seemed only too ready to believe in the bishop's guilt. Linking New Zealand's own traumatic war experience with Liston's alleged insult to the British forces added sting to his rebuke; however, this view of the Irish rising as calculated treachery in the interests of the enemy powers was one firmly held by many non-Catholic New Zealand citizens.[27]

Leys next raised the thorny issue of rival allegiances: 'Dr Liston and the local Irish community generally may fairly be asked whether they wish to be considered British subjects.' The test of this desire was an Irish one: were they for the Irish Free State or for 'the irreconcilables'? The *Star* then generously gave Liston and his supporters a further chance to redeem themselves.

> At the outset we invited our Irish friends to place themselves publicly behind the treaty, but we have never heard that they did so. Their silence breeds the suspicion that they are either vacillating, lacking the moral courage to declare themselves, or that they secretly wish that De Valera may prevail. We appeal to them again to throw their weight publicly into the scale of that peace and reconciliation which their commonsense as well as their Christianity should tell them is the supreme need of Ireland, New Zealand and the whole world.[28]

The New Zealand press had led the cheering when news of the Anglo–Irish accord first arrived. Pressure was immediately placed upon local Irish spokesmen to endorse the treaty as a full and fitting settlement of the long quarrel between England and Ireland. While the Wellington Catholic lawyer Patrick O'Regan welcomed the agreement as President of the Irish Self-Determination League of New Zealand,[29] Liston refrained from public comment after taking advice from his episcopal colleagues in Australia and Ireland.[30] The *Auckland Star* repeatedly spelt out the duty of Irishmen both at home and abroad. The press would permit the New Zealand Irish to speak about Ireland – but only at the time and in the way it deemed most appropriate.

Undeterred by this double dose of editorial bile, Liston went about his episcopal duties on Sunday, 19 March. He said mass at St Benedict's church in the morning and laid the foundation stone of a new primary school at Epsom in the afternoon.[31] A large crowd braved the torrential downpour which almost ruined the ceremony; that storm was nothing to the one that was about to break over the bishop's head in the week that followed.

3

A Protestant With Backbone

Auckland, an Empire's outpost, alone,
untroubled, serene;
You have won a place in our secret
hearts that will live through the
years between.
New towns may come, new faces go,
our cruise must have an end;
But Auckland stands pre-eminent,
a very loyal friend.

(Log of HMS *Renown*)[1]

The Mayor of Auckland read his Saturday-morning *Herald* with rising incredulity. Nothing remotely resembling the Town Hall speech had been heard from such a source in Auckland before. Convinced that Britain stood 'for truth, righteousness and justice' throughout the world, James Gunson found the gibes directed at England and the Empire deeply provoking.[2] If Bishop Liston was to be credited with the authority claimed in his first sentence, Auckland Catholics were apparently rejecting their allegiance to the British Empire; England to them was a foreign nation, her troops foreign murderers. The entire St Patrick's Night celebration seemed like a calculated and deliberate insult.

Gunson's amazement at the speech owed much to his earlier impressions of the speaker. He found it impossible to recognise the mild-mannered cleric who had officiated at his friend P. J. Nerheny's funeral three months earlier in the platform firebrand now revealed. Gunson had then considered the coadjutor bishop to be 'a quiet, inof-

James Gunson resplendent in his mayoral robes. ATL

fensive man'.[3] This belief now caused him to pause before passing judgement on the Town Hall speech. The mayor at oncc wrotc Liston a short note inquiring whether or not he had been correctly reported in the *Herald*.[4]

Few Aucklanders were in a better position than Gunson to weigh the worth of Gordon Stanbrook's report. He might have called on his brother-in-law, Fred Wilson (a *Herald* director), or phoned Robert Hackett to congratulate him on his trenchant editorial.[5] Had he done so, Gunson would have learnt of the high esteem in which the reporter was held; also that he was willing to make a sworn declaration in support of his version of Liston's remarks. The mayor did not mention these precautions in his subsequent public statement, noting merely that 'long experience of the press in Auckland gives me no cause to doubt the accuracy of the report'.[6] The Auckland Catholic journal, the *Month*, later jeered at Gunson's 'touching faith in the disinterested accuracy of the Auckland daily press', as the *Herald* had been one of the mayor's most vocal supporters during his rapid rise in local body politics.[7]

Gunson's belief in the *Herald* report was surely redoubled when the identical text appeared in the *Auckland Star* later that afternoon. Needing no further justification or corroboration, he began to draft a public statement on behalf of Auckland's citizenry. The fact that (with no Sunday mail deliveries) Liston could not possibly receive his letter of inquiry before Monday morning no longer concerned the mayor. That the *Star* carried neither disclaimer nor correction from the bishop seemed in itself to be a telling indication of his guilt.

Gunson may also have wanted to administer his censure before everyone else had done so. Already both local editors had unburdened themselves. Was the leader of the community to be the last to speak? This would not have been the James Henry Gunson Aucklanders had come to know. The forty-five-year-old mayor usually led from the front. Proud of his native city and fiercely jealous of its reputation, Gunson was sure to react swiftly to any slur on Auckland's loyalty to King and empire. (Five months earlier, after viewing his growing city from the air for the first time, Gunson declared, 'I love Auckland more now than ever'.)[8]

Gunson's role in the Liston case needs to be considered in the context of his meteoric political rise which had brought him, at thirty-eight years of age, to the helm of New Zealand's largest city. Born in Auckland in 1877, he left the Grammar School at the age of fifteen to work in his father's grain and seed business. After inheriting this, Gunson ran it for over a decade before selling up in 1916 to devote himself to public life. Success came quickly as his talents were recognised. Both the Auckland Harbour Board and the Chamber of Commerce chose him as their chief after a mere two years of service. Following his election as mayor in 1915 he held what has been described as 'a veritable mortgage' on the office; his only contested election in a record five terms was the first one. Indeed, his supporters had difficulty in persuading Gunson to remain in harness, especially after his wartime exertions.[9]

The press was quick to estimate Gunson's native worth and to predict a rosy future for him in national politics. His business acumen, sound judgement and youthful energy impressed most observers. Others, however, were less enamoured of his imperious style of leadership, referring to him as 'the civic dictator'.[10] Gunson's manner of dealing with men and measures was shaped by the high self-confidence born of rapid political success despite a limited formal education. His tendency to bully competitors was most evident in relations with the central government. One favourite tactic was to stampede the latter

Gunson takes on the Defence Department in 1916. NZO

into a desired course of action by whipping up local feeling to back his strongly expressed public lobbying.

As part of an agitation in 1915 to have a military camp sited near Auckland, Gunson led 'a roaring phalanx' of twenty-eight mayors in what the Wellington *Evening Post* saw as a blatant attempt to bulldoze the national government.[11] A year later he levelled a series of charges against the Defence Department, alleging neglect of the returned servicemen. On this occasion the *New Zealand Free Lance* took issue with Gunson's tactic of shooting first and asking questions later.[12] In 1917 the mayor again attempted to hustle Wellington into acting against those 'enemy aliens' who were allegedly buying up large tracts of North Auckland. Unless the 'intolerable position' was ended, Gunson warned, 'some drastic step would have to be taken by the community'. His imprecations against the so-called 'Austrians' – 'these men are enjoying the privileges and freedom afforded by British protection' – were to be heard again in 1922.[13]

Another argument took place in late 1918 over exactly who was to blame for the heavy toll of the influenza epidemic in Auckland. Several aspects of this unedifying squabble throw light on what would become known as the Liston case. Gunson was furious with what he saw as laxity by the Health Department in allowing ships suspected of carrying a deadly cargo of disease to berth in Auckland. He threatened to take local action if the government continued to neglect its duty.

An over-worked health minister, G. W. Russell, responded by publicly blaming the rapid spread of the plague on Auckland's notorious slums. He also accused Gunson of inciting Aucklanders against his department in an effort to distract public opinion from 'the revolting conditions proved to exist in your city, and for which you must, as Mayor for several years, be held morally responsible'.[14]

Auckland's City Council, press and local bodies at once fell in behind the mayor. Several public meetings were held in the Town Hall at which Gunson explained his version of the affair. He denied that it was a personal matter, but the accusations of incompetence and neglect had surely stung. Believing that the interests of his city were now jeopardised, Gunson bombarded Prime Minister William Massey with expressions of civic indignation at Russell's 'abusive and insulting' telegram. He was especially disturbed by the health minister's discourtesy in handing his censure first to the press, thus taking him to task publicly on false evidence. 'This telegram was actually published in the Auckland morning paper before it reached me', he said.[15] In the light of Gunson's subsequent treatment of Liston, the complaint has an ironic touch.

Two Irishmen with bit parts in this unsavoury drama would later star in the Liston case. One of Gunson's supporters in the dispute with Russell was Bishop Henry Cleary. He spoke strongly at two public meetings before moving a motion endorsing the city council's protest.[16] For his part, William Massey was repeatedly hauled over the coals by the importunate Mayor of Auckland, who refused to deal with the Health Department while Russell remained at its head. Gunson, insisting that the Prime Minister solve the imbroglio before leaving the country for the Versailles Peace Conference, handed his placatory telegrams to the Auckland press (which duly dismissed them as inadequate). Throughout the affair Gunson posed as the defender of his city's honour.[17]

One wonders what lasting effect these disputes had on Gunson's chances of a seat in Parliament. His name had been mentioned in this context as early as 1912. Two years later he declined an invitation to contest the Auckland East seat (his refusal to compete with the Liberal ex-Mayor of Auckland, Arthur Myers, giving a slight indication of his political leanings).[18] The conspicuous success of previous Auckland mayors – Edwin Mitchelson, Arthur Myers, Christopher Parr – gave him grounds for optimism.[19]

Gunson's aim had always been to move from local to national politics. In 1919 and 1921 his Auckland supporters had to work very hard to dissuade him from giving up the mayoralty. But if his talents were valued in municipal life, it was quite otherwise where higher representative honours were involved. Events seemed to conspire against the realisation of his ambitions. After an approach by a group of Roskill electors in early 1919, Gunson agreed to stand for the new seat, declaring himself an 'Independent'. His refusal to enlist under the Reform Party's banner was due not solely to an unhappy relationship with its leader, William Massey. The wartime coalition of Reform and Liberal still staggered on, with no sign of the tremendous momentum that Reform's electoral bandwagon would later achieve. Gunson's cry of 'new men and new measures' was aimed at both traditional political groupings; it was clear that he regarded himself as among those 'new men' who would have to be accommodated in future.[20]

Gunson's best chance of entering Parliament came in the 1919 general election. First in the field for Roskill, freshly decorated as an OBE for his war relief work, he probably felt that the seat was his for the taking. He had no argument from the Auckland press, who referred to him as a 'practical certainty' to be elected.[21] Was his decision in July 1919 to take a four-month holiday in the USA due to over-confidence? When his departure was announced, the possible benefit of the trip to his health was mentioned; by the end of the campaign Gunson's supporters were painting their man as a patriot broken in the service of his country whose doctors had insisted on an immediate convalescence abroad. If so, he was to demonstrate impressive powers of recuperation by driving his own car over 14,000 kilometres around the western United States.[22]

His holiday over, Gunson found it impossible to secure a berth on the only ship which would return him to New Zealand in time for the election campaign. After frantic bargaining, the earliest passage he could obtain landed him in Auckland just after the polls had closed.[23] At first, Gunson's absence did not seem to endanger his electoral chances, as a pre-signed nomination form had been lodged on his behalf. However, in early October it assumed a more serious aspect, when a rival candidate appeared. Lieutenant Vivian Potter, newly returned from three years' service with the New Zealand Expeditionary Force, had agreed to contest the Roskill seat in the Reform interest.

Potter was a popular speaker and an able campaigner. He had seen action also in the Boer War, while his well-known opposition to local socialists, the 'Red Feds', during and after the Waihi strike of 1912 was proof of his anti-Bolshevik credentials. Enjoying Massey's unequivocal endorsement, Potter mocked the attempts of Gunson's sup-

ROSKILL.
J. H. Gunson (in Vancouver, awaiting a boat home)
Why did I leave my little old town, the Queen City?

Gunson misses the boat and a seat in Parliament at the 1919 general election. NZO

porters to portray their candidate as all things to all men. He referred to the absent mayor as a 'political weathercock', and hinted that Gunson's continued absence was due to an unwillingness to face the voters.[24]

The shifting political wind left Gunson badly exposed. Massey's Reform Party was on its way to a huge electoral victory, the only decisive win at the polls the Irishman was to score in his long political career. In Gunson's enforced absence, his friends were obliged to improvise. But if their candidate was a late arrival, so was the platform upon which he stood for election. A month before polling day his supporters were as much in the dark on this score as his opponents. They made a virtue of necessity by boasting that Gunson was under obligation to neither Liberal nor Reform; then came a clumsy attempt to clamber onto the Masseyite bandwagon. Gunson was said to be in accord with Massey's programme, so much so that Massey would be pleased to see him returned. (Had not the Prime Minister requested the voters to send to Parliament 'the best brains you can find'?) The crowning nonsense was a claim that 'instead of Mr Gunson swallowing Mr Massey's platform, Mr Massey had adopted Mr Gunson's'.[25]

Vivian Potter, the successful candidate for Roskill in 1919. NZO

When Gunson's programme eventually appeared on the eve of the poll, it was pure Reform without the label. He adopted a strongly anti-revolutionist stance, agreed with Massey's administrative policy, and announced his intention to vote for Reform on a motion of no confidence. This belated declaration did Gunson no good. He landed in Auckland in time to read the poll results fresh off the presses – Potter had beaten him by a margin of two to one. Gunson did not have even the consolation of casting a vote for himself.[26]

It was not just that Potter ran an active campaign while his main rival was ploughing the high seas between Vancouver and Auckland. The ex-soldier possessed two cards which Gunson could not trump. To offset Potter's military record, the mayor's supporters cited their candidate's work as president of the Auckland Provincial Patriotic and War Relief Association and as a member of the National Efficiency Board. But Gunson, despite being of military age, had chosen to fight his war on the home front. While urging single men to join up, he protested at the suggestion that married men should be called upon to volunteer. (He had himself been married for ten years.) In late 1916 attacks on the mayor as a 'shirker' drew a memorandum of 'protest and sympathy' from the Auckland City Council; a year later the writer of a pamphlet which repeated the charge was prosecuted and jailed.[27]

The soldiers gave their own view of the matter when Gunson attempted to farewell the 27th Reinforcements (composed mostly of conscripted men) from the Auckland Drill Hall in March 1917. The *Herald* reported that, because 'the noise was still proceeding' when he rose to speak, the Mayor had 'confined himself to the briefest of remarks'. Another witness to the scene told a different tale:

> After one or two officers had farewelled us with advice etc. Mr Gunson proceeded to address us. However he didn't get very far before he was bombarded from several quarters with the question 'why wasn't he going himself' and then the reinforcements quickly 'counted him out'. He is one of those 'Lip Loyalists' that preferred to see the other man do the fighting.[28]

Potter the war hero was also very much the candidate of the bigots. The Protestant Political Association (PPA) had helped to persuade him to run and backed him vigorously, after receiving his 'satisfactory' answers on matters dear to its heart.[29] (He was probably not questioned too closely; the PPA was out for Gunson's head and Potter seemed likely to deliver it.) Gunson had offended by adopting an impartial attitude towards the contending sects that represented organised Christianity in New Zealand. Whether it was a case of welcoming delegates to the Presbyterian General Assembly, or greeting the new minister of the Auckland Baptist Tabernacle, or playing host to the Papal Delegate, he was willing to serve in his official capacity. A Methodist himself, Gunson was praised by the *New Zealand Methodist Times* for his even-handedness on such occasions. Others felt that he was too ready to serve the interests of one denomination in particular, and attacked him as a 'wobbly Protestant' soft on Rome.[30]

For granting a civic reception to Bonaventura Cerretti (Pope Benedict XV's envoy) on his tour of New Zealand in 1916, Gunson was subjected to scathing criticism in another anonymous pamphlet, 'The Papal Delegate and the Mayor'.[31] When mass was then celebrated in the Domain as part of the St Patrick's Day celebrations, Gunson and his council turned a deaf ear to the howls of protest from enraged local Orangemen.[32] As preserving an impartial attitude became increasingly difficult, Gunson pursued a Pilate-like approach to the rival parties. Unlike the mayors in other cities, he refused to chair PPA meetings; nor would he preside over a reception for his friend Henry Cleary in late 1917, when the bishop returned from his spell as a war chaplain in Flanders.[33]

The Auckland correspondent of the *New Zealand Tablet* was unstinting in his praise of James Gunson. The 'worthy and capable' civic leader of February 1917 was still 'our enlightened and progressive Mayor' four years later.[34] The retention of this warm Catholic endorsement in a period of savage sectarian conflict was not due to any sympathy on Gunson's part for Irish self-determination, the *Tablet*'s most burning cause. Like many public figures during these turbulent years, Gunson became ever more vocal in his expressions of imperial devotion. Even Massey received his meed of praise; when the Prime Minister was leaving to attend the Imperial Conference of 1921, Gunson gave him a rousing send-off in the Auckland Town Hall. 'We have always admired that patriotism of Empire you have voiced at all times. We are privileged to follow your lead in Imperial matters.'[35]

An opportunity to parade Auckland's devotion to throne and Empire came in April 1920 when the Prince of Wales toured the Dominion. The northern city succumbed to 'Princeitis' as more than 100,000 people flocked to welcome 'The Greatest Young Man in the World'.[36] The press gushed loyalty, editors ransacking their dictionaries to describe the atmosphere of joyful celebration. Britain was dubbed 'the champion of freedom, the home of democracy, and the repository of all that is best and noblest in human history'.

The scene outside the Auckland Post Office during the welcome to the Prince of Wales in 1920. ATL

Gunson presides at the civic reception for the Prince of Wales (on his right). Prime Minister W. F. Massey is sitting to his left. APL

> The Prince had come half way round the world to visit the most distant part of the Empire. Loyalty thrilled to the thought that the Heir to the Throne, so long familiar through photograph and pen picture, was among us. Patriotism glowed as a representative ship of the British Navy swung into her berth, as a guard of New Zealand soldiers marched past, as the Royal motor traversed the streets of Auckland. For is not the Throne the one visible symbol of the unity of our Empire.[37]

Prince Edward's first port of call in New Zealand, Auckland almost overwhelmed him with its uncritical adoration. The Town Hall was packed to overflowing, its galleries draped with red, white and blue bunting and a large Union Jack covering the organ loft, while the flags of the allied nations decorated every wall. Moved by his reception, the Prince made the unusual gesture on the platform of shaking hands with the mayor and mayoress, all the city councillors and their wives.[38] Gunson's subsequent appointment as a CMG in the 1922 New Year's honours list was probably a belated recognition of this warmest of welcomes. A letter from the Prince's private secretary arrived soon afterwards, expressing the royal 'delight' at Gunson's promotion.[39]

The honour came at a time when the mayor's loyal reputation was under heavy attack. In late 1921 Gunson had signed a testimonial to

Auckland lawyer and Irish enthusiast, Alfred Hall Skelton. NZ Truth

Alfred Hall Skelton, a three-term Auckland city councillor who had been narrowly defeated in the recent municipal elections. Since his reverse at the polls, Hall Skelton had conducted a quixotic personal campaign in favour of self-determination for Ireland, the land of his parents. His energetic platform performances on behalf of the newly formed Irish Self-Determination League won him selection as a delegate to the Irish Race Convention due to be held in Paris in early 1922. An illuminated address (with Gunson's signature at its head) was presented to Hall Skelton at a ceremony in the Town Hall, along with a cheque for £1000 raised by Auckland's Irish community.[40]

The departing delegate predicted that Ireland would emerge from its current turmoil as 'one of the most important self-governing countries in the British Empire'.[41] This loyal note did not placate those critics who saw only treachery in any advocacy of Irish national rights. Their fury grew as Gunson's signature was published in seeming endorsement of the Sinn Fein cause. A sharp debate broke out in the Auckland press as those councillors who had not signed dissociated themselves from the testimonial. It was advanced in Gunson's defence that he had not acted in his capacity as mayor, and that he had been 'surprised and indignant' when this claim was published. While some critics refused to allow a separation between the man and his office, others challenged his right to sign even as a private citizen.[42]

The PPA was predictably angry, its Auckland president reminding a crowded meeting of Gunson's past dalliances with the enemies of the empire. What was the Irish Self-Determination League but Sinn Fein in cunning disguise?

> Their policy being the dismemberment of the grandest and noblest Empire in the world . . . Gunson had no right to sign unless he sympathised with the aims and aspirations of Ireland. If he did so it was his duty to let the people know that he was in sympathy with the League's views. (Applause).[43]

Clearly, Gunson was not the PPA's sort of mayor. He kept silent during the testimonial affair, but must have worried about the damage done to his chances of success in the general election due later that year. A rumour had circulated that he was planning to contest either Auckland East or Auckland West; if the PPA carried the same electoral punch as it demonstrated in 1919, he might end up losing once again.[44] All these thoughts would have been running through Gunson's mind as he considered how best to respond to Bishop Liston's reported speech. While such flagrant disloyalty from the stage of the building that symbolised civic unity called for an immediate disavowal, the results of similarly firm action by municipal authorities in Australia were not encouraging.[45]

Like Liston, Gunson felt a duty to speak out on behalf of the people he represented.[46] Were the flames of his indignation, sparked by the *Herald* report and fed by the *Star*'s confirmation, further fanned on Sunday morning when he attended to his religious duty? (Gunson's fellow Methodists later applauded his stern condemnation of the 'blatant sedition-monger'.)[47] At church services throughout Auckland, the Town Hall speech was the main topic of conversation. The Reverend Jasper Calder addressed his congregation at the Auckland City Mission:

> I have learnt that the Irish Romans at their national concert on Friday night, instead of making it a happy holiday, with everybody smiling and contented, made it so that it reads like a night of political bitterment. I have no remarks to make about it just now. Instead will all those who are willing kindly stand and sing the National Anthem?[48]

Some 1200 people immediately rose in a body and sang 'God Save the King' with great enthusiasm. By contrast, James Gunson had plenty to say about the speech; late on Sunday afternoon he completed his statement and handed it to the press.

4

Studied Insults

BISHOP'S UTTERANCE

PROTEST BY THE MAYOR
INSULT TO LOYAL CITIZENS
FURTHER ACTION PROPOSED

The following statement was made yesterday by the Mayor of Auckland, Mr. J.H. Gunson:-

'The speech of Bishop Liston as delivered in the Town Hall on Friday evening calls for immediate action on my part as Mayor on behalf of our citizenship.

I wrote to the bishop on Saturday morning asking him to advise me as to whether he had been correctly reported, though my long experience of the press in Auckland gives me no cause to doubt the accuracy of the report.

The speech as reported is avowedly and openly disloyal to King and country, and is an affront to our citizenship. It is seditious and designedly calculated to cause disintegration of all that Britishers hold dear. It is a studied insult to the citizenship of the Empire to which New Zealand is proud to belong.

The repudiation of England, the sneering reference to her as a 'foreign nation,' and the entire dissociation with disdain of the speaker and those for whom he said he spoke, as 'a right,' from all that pertains to the Empire, challenge all loyal citizens to raise their voices in protest.

The reference to British soldiers as foreign murderers is especially offensive and unwarrantable. I take this first public opportunity of saying with all the emphasis possible that the citizens of Auckland will not tolerate for one minute such a studied and deliberate act of disloyalty, and of insult to British manhood and womanhood. And in making this intimation I wish to say that such a seditious and ruinous speech will not be allowed in the Auckland Town Hall, or in any place which the city administration controls or licenses. The bishop and others holding views such as reported are not fit to longer enjoy the privileges and rights of our British Commonwealth, and the protection

> of the British flag. This speech will be brought under the notice of the Attorney-General, and it will be my duty to advise the City Council to take other appropriate action. In the meantime, on behalf of the citizens of Auckland, I enter an emphatic protest in the foregoing terms.'[1]

Forthright and superior in tone, Gunson's statement displayed the same lack of restraint he criticised in the bishop. By twice describing the speech as 'seditious', the mayor went beyond mere protest. It was not for him to pronounce on the legal status of the bishop's alleged remarks. Gunson also imputed motives to Liston by using the phrases 'designedly calculated' and 'studied and deliberate'. What, one wonders, were his own remarks 'designedly calculated' to bring about? The *Month* later mocked the mayor's 'wonderful sequence of partially-accepted premise, probable guilt and then fitting penalty'.[2] Gunson had opened up a further line of attack by referring the speech to the Attorney-General. Evidently, Liston's future enjoyment of the privileges, rights and protection of the British flag was now at risk – in Auckland at least.

The mayor was surely cheered by the *Herald*'s Monday editorial on his statement. It cited his well-known impartiality in sectarian issues and recalled the unfair criticism he had recently incurred on this score. Choosing not to dwell on the details of Gunson's statement, Hackett deemed his motives in protesting to be beyond reproach. The loyalty owed by Auckland to the King had been repudiated; it was the mayor's duty to prevent the recurrence of such a heinous act.

> As Mayor of Auckland, Mr Gunson is not concerned with the private opinions of individuals on political questions, but when the head of any section of the community claims the right by virtue of his position to proclaim its attitude in terms that are offensive to every other section, the Mayor is certainly entitled, and is probably under an obligation, to say plainly that such sentiments are not endorsed by the city.[3]

The mayor had a busy Monday morning. He despatched copies of Stanbrook's report and his own statement to Attorney-General Sir Francis Bell, 'with a view of your taking whatever action appears to you to be necessary in the interests of the Country'.[4] Gunson was even more direct when writing to the Prime Minister, describing the speech as 'disloyal and seditious'. He seemed confident that Massey would agree with his verdict: 'I feel that I have only to bring this grave matter under your notice to ensure adequate action being taken'.[5] Part of

Gunson's morning was spent closeted with the City solicitor discussing the legal aspects of the speech and the best means of carrying out the preventive measures threatened in his statement. Whatever action the government might or might not take, the Auckland City Council was able to apply sanctions immediately.

All this activity meant that Gunson was unable to attend the Auckland Rotary Club's weekly luncheon at the Town Hall. In apologising for his absence, the club chairman referred to the mayor's 'thrilling' statement of that morning. The *Star* reporter later described the sequel.

> A scene of enthusiasm followed, members rising and cheering the Mayor, and loudly applauding the remarks of Mr Rhodes. 'I am not going to say another word, but I have no doubt that your expression of feeling will be conveyed to the Mayor.' (Applause.)[6]

The Rotarians were then addressed on 'Effective Citizenship' by John James Virgo, an Australian who was touring the country in his capacity as organising secretary of the YMCA. Virgo took the opportunity to expound on the duties of loyalty: 'If the speaker could not be loyal to the Empire that conferred so many benefits upon him, he would feel that he was about the meanest cad possible, and would consider it his duty to leave the King's Dominions and take himself off somewhere else. (Hear, hear.)'[7]

Equal belligerence was displayed by the large audience who filled the Town Hall that same evening to hear a visiting American Methodist bishop, C. E. Locke. When Mayor Gunson stood up to introduce the speaker, it was he rather than his guest who received a hero's welcome. All those present rose and repeatedly cheered for several minutes. After the din had subsided, Gunson condescended to make a brief reply.

> Fellow citizens, I understand this to be an impersonal tribute to the attitude your civic head of administration has taken in connection with a very disloyal and seditious speech delivered in this Town Hall on Friday evening last. (Applause.) I take it that such is the case. (Hear, hear.) It was my duty as a citizen and as your civic head to take the stand I did . . . There is an inherent privilege of free speech dear to us all as Britishers, but there is also a question of loyalty – loyalty to throne and to realm – which we also as Britishers gladly prize. (Applause.) That is all I have to say. (Applause.)[8]

Not to be left out, Bishop Locke quickly praised the loyalty of both Gunson and his hosts. 'I can assure His Worship that the Methodists

Above left: John James Virgo, organising secretary for the YMCA. Above centre: Bishop Locke, a visiting American Methodist. Above right: Mayor Donaldson of Newmarket. NZO

of New Zealand are loyal to the good old British Empire, loyal to dear old England, and loyal to your noble and exalted ruler, King George. (Cheers.)' The chairman of the Auckland Methodist district next assured Gunson that they were all behind him 'to the last ditch'. The proceedings concluded (as they had begun) with a rousing rendition of 'God Save the King'.[9]

Having given such a decided lead, Gunson must have been gratified by the support rapidly forthcoming from both public and private bodies in the city. His former colleagues on the Auckland Harbour Board set the pace on Monday afternoon by unanimously congratulating him on his 'manly and British sentiments' and applauding his action 'to suppress disloyalty and uphold the honour and freedom of the Empire'. Later that day the Auckland Hospital Board echoed these sentiments, its chairman expressing his pleasure that the sole Catholic member of the board had also disavowed the speech.[10]

Other municipal bodies soon joined the chorus. At a social to mark the inauguration of the Devonport roads improvement scheme, Mayor H. S. W. King told those gathered how glad he was 'to have the opportunity of expressing his approval'.[11] On Wednesday evening, and without pausing for discussion, both the Devonport and Birkenhead borough councils passed unanimous resolutions endorsing Gunson's protest.[12] The closest thing to a debate on the speech took place the same evening in the Newmarket Borough Council.[13] When Mayor Donaldson proposed a motion congratulating Gunson, Councillor F. J. O'Meara rose immediately to object. He refused to criticise Gunson's statement, merely pointing out that Liston had been condemned unheard. ('I am not here to defend Dr Liston. I have not seen him about the matter, was not at the concert, nor do I know that he said the words.') Gunson's letter was published before any reply could be sent; O'Meara suggested that the threat of legal action it contained had probably persuaded the bishop to reserve his defence. Was this the British fair play of which they all boasted?

O'Meara refused to place absolute faith in the accuracy of the press reports. He considered Liston's remarks on the 1916 rising to be 'very strange'. How could the Irishmen in the British army who had helped to crush the rising be called 'foreigners'? As a Catholic, O'Meara objected to the press taking Liston's private opinions as representative of Catholic views. He believed that the issue was being exploited primarily for sectarian purposes, but the amendment he moved deprecating this fact failed to find a seconder.[14]

Mayor Donaldson would have none of this. He denied that religious motives underlay the public protest; it was 'simply a question of loyalty against disloyalty'. If Liston had been wrongly reported, no one would be happier than him to hear it. Liston's position as a Catholic leader gave his private opinions added significance. Donaldson softened his criticism by acknowledging that 'a large proportion of the Roman Catholics were just as loyal as any English'. Satisfied by this concession, O'Meara chose not to dissent from the original motion, which then passed unanimously.

Several organisations took the opportunity to display the loyal hearts upon their sleeves. The New Zealand Welfare League quickly informed Gunson of its abhorrence of Liston's 'anti-British and seditious' utterance: 'Such a speech can only tend to engender bitterness and strife among our people, and encourage those whose efforts are directed at the destruction of the Empire.'[15] At a special meeting on Thursday evening, Auckland University College students passed a resolution congratulating Gunson, adding that 'in view of various aspersions cast on the loyalty of university students in New Zealand this meeting also hereby expresses its unswerving loyalty to the King, the British Empire and the flag'.[16]

On Wednesday evening the local adherents of the British Israel Association gathered in the Town Hall concert chamber. According to this select group, the British were descended from the ten lost tribes of Israel and their Empire was the special creation of Providence. Gunson's deputy on the Auckland City Council, A. J. Entrican, was a leading light in this organisation, which also numbered Prime Minister Massey among its members. Predictably, the meeting backed the mayor in his protest and urged that legal action be taken over 'the libel of the soldiers of our Empire'.[17]

The *New Zealand Methodist Times* evinced understandable pride in its leader on the mayor's action, entitled 'Straight from the Shoulder'. Recalling the 'boiling over of wrath' in some Protestant circles over the civic reception Gunson had accorded the Apostolic Delegate in 1916, the Reverend W. J. Williams concluded that 'it was the treatment of Monsignor Ceretti [*sic*] that made possible and consistent the treatment of Dr Liston'. The bishop had revealed himself to be 'a blatant sedition-monger' and needed to be handled 'with the gloves off'.[18]

The *New Zealand Baptist* cried 'Bravo!' to Gunson's vigorous action over the speech. Its editor, the Reverend J. J. North, felt that Archbishop Redwood should have been prosecuted for his post-treaty remarks, while Dr James Kelly 'ought to have been in the dock over and over again'. Surely many Catholics resented 'the frothings of these clerical firebrands', he continued. What was to be done with those priests who used religion as a cloak for their malice?

> Too many of these clerical traitors have been allowed 'privilege of clergy' of late. Romanists must be taught quite sharply that the Democracy knows nothing of their priests and bishops as such. They are in the eyes of the law simply and only citizens. Treason on their lip is as deadly and as directly punishable as on the lip of the humblest Red Fed.[19]

North had already excoriated Liston at a meeting of the Council of Christian Congregations held in Christchurch on Monday night. The council's lengthy discussion, which was reported in all the major dailies, deserves closer examination. Was it marked by the bigotry which many Catholics saw as the principal motivation of Liston's critics? The key motion was introduced by North on behalf of the executive:

> The Council of Christian Congregations regrets exceedingly that prelates of the Roman Catholic Church in New Zealand should more than once have used the occasion of the Irish Treaty, which has been approved by the Parliament of Great Britain and by the Irish National Assembly, and by the world at large, to express suspicion of the honesty of the intentions of the Mother Country, and their discontent with the treaty itself and generally to malign the Empire. The Council is unable to believe that any man is a good New Zealander who defames the Empire.[20]

North began by denying any sectarian motivation; the executive had considered Liston's remarks solely 'from the social welfare point of view'. Such sentiments coming from a community leader could have

The Reverend J. J. North, a pugnacious Baptist cleric. NZFL

only an unsettling influence on his people. It was rank disloyalty 'to suggest in a most awkward fashion that this country was one thing and the Empire another'. By claiming 'that a man could be a New Zealander and not a Britisher', Liston had tarnished the honour of the dominion. At a critical juncture in the empire's affairs Redwood and Liston had 'spoken most offensively of the negotiations and the negotiators'. All sensible Britishers abhorred the probable consequences should these sentiments be disseminated 'among a section of the people'.[21]

Gunson's name was warmly applauded by the council, but North wanted the mayor's protest to be more formally endorsed. 'If no indication was given that the people of the country did not resent the words, we should have failed to play the game. (Hear, hear.)' The resolution had been cautiously drawn up and should appeal to many Catholics, he continued, though mainly the non-Irish ones who resented Liston's aspersions on the empire. He expressed pleasure at Gunson's 'stern attitude' along with the hope that such utterances would end 'voluntarily'.

Possibly expecting some resistance from other council members,

North was unusually circumspect in his remarks. The Reverend C. E. Bevan Brown registered a personal protest at the phrase 'murdered by foreign troops', contrasting it with Liston's silence over the recent killing in Belfast of two policemen sick in hospital: 'He tried to inflame his own people by such reckless remarks.' Nevertheless, Bevan Brown thought that the words 'Roman prelates' should be deleted from the resolution, thus limiting its censure to Liston alone. The Reverend T. A. Joughin retorted that the speech was not a solitary incident. When Dean Carrington also opposed a general charge being made against the Catholic hierarchy, North agreed to alter the motion accordingly.[22]

The Reverend J. Paterson then spent several minutes defending the executive's decision to involve the council in the affair. Despite some doubts whether it came within the scope of their work, it was agreed to challenge those dividing the community over the Irish issue. Canon Mutter asked why the council had said nothing against the Protestant Political Association on these same grounds. A call to move on to other business was then lost on the voices, although the Christchurch *Sun* claimed that it was 'fairly strongly supported'.[23] The Reverend J. Napier Milne urged that the discussion proceed. He denied having any sympathy with the PPA; indeed, his congregation had recently criticised him for condoling with Catholics over the death of the Pope. After a few final remarks from North explaining the necessity for action, the motion of censure was carried with only two dissenting voices out of fifty.

If the council's proceedings were somewhat restrained, there were many other bodies eager to add their ingredients to the sectarian stew. The Loyal Orange Order quickly seized its opportunity; on Monday evening eleven suburban and city lodges met in Auckland to endorse Gunson's 'courageous, well-timed and well-deserved' denunciation. They wanted the focus shifted from Liston on to his approving audience:

> It is undoubted that the expressions of enmity to the Empire were not only supported by the 3000 people in the Town Hall on that evening, but are also voiced by the great majority of their co-religionists throughout the Dominion, and that the rank and file of the Roman Catholic Church are in complete accord with such expressions of disloyalty.[24]

The Protestant Political Association also climbed aboard with alacrity. It did not know whether to laugh or cry over the speech, which was the vilest form of treason, but also a justification of every charge the PPA had levelled since its inception. While condemning

Howard Elliott reads the offending speech. NZO

Liston's address, the PPA executive had the grace to add that 'the unrestrained expression of the real thought of the Roman ecclesiastic has proved the contention of the PPA that the Papacy in Australasia and throughout the world is the enemy of the British Empire'. Unfortunately for Rev. Howard Elliott, the association's founder and chief spokesman, ill health kept him out of action from March to May and thus unable to bring his remarkable histrionic talents to bear on the controversy.[25]

Entitled 'Dropping the Mask', the PPA's view of the affair was broadcast up and down the country on Thursday. Vice-President George Harwood likened Liston to a snarling tomcat, while lauding Gunson as 'a Protestant with backbone'. 'Bishop Liston had done more in five minutes than their organisation had managed to accomplish in twelve months – he had stirred the people.' In 1916 Ireland had stabbed the Motherland in the back, yet Liston called the troops who suppressed the rebellion 'murderers'. What should they do with him? Harwood asked his audience. 'Tar and feather him' came the reply.

> Liston posed as a good New Zealander. Well, he should love it well enough to get out of it – he was not fit to live here. The Hibernian Society in Auckland had backed him up. What could they do with such men – they could not excuse their action on the ground of ignorance. It meant that Catholicism had dropped the mask. No apology could atone for this nor would it be sincere.[26]

A singular contribution to the argument was published in the *New Zealand Herald* on Friday. Described as a 'dignified Maori rebuke', it bore the signature of one Keremeta Ngahuripuke, who professed to speak for all the Northcote Maori.

> I read with pain of heart, O Bishop, your words. Here we are – Catholic Maoris living on this Catholic Maori reserve – under the shadow of the Church. I feel it my duty to protest for our people and at their request after proper meeting this day, and so make known our objecting to foolish words so lightly spoken.[27]

Previous bishops of Auckland had taught them to honour both God and the King, Keremeta claimed. While Irish history was a tragic tale, he believed that it was no sadder than Welsh, Scottish or English history. For that matter, Maori experience of British rule was equally bitter: 'War also and like sorrows came with the loss of homes and the tribal lands.' Irish soldiers and administrators had helped to conquer them – Maori and Irish blood flowing on the same battlefield. Had not Governor Grey, an Irishman, taken their lands as the price of war?

> But we have in these few years since then past forgotten all those things our fathers thought wrong. We have settled down; tribal wars have ended forever. We are happy and prosper; are increasing in number; enjoy all those good things brought by rule under that Empire and the Union Jack which the bishop condemns in error. For there cannot be much wrong with that Government, if our State is as I describe it – I claim correctly – in this country.

If the Maori had forgotten their grievances in so short a time, he wondered, why could the Irish not do the same in the hundreds of years at their disposal? Christian teachers had taught them to reject as evil the sweetness of revenge. Maori lads of all tribes, himself among them, had fought in far-off Europe to defend the Empire's cause. 'Many indeed stayed beyond there; they sleep forever on those battlefields.' Catholic Maori loyalty had been proved in deed as well as word. 'Follow, Irishmen, the example of your Maori younger brothers in the Empire net.'

Keremeta held firm views on the appropriate punishment for dissent, recalling a recent example of government action against alleged Maori law-breakers. In 1916 the prophet Rua Kenana was arrested, convicted and jailed, during which police action his son was killed.

> If a people oppose the law – they will be shot. Rua opposed the law; his son was shot. Our foolish young men oppose the law; they are punished in prison. These penalties are quite right. If right here – so they are in Ireland. It is the same law, the same King who rules us all – who shoots and prisons the wrong and protects the good.[28]

The Auckland City Council 1921–23. Standing from left: W. J. Holdsworth, T. H. Bloodworth, M. J. Savage, G. Davis, J. Dempsey, E. H. Davis, H. N. Bagnall, G. Knight, J. A. C. Allum, F. W. Brinsden, M. J. Bennett. Seated from left: J. W. Hardley, J. A. Warnock, E. Meville, J. H. Gunson (Mayor), G. Baildon, J. Robertson, J. B. Paterson. Insets from left: P. M. MacKay, H. D. Heather, E. H. Maguire, G. R. Hutchinson (Deputy Mayor). APL

The open letter concluded with an eloquent appeal for Liston to make the *amende honorable*. Impressed, the *Herald* felt that its readers would take 'exceptional interest' in it.

> Yes – oh Liston – your words are wrong. It is such words that are indeed foreign, at least to the ear drums of us Maori Catholics – children of Pompallier. Your words are as thrusts of dangerous spears. Now, this is our proverb: 'The spear by the warrior, its thrust can be parried; but not so the thrust of false words – those cannot be parried.' Again, 'A bird fled from the net will yet be caught – but a word let go cannot be caught.' Go, oh bishop – heal the the wounds you have made. We cannot parry your words – nor stop their flight.[29]

Did the flood of approval Gunson received early in the week encourage him to step up the pressure on Liston? The bishop had responded to his letter of Saturday by publicly chiding Gunson for his presumption and discourtesy.[30] Several critics had also pointed out the mayor's repeated acts of supererogation.[31] Was Gunson more than usually anxious for the backing which his colleagues on the city council had given him on so many previous occasions? He chose not to convene a special meeting, preferring to wait for the council's regular session on Thursday afternoon. After consulting the City solicitor, he outlined a series of penalties to be imposed on the unrepentant offenders of St Patrick's Night. Gordon Stanbrook supplied him with a sworn statement of the speech as he recalled it.

What the council was not allowed to see was the Attorney-General's cautionary reply to Gunson's letter of Monday. While Sir Francis Bell endorsed the mayor's strictures on the speech and approved of future controls on the use of public buildings by anyone likely to repeat Liston's remarks, he was not convinced that the latter deserved to be termed seditious. He pointed to the distinction between laudation of sedition in the past and incitement to it in the present or future, implying that Liston was guilty merely of the former. As for a prosecution, 'defiance of propriety and disregard of duty are not alone sufficient to constitute an offence against the criminal law'.[32] Did Gunson read a rebuke between the lines of Bell's letter for his repeated denunciation of the speech? In reply, he cited local legal opinion that the speech was indeed seditious in both the respects mentioned by Bell, adding that he was treating their correspondence as private.[33]

The Auckland city councillors who gathered on Thursday evening had no desire to be fouled by the pitch of religious bitterness. Most of them had publicly deplored its introduction into municipal elections over the previous six years.[34] When the council's sole Catholic died four months earlier, his funeral provided an opportunity for a number of them to meet the new coadjutor Bishop of Auckland in person.[35] Other members, stung by criticism of their involvement with Hall Skelton's testimonial, probably welcomed the chance to reassert their credentials as loyal Britons. At least two councillors had no concerns on that score: J. B. Paterson and M. J. Bennett were stalwarts of the Auckland central branch of the PPA.[36]

Gunson began the council meeting by explaining the circumstances of his statement.[37] Although six days had passed since he had first read Stanbrook's report, his anger seemed unabated. 'Owing to the disloyal, seditious and offensive nature of the speech I considered it my duty on behalf of yourselves and of our citizens generally to immediately publish a protest.' He had done this after convincing himself of the report's correctness; the council was now shown a sworn declaration by the *Herald* reporter of what he had heard. Bell's caution regarding prejudgement forgotten, Gunson puffed himself up large for his next delivery.

> The question is the gravest that has confronted the civic administration of Auckland. It is a challenge to our loyalty as a community to His Majesty King George V and to our British manhood and womanhood. It is a question we could not ignore without losing our own honour and wounding our own self-respect. If we failed to vindicate those things that as citizens we most value from the attack of disloyalty and sedition we should

> be encouraging those pernicious forces that are alien from all that is best and noblest in our British civilisation.

An occasional preacher at Methodist services, Gunson went on to deliver a homily on loyalty. While properly refusing to take sides in mere sectarian or political controversies, the council was obliged to 'discourage and suppress every form of disloyalty to the Crown and the Empire'.

> The benefits, rights and privileges of our citizenship, won at great cost and now so wide and beneficent are not available for propagators of sedition, whether such be of the humblest calling or of the highest rank. And the facilities of the city cannot be available for organisations under whose authority or with whose support the doctrines of disloyalty and sedition are propounded and disseminated.

Several measures were then proposed to carry this threat into reality. The city solicitor was to redraft the terms for letting the Town Hall and the by-laws relating to public use of the Domain, parks and other open spaces. The plan was to extract from anyone using these facilities a guarantee that all proceedings would be conducted in an acceptably loyal manner. The council gave itself a wide safety margin: any future use would forbid conduct 'constituting an affront to its citizens'. In particular, any request from those connected with the St Patrick's Day celebrations would be denied 'until the sentiments expressed in the speech and evident in the proceedings are disavowed and assurance given against any repetition of such statements'.[38]

Gunson was asking the council to repeat his public strictures on the speech; the punitive resolution was spiced with phrases echoing his earlier denunciation. After affirming the council's loyalty and allegiance to King George V and the British Empire and deploring Liston's 'disloyal and seditious speech', the motion continued:

> (1) That this Council hereby records its condemnation of the said lecture and declares its opinion that no person capable of making the statements reported to have been made by Bishop Liston is worthy of British citizenship.
> (2) That the speech be brought under the notice of the New Zealand Government with a view to its taking appropriate action.

The mayor ended by publicly acknowledging, 'on behalf of the civil authority', the flood of telegrams and letters he had received from up and down the country. (The *New Zealand Observer* cartoonist sketched him swamped by a pile of congratulatory messages.)[39] Gunson clothed all his statements in official robes, making the clearest

Gunson engulfed by congratulatory correspondence. The Observer *contrasts this with Liston's public silence.* NZO

distinction between man and mayor. Had he learnt this lesson from the Hall Skelton testimonial incident?[40] Another member of the council with reason to regret the same episode now stood up to second Gunson's resolution. H. N. Bagnall's name had been omitted from the list of councillors who had declined to sign the offending testimonial. He wrote an indignant letter to the *New Zealand Herald*, claiming to have been the first one to protest, and later had the council's minutes corrected to record this event.[41]

In a rather confused contribution to the discussion, Bagnall condemned 'the raising of dissension in a country which was so far away from the seat of the Irish trouble and in which hitherto there had been loyalty among the citizens'. Punishing Liston would help not only to preserve the fragile Irish peace, but also to protect Catholic workers in New Zealand from retaliatory discrimination. Bagnall reminded the council of its duty to prevent utterances 'likely to provoke dissension among various classes of the community'.[42]

When Councillor J. B. Paterson rose to his feet, those present were probably expecting a scathing denunciation of the bishop, as Paterson's views were no secret. The *Herald* reported what happened next:

> Instead of speaking, however, he commenced to sing the National Anthem. Instantly the members of the council, the staff, the press representatives,

Liston and his friends learn of the ban on future use of municipal facilities by those deemed to be disloyalists. NZO

> and some twenty citizens who had assembled in the public gallery, seized Mr. Paterson's point, and, also rising, they all joined in the singing of the first verse of the anthem. No one present hesitated to join in this spasmodic [sic] demonstration of loyalty.[43]

Tom Bloodworth next took the floor, complaining that he would have spoken earlier had he been aware of Paterson's intentions. ('We know that, Councillor Bloodworth', retorted Gunson.) As Liston's sole apologist in the chamber, the Labour member faced an unenviable task.[44] He started by deploring the bishop's speech 'as much as anyone'. Ireland's delicate state and the spread of similar troubles throughout the Empire made it singularly ill advised. Even so, the mayor should have deferred his rebuke until Liston had sufficient time to reply. Bloodworth's concern was more for the Catholic working man than for the bishop. He reminded his listeners of the many Catholic soldiers who had lately given their lives for the Empire. Had not the council itself recently lost a lifelong supporter of the cause of Irish freedom?[45]

Did Bloodworth's plea to the council not to be 'harsh or hasty' in judgement contain an implied criticism of the mayor? Liston's speech was now before the competent authorities and he urged that they be left alone to pronounce upon it. Bloodworth's defence of the Bishop was carefully measured. He claimed to have 'analysed' the offending

The New Zealand Herald *cartoon which gave enough offence to Auckland Catholics to prompt thoughts of legal action.* NZH

speech and 'could not find that it contained other than improper and unwise statements'. Bloodworth balanced Liston's worst phrase, 'murdered by foreign troops', by quoting from British sources to show that much stronger statements had been made openly by prominent men without interference. Free speech, 'the greatest privilege of British citizenship', was enjoyed in Britain to a much greater extent than in New Zealand, he concluded.[46]

When Bloodworth moved to delete the words 'disloyal and seditious' from the resolution and to omit the clauses restricting the use of public facilities, neither of his amendments found a seconder. J. A. C. Allum, the final speaker, 'unhesitatingly' supported Gunson's resolution. Liston had set the worst possible example at a time when community leaders were looked to for guidance; they could not simply let the matter pass. 'They must stand together on the main issue of loyalty to one another, loyalty to their King, and loyalty to their Empire.'[47] The motion was then carried on the voices, Tom Bloodworth abstaining.[48]

The Auckland City Council now expected the government to adjudicate on the speech, having ensured that a white-hot glare of publicity would illuminate that process. After arousing a hornet's nest, Gunson and his colleagues directed the swarm south. They had given the newspapers plenty of ammunition to use against Liston and his friends. As the next chapter will show, press comment on the bishop's reported remarks often twisted and embroidered them. Increasingly, the events of St Patrick's Night came to be seen as through a distorting mirror, well illustrated by the *New Zealand Herald*'s Saturday supplement of 25 March. It carried a cartoon of an enraged James Liston, shillelagh in hand, furiously trampling the Union Jack into the Town Hall stage.[49]

5

Horribly Vulgar and Unspeakably Low

Instead of following public opinion, the press now leads it.

Gunson to a gathering of newspaper editors,
New Zealand Herald, 17 June 1918

Four years after making the bold claim above, James Gunson gave the New Zealand press a perfect opportunity to prove its truth. By speaking out on Sunday he allowed the Press Association to transmit his statement (and Stanbrook's report) throughout the country for comment the following day. The resulting tidal wave of editorial censure threatened to sweep away the offending prelate and his sundry apologists. The protest gathered momentum as the week unfolded. The major dailies supplemented their own critiques with selections from one another's columns, while lesser organs cribbed shamelessly; the Pahiatua *Herald* lifted most of the Wellington *Evening Post*'s editorial without acknowledgement.[1] Confident in their ability to voice the public mind, the editors struck loyal poses and parroted righteous indignation.

Nor was this assumption of editorial omniscience challenged by correspondents. On the contrary, public pressure was applied to any editor whose censure was deemed to be tardy or insufficiently vigorous. When the *Lyttelton Times* did not immediately condemn the bishop, it received a letter from 'Loyalist' asking when this action might be expected.[2] There was a small revolt by readers of the *Manawatu Daily Times* when its editor dared to differ from them in his apportionment of blame between mayor and bishop.[3] The editor of the *Franklin Times* was more accommodating. 'The Times hastens to join the loyal press of this Dominion in the general expressions of disgust at the disloyal and insulting speech.'[4]

Pens were dipped in acid as Liston's note of racial scorn was returned in full measure. Ireland was cursed with orators and 'glib-tongued patriots', declared the *Sun* (Christchurch), 'and the plague has spread to all those countries afflicted with Irish immigration.'[5] The *Dannevirke Evening News* wondered whether the bishop had deliberately spoken seditiously 'or whether he lost his head and allowed his Irish tongue to run away with him'.[6] He must have been under some strain when speaking, commented the *Wanganui Chronicle*, 'for the speech as reported lacks any trace of the astuteness which usually characterises disloyalists of his type'. Perhaps it had been made 'under the influence of that national elation to which the Irish are prone on St Patrick's Day'.[7]

Most editors backed Gunson uncritically. His 'dignified and whole-souled condemnation' won the heartiest approbation of the *Northern Advocate*. The mayor had 'voiced the feelings of an indignant populace'.[8] The *Wanganui Chronicle* described the speech as 'in its flagrant disloyalty an offence to every loyal citizen of New Zealand'.[9] From the *Coromandel County News* came undiluted praise for Gunson: 'New Zealand may well be proud of a city magistrate who so promptly and fearlessly and in such forcible and dignified language rebuked the speaker and vindicated our self-respect.'[10] The *Evening Post* was still more effusive:

> We cannot recall a criticism of any of our public men by any other that is comparable in severity to Mr Gunson's censure of the Bishop, nor, we may add, one that was more richly deserved. Not only the citizens of Auckland for whom he speaks, but the whole of our people, are indebted to the Mayor, who in this prompt, decisive, and memorable fashion has vindicated our common loyalty and our faith in the honour of the statesmen and soldiers of Great Britain from the outrageous slanders of the Coadjutor Roman Catholic Bishop of Auckland.[11]

Only two commentators saw Gunson's promptness as precipitancy and his forcefulness as weakening the dignity of his protest. The Christchurch *Press* considered him rather severe in his comments on the alleged intention of the speaker, although it added, 'we can think of no point of view from which the speech is not utterly deplorable'.[12] While conceding that Gunson had acted in what he thought were the best interests of the country, the *Manawatu Daily* Times expressed strong reservations about his public statement:

> It is questionable, however, whether he has displayed prudence or good judgement in his selection of terms. He should have been satisfied to refer the matter to the Attorney-General and to allow the Courts to determine,

TRUTH, SATURDAY, MAY 6, 1922

LISTON'S LAPSE

OUT OF THE HURLY BURLY

Irish Friends Or Irish Foes

PRELATE'S PERFERVID PRECEPTS PROVOKE PROSECUTION

The Magistrate's Court, Auckland, was packed on Monday, when the charge of making a seditious utterance preferred against James M. Liston, Co-Adjutor Bishop of Auckland, was heard before Mr. J. W. Poynton, S.M.

Mr. V. R. Meredith, Crown Prosecutor, prosecuted, and Mr. J. L. Conlan appeared for accused.

DRIVEN FROM THE COUNTRY

in which they were born and in which they would have been content to live. Why did they leave their country? Because their foreign masters did not want Irish men and women peopling their own land, but wished to use it as a cattle ranch for the snobs of the Empire. I am a native of New Zea-

Perhaps acting on legal advice New Zealand Truth *later altered its headline to 'Prelate's Alleged Lapse'.*

> if necessary, whether the language was disloyal or seditious. Mr Gunson may place his own interpretation upon the words of the Bishop, but he has no right, in his official capacity, to describe as 'seditious' an utterance that might be held by the Courts to be otherwise.[13]

Had Gunson blundered in his capacity as mayor just as badly as Liston had as bishop? Many *Manawatu Daily Times* readers did not think so. 'Britisher' took his editor to task at once, urging all loyal citizens to demand the prosecution of 'these demi-gods' Redwood and Liston. 'Those Roman Catholics who cannot live in harmony under our flag should forego the benefit of our rights and privileges, and withdraw to a Roman Catholic country.'[14]

The *Times* had indeed devoted more space to condemning Gunson than to censuring Liston, whose address was deemed merely 'unfortunate' and 'ill-advised'. This imbalance was pointed out by another correspondent, who recalled similar speeches by Archbishops Mannix and Redwood. Their insults to the British Empire were all 'garbed in the cloak of religion'. Why then upbraid Gunson for being 'a little zealous'? The editor rapidly retreated before his critics, claiming that he had refrained from abusing Liston because violent language would not contribute to peace in the community. 'We asked if the speech of Dr Liston was loyal, and the answer of our correspondents appears to be entirely in the negative.'[15]

The *Southland Daily News* thought that Gunson should simply have ignored Liston as unrepresentative of his people. It seemed to believe that disloyal Catholic prelates, like Labour extremists, would wither away once post-war social dislocation had run its course. 'If some mem-

AN EPISCOPAL BOWMAN.—A ST. PATRICK'S DAY SPORT.

The Observer *captures the wounding effect of Liston's bitter phrases.* NZO

bers of each organisation are less than British, the majority of them are at heart loyal citizens of the Empire, and it would be wise to treat with majorities only until the world is sufficiently revived to make a closer analysis of conditions.'[16] Showing rare wisdom, the *Dannevirke Evening News* refused to comment on the details of the speech as practically *sub judice*; it also noted with disapproval the rival forces assembling behind mayor and bishop respectively.[17]

Few editors thought to query the accuracy of the Press Association report. While the *Northern Advocate* felt that it gave enough of the speech and its sequel 'to make it quite clear what has happened', both the Christchurch *Press* and the *New Zealand Times* prefaced their condemnations with the assumption that the bishop had been correctly reported.[18] The *Timaru Herald* made a telling point:

> Bishop Liston of Auckland has neither denied nor yet admitted the speech attributed to him at the St Patrick's Day concert. Our comment therefore must still be tentative. But it can hardly be suggested that his Lordship has not had ample opportunity of correcting any possible misrepresentation, or that the matter is of so little importance that he can afford to ignore it. Neither Dr Liston nor any one else may do that.[19]

The *Wanganui Chronicle* cared little whether the report was accurate. Its bitter editorial, headed 'Flagrant Disloyalty', made it clear that Liston was damned if he did and damned if he did not.

> While we are loath to believe that this church dignitary so far forgot himself as to say what he has actually been reported to have said, and while we question whether he will acknowledge his statements as published are correct, we have no doubt that the words really express his sentiments.

> 'Scratch a Russian and you will find a Tartar' is an old saying which is not perhaps without application in this case.[20]

Liston's historical references drew a sharp rejoinder from the *Rotorua Chronicle*. Had not England 'pampered and fed' the Irish over many long and weary years? Repeated concessions had been made to generations of Irish nationalists with the British taxpayer patiently bearing the cost – all to no avail. 'Every fresh advance has been followed by the bitterest recrimination, accusation, calumny and falsehood.'

> The 'Wrongs of Ireland,' the slogan to evil deeds and unjust thoughts, has to go back centuries for its justification . . . Looking back over all recorded history, one is tempted to think that were all national wrongs so held in remembrance as are the wrongs of Ireland, the world would be one vast Golgotha. What keeps this burning hate alight? Who feeds this quenchless fire?[21]

According to the *Southland Daily News*, Catholic prelates were simply reading from the wrong script. 'While Archbishop Redwood and Bishop Liston persist in quoting dark history instead of considering the blessings they might assist in conferring on Irishmen, there are certain to be reprisals and sectarian bitterness.'[22] ('Reprisals' was an unfortunate choice of word, given that they were very much current history for the Irish.) Liston stood accused of distorting Ireland's present as well as its past; the Christchurch *Star* described his summary of recent events as 'about as one-sided as it could possibly have been'. His viewpoint seemed deliberately perverse. 'The troubled course of the Irish question is watched by these people with a prejudiced vision, which transforms the Sinn Fein gunmen into noble patriots and the Imperial soldiers into foreign murderers.'[23]

These rival perceptions came into sharper focus once the press began to analyse Liston's reported remarks in detail. Despite reproducing the Press Association report elsewhere in their columns, several editors published a phrase-by-phrase dissection of the speech. The case for the prosecution was summarised by the *New Zealand Times*: Liston had 'raked up the bad past of ages, mingled discontent with his satisfaction for the present, and encouraged the idea of a future of bloodshed'. Rather than bury the hatchet, the bishop had brandished it in the air.

> Was it a time to glorify the rebellion of 1916 and denounce as murderers the troops who fought for the Crown against that rebellion? Was it a time for raking up the wretched past of the centuries with bitterness excessive? Was it a time to tell Irishmen by implication that it is the will of

> God that men and women must shed their blood to obtain the completeness of the freedom which he alleges they have only partially attained?[24]

The press refused to accept either Liston's Irish descent or his ecclesiastical position as justification for such 'poverty of judgement'. His prediction that many would fight for complete Irish freedom brought a telling rejoinder from the *New Zealand Times*. 'Of course, this does not mean a definite offer to rebellion of Divine approval, and a solemn promise for its success of Divine assistance. But if the extreme view is taken that he did mean these things, Bishop Liston will have no-one but himself to blame.'[25]

Liston's references to the Irish rising drew the heaviest fire. The Christchurch *Press* singled out his 'wrong and bitter phrase' on foreign murderers as the prime cause of complaint, while it 'passed the comprehension' of the *Waikato Times* how anyone could glorify the bloody rebellion.[26] 'A glorious attempt indeed to cripple Britain and the Empire, including New Zealand, in the death struggle with Germany', the *Dominion* commented scathingly, reminding its readers that Germany had supplied weapons to the Irish rebels.[27] For that matter, were not speeches like Liston's the root cause of the 1916 revolt?

> The rebellion of 1916 was largely the fruit of Irish oratory which inflamed the passions of the Irish mob, and spurred them to deeds of the blackest treachery and dishonour. The brand of Cain is imprinted equally on the brows of orators who killed the English with their mouths, and the misguided fools who listened to them, and took up arms against the Crown at a time when England and the rest of the Empire were fighting for liberty. If Dr Liston and his Sinn Fein friends had had their way Ireland might have been Germanised here now.[28]

Had Liston forgotten that 'at the very moment English troops had to be sent to quell the rebellion in Ireland, New Zealand soldiers, including men of his own church, were giving up their lives in France, in company with other units of this so-called foreign army?'[29] The Anzac link was re-emphasised by the *Dannevirke Evening News*. The Irish rebels, over whom Liston 'slobbered', had been 'in league with Germany to betray every soldier that went from the Dominions Overseas to fight for the Empire'.[30] The *Wanganui Chronicle* was predictably severe in its conclusions.

> Apparently Bishop Liston glories in the rebellion of Easter 1916, because it was a rebellion against the British flag, and he evidently rejoices in the deaths of British Protestant soldiers, 'foreign murderers' he calls them, in

De Valera addresses Dail Eireann in 1921. Camera Press

putting down the rebellion and for the serious effect this rebellion had in keeping so many British troops from the Western front.[31]

Liston, it appeared, would give only one small cheer for the partial freedom Ireland had achieved, while reaffirming the country's right to the whole of it. To the *Wairarapa Age* this seemed to impugn the basis of the Anglo–Irish Treaty. Liston had called upon Irishmen 'to regard it merely as an instalment and to claim that whole freedom which can only mean a republic'.[32] Far from ascribing the treaty to England's financial weakness (Redwood's view), or to the military victory of the Irish Republican Army (Dr Kelly's boast), the press preferred to emphasise the magnanimity of British statesmen. 'Even the most generous concessions ever offered by a great nation to a small one fail to extract the faintest semblance of gratitude or goodwill', grumbled the *Evening Post*.[33] The Christchurch *Press* had 'only indignation for any attempt to keep the Irish question alive here.' Its city rival reminded readers that the treaty still had to go before the Irish people for confirmation, 'and the work in opposition to it is being done by men of like mind to Dr Liston'.[34]

Several papers coupled Liston and de Valera as men who would risk civil war in Ireland and disruption of the British Empire in order to achieve their impossible goals.[35] Although Liston had not mentioned the Irish leader by name, his allusion to the man who would ensure that Ireland was not 'duped by England' was unmistakable. The *New*

Zealand Times expressed surprise that such a statement had emanated from a bishop rather than 'a rash, ignorant schoolboy'. It was said of a man 'who is fighting a minority fight to incite discontent, repudiation of the Treaty, and renewal of the bloody struggle which was ended by the Treaty'.[36]

British tolerance was being mistaken for weakness, claimed the *Evening Post*; to this it ascribed 'the contempt and even the hatred' displayed by men like de Valera and Liston. 'By more hatred, more ferocious rhetoric and more bloodshed – Mr de Valera uses this very word, and it is implied in the passage above quoted from his disciple – the weakness of Britain may yet be exploited still further, and the virtual independence of Ireland be made absolute.'[37] The two rebels were finding sterner opponents in the vigilant editors of New Zealand's daily press, and none more so than the editor of the *Auckland Star*, that erstwhile candid friend of Irish nationalism.

> The spectacle of Eamon de Valera rushing through Ireland in a whirlwind of hate must make all true friends of Ireland grieve and shudder. There is something horrible, something fiendish, in his speech at (of all places) Killarney, in which he 'forecasted and pleaded for civil war.' To gain full freedom Ireland must war against not only 'foreign soldiers,' but her own sons. Republicans must march over the dead bodies of their own brothers; they must 'wade through Irish blood.' Are we listening to the words of a civilised man or to the ravings of a Zulu witch doctor?[38]

Several papers expressed sarcastic gratitude that Liston had declared his love for New Zealand, his native land. It was as well to have this assurance, commented the *Evening Post*, because it was impossible to infer 'from the whole drift and spirit of his argument'.[39] Liston's claim to be a loyal New Zealander, however, could not be go unchallenged. The Christchurch *Press* read the lesson. 'One cannot be a loyal New Zealander and at the same time either applaud antagonism to the Empire and enmity to Britain, or hope for any weakening of the solidarity of the Imperial structure.'[40] No dual allegiance was permissible – other than that enjoyed by 'British' New Zealanders, of course. The *Gisborne Times* expanded on the crucial issue of identity: 'If Britain is a foreign nation so far as Ireland is concerned – and that is, of course, not in accordance with fact – so would be New Zealand and all the other units of the Empire.'[41]

Not satisfied with denying the bishop's right to speak for his fellow-countrymen, the *Rotorua Chronicle* accused Liston of 'base treachery' to his country. While Irish agitators who abused Britain were an unhappy fact of American political life, 'here in our own land, surrounded by all the freedom that the British freeman enjoys, protected by its laws, using its privileges, and kept in safety by its arms, born in the land and living on its wealth, high in the confidence of the church he represents, is one who infamously traduces those to whom he owes his all'.[42]

The *Evening Post* reminded its readers that those 'foreign' soldiers maligned by Liston had saved New Zealand from the terrors of foreign invasion and made it possible for the bishop to speak at Auckland on Friday evening. The paper further explored the motives of self-interest which should prompt a unanimous censure of the speech.

> The insurrection . . . of 1916 would have let the Germans not only into Dublin but into London, Auckland and Wellington too, if it had succeeded. . . . Without the help of these foreign murderers and of their fellow cut-throats in the Navy, the liberties of New Zealand could not have been preserved any more than those of Ireland. St Patrick's Day would have been celebrated with the German flag above that of Sinn Fein if the soldiers and sailors of this 'foreign nation' had failed us. New Zealand still needs the protection of these forces, and those of us who are not blinded by prejudice and passion can see that, if Britain allows the establishment in Ireland of an independent republic animated by the spirit of Mr de Valera and Bishop Liston her power would probably fail to protect us in the next great war.[43]

This press unanimity was based on something more than smug self-certainty. No one had challenged the accuracy of the *New Zealand Herald* report, which had also been endorsed by the *Auckland Star*, the NZPA and the mayor of Auckland. Not content with censuring the errant bishop, several editors turned to dictating a course for the government to follow. 'There is a law on the Statute Book regarding sedition', declared the Christchurch *Sun*, 'and Dr Liston should be taught that his rank and position do not confer upon him any privilege to talk treason when the spirit moves him.'[44] 'Muzzle the sedition-monger', demanded the *King Country Chronicle*, while the *Gisborne Times* agreed that Liston could have no complaint if asked to explain himself by the Attorney-General.[45]

There was no lack of suggested sanctions to be imposed on the bishop and his supporters. The *Franklin Times* called for their immediate disfranchisement or deportation – surely life in a non-British country would be more comfortable for someone holding the views ascribed to the bishop?[46] The *Evening Post* urged Liston to 'go and help Mr de Valera in his relentless vendetta, not against the hated Sassenach but against his own fellow-countrymen'.[47] The only consolation the Christchurch *Sun* could find in the emergence of the Irish Free State was that its citizens would now be reduced to fighting each other.[48] The *Rotorua Chronicle* valued the new creation solely as a place to dump disloyalists like Bishop Liston, predicting that 'when they are removed from the personal safety zone of the Dominion, from the ideal and safe to the real and dangerous, they will be more chary of expressing their opinions'.[49]

Thus, within a week of his St Patrick's Night address, the newspaper editors of New Zealand had effectively tried, convicted and passed sentence upon James Michael Liston. While the bishop had not formally admitted his guilt, his silence was regarded as eloquent testimony for the prosecution. All that remained was for the government and the judiciary to do their duty.

6

Disgusted

> While tolerant of the views of others, this paper will not ventilate the opinions of those whose writings can be construed into an expression of hatred and contempt towards English rule and sympathy and friendship towards her enemies.
>
> *Hawke's Bay Tribune*, 23 March 1922

The chorus of editorial approval and the pile of congratulatory resolutions on Gunson's desk represented a vote of confidence by the establishment in the mayor's judgement and integrity. More popular feeling on the issue was expressed in the cheers, applause and fervent patriotic singing of various congregations and assemblies. Unfortunately, the sheaves of letters Gunson received during his week in the limelight have not survived, nor were they published at the time (save in cartoon form).[1] As the more enthusiastic of Gunson's correspondents may have written also to the local papers, the contents of their correspondence columns enable us to examine individual responses to the controversy.

The *New Zealand Herald* invited its readers to comment on the speech, again printing their contributions under somewhat leading shoulder headings: 'Disloyal Parsons', 'Fomenting Hatred', etc. Despite selecting from a heavy mailbag, the editor did not turn away those critics of the bishop who preferred to remain anonymous. By contrast, the *Auckland Star*, considering the matter 'in a large measure personal', refused to publish correspondence over noms-de-plume.[2] Some seventeen letters appeared in the *Herald* in the week following the speech, only six of which bore the author's name. Less suavely worded than most of the editorials, the letters revealed a narrower, sectarian focus and called for sterner penalties to be imposed upon Liston.

F. A. Carling condemned both Whyte and Liston for their 'unfortunate utterances'. (Bishop Whyte had criticised the government's refusal to allow state scholarships to be taken out in Catholic schools.) 'Probably only Irishmen could draw so deeply upon their imagination for a description of the acts and deeds of the Governments of Ireland and New Zealand and still retain their self respect and the respect of their adherents.' Carling's advice to New Zealanders was to stand firm for an uncorrupted secular education system. 'Happily unbiased education has freed most of us from the fetters of religious bigotry', he concluded smugly.[3]

Other *Herald* correspondents expanded on the educational theme. How could Liston have spoken otherwise, asked 'The Native Born', when 'it is part of the regular curriculum of Roman Catholic schools that the scholars shall be taught hatred of England and disloyalty (more or less) to the Empire'? Surely Protestants owed Liston a debt of gratitude.[4] 'M.B.' also considered the speech to be 'a splendid argument against loyal British subjects supporting those schools which refuse to teach the scholars to "Fear God and honour the King"'.[5]

'Teacher' wanted the same oath of allegiance to be administered to ministers of religion as was being asked that very month of every schoolteacher: 'For, if a teacher, with only the fear of the cane behind him, can by his seditious talk cause a rot in the community, how much greater harm can a disloyal priest accomplish, when he can back up his talk with the pain and pangs of hell?'[6] 'Proud Britisher' would extract an oath of allegiance from every public servant: 'Such employees are undoubtedly in the service of the King, and let them either own such allegiance or get out.'[7] George Johnston suggested the application of oaths all round:

> My own idea is that no minister, parson, priest, or other person should be permitted to preach in a church or chapel or hall, or deliver a lecture or address, religious or political, either in a building or at Grey Statue or the foot of Queen Street or the wharf or other public place who has not previously taken the same oath that teachers are now required to take.[8]

Why not a by-law requiring the national anthem to be sung at the start of every Town Hall gathering? 'Loyalist' also wanted the Union Jack to be on permanent display in the auditorium. While he or she believed that loyalty should not have to be thrust down the throat, such action was needed when dealing with 'certain small, though loud-voiced sections of the community.'[9] 'The Native Born' wished to remind Liston that patriotism was not an attribute of Irishmen alone. 'Although the English-born do not proclaim their love of country from the housetops in the frothy and "spill-over" Irish way, the English-born are nevertheless deeply patriotic.'[10]

John Liddell Kelly roundly denounced the speech in his letter to the *Auckland Star*: 'as wanton as it was provocative, and as unwise as it was untrue'. If Liston's superiors in Rome did not reprimand him, Kelly wanted the Governor-General to recommend punitive action by the imperial authorities; perhaps threatening to recall the British Ambassador to the Papal Court might do the trick. A lifetime supporter of Irish home rule and an opponent of sectarianism, Kelly boasted that some of his best friends were Catholics – a relative had even married one!

> Up till quite recently I have always upheld the Church of Rome as the leading Christian sect and have strenuously resisted the contention that she could possibly be Babylon, the Scarlet Woman, or the Beast of Revelation. But the events of the past six years have slowly but surely undermined my faith in the Irish as a people and in the Romish Church. The former, I begin to perceive, are incurably hostile to the British; the R.C. Church begins to assume the form of Anti-Christ.[11]

For this change in his views, Kelly blamed 'the Listons, the Redwoods and the Mannixes of the Romish prelacy'. He sympathised with Irish people 'duped and misled by such men as these prelates and by a half-crazy visionary like de Valera'. 'The Native Born' voiced similar concerns in the *Herald*. 'There is little doubt that slowly but surely there is arising within this Dominion a strong and very deep feeling of resentment, anger and distrust of the Roman Catholic hierarchy and of that church.'[12]

Correspondence published outside Auckland followed similar lines, distance not lessening the strength of feeling caused by Liston's remarks. Ex-servicemen seemed to take especial umbrage. 'Returned Soldier' in the *Taranaki Daily News* objected to being classed as a murderer: 'Well do I remember with what disgust the Dublin rebellion was received by our troops in France. While we were going through hell . . . there were these rebels in Ireland stabbing us in the back. Surely they out-Hunned the Hun, the diabolical murderers.'[13] Returning the bishop's bitter epithet, he recalled the events of 'Bloody Sunday' (21 November 1920), when the IRA 'murdered fourteen English and Scottish officers, in their beds, defenceless, and in the presence of their wives!' Liston had rejoiced in 'deeds which we

Liston was widely berated for encouraging the revival of sectarian antagonism. NZO

associate with Egyptians, Turks, Bedouins and other partially-civilised, non-Christian races'.[14]

There was scant sympathy for the bishop's tragic personal history. 'Loyalist' commented tartly in the *Lyttelton Times*: 'If Dr Liston's parents were driven from Ireland, as the doctor says, I presume it was for their country's good, but it is a pity they did not go elsewhere.'[15] 'Disgusted' in the *Otago Daily Times* attributed the growth of sectarian feeling in New Zealand over the past decade to the sentiments expressed so freely by Liston and Dr James Kelly.[16] Several correspondents had a shilling both ways, condemning the PPA but blaming Catholics for its existence. 'Britisher' in the *Manawatu Daily Times* saw Liston's speech as 'a recruiting agency' for Howard Elliott's organisation, while 'Unshackled' in the *Waipawa Mail* was closer to the mark when placing some of the blame on the fiery *New Zealand Tablet* editor:

> Of late years the Roman Catholic paper published in Dunedin, and the bishops of the Church, have seen fit to make a 'dead set' on our Imperial connection and have belittled England in every possible way, so that there has arisen a growing section who are joining hands with the only leader offering himself, and thus establishing the P.P.A.[17]

'Where is it going to end?' asked 'Returned Soldier' plaintively. 'Is our beloved New Zealand to be turned into another Ireland?' Liston was 'preaching racial hatred of the worst kind'.[18] While claiming to be a New Zealander, he seemed determined to fight the religious battles of the Old World. 'Disgusted' demanded that Liston be presented with his passports and made to leave the country within twenty-four hours.[19] H. Irwin in the *Hawke's Bay Tribune* also urged Massey to order Liston's immediate deportation, adding that his good example in this respect might well be followed by W. M. Hughes, the Australian Prime Minister, in dealing with Archbishop Mannix of Melbourne.[20]

> During the war Mr Hughes continually threatened Mannix with punishment unless he ceased his disloyalty and seditious speeches but there it ended. Will Mr Massey show a little more backbone than Mr Hughes, and act, without threatening? It would be pleasant to find that we had one politician in the Empire who is not afraid of the Roman Catholic hierarchy.[21]

The reaction of Liston's Town Hall audience had tarred the Irish Catholic community with the brush of disloyalty. Stanbrook's report gave no indication that anyone had objected to the bishop's remarks; rather, those attending had indicated their noisy approval. Several editors could not quite bring themselves to accept this sad fact. The *Dannevirke Evening News* wept for the loyal Irish Catholics ('who realise the blessings of this free country') distressed by the speech, while the *Franklin Times* regretted its consequences for those Catholics who had proved their 'splendid loyalty' during the war.[22]

By stressing his episcopal status, Liston had put the onus on 'loyal' Catholics to disavow his sentiments. The *Auckland Star* challenged them to do so by publicly backing the Anglo–Irish Treaty.[23] The *New Zealand Herald* stepped up the pressure as the week unfolded. Newmarket Borough Councillor F. J. O'Meara's plea that judgement be reserved until the bishop had been heard was contrasted with Liston's contemptuous reply to the mayor (see Chapter 7).[24] After the Auckland City Council meeting on Thursday evening, the *Herald* was still more importunate in its demands for a public disavowal:

> No person or no organisation is asked to apologise for what may have been an individual expression of opinion. But since Bishop Liston presumed to speak for others it is necessary that these others should dissociate themselves from his speech or share his condemnation. If they do not, the public can only interpret their silence to mean approval, and the resolution of the City Council will apply to them.[25]

The *Auckland Star* wondered how anyone could find a word to say in favour of the beleaguered prelate. It questioned the identity of those behind the supportive Hibernian and Irish National Association resolutions published in its own columns; at least Liston had come out into the open with his disloyalty. 'It is desirable in this matter that we should know those who are loyal to the flag, the protection of which they enjoy, and those who are disaffected. There would appear to be no reasonable middle course.'[26] Laurence Johnstone quickly endorsed the *Star*'s demand; if these people represented genuine local Irish opinion 'then it is high time that we settle who are the foreigners in this Dominion'.[27]

To judge from the correspondence columns, Auckland Catholics were only too eager to oblige. On Tuesday the *Auckland Star* received several letters from Catholic readers 'deprecating the utterances of the Coadjutor Bishop and protesting the loyalty of Catholics to the country of their birth or adoption'.[28] To the fore were those Catholics with reputations to protect, notably William Joseph Napier, who wrote to both Auckland papers. Napier was founder and president of the Navy League and the Victoria League, so his reaction to the speech came as no surprise. Confident that few intelligent Catholics would care for Liston's 'ill-timed and misleading remarks', he condemned the reopening of old sores between England and Ireland. An ardent home ruler, he had warmly embraced 'the great Treaty of Peace and Reconciliation'.[29]

Napier's recent return from a year-long visit to England and Ireland added weight to his analysis of Irish political opinion. He believed that North-east Ulster was only temporarily estranged and a united Ireland not far off. Ireland's rejection of 'the hybrid Spaniard' (de Valera) and her embrace of 'true Irishmen like Collins and Griffith' was proof of the treaty's popular support; the cry of lay and clerical diehards for complete independence had no solid support in the country. Napier scorned the suggestion that God's desires tended towards an Irish Republic:

> I do not pretend to have the ear of the Almighty, but I prefer to accept the settled judgement of four generations of Irishmen from O'Connell to John Redmond, that Ireland wants only self-government within the Empire rather than to believe the irresponsible ipse dixit of a colonial bishop.[30]

The Irish-born Napier clearly resented having to speak up for the Irish landlord, whose misdeeds he had long denounced. He challenged Liston's right to reopen the Irish land question (solved some twenty years ago) and dismissed the Dublin Rising as 'a wild escapade during the Easter holidays of 1916' by 'patriotic but misguided young men'. To say that British troops had murdered them was 'a gross travesty of

William Napier was perhaps the Auckland Catholic under most pressure to disavow his Bishop's speech. NZO

the facts': 'The soldiers of the King had to do their duty of suppressing the rebellion, and all contemporary records prove that they did it with the humanity that has always characterised "Tommy Atkins".'[31]

Napier predicted that Ireland and New Zealand would long remain contented units of the 'Anglo–Celtic Empire'. (He preferred this description because 'Irishmen have largely contributed by their labour and talents to build up the Empire'.) As for Bishop Liston, born a New Zealander and therefore a subject of the King:

> [W]hatever justification his progenitors may have had for hating England, he has none, but rather owes a debt of gratitude to the Mother of Parliaments for the great benefits of New Zealand citizenship. It is to be hoped therefore that he will not by unguarded speech sow the seeds of disloyalty to the Throne and Empire – that Empire which I venture to say is the most potent instrument created by Providence for the spread throughout the world of civilisation, justice and peace.[32]

Maurice Foley, an Auckland insurance agent, also responded to the invitations of the Auckland press. Limiting his remarks to the Anglo–Irish Treaty, Foley spoke for the New Zealand Irish as confidently as had Napier for those in Ireland:

> I speak with authority on the subject, as I have had much intercourse recently with men of Irish birth from different parts of New Zealand. I am satisfied that as far as England is concerned she has done her part, so now the quarrel must be between Irishmen themselves. Ireland as a republic does not enter our thoughts. I have not met anyone among the Irish people who advocates it. In fact, we are dead against it.[33]

Foley's self-restraint contrasted with the outspokenness of Patrick Darby, a manufacturer's agent and member of a prominent local Catholic family. Patrick's brother, Joseph Croke Darby, was an Auckland priest who had recently been suspended from clerical duty pending an appeal to Rome.[34] Several Catholic commentators suspected fraternal collusion in this letter of protest, which was published in both Auckland daily papers. 'Pained and surprised' at the speech, Darby expressed sympathy for his non-Catholic fellow-citizens; Liston had no right publicly to insult them, still less to cite his episcopal rank as supporting his remarks. Had not Pope Benedict XV enjoined restraint on the clergy when speaking on such matters?

> He has no more right than any ordinary layman, Catholic or non-Catholic, to dictate to him his political views. His duty, in conjunction with all other bishops and priests, is to attend to the spiritual wants of his people and not to try and stir up strife and dissension amongst people.[35]

Darby dismissed the supportive resolution of the Auckland Hibernians (another of his priestly brother's bugbears) as representing 'only a fractional part of the Catholics in Auckland, and on a par with the three tailors of Tooley Street'. He ended by advocating a loyalty test far beyond anything suggested by Liston's harshest non-Catholic critic.

> The time has evidently arrived when not only the school teachers, private and public, should be called upon to take the oath of allegiance, but every adult in the Dominion, and those who refuse to take the oath be given the option of leaving the Dominion to settle in lands more in keeping with their sentiments.[36]

In George Graham's view, Liston's comments were 'inexcusable and must not pass unchallenged'. As a Catholic, he objected to the bishop's views being taken as official teaching: 'Roman Catholics yield the palm to no section of this or of any other part of the Empire in loyalty to the Crown.' Had they not helped to wrest the land from the Maori ('now happily our friends and allies in Empire building')? Again, in the Great War, 'Catholic wealth and blood flowed freely to defend our Empire and all it means.' Graham hinted that obstacles might be placed in the way of Liston's succession to the Auckland see should he fail to retract. Drastic action should be taken against all disturbers of the community peace – the higher the perpetrator's rank, the more severe the punishment. Graham maintained that Gunson, rather than Liston, commanded the whole-hearted support of the Catholic community.[37]

The *New Zealand Herald* allowed several Catholics to express their indignation from the shelter of a comfortable anonymity. 'C.C.C.' was an Irishman with scant regard for his fellow-countrymen. 'For centuries England has striven to understand a temperament which is almost un-understandable.' Who could blame the English for concluding that nothing but Cromwellian severity would now meet the case? He advocated withdrawing the civil rights of those who endangered New Zealand's domestic peace 'by this artificially fomented hatred of England'. It was sheer perversity constantly to claim that England desired 'the enslavement of Ireland to Empire aggrandisement' when all the evidence was against it.[38]

Most Catholic correspondents prefaced their censures with a fervent declaration of loyalty to God, King and Empire. 'Atra Dies' had 'done his bit' overseas. He was alarmed at the thought of his co-religionists being branded as disloyal, a fate that had befallen Australian Catholics through the activities of Archbishop Mannix. 'Thus, we may fearfully visualise the day when we Catholics shall be relegated to the gutter as things that are unclean.'[39] For his or her part, 'Mens sibi conscia recti' wanted a public apology from Liston; only thus would the Catholic reputation be rescued.[40]

The Wellington *Evening Post* had handled Liston roughly in its Monday afternoon issue; he was also targeted in its correspondence columns, with Catholics contributing at least three letters. 'New Zealander' criticised Liston for playing into PPA hands and endangering the political interests of the church:

> Catholics individually are, according to their upbringing and views, in all political and national parties, but Catholicism is not allied to, or in any way incorporated in or with, Masseyism, Sinn Feinism, Liberal-Labourism, Red Flagism, Lloyd Georgeism, or any other 'ism, and it is the bounden duty of Catholic religious leaders to refrain from giving colour to any suspicion to the contrary.[41]

'Another New Zealander' was a Catholic of English descent. He saw the speech as injuring those who shared Liston's faith but not his nationality: 'One would sometimes think that there were no English Catholics in New Zealand.'[42] This theme was taken up by 'Semper Fidelis' in a stern lecture:

> He may not be aware the Catholic Church is universal, not Irish as he would make us believe. In this spiritual capacity racial conflicts and politics should have no call, and should form no part of any clerical discourse, especially in the Church which embraces all nations.[43]

Outside the religious sphere, Liston's utterances were 'on a par with the ordinary twiddle-twaddle of the man in the street'. Nevertheless, 'Semper Fidelis' believed that Liston had set a dangerous precedent; another priest – perhaps a Bolshevik one – might use the glamour and protection afforded by his sacred mantle to subvert society. What could be done to prevent such a calamity? One possible safeguard would be a New Zealand agent at the Vatican capable of lodging a formal complaint and ensuring that any clerical firebrands were hauled over the ecclesiastical coals.[44] 'Semper Fidelis' also proposed the intriguing idea of a strike by loyal Catholic laity. Could the latter be blamed for rejecting the spiritual ministrations of a disloyal pastor? Or refusing to contribute further to Catholic schools and seminaries?

'Semper Fidelis' raised a wider issue by guessing (wrongly) that Liston had received his education in New Zealand. Surely the laity should exercise better control over their schools and seminaries if the bishop was a fair specimen of the fruits of Catholic educational methods. Their money was not given 'for the purpose of making their schools a hotbed for sedition and the training ground for mischief-making clergy.'[45] Indeed, Liston may well have risen to his present eminence thanks to the generosity of English Catholics: 'Possibly had it been otherwise, he might be a simple hewer of wood and a drawer of water, labouring among his own people.'[46] 'Semper Fidelis' scarcely needed to assure *Evening Post* readers that he was not an Irishman.

The long-suppressed resentment of many non-Irish Catholics found release in this assault on Liston. While 'English Catholic' warned the *New Zealand Herald* against confusing Irish opinions with the teachings of the Catholic church, 'Cut It Out' explained how the confusion had arisen. 'Catholic priests of the Liston-Mannix type evidently place their tinpot feuds and politics first, and their religion second.'[47] An Australian Catholic of Irish parentage, he declared himself 'fed up' with the wrongs of Ireland and with those who bleated about them from the pulpit.

> Their national hatreds and bitterness take precedence, to the great detriment and scandal of the Catholic faith. Our Catholic faith is of all countries, and not, as many Irish people unconsciously believe, a special privilege of the Irish. Even numerically, Ireland's Catholics are as a grain of sand on the seashore of the great and grand ocean of Catholicity. They have

> the faith, but not a monopoly of it, as many of the sermons we hear would lead us to infer. There were other saints than Irish saints, and other martyrs than Irish martyrs.[48]

Impatience and frustration was the keynote struck by all the Catholic correspondents; they did not want old hatreds perpetuated in their new country. 'We want to live in peace and happiness with our neighbours, no matter what their religious beliefs may be, or their politics either.'[49] The strength and unanimity of Catholic feeling, at least as manifested in the press, probably lessened the explosive effect of Liston's speech. That Catholics were foremost in condemning their bishop, and in advocating extreme penalties for any future failing on his part, reassured the non-Catholic community and helped to retard the development of an unambiguous sectarian cleavage. What it did for James Liston and his supporters was quite another matter.

7

I Weighed All My Words Carefully

Not understood. Poor souls with stunted vision
Oft measure giants by their narrow gauge;
The poisoned shafts of falsehood and derision
Are oft impelled 'gainst those who mould the age,
Not understood.

'Not Understood', Thomas Bracken[1]

On the morning of Monday 20 March it was Bishop Liston's turn to have his breakfast ruined. The *New Zealand Herald* was brought in to him at 8.15; Gunson's letter of inquiry arrived one hour later. Liston considered the mayor's statement to be hasty and intemperate. The *Month*, published under his supervision, dubbed it 'a remarkable effusion'.[2] Less convinced than the *Herald* of the purity of Gunson's motives, Liston considered the outcry 'simply a clever plan to put the Mayor of Auckland into Parliament and to further the cause of the Reform Party.' Had not the latter displayed 'shocking bigotry' towards his Church over the previous eight years, 'under the personal stimulus of the bigoted Mr Massey'?[3] Liston saw himself as the innocent victim of a cruel plot. He described the flurry of press censure over the next few days as 'horribly vulgar and unspeakably low'.[4]

Only two small voices were raised in his defence: Members of the Hibernian Society and the Irish National Association (INA) held separate meetings on Monday evening and passed resolutions condemning the attacks on the bishop. The St Benedict's Hibernian branch expressed its 'warmest appreciation and unbounded and unalterable confidence' in Liston, while the INA sternly rebuked those Irishmen who had criticised him.[5] Published in Tuesday's *Auckland Star*, these resolutions were reprinted in newspapers throughout the country.

When the storm first broke, Liston took the precaution of consulting the several lawyers among his parishioners. It was later claimed that they urged him to stay silent in view of the threatened legal action. His own attitude is revealed in the letter he wrote on Tuesday to the Wellington lawyer, Patrick Joseph O'Regan: 'Though a stranger to you I feel no hesitation in appealing to you for advice. I'm in hot water, and for the usual reason – Ireland.'[6] O'Regan had not only made a specialty of defending alleged seditionists, but, as President of the Irish Self-Determination League of New Zealand, was the country's best-known lay advocate of Irish nationalism.

Liston fired off a volley of questions at the lawyer. Was there any sedition contained in the *Herald*'s version of his remarks? 'I weighed all my words carefully and don't think I fell in.' Had Gunson the right to refuse Catholics the use of the Town Hall? What should he do if proceedings were begun? Could the Attorney-General rely on a newspaper report? Liston explained his public silence with alarming candour: 'I think it better to wait till the storm has abated and then repeat my remarks.' There was no hint here that the newspaper report had distorted or misrepresented his speech. Nor did he seem unduly worried about his legal position: the threat from the City Council rather than the Crown Law Office was causing him most concern.

Twenty-four hours later the temptation to respond to the mayor and his acolytes grew too strong for Liston to resist. He decided to copy Gunson's tactic of an open letter through the press. It was a calculated snub to the mayor; his question was left unanswered, his 'protest' mocked, and his manners corrected.

> I beg to acknowledge the receipt of your letter of Saturday. I notice that Your Worship issued your 'protest' before I could possibly have received your letter.
>
> Seeing that Your Worship had not the courtesy, not to say the sense of fair play, to await my reply to your question, before handing your condemnation of me to the press of New Zealand, it seems to me quite unnecessary that you should have written to me at all, and it is certainly unnecessary that I should answer your question.
>
> As Your Worship has made this matter public, I am handing this letter to the press.[7]

This stinging rebuke was also Liston's revenge on those editors who had importunately demanded apologies and explanations from him.

He dismissed the whole affair as 'contemptible and muddle-headed', and was not slow in expressing his contempt.[8] Liston's friends greatly relished the reply, the *New Zealand Tablet* rejoicing in the snub administered to mayor and press alike.[9] However, few of the bishop's critics were impressed by its tone of injured innocence, while the letter probably steeled Gunson in his determination to secure a renewed condemnation of the speech from his fellow councillors on Thursday evening.

After reading the Auckland City Council's pronouncement in Friday's *Herald* (along with the inevitable editorial in its favour), Liston took the train to Wellington, where he was due to officiate at the opening of St Mary of the Angels in Boulcott Street. He was also planning to consult O'Regan, an appointment that must have seemed more urgent on Friday than when originally made three days before. Liston's concern had increased as the week passed and the public protest snowballed. Shocked by the attacks in the Auckland press, he could not but note that their columns were bulging with Catholic critics. His own mailbag, however, had never been heavier. Father John O'Hara of Waihi summed up the feelings of many of Liston's correspondents.

> All the Catholic people, priests and Sisters of Waihi at a unanimous meeting today expressed their sincerest sympathy for you; as well as their wholehearted fidelity and fullest confidence in you. I am glad that you did not respond to Mr Gunson. He took you short and wanted to have a shot at Catholics through you well knowing the crowd that would back him up; so don't worry stick to your guns. What you said was too true for them and the applause you received from your Irish Catholic audience I am sure plainly showed that they approved of your words. You have all your own with you to the last.[10]

O'Hara was untypical of the Auckland clergy in his prompt vote of confidence. Was it merely diffidence that prevented many of his new charges from rallying immediately to their bishop's side? Priests from the south who knew Liston better were quicker to offer support. Telegrams arrived from Fathers James O'Neill (Invercargill), Daniel O'Neill (Riversdale), Eugene Kimbell (Fairlie), James Long and James Kennedy (Hokitika), among many others. They conveyed a consistent and heart-warming message: 'Truth will out; long live spirit evoked.' 'Congratulations on your speech St Patrick's Night, hostile press propaganda notwithstanding.' 'Congratulations fearless speech; Gunson has discovered you, your future made.' 'Heartfelt sympathy unwarranted attack confidently hope complete vindication.'[11]

This note of warm approval was echoed across the Tasman. The Vincentian superior, Paul Cullen, led the cheering from Sydney. 'Bravo! We were all delighted to see that you gave the "others" something to chew.'[12] Father Xavier O'Brien, a visiting Australian, told Liston of the delight with which the Hamilton clergy had greeted his 'great speech'.[13] The bishop's former fellow-seminarians at St Patrick's College in Manly also wrote to offer praise and sympathy; its President, Father Thomas Hayden, applauded Liston's straight speaking: 'What you stated is historically true and if the history of Ireland is unpleasant reading for some people, well, let them look to it.' Hayden sent Liston a message from the staff and students: 'Your Alma Mater believes in you and is proud of you.'[14]

Liston's lay correspondents were predictably severe on the Mayor of Auckland. W. H. Watson of Waikumete commented, 'We are not surprised when we hear what asses like Gunson say that it's hardly 2000 years since our fathers were wearing woad and worshipping fire.'[15] J. P. O'Sullivan of Oamaru and W. H. Mulcahy of Auckland agreed that the whole business was 'an electioneering stunt'.[16] The clerical verdict was even sterner. Father Farragher cabled from Gisborne: 'Mayor's bombastic impulse, audacious pomposity and arrogant display the froth of bigotry.'[17] Father James Lynch of Wrey's Bush declared, 'The twaddle of that Mayor of Auckland as it appears in Southland papers is very audacious and contemptible.'[18]

Gunson's premature handing of his protest to the Press Association incensed many Catholics. 'Yet this is conduct that is regarded as worthy of all praise by the PPA and their sympathisers. What a striking example of British fair play,' remarked Father Lane bitterly.[19] Liston's friends begged him not to give in to the mayor. 'Pitch into him and his gang and you will have the goodwill and prayers of the whole people to assist you.'[20] Clearly, some Catholics were spoiling for a fight over the issue. John Walls, the *New Zealand Tablet*'s business manager, urged Liston to 'just rub it into Gunson a little bit harder, and don't forget a bit for Bill Massey at the next election'.[21] O'Sullivan, a recent arrival from Ireland, took great satisfaction from the speech:

> The mad mullaghs of Brithunism and Empireism are raging. Evidently they don't like a few home truths such as you expressed. It is just about time that we took a twist out of the supporters of Brithunism in this country so you are to be congratulated heartily.[22]

The Liston camp took a largely dismissive view of the affair in its early days, well expressed in Bishop Whyte's telegram, 'Friends amused at puerile criticisms and resolutions.'[23] Another lay correspondent assured Liston, 'After all it will be only a nine days wonder and by the time they have sung "God save" a few times they will have cooled down and commonsense will have returned.'[24] Father Riordan of Ross saw no reason for regret: 'It's a good thing some one comes out occasionally and tramps on the flag flappers' pet corn. Nuff said about them they make me sick.'[25] St Patrick's Day was always a thorn in some people's flesh, Joan O'Leary of Kapuka told Liston, 'well, they would not remember it was there if it didn't prick occasionally'.[26]

Meanwhile, others were urging the bishop to counter-attack. Father Kennedy suggested a libel action against the mayor; with a good lawyer he need have no fear of the result 'even if the Chief Justice presided'.[27] Father Lane of Gisborne promised Liston financial support from the priests and people of Poverty Bay 'in any action you may be pleased to take or may be called upon to defend to vindicate your position'.[28] Any worries Liston may have had were soothed by his correspondents. The attacks would draw his new flock closer to him; indeed, the whole affair might even be a blessing at the beginning of his episcopate. As Father Lane observed:

> It may be gratifying and consoling for you to know that the unwarranted attacks made upon you by the enemies of our race and creed have evoked expressions of the strongest condemnation among your people in Poverty Bay, and have intensified their devotion and loyalty to your office and person.[29]

Few writers referred to the details of Liston's speech beyond a general endorsement of its truth. Welcoming his call for vigilance against possible trickery by British politicians, J. P. O'Sullivan cited the delays in ratifying the Anglo–Irish Treaty as proof of 'deep perfidy'.[30] Father Patrick Lagan of Rotorua, much moved by Liston's 'generously-worded reference to the land we all love', unwittingly brought the speech closer to the charge of sedition by suggesting its likely effect in Ireland: 'Patriot hearts at home will be cheered by your words.'[31] And not just at home – the Te Kuiti adherents of the Irish Self-Determination League had wept 'tears of gratitude' when reading his speech.

> We admire your manly and courageous defence of the men of 1916, and thank you sincerely for your words of encouragement to the men who are still fighting Ireland's battles. We venture to assert that you are worthy to take your place beside De Valera, Archbishops Mannix and

> Redwood and the other champions of oppressed Ireland. It is our earnest prayer that you will be long spared to defend Ireland and to see her completely free.[32]

The exact content of Liston's address was of little importance to some. Sister Mary Stephena was one of many nuns who hastened to sympathise with the bishop. 'I haven't seen your speech so I don't know what you said and I don't care either. That you made it is enough for me, I know it could be nothing but right.'[33] The insults being heaped upon Liston were deeply provoking. 'My heart is bursting over the rotten business', Bryan Flannery wrote.[34] Joan O'Leary expressed similar sentiments, albeit more colourfully:

> When I read the paper I could 'hit the roof.' In some ways I am a bad tempered savage woman, and oh my Lord I can't bear anyone to say a word against you. To read their flurried resolutions is just like hitting me. I'd dearly love to give them all a black eye, which would remain so till on 17th March 1923 it would turn green.[35]

Liston may well have suspected the motives of two of his keenest sympathisers. J. P. O'Sullivan ended his letter of support with the suggestion that he come to Auckland to spread knowledge of the Gaelic language and culture. 'I wish I could lecture amongst our people. Go up and put them on their metal [*sic*]. Together with teaching our Irish language.'[36] This would, he claimed, offset the compulsory saluting of the Union Jack which came into force in all schools on 1 April. O'Sullivan received no encouragement from the bishop.

W. H. Mulcahy had a much more ambitious vision – a nationwide Catholic co-operative network. Anticipating yet greater disabilities being imposed upon Catholics, he had devised a scheme 'to institute a measure of protection to our own people – by our own people – ourselves by ourselves to be defended.' He wanted Catholics to band into one huge organisation 'to cater for all requirements, to produce or manufacture wherever possible all supplies, and at the same time to create remunerative employment without anxiety to a large number of our men'.[37] Mulcahy was convinced that most Auckland business firms were deeply hostile to Irish Catholics, and either open or covert supporters of the PPA. Had not the Farmers' Union Trading Company refused him a job solely because of his Catholic faith? Liston answered nearly every letter of support he received during his two months of worry; Mulcahy got no reply.

Although more than 200 letters and telegrams arrived to cheer the bishop, there was little sign of this groundswell of support in the newspaper correspondence columns.[38] This was due only partly to the informal censorship exercised by those like the editor of the *Hawke's Bay Tribune*, who would not permit their loyal columns to be sullied by the apologists of sedition-mongers.[39] As Peter Dowd of Otorohonga complained to the bishop: 'Any letter written to the press in your favour would not be printed, as it's only those whose views suit get into print.'[40] Father Michael Edge of Te Awamutu had his own way of redressing the balance. He sent Liston an ostensible 'letter' intended for publication in the *New Zealand Herald*. 'Loud-mouthed patriots are influenced more by their own interests than by anything else. If the letter is published you will not, of course, be in any way bound to follow its advice.' Despite its impressive nom-de-plume, 'John Bull', it did not appear.

> Sir, Will you kindly allow me to suggest that it is quite time to call a halt to the easy loquacity that pours condemnation on Bishop Liston? I would suggest to His Lordship to bring matters to an early and conclusive issue by instituting proceedings for libel against those who have so readily labelled him 'seditious', traitor', 'disloyal' etc. Such action will cost a large sum of money but I will assure His Lordship that if he consents to adopt this course every penny required will be forthcoming within a fortnight.[41]

Auckland Catholics who wrote to the press in support of their spiritual leader ran obvious risks. Most of them belonged to the working class or were otherwise reliant upon Protestant patronage for their living. The post-war economic recession had begun to bite and the Auckland Returned Soldiers' Association several times publicly expressed concern over the numbers of ex-soldiers out of work and destitute.[42] Accusations of sectarian bias by employers had been heard frequently over the past six years. One wonders whether W. H. Mulcahy's dire prediction caused Liston any sleepless nights.

> The incidents of the last few days in Auckland, offering a long sought opportunity for the safe disgorging of bitter, bigoted hatred and malice against the Church, and Your Lordship personally, will surely carry in its cowardly trail a sinister sacrifice of many Catholics holding positions of employment, particularly as this palpable advertising dodge for Mr Gunson's next political campaign will be industriously fanned by the PPA and other mongrels.[43]

Liston later told Bishop Cleary how 'our people here at first were taken aback by the fierce onslaught in the press and, as you can guess, were not demonstrative in their support'.[44] Those daring to speak publicly in Liston's favour seemed less interested in defending his reported views than in rebuking his Catholic critics. Jeanne Hall told the *New Zealand Herald* of her bishop's personal qualities, adding that while many Catholics might not agree with his Town Hall sentiments, all save Patrick Darby were 'grieved to admit it'. She dismissed Darby's letter as 'a masterpiece of bad taste'.[45] The INA expressed its 'utter contempt of assertions made by shoneen Irishmen, who voice no opinion than that of their own'.[46] Liston was well aware of the 'shoneen' factor, as he informed Cleary:

> I think what more than anything else made our good people resent the attack on the Bishop was the contemptible attitude of the few 'leading Catholics,' who rushed into print to tell the world what intelligent men they were, that they didn't follow Pope or Bishop in politics, that they were loyal etc, that Bishops and priests were always bad politicians and anyhow had better not abuse the privileges of British citizenship, etc, etc. . . These contemptible people have got many a dressing down since from Catholics and non-Catholics alike. I am really grateful to them, because they have done us a good turn in awakening our own.[47]

As Auckland Catholics seemed to need a great deal of awakening, it was hoped in the south that Liston's speech might do them some good. Father Lynch of Wrey's Bush touched on the regional factor in reactions to the address: 'Evidently Auckland has some "ardent patriots" and a little education on sound lines is much needed. Down here your speech would be considered by the Philistines mild and merciful.'[48] Joan O'Leary of Kapuka also urged the bishop not to worry 'over those Orangemen and half-hearted Irishmen that you have up there'.[49] While reluctantly acknowledging Liston as a local product, the *Otago Daily Times* could not resist taking a backhanded swipe at the *New Zealand Tablet*.

> It was in the South that he acquired all the strange knowledge his possession of which has excited the wonder of the North. And anyhow those who peruse the pages of the organ of his church in the South can read every week what was said at the St Patrick's Day concert last week and is to be heard only once a year on the public platform.[50]

The *New Zealand Herald* professed ignorance as to exactly what was a 'shoneen' Irishman – 'is he a good chap or a bad, dark or fair, north or south?' – and suggested that Gunson lodge another protest at their controversies being conducted in a 'foreign' language.[51] New Zealand Catholics hardly needed the term to be translated, as Dr James Kelly had been accusing them of shoneenism for over five years.[52]

The slide into shoneenism was frequently charted as an awful warning to *Tablet* readers.

> They forget the pride of their Irish birth or ancestry; and then they forget their religion and their duty to God; and then they become the most despicable and vile things on this earth. There is no deeper depth of degradation than theirs; they have fallen beneath contempt.[53]

They would have to fall very far indeed to be beneath Kelly's contempt. He had a low opinion of colonial Catholics: they were lax in their religious duties, apathetic towards wider Catholic concerns, too keen to marry Protestants, and insufficiently supportive of the Catholic school system. They also sorely needed education in the tragic history of Catholic Ireland, despite possessing what Kelly termed 'the proudest heritage of all nations, and through it the strongest obligations'. The sad fact remained that there were probably more shoneens than patriots even among readers of the *New Zealand Tablet*; the very frequency with which Kelly felt obliged to condemn shoneenism was strong evidence of its ubiquity.[54]

Many rising, middle-class Catholics resented being dragged back down into the catacombs or soiled with the pitch of Irish disloyalty. Jeremiah Twomey, a Timaru Catholic journalist, bemoaned the effect of Kelly's aggressive policy on Catholic social integration and material progress: 'We are only 14 per cent of the population, and should not incite antagonism. I spent about £2000 on the education of [my] children. They are out in the world now and this sort of thing will handicap them.'[55] Here was the authentic shoneen voice. Twomey also lamented the withdrawal of community support for Irish nationalism once Sinn Fein had replaced home rule as its expressed goal.[56]

Michael Joseph Sheahan was another stalwart of Irish home rule; the Auckland real estate agent was as passionately involved in Irish politics as a distance of 20,000 kilometres would allow.[57] Clinging to home rule long after it had gone down in flames, Sheahan strongly disapproved of Kelly's Sinn Fein line and the support it received in clerical circles. From 1918 he served as Bishop Cleary's lay agent in controlling the divisive effect of the Irish issue in the Auckland diocese, earning Kelly's bitter rebuke as 'a traitor to the movement'.[58]

This was hardly fair. While Sheahan regretted the supersession of constitutional nationalism, his main aim was to preserve a united front against Ireland's enemies, and he welcomed the creation of the Irish Free State ecstatically.[59] Sheahan, who had rejoiced in 1900 at the prospect of 'no more shoneen rule' in Ireland, was by 1922 widely

Land agent and stalwart of the Auckland Rugby Union, M. J. Sheahan was another Catholic placed in a dilemma by Liston's speech. NZO

regarded as himself a shoneen.[60] However, the conflicting pressures on men like Twomey and Sheahan need to be appreciated – shoneenism, like patriotism, was in the eye of the beholder.

It was, of course, much easier to denounce Liston's critics than to defend his reported views. The bishop's own silence did his apologists no favours. The *New Zealand Herald* sneered at F. J. O'Meara's 'halting and partial defence', and stressed Tom Bloodworth's admission that the speech was 'extremely ill-advised,' and contained 'improper and unwise statements'.[61] J. A. Lee was moved to write to Liston apologising for Bloodworth's 'half-hearted' performance.[62]

The New Zealand Labour Party had been using the Irish issue as a stick to beat both Liberal and Reform parties for almost five years.[63] Was the fact that Parliament was not sitting the only reason why Labour did not take up the case now? Given the post-war obsession with 'loyalty', and with a general election on the horizon, the Labour spokesmen were probably wise to keep quiet. Liston had to content himself with their private messages of support, as when Pat Hickey congratulated him on his 'fearless' speech: 'If you had said anything with which either the "Herald" or "Star" could agree and as a result earned their congratulations then indeed you might with justification be "suspect" by all lovers of Ireland.'[64]

Labour's newspaper, the *Maoriland Worker*, made but one brief reference to the case.[65] When the *Grey River Argus*, the only other Labour journal, published a supportive editorial entitled 'The Prussianists and Dr Liston', its arguments in favour of free speech were closely scrutinised by the Crown Law Office.[66] Throughout, it was the bishop's right to speak his mind, rather than the rights and wrongs of what he said about Ireland, that exercised the Labour Party.

On Friday, 24 March, exactly one week after Liston had spoken, the Auckland Catholic clergy at last moved to support him. Eighteen of the city and suburban priests met in the presbytery of St Patrick's Cathedral and unanimously passed two resolutions, published in the *Auckland Star* under the headings, 'Priests Support Bishop. Unanimous Devotion. Irish Loyalists Repudiated.' The second resolution was aimed at those Catholics who had broken ranks by censuring their bishop.

> (1) We express our loyalty and devotion to His Lordship, Dr Liston, and our sympathy with him in the bitter attacks being made upon him, and the misrepresentation to which he has been subjected. We assure him, moreover, that he has our cordial support.
> (2) We repudiate the action of certain, self constituted spokesmen who assailed Dr Liston in the columns of the Press. Their assumption of authority to express Catholic or Irish views is altogether unjustified.[67]

The initial resolution must have surprised many readers. It was the first public intimation that the *Herald* report had failed to do Liston justice. Several of the bishop's own correspondents had immediately spotted flaws in the published summary of his address. The Catholic clergy saw clearly where Stanbrook had gone wrong. Father Riordan of Ross realised that Liston was referring to the period 1920–21 when speaking of foreign murderers: 'They can call the Irish murderers and worse but yet when Black and Tans England['s] scum are called something similar there is an explosion.'[68] Father Kennedy also understood the epithet as aimed at the notorious Black and Tans: 'I can only sympathise with you in the gross distortion of your remarks, made it would seem for some ulterior purpose. The distortion must be evident to any unbiassed person reading your remarks as telegraphed and the Mayor's protest.'[69]

Three of Liston's episcopal colleagues were absent in Rome during his hour of need. O'Shea and Brodie are on the lowest step, Cleary is holding the rail.
ACDA

The *Herald* editor refused to accept that any mistake had been made. Hackett had earlier rejected F. J. O'Meara's plea to withhold judgement until Liston's version of events had been heard: 'We are responsible for the report and we have no hesitation in affirming both its accuracy and its fairness.'[70] Nor was he impressed by the Auckland clergy's new charge. While finding their devotion to Bishop Liston 'all very intelligible and admirable', he suggested that they place their own attitude beyond the possibility of any similar 'misrepresentation'.

> When they refer to 'the misrepresentation to which he has been subjected' it would be well that we should know what they mean. The issue is very simple. The Bishop made a speech a week ago which was publicly reported at the time. If the priests meant to question the accuracy of that report it was open to them to do so and to state in what particular it misrepresented the speaker. They have not done so, and the tenor of their second resolution leaves the very broad inference that they have no intention of doing so, but, on the contrary, that in addition to their loyalty, devotion and sympathy the Bishop also has their approval of what he said on St Patrick's Day.[71]

An unflattering portrait of P. J. O'Regan. NZ Truth

This proof of his clergy's support must have comforted James Liston during his long train journey to Wellington on Friday evening. The official opening of St Mary of the Angels was a providential opportunity for those members of the Catholic hierarchy then in New Zealand to get together. With three bishops away in Europe, only Francis Redwood and James Whyte remained for Liston to turn to for advice and support.[72] Then there was P. J. O'Regan, with whom he had arranged to meet on Saturday afternoon. Four months previously O'Regan had carried out a long-promised resolution and began to keep a detailed account of his professional life; his journal over the next two months contains a daily record of what was soon to become the Liston case.[73]

Liston and O'Regan met for the first time at the presbytery of St Mary of the Angels. Both New Zealand-born sons of Irish immigrant parents, they shared a deep devotion to their two countries. At fifty-three, O'Regan was the elder by twelve years. His first impressions of Liston were favourable: 'A mild-mannered, soft-voiced and self-possessed man. Not the slightest intention of backing down.'[74] Stung by the criticism of his speech, the bishop had initially considered repeating his remarks once the fuss died away; by now he had chosen a contemptuous silence as the more appropriate response. Did this change of mind reflect a growing appreciation of the seriousness of his position? Liston's concern must have deepened towards the end of the meeting with O'Regan when the *Evening Post* arrived containing the official announcement that he was to be prosecuted for sedition.[75]

8

Sacred Traditions of Sorrow

In the evening I was in a whirl; my mind jumped from a snatch of song to a remembered page of economic history.

Ernie O'Malley, Easter Week 1916[1]

My parents were driven from the country in which they were born and in which they would have been content to live. . . . They came to this country with the memory kept sacred of their privations and wrongs. They have left to us the sacred traditions of their sorrow.

Bishop Liston on St Patrick's Night, 1922

Whatever drove Bishop Liston's father and mother from Ireland, they had plenty of privations and wrongs to pass on to their colonial-born children. James Liston senior was born in 1844, his future wife Mary Sullivan three years later; both came from Barefield, County Clare, in the south-western corner of Ireland.[2] The country was then on the verge of the Great Famine: several years of misery, disease and death, during which the Irish population declined by over three million. This blunt figure conceals unspeakable horrors; Bishop Liston's parents reached adolescence having witnessed great suffering and devastation. It is likely that they shared some of their experiences with their youngest son.

> My parents were born during the terrible years of Ireland's famine 1846–51. This famine was artificial, because there was plenty of food in the country, but it was transferred by the military. . . . While my father

Death wagons in County Cork, 1847. NLI

> and mother were growing up in Ireland, 1 million lives were lost through sheer starvation and over a million were forced to clear out. During 50 years 3,688,000 souls were evicted from the homes of their fathers by alien landlords.[3]

The harrowing scenes that accompanied these events made an indelible mark on those who witnessed them, as also on the collective memory of their descendants.[4] Liston's parents survived the ordeal only to be faced with a potential recurrence barely a decade later. During the depression of 1859–64 a succession of heavy rains followed by parching drought brought damaged crops, diseased livestock, and widespread fears of famine on the horrendous scale of the forties. While the ready availability of Indian corn prevented such mass starvation, evictions rose sharply as the crisis deepened.[5]

This renewed misery probably helped to convince many Famine survivors to cut their losses and leave the country. James Liston and Mary Sullivan (and thousands like them) were now old enough to vote with their feet. Were they evicted? We have their son's repeated word for it; but the terms 'eviction' and 'emigration' held the same meaning for him. He referred to all who left Ireland as having been 'evicted' from home, land and country, including his mother, whom he described as 'an exile'.[6]

The seventeenth-century confiscations by the English in Ireland had resulted in the imposition of an alien landed oligarchy; it became part of the Irish nationalist canon that these landlords and their descendants – Ireland's 'foreign masters' – were responsible for most of the ills suffered by their unfortunate country. Cast as principal

A harrowing eviction scene. Mansell Collection

villain, the stereotypical landlord was cruel, rapacious and desperate to maximise his profits. Protestant (or worse), preferring cattle to Christians, the landlord and his agent were regarded as foreign in every sense of the word.[7] (For Bishop Liston and many others, such tyrannical behaviour left them deserving of the bullets that came their way during the land war of the early 1880s – killing them was no murder.)[8]

However, the comforting simplicities of this story of predatory landlord and oppressed tenant have not stood up well to the rigours of modern historical research. Irish rents were quite low by English standards, rackrenting uncommon and evictions relatively infrequent; nor was the country uniformly poor or endemically violent. To complete the refutation of what might be termed the heroic version of the Irish land struggle, it appears that the average tenant markedly improved his position at the landlord's expense in the post-Famine era. Indeed, as one historian has provocatively suggested, it could be argued that 'an unloved but not oppressive landlord class was overwhelmed by a rapacious tenantry'.[9]

Tenant farmers emerged as the real winners from the Great Famine; while their numbers remained relatively stable, the ranks of landless labourers, cottiers and small-holders were decimated. The reduced competition for land benefited the 'hard-faced men' who remained. The latter often considered themselves the victims of the disaster; they were in fact the legatees of those removed.[10] Their prosperity was based largely on a buoyant livestock market. Bishop Liston might lament the growth of pasturage over tillage as a feature of Irish rural life, but it was his own people who were turning the country into a cattle ranch. Irish farmers were simply responding to the market; given the conditions of soil, climate and return on labour, the move was a logical one.[11]

Can we interpret the emigration statistics in a similar light? Or, to put it another way, would Liston's parents have been as content to remain in Ireland as their son believed? David Fitzpatrick has aptly described nineteenth-century Ireland as a land which most people wanted to leave.[12] While the Famine years had seen millions of starving peasants flee a stricken country (some two and a half million leaving between 1846 and 1856), the exodus was to continue long after the Irish economy had recovered. From 1855 to 1914 another four million Irish people left, while between 1801 and 1921 a total of more than 8 million emigrated (a number almost equivalent to the entire Irish population at James Liston senior's birth).[13]

Nationalist historians have traditionally viewed the Irish diaspora like the Famine, as the culmination of a nefarious policy aimed at keeping Ireland under the British heel.[14] Recent writers have been more willing to acknowledge the material factors behind this massive movement.[15] The emigrant tide was continuous and intense, from virtually every Irish county, and involved men and women in equal numbers, most being young and unmarried. It was also a carefully calculated process, well informed and directed, and subject to short-term and cyclical fluctuations.

Priest, pressman and politician all professed to abhor the drain of humanity, but could do little to halt or slow it. (Even the creation of two Irish states in 1922 failed to staunch the flow.) Its key determinants were structural changes in post-Famine Irish life, heavy foreign demand for immigrant labour and chronic under-employment at home. Cut off from access to land and marriage, the surplus children had to seek these things elsewhere – 'growing up in Ireland meant preparing oneself to leave it'.[16] Put simply, it was as sensible for the many to leave and prosper abroad as it was for the few who remained to run cattle on their farms.

James Liston and Mary Sullivan neatly fit the profile described above; both were single, young adults. The typical emigrant from County Clare was a semi-skilled farm labourer who had lost employment through the rapid contraction of tillage farming.[17] (The depression of 1859–64 also hit particularly hard in the west and south-west.) The available statistics allow us to distil distinct streams of emigration; that from Clare led to Victoria in Australia, where the Irish were adept at using the nomination system by which government assistance was granted to help bring out their relatives.[18] Did a brother or cousin subsidise James Liston's passage, just as he would later pay for his sister Hannah? This 'chain system' sometimes worked so well as to bring out entire family groups, leaving no trace of them in Ireland – a fate that may have befallen Mary Sullivan's people.[19]

Part of the attraction of Australia for James Liston senior may have been the prospect of striking it rich on the goldfields. Arriving in 1864, he spent three years there (first in Adelaide and then Victoria) before joining the exodus to the West Coast of New Zealand's South Island. He was among thousands of hopeful immigrants, lured by reports of the latest marvellous gold strikes. Perhaps learning from his Australian mistakes, James chose to supply provisions to the growing hordes of miners rather than joining them on the diggings.[20]

The post-Famine Irish emigrant of repute was a highly politicised creature, ripe for involvement in exile politics.[21] James Liston had an opportunity to demonstrate his patriotic fervour immediately upon his arrival in Hokitika. Feelings were running high in the Irish Catholic community over the execution of the 'Manchester Martyrs', three Irishmen convicted of killing a policeman during a Fenian escape attempt in England.[22] Mock funeral services and marches took place in several West Coast settlements in early 1868. After Father William Larkin led a procession to the Hokitika cemetery and planted a memorial Celtic cross, he and several others were arrested, convicted and jailed. Although no record has survived of James Liston senior's direct involvement in the affair, his subsequent service to the Irish nationalist cause is very suggestive. The colourful episode was recalled by several commentators as Bishop Liston prepared to enter the dock on the same charge exactly fifty-four years later.[23]

In many of the countries where they settled, Irish Catholic immigrants were given an unfriendly reception by the host population. They responded by sticking closely to their own. 'Ethnic defensiveness was manifest in settlement patterns, marriage choices, political and social networks, religious participation, drinking patterns and persistent involvement in Irish affairs.'[24] While the West Coast was no hostile new frontier for an itinerant Irishman – Irish Catholics were a quarter of the population of some 26,000 in 1867[25] – the Hokitika incident showed that much depended on how they expressed their Irishness. Allegiances were fierce and emotions raw in the rough mining communities; sparks from abroad (fanned by a hostile colonial press) could easily ignite a powder keg of passion among the

The Bishop's father, James Liston senior.
ACDA

three quarters who were not Irish. Irish Catholics found that they could not escape their ethnic or sectarian identity; 1868 was not the last time they would have to defend their priest and the symbols of their national pride.

James Liston senior's part in these stirring events was probably as a silent participant or an anxious spectator during the subsequent trial – the Irish pantheon had to await another generation for a Liston to be numbered among its members. Indeed, as a trader reliant largely upon a communal clientele, he may have benefited from the heightened ethnic and sectarian consciousness provoked by the affair. By 1874 he had done well enough to contemplate marriage and a family; on 17 February he married Mary Sullivan in Hokitika, the ceremony being performed by Father Aimé Martin.[26] Five years later the Listons decided to move to Palmerston South, where James took up another traditional Irish occupation by becoming the proprietor of a hotel.[27]

The refugee had found respectability, the evicted tenant was now a landlord. The Liston family's growing prosperity can be traced through the succession of pubs run by James in the last two decades of his life. After moving to Dunedin in 1880, he held in turn the licences of the Robbie Burns (1881), the Douglas (1883–92), and the

Criterion (1894–99).[28] Liston became one of those 'lace-curtain Catholics' of whom Bernard Cadogan has written so vividly.[29] He and his wife joined a close-knit Irish Catholic tribe set belligerently apart from the Scottish Protestant majority. Theirs was a tight circle of home, school and church; segregated education insulated their children from the dangers of an overwhelmingly Protestant society, while the effort to maintain the schools and to secure state funding for them mobilised and unified the Catholic community.[30]

James Liston senior was generous in his financial contributions to Catholic causes, also serving as a director of the *New Zealand Tablet*. Mary Liston gave of herself, earning a reputation as 'a saintly person noted for her works of charity' before her tragically early death in 1902. James had predeceased her by two years, after a sudden illness which caused him to retire from hotel-keeping.[31] By then they had made their greatest gift to the church in the shape of their youngest son. Given the Irish Catholic proclivity for publicanism, it was not unusual for a priest to emerge from a hotel, as it were. In early Otago the bar-room had often served as a convenient place for an itinerant clergyman to celebrate mass – the spiritual influences in Irish Catholic pubs were not confined to those sold across the bar.[32]

It is possible that the future bishop was born in the Robbie Burns Hotel, on 9 June 1881.[33] Ten days later James Michael Liston was baptised in St Joseph's Church (later Cathedral), thus beginning a long association with that place of worship; his family attended regularly, and his own first holy communion, confirmation, ordination and consecration would all take place there.[34] The first two of these sacraments were administered to the young James Liston by Bishop Patrick Moran. By 1881 this inspiring and pugnacious Irishman had led the Dunedin diocese for a decade, staffing it largely with imported Irish clergy and bringing an uncompromising leadership style redolent of the sectarian conflicts of the Old World.[35]

Throughout his episcopate Moran struggled to obtain a supply of priests sufficient to cope with the demands of his burgeoning diocese. On a trip back to Ireland in 1881, he recruited a young seminarian, Patrick Maguire Lynch, who came out a year later to be one of the first priests ordained in Dunedin. Lynch was no stranger to New Zealand; born in County Cavan in 1858, he had arrived in Hokitika with his parents at the age of ten. His nascent vocation was fostered by Father Martin, and he returned to Ireland in 1872 to train for the priesthood. As a self-styled 'wild Maori', Lynch would study at various Irish institutions for the next nine years, finally at Holy Cross

Mary Liston and her son, James.
Dunedin Dominican Archives

College, Clonliffe (Dublin), where Michael Verdon was vice-rector.[36]

Patrick Lynch was to play a crucial part in young James Liston's life. He was determined to foster a native priesthood from the sons of pious Irish Catholic immigrants, an ambition which came closer to realisation in 1888 when Michael Verdon arrived in Sydney to head the newly established St Patrick's College at Manly. Lynch saw this 'Australian Clonliffe' as the answer to his prayers; the new seminary would remove the need for young New Zealanders to make the long, expensive journey to Europe to pursue their vocation. Starting with James Delany in 1890, Lynch sent the best and brightest of Dunedin's Catholic youth to attend the infant institution. 'If these boys do well others will follow', he informed Verdon in January 1893. 'Once the stream begins to flow we shall not want [for] vocations in this diocese.'[37]

Lynch found his most promising candidate in the youngest son of his close friends at the Douglas Hotel. Attentive at the altar, clever in school, quiet and intelligent, with devout, well off Irish parents, the boy had excellent qualifications.[38] Liston later claimed that he made up his own mind about entering the priesthood, and that nei-

Father Patrick Lynch, who fostered young Liston's vocation.
DCDA

ther parent was responsible for his decision. However, his faith had been learnt at his 'saintly' mother's knee and reinforced by daily family prayers in the hotel's private sitting-room, while his father made it all possible by paying for his seminary training.[39]

In February 1893 Liston left Dunedin for Sydney, aged just over eleven and a half. A small boy both in years and in appearance, he began life in St Patrick's College at the very bottom (53rd on a seniority list of 55).[40] Despite his size he lacked nothing in determination. Lynch warned Verdon that 'young Liston may possibly endeavour to do too much in the anxiety to keep up with, or not far behind, the others'.[41] There were several New Zealanders at Manly, whose sense of solidarity was sharpened by the fact that students were grouped by state of origin. They included two Aucklanders (also sons of publicans) who were to become close friends of the newcomer, Matthew Brodie and Joseph Croke Darby. Brodie was a popular and influential prefect during Liston's time at Manly. Another classmate was James Kennedy, the son of the Greymouth gasworks manager, while one of Liston's first professors – a tall, stately Irishman named James Whyte – would be raised to the episcopate twenty-eight years later alongside his then tiny pupil.[42]

Liston's fragile health was gradually undermined by the tough Manly regimen. When he returned to Dunedin for the Christmas vacation in 1896, his parents were alarmed at his weakened state. Michael Verdon, who had succeeded Patrick Moran as Bishop of Dunedin some nine months earlier, complained to the new President of Manly:

> My most promising subject James Liston will not be allowed to return to St Patrick's College. He was in very poor health indeed when he came home in December and his parents were greatly troubled about him. They brought him to the best doctor in Dunedin who forbade them to send him again to Manly. His parents will keep him at home for some months and then they will probably send him to Ireland to continue his studies.[43]

The process by which Liston's seminary rector became his bishop deserves brief discussion here. The ailing Moran had wanted Patrick Lynch, his trusted friend and right-hand man, as his eventual successor. While the other bishops agreed that Lynch possessed all the necessary qualities, the Dunedin clergy felt otherwise, preferring not to include Lynch among the three candidates they endorsed, a selection known as the 'terna'. Two of his severest critics were the Irishmen Dean William Burke and Father James O'Neill. (Burke's achievement of first place in the clergy voting was devalued by the widespread suspicion that he had voted for himself.)[44]

The feeling against Lynch was sufficient to rule him out; did he then persuade Bishop Moran to plump for Michael Verdon as a compromise candidate? Moran's second wish was to be granted, although he did not live to see it. Dean Burke later complained of the 'Paddy Lynch hysterics' which greeted Verdon's appointment in early 1896. Lynch's joy was partly because he would now be able to fulfil a long-held ambition to join the Redemptorist order; Moran had depended too much upon his talented kinsman to agree to his earlier requests for release.[45]

Events conspired to send Liston off to Holy Cross College, Clonliffe, Dublin. Verdon was dissatisfied with Manly under its new chief, while the Irish seminary was *alma mater* to both Lynch and Verdon.[46] It was also acceptable to Liston's parents, who were footing the hefty bill for his education. Lynch was travelling home to Ireland to undertake his Redemptorist novitiate; he could thus keep an eye on Liston during the early years of his training.

Clonliffe was a tough proposition for the sixteen-year-old boy. It meant a painful separation from his family, with no prospect of returning for holidays (as he had been able to do from Sydney). In

Liston in Rome around 1901.
Dunedin Dominican Archives

one sense it was a return to the land of his fathers; it also meant leaving his parents forever. He was never to see them again. He arrived in September 1897 and remained until July 1900. Years later his memories were decidedly mixed. 'Being immature I learned many things slowly and had many lonely days at Clonliffe.'[47] There were no fellow-New Zealanders with whom to share achievements, discoveries and complaints. One of his contemporaries later presented a slightly different picture:

> He was an apt student whilst there, and a great favourite with the Irish boys and the Irish clergy. What time he spared from clerical society he gave to a close study of Irish folk lore. He passed his vacations with the relatives of his parents, and in this way verified for himself all the old Irish national traditions of faith and fatherland that from his childhood he had learned from his good Irish father and mother.[48]

It seems that Liston's romantic image of Ireland survived prolonged exposure to the realities of life there. The severe Irish winters cannot have helped to assuage his painful homesickness. In 1962 he wrote, 'the years have made me aware of my debt to Clonliffe for what it gave me of training and of love for Ireland'.[49] There was always Patrick Lynch to confide in and to offer encouragement; the apprentice Redemptorist was close by in Dundalk. In 1899 Lynch reported Liston as looking 'stronger' than he had a year earlier.[50] Lynch had just been visited by Bishop Verdon who was en route to Rome and was taking Liston with him to the Irish College, where the young man was to complete the theological part of his priestly training. (Verdon had been vice-rector there from 1880 to 1888, so Liston now attended the third of his bishop's former seminaries.)

By this stage Liston had found his feet abroad, and enjoyed Rome immensely. The Irish College rector, Michael Kelly, was kind to him, while his nephew, James Kelly, became one of Liston's classmates and closest friends. There were also three other Dunedin students to swap New Zealand stories with after daily lectures. Rome also brought sadness. Just after his arrival he learnt of his father's death; a harder blow fell two years later when his mother died. The highlight of Liston's days in Rome came in July 1901, when he received the blessing of Pope Leo XIII. On completion of his studies in late 1903 (at twenty-two well short of the canonical age of ordination), he returned to New Zealand via Ireland and Australia.[51]

Meanwhile, Bishop Verdon was in desperate want of priests to run his new seminary. Founded in 1900, Holy Cross College, Mosgiel, had grown so rapidly that he was obliged to lecture there himself for much of 1902.[52] Needing a clever professor to establish a philosophy course, the bishop saw his Roman students as his salvation. On 31 January 1904 Liston was ordained by Verdon in St Joseph's Cathedral. With a Roman doctorate of divinity among his impressive academic achievements, he was at once despatched to Mosgiel to teach sacred scripture and dogmatic theology.[53]

Accustomed to seminary life from childhood, Liston was well equipped for the rough and primitive conditions of the new institution. The hard scholastic years had formed his habits: solitary, disciplined, abstemious and dedicated. It was said that he 'cheerfully made asceticism a deliberate part of his daily life'.[54] A colleague remembered him 'wrapped in a Roman cloak, seated in an uncarpeted, austerely furnished room, bent over his books in preparation for the morrow, often until midnight'.[55] This was his schedule for six days, with shared parish duties for Mosgiel and the surrounding Taieri district on Sunday.

The Holy Cross teaching staff. From left: James Delany, Liston, Michael Verdon, Daniel Buckley, Michael Ryan. DCDA

After his appointment as rector of Holy Cross in 1910, Liston had the chance to shape the college in his own image. Everyone at Mosgiel immediately felt a new energy at work. He drove his charges almost as hard as he drove himself. Father E. J. Lynch later recalled those years in the Holy Cross golden jubilee history: 'Will it be surprising if we admit that it was no child's play to follow, to try to follow, the eager strides of this athlete of Christ.'[56] As rector, Liston never favoured the easy way; a strict disciplinarian, he would allow no compromise with the rules and was inflexible once he had made up his mind.

It was not all work and worry. For recreation Liston raced around the Taieri roads on one of the first motor-cycles ever seen in Otago, a belt-driven, French machine that caused great excitement when it reached 25 mph (40 km/h).[57] He also played some rugby, reversing Verdon's ban on the game and on the wearing of woollen jerseys (it had been a strict rule that no student was to lay hands on another). This love of rugby stayed with Liston all his life. He long remembered the heroic players of his Dunedin boyhood, and later attended or listened to all of the major games at Auckland's Eden Park.[58]

Holy Cross became his home, its staff and students his new family. He would later speak often of his 'sixteen supremely happy years' there.[59] One especially joyful moment came in December 1909 with the ordination of the first priests to receive their complete clerical training at Mosgiel. Holy Cross College spared young New Zealanders from sacrificing all that was familiar and dear to them in order to follow their spiritual vocation. Liston's personal vision was a native-born priesthood along the best lines – which for him were Irish ones. He had no doubts as to the quality of the local product.[60]

From 1910 Bishop Verdon's gradual retirement thrust more responsibility upon Liston as a spokesman for his church. He wrote frequently in the religious and secular press on public issues, advocating state grants to Catholic schools and greater Catholic representation in Parliament. The withdrawal of state aid from 1877 had encouraged Catholics to build a separate school system based on the pennies of the faithful and the largely unpaid services of a host of religious teachers.[61] The double taxation thus inflicted upon New Zealand Catholics gave them, in Liston's view, 'the sharp experience of stinging injustice'.[62] Had not his own parents worked hard, and sacrificed their health, to provide a large family with the education to fit them for both this world and the next?

In August 1914 New Zealand Catholics went to war with gusto. They were soon made aware of the depth of their sacrifice as the faces of their dead sons stared out each week from the pages of the *New Zealand Tablet*. Despite this, they found themselves cast as scapegoats for a host of wartime ills. By 1917 it seemed to many Catholics that bigotry had invaded even the corridors of power. Did Massey and the Orangemen secretly plan to rid the country of their priests, to cripple their schools, and to brand them as disloyalists unworthy of New Zealand citizenship? Was the national government allowing itself to be used as a tool of the PPA?[63]

The wartime issue that above all alienated and radicalised Catholic leaders arose over religious conscription. The bishops felt betrayed by a cowardly government. They had supported conscription only after being assured that their key personnel – priests, religious teachers and ecclesiastical students – would be in effect exempted. In early 1917 it seemed that these undertakings were being shamelessly broken. The threat to ordained clergy, although irritating, was easily circumvented; it was soon arranged that all priests of military age should present a government certificate to the appropriate military service board stating that their call-up was against the public interest. Liston felt this to be a 'miserable and humiliating' procedure;

nevertheless, Bishop Brodie, Dr Kelly and Liston himself were all required to perform the charade.[64]

When the production of exemption certificates failed to prevent a couple of boards from rejecting the appeals of several ecclesiastical students, Liston was beside himself with fury – Mosgiel was being turned into a preparatory school for Trentham Military Camp! When the closure of his seminary seemed possible, Liston's exasperation and outrage were replaced by defiance. He obtained permission to hurry the tonsure of several endangered students, effectively making them clerics; for the rest, he advocated a policy of non-co-operation with the authorities: 'Isn't it up to us to take no more notice of the whole business, and if they want these students let them come and take them?'[65] The supply of clergy was a critical issue for the bishops, especially as the need to provide military chaplains had already stretched priestly resources to the limit. The *New Zealand Tablet* mingled sadness at the toll of lives in Europe with ringing declarations that no Catholic priest or student would be allowed to add to it.[66]

The bishops had hoped for state aid for their schools as recognition of the Catholic war effort; instead they found their very existence at risk. It was widely believed that the Catholics, motivated by cowardice or disloyalty, were demanding special privileges over military service; Catholic schools were said to be flourishing while loyal Protestant ones declined. As the community polarised over these issues, the PPA began to find an audience for its peculiar world-view. While few people were convinced by its seductive argument that the Pope had caused the war, sectarianism gave many frustrated believers a chance to fight the Hun at long distance. The Irish imbroglio seemed to reveal a deep Catholic malevolence towards the British Empire. Even Howard Elliott's worst excesses could not obscure the groundswell of anger at those who seemed to be cheering for the wrong side in the great struggle with Germany.[67]

Apart from an occasional rebuke, Liston ignored the PPA and its apologists. In December 1917 he chided the Reverend John Dickie for sectarian muck-raking, which he deemed 'wantonly cruel to Catholic soldiers at the front as well as Catholics at home who are serving their beloved New Zealand with brains and brawn'.[68] While the PPA had relatively little success in the south, which was well used to the rough and tumble of sectarian debate, Liston's confidence that 'the puny efforts of the Church's enemies are futile' was to be shaken after the war.[69]

From 1920 the PPA extracted a series of anti-Catholic measures from a compliant Reform government, culminating in legislation to penalise Catholic marriage teaching. While Liston attributed the betrayal over conscription to 'a combination of bigotry, political cowardice and treachery',[70] he saw merely stupidity behind the Marriage Amendment Act.[71] This Act included a controversial clause making it an offence to allege that any one legally married was not 'truly and sufficiently' married. It was widely claimed that the papal decree *Ne Temere* (1908) impugned the validity of any marriage not celebrated by a Catholic priest. After the Act had become law (despite fierce Catholic resistance), Liston took a dismissive line when condoling with Bishop Cleary. 'If the bigots have won in the meantime it certainly is no fault of yours and no credit to them. The whole business is no doubt a studied insult to us, but that's the end of it and they are welcome to whatever good that will do them.'[72] Liston shared Cleary's view that a tiny group of anti-Catholics were enjoying a temporary ascendancy due to wartime stresses, political bungling and the divisive effect of Irish and Australian politics.[73]

For Liston's friend and fellow-seminarian, James Kelly, the rise of the PPA merely revealed the bigotry that surrounded Irish Catholics throughout the British Empire.[74] His response was to declare war upon the enemies of his faith and fatherland through the columns of the *New Zealand Tablet*. Once at the helm of the weekly paper, from February 1917, Kelly refused to curb his belligerence, ignoring the repeated requests of an increasingly exasperated hierarchy.[75] Liston, who had helped to persuade Kelly to take the job, stoutly defended his aggressive line to an infuriated Bishop Cleary. He cited as partial justification the provocation offered by the *Otago Daily Times*, whose attacks on Sinn Fein and papal neutrality had caused its name to 'stink in the nostrils' of local Catholics.[76] Another senior priest prepared to sanction Kelly's confrontational tactics on these grounds was Father James Coffey, the Irishman who largely ran Dunedin diocese on behalf of his ailing bishop.[77]

Michael Verdon's death in November 1918 came as a tremendous blow to Liston. As teacher and bishop he had guided the young man's vocation, setting him on the path to Dublin and Rome. After Liston's return to New Zealand as an orphan, Verdon had practically adopted him. The bond between the two men was strengthened by their shared love for Mosgiel (the fourth seminary they had in common). Verdon also recognised Liston's talents by giving him power and preferment at an early age; appointed a professor at barely twenty-three, he became rector six years later. Holy Cross College flourished under his leadership, as all the other bishops heartily agreed when discussing who should fill the vacant see of Dunedin.[78]

The late bishop had left no one in any doubt as to his preferred successor, having carefully groomed Liston for the position which both the clergy and laity of Dunedin expected him to occupy. When Archbishop Cerretti visited New Zealand in 1916, Verdon took every opportunity to whisper the name of his protégé into the Apostolic Delegate's ear.[79] In the circumstances, Liston could be forgiven for believing that the mitre was his for the taking. In 1916 he had attended the consecration of Matthew Brodie as the first New Zealand-born bishop; three years later it looked highly likely that Brodie would soon be returning the favour for his 'friend and brother'.[80]

Most of the senior Dunedin priests had secretly agreed to resist Liston's appointment at all costs. It was known that James Coffey, the only other likely candidate, was determined not to allow his name to go forward. The search soon began for an acceptable outsider, one with credentials good enough to match those of the local favourite. So notorious was this canvass that the result of voting at the terna meeting in January 1919 came as a surprise to few. Michael O'Farrell, an Irish-born Australian priest, led with ten votes, Coffey scored four, while Liston trailed in with three. Several voters were well aware of the similarities with 1895, when Patrick Lynch was excluded; indeed, not only was history repeating itself, but the very same men (principally William Burke and James O'Neill) were actively ensuring that it did so.[81]

Such clerical plotting was anathema to the New Zealand bishops, who roundly condemned it when reviewing the terna results for transmission to Rome. Liston was their unanimous choice – their only choice – and they stuck to him even after a complaint from Rome about their refusal even to discuss his potential rivals.[82] The dissident Dunedin clergy further muddied the waters by petitioning the Apostolic Delegate in Sydney, Bonaventura Cattaneo, in favour of O'Farrell – Burke and O'Neill being again the prime movers.[83] Despite their obviously personal motives, Liston's critics deserve serious attention here; a paltry three votes out of twenty was a devastating expression of no confidence in the Mosgiel rector. Were the local clergy really terrified at the prospect of firm discipline after the laxity of Verdon's day, as claimed by the hierarchy? Or had they chosen O'Farrell after being impressed by his episcopal qualities?[84] Perhaps the strongest point in their memorial to Cattaneo was the complaint that Bishop Verdon was effectively bequeathing the mitre to his favourite.

Dr James Kelly's view of the affair is also worth considering. Based in Dunedin merely as *Tablet* editor, he did not have a say in the choice of bishop. Had it been otherwise, his vote would have gone to Coffey. Despite their long friendship, Kelly felt that Liston was unfitted for the task. During the interregnum of some eighteen months, Kelly kept John Hagan, rector of the Irish College in Rome, informed of events as they unfolded. His letters contain a savage critique of Liston: narrow, obstinate, unapproachable, unpopular. Kelly claimed to have learnt much of this from the staff at Mosgiel (possibly from Father E. J. Lynch, Dean Burke's nephew). Kelly's sympathy with Burke and O'Neill helped to shape his views, as did his fear of being landed with a bishop insufficiently sound on the Irish issue. Nevertheless, he described Liston's faults with the accuracy that only a friend could muster. As bishop, Liston would be too much the seminary rector – the senior Dunedin clergy preferred to choose a devil they did not know.[85]

Gossip and rumour flew as 1919 passed without an appointment to the vacant see. When an announcement was made, in April 1920, it was a veritable bombshell; Rome had given Dunedin an Irish–Australian outsider – but not the one agitated for by the clerical malcontents. In another replay of 1895–96, James Whyte, the Chancellor of Sydney archdiocese, crossed the Tasman to become the third Catholic Bishop of Dunedin, while James Liston was sent north to fill the unenviable role of Bishop Cleary's coadjutor.[86]

Liston's reaction to his appointment was well recalled by a fellow professor at Mosgiel: 'One could see that he had been taken unawares and literally swept off his feet'.[87] The job of assisting an erratic genius like Cleary was enough to make anyone hesitate. There were also more personal reasons for Liston to dread a move north. It would be a second exile, another reluctant parting from all he held dear. After his studies in Australia, Ireland and Italy, Liston had returned to New Zealand 'to find he loved the country deeper than ever'.[88] Holy Cross College had then given him a new home and family; the wrench of leaving it was deeply affecting. When choosing Dunedin as his place of consecration he mentioned to Cleary the pleasure this would give his students and friends 'from whom I shall be cut off in future'.[89]

What awaited him in Auckland? A sick and unpredictable bishop, a laity notoriously laggard in Catholic and Irish causes, a group of priests who would probably regard him as an episcopal carpetbagger. (The Auckland clergy had voted solidly for three of their own number as Cleary's coadjutor.)[90] Small wonder that Liston agonised

Liston and the Dunedin clergy at his consecration in 1920. DCDA

over accepting Rome's decision, or that his first steps in Auckland were nervous. He did not disguise his feelings on arrival: 'I confess that I should have been glad to spend all my life in the work of training aspirants to the priesthood. I should have preferred to remain a soldier in the ranks than become a leader in the fight.'[91]

His early days in Auckland were encouraging. Cleary was 'wonderfully kind and considerate', Liston told Brodie. 'He wishes me to take full charge.'[92] Cleary ensured that this happened by withdrawing into the Mater Hospital for almost six months, before leaving on an extended trip to Europe in September 1921. Liston spent most of his first year on a series of visitations throughout the vast diocese. After meeting the Auckland clergy, he confessed that his 'fears in that direction' were gone.[93] Nevertheless, there were hints of storms ahead. When Cleary complained to Brodie in May 1921 of 'administrative difficulties' involving Liston, the Christchurch prelate suggested 'a friendly tête-à-tête so that all steps would be taken with your sanction and approval. Our mutual friend is inclined to make the rash mistake of acting without advice and thus get on the nerves of the priests.'[94]

Liston's busy start did not keep his sadness completely at bay. He confided to a friend, 'I am still horribly lonely, and when I came across "Dunedin St" the other day I could have sat down and wept.'[95] As the only active bishop in the diocese, Liston was obliged to come out of his shell. He attempted to 'infuse life' into the moribund Catholic

Archbishop Redwood leads the procession into St Joseph's Cathedral for the joint consecration of Liston and Whyte. DCDA

Federation and the Hibernian Society by striking an aggressive note (both in private and in public) from the very start.[96] In early 1922 he warned the Minister of Education that Auckland Catholics were 'greatly incensed' over the government's failure to deal fairly with Catholic orphanages.[97] If his people were not quite as angry as he claimed, then Liston was determined to make them so. The speech he gave at his reception was proof of this.

> By historical tradition, by force of circumstance and by the sharp experience of stinging injustice, we Catholics of New Zealand are essentially a fighting race . . . . Is not an inheritance like this something to be proud of and openly to profess even if the acknowledgement entails some temporal disadvantage. . . . Shall we not also burn with pride as we recall the sacrifices even unto death made by many generations of our race in order to hold fast to the precious possession of faith?[98]

In his eagerness to mobilise an apathetic laity, Liston would frequently remind his listeners of their Irish heritage; as children of a fighting race they might find sufficient courage to face their foes. He himself drew inspiration from the sacred traditions of Irish sorrows: 'It is our proud boast that the spirit of our Mother, the Irish Church, has passed to us her children'.[99] Liston had won a reputation in the south as a vigorous defender of Ireland's good name. At a farewell social in his honour it was stated that 'by his cultured and convincing writings he has successfully countered attacks of calumny and misrepresentation and on many occasions paid his tribute of love for

Ireland'.[100] However, his references to the current Anglo–Irish conflict were carefully phrased, as when he addressed the Auckland Hibernians in March 1921:

> The land of our forefathers is today undergoing a severe test, but we should, even under the heavy burden which Ireland was enduring, be hopeful. I would say 'Sursum Corda' – 'Lift up your hearts' – because the hearts of the people of Ireland are free, and, with that freedom deeply imbued, Ireland will surely attain to her aspirations.[101]

Liston was still more circumspect in Gisborne two months later, predicting 'firm friendship' between England and Ireland if only self-determination was granted to the smaller country.[102] His natural caution was heightened by the prosecution of others guilty of more extravagant comments on the Irish situation. Nor had the presence of police reporters at Irish and Catholic gatherings gone unnoticed. In August 1921 Liston warned Alfred Hall Skelton to tread warily when speaking on the subject from the stage of the Auckland Town Hall; five months later he consulted the Australian bishops for guidance on the safest response to the ratification of the Anglo–Irish Treaty.[103]

As one whose political utterances would carry considerable weight, the fledgling bishop faced a difficult choice of Irish styles. Was he to follow the aggressive Sinn Fein lead of Mannix and Kelly, or to play down the divisive issue as Cleary had done? In effect, Liston managed to do both in turn. In cold blood he could muster up the control and moderation needed when speaking publicly of Irish affairs; but this calculated approach co-existed with a romantic emotionalism which was apt to surface whenever he left the historical past to dwell on more recent privations and wrongs. Was it not his filial duty to remember – to celebrate – the sacred traditions of sorrow left by his exiled parents and their generation?[104] In May 1917, when addressing mourners at the funeral of one of Bishop Moran's Irish priests, Liston might well have been speaking of himself:

> He had the blood of martyrs in his veins – what Catholic Irishman has not?. . . . He was Irish to the bone. He had read the pages of Irish history and seen on them thickly scattered stains of blood; he had looked into Ireland's soul and saw there cut by the sword, or branded by the fetter, sensitive wounds of outrage, and the indelible scars of wrong. Could he forget?. . . . His love for Ireland deepened with the years; his belief in her destiny never faltered; no power on earth, he thought, can wither the persistent and insistent presence of a true and holy cause.[105]

9

Mr Massey is Much Concerned

This country is British and is going to remain British. Those who preach these [seditious] doctrines are enemies of the country and enemies of the people, and are acting against the best interests of the country. It has got to be put down.

Massey to Parliament, 1 October 1920[1]

James Gunson had put Massey and his colleagues on the spot once again. His denunciation of Liston's speech and the subsequent endorsement of his comments by the Auckland City Council were circulated throughout the country by the Press Association. He also let the papers know of his letters to Massey and Bell.[2] While the avalanche of press criticism greatly reduced the government's room to manoeuvre, the Prime Minister did not react quite as expected. Massey chose not to make a public statement or even to comment privately on the mayor's actions; when referring the matter to the Attorney-General, he asked Bell merely 'to ascertain whether there is sufficient authority in the present law to enable Govt. to act in case of necessity'.[3] There was no sign here of a burning desire to haul the offending prelate into court.

Liston's friends agreed with Gunson on Massey's likely reaction, regarding him as an arch-bigot only too eager to seize the opportunity to persecute a prince of the Catholic Church. Had not Kelly predicted something of the sort in the *Tablet* barely fifteen months before? ('Some of us would not be surprised if Mr Massey went further on his slavish course and imprisoned certain persons among us.')[4] The *New Zealand Sentinel*, the organ of the PPA, had long clamoured to see a Catholic bishop in the dock. Even before Liston spoke, its editor was demanding severe action by the authorities against Archbishop Redwood: 'Is the Government afraid of the Romanists, or is it the desire of the Cabinet to conciliate the Church which has cursed them collectively and individually by "bell, book and candle"?'[5]

On the face of it, there were strong surface grounds for believing the worst of the dominion's chief citizen. An Ulster-born Presbyterian, Massey had acted as leader of his local Orange Lodge in South Auckland. Ten years after his entry into national politics in 1894, he had risen to head the small, conservative parliamentary faction in opposition to Seddon's Liberals.[6] Catholic voters were responding favourably to the latter's progressive land and labour legislation, as well as to its embrace of Irish home rule; a disgruntled opposition began muttering about corruption behind the scenes, with Catholics allegedly favoured in government appointments.[7] These complaints grew more frequent after the Catholic Joseph Ward succeeded Seddon as Premier in 1906. Ward's vulnerability on the sectarian issue was exploited by the opposition; after his fall from power in 1912, he complained bitterly that 'a lying tale' had been told against him throughout the country.[8]

So far so bad for Massey's reputation in Catholic eyes; however, there is another side to the story. Massey had left his native Ulster at the age of fourteen (he described himself as being 'of Irish birth', rather than as an Irishman). As a young man with political ambitions it was only natural that he become an Orangeman; he also joined the Freemasons and the Oddfellows.[9] It made good political sense for Massey and his colleagues to attack the Liberals on their vulnerable sectarian flank; his own party was criticised in its turn for allegedly favouring Protestant sectional causes. While these tactics were adopted by both sides, only Massey has been castigated by posterity for his alleged misdeeds.[10]

Massey's attitude towards the Catholic Church has been assumed rather than examined by most historians, who have denied him credit for escaping the constraints of his Orange heritage. As Prime Minister from 1912 to 1925 Massey revealed himself as an astute politician determined to hang on to the office he had sought for so long. The Catholic bishops were especially delighted by his willingness to allow state scholarships to be taken up in Catholic schools.[11] Another worry for the hierarchy was the vigorous public campaign waged from 1911 to 1914 for a referendum on the introduction of Bible reading in the state schools, seen to present an unacceptable risk of proselytism for

William Massey in Masonic regalia. AWN

Catholic pupils. Massey at first declared against any change to the existing secular education system, but ended by voting for the referendum.[12] He balanced this act with private assurances to the Catholic bishops of Reform's lack of sympathy for the referendum, which was later heavily defeated in Parliament.[13]

The outbreak of world war initially allowed Massey to distance himself further from the charge of sectarian bias. In 1916 he welcomed the Apostolic Delegate on the latter's brief visit to New Zealand.[14] Domestic harmony was to end all too soon, however: the Irish rebellion and the rise of Sinn Fein, bitter arguments over religious conscription, and guerrilla warfare between the Catholic Federation and the PPA, all combined to poison the political atmosphere. On returning from Europe in late 1917, Massey and Bishop Cleary were both shocked by the savage sectarian conflict they found raging on the home front.[15]

Massey was frequently accused of flirting with the PPA, mainly for refusing to curb the activities of its leader and by promoting its principal apologists. The Reform Party undeniably enjoyed noisy PPA support during the 1919 election. After the poll Howard Elliott took up a new role as lobbyist in Wellington, touting his creation as 'the most powerful political organisation in the country'.[16] He spent the next two years collecting political debts, as the Reform government granted a stream of his anti-Catholic wishes: concessions on travel and fees were withdrawn from Catholic teachers and pupils, state scholarships were made no longer tenable at Catholic schools, the *Ne Temere* decree was challenged by an act of Parliament, restrictions on the importation of anti-Catholic literature were removed, while a ban was placed on Sinn Fein material (including badges and emblems bearing de Valera's image).[17] The *Tablet* editor saw all this as persecution, adding pugnaciously, 'let us have more of it by all means. It is just what we want to unite us.'

> It is hardly necessary to make it clear that we consider the Government of this country today as a PPA Government pure and simple. The PPA boasted that they elected the majority of the so-called Reformers. They numbered and weighed their tools after the election. And since the election they have pulled the strings and the puppets have danced.[18]

James Kelly's remarkable talent for abuse was fully exercised in these years. He excoriated Massey and his colleagues, the New Zealand press, the British Empire and all it stood for. Yet, if Massey left Elliott unhindered, he also declined to rise to Kelly's bait. Despite the Solicitor-General's repeatedly recommending Kelly's prosecution for sedition, Massey chose not to risk the storm that such an action would provoke.[19] By refusing to repay Kelly in kind, Massey avoided the unedifying slanging match that developed between his Australian counterpart and Archbishop Mannix.[20]

A wave of anti-Catholic feeling passed across most English-speaking countries in the immediate post-war years.[21] This phenomenon was exploited in New Zealand by the PPA, where Howard Elliott seemed to capture the country's mood – as evidenced by Ward's crushing defeat in the 1919 general election.[22] Catholics had appeared to use the crisis of the Great War for sectional advantage. There was also deep concern at the growing threat posed by denominational schools to the state system. With his party's electoral machinery in disrepair after five years of inactivity, could Massey be blamed for not rejecting PPA assistance? Despite all claims to the contrary, the PPA ran its 1919 campaign solely in the Reform Party's interest. Its actual impact on the result is debatable, especially given the policy of 'nominating' the likeliest candidates and then claiming credit for their return. Elliott's real victory lay in his ability to persuade at least some of the winners that they owed their return to his good offices.[23]

Massey may well have felt grateful for the PPA's assistance in winning his only convincing electoral victory and ridding him of his perennial political rival. However, he had now to deal with a confident sectarian organisation, flushed with success and having strong popular backing for its demands. The gains made by the Catholic Church during Massey's first administration were the fruit of concerted pressure and skilful propaganda; from 1920 it was to be the PPA's turn. The jewel in Elliott's crown was the Marriage Amendment Act, deeply resented by New Zealand Catholics as an attempt to ban their teaching against mixed marriages. There were men in the government, claimed the *New Zealand Tablet*, who would rejoice to see every Catholic church in New Zealand razed to the ground. Kelly challenged his readers:

> Catholics of New Zealand! Do you want further evidence of the spirit of religious persecution with which we have to contend? Do you want further proof that the time has come for us to organise seriously and to be ready to defend our religion, and even our rights as citizens? We come of a stock that never hesitated to prove to any Government that Catholics can defend their rights, and die for them if need be. Does Mr Massey want us to prove that?[24]

For Kelly, the Reform administration was 'first and last a Government for the bigots, by the bigots and of the bigots'. He urged Catholics to cut out the final voting list on the marriage legislation and paste it up in a prominent place. 'Teach your children to realise as soon as they can read that the list is meant to warn them against the enemies of their religion and to remind them who their friends are.'[25] The progress of the Marriage Amendment Bill seemed to measure Reform's guilt – of either its bigotry or its willingness to pander to bigotry.[26]

The Bill passed on a clear party vote, with Reform almost unanimous in support and the Liberal and Labour members mostly opposed. The lengthy debate saw a procession of speakers denouncing both the Bill and Reform's alleged collusion with the PPA over it. However, rather than being the gift of a grateful government, the legislation was Elliott's personal triumph, coaxed through Parliament by a mixture of skill, cheek and persistence. It could even be argued that it was forced on Reform by the need to keep the rival sectarian bodies from each other's throats. In this respect the affair bears a striking parallel to the Liston case: bitter arguments in the press and from the platform threatened the peace of the community. By allowing the legislature and a jury to decide the respective cases the government did no more or less than its duty.[27]

It has been claimed that Reform passed the Marriage Amendment Bill as a means of drawing PPA support 'on a permanent basis'.[28] Rather, it was the PPA who sought influence as of right on Massey's administration. During the debate in Parliament its principal apologist and co-founder, J. S. Dickson, threatened to expose those Reform members who he believed were reneging on pledges to support the Bill. Dickson's ambitions extended to Cabinet rank and he was said to be 'disgruntled' at Massey's failure to promote him. In mid-1920 he complained to his fellow-Orangemen that the Prime Minister seemed reluctant to acknowledge his large debt to the Protestant community.[29]

Massey was not a man to be railroaded in this way and his irritation with Elliott's constant presence in the political lobbies was soon made known.[30] He was also aware of the damage that too close an identification with the PPA could do to his image. Both Liberal and Labour parties made great play with any opportunity to brand him a religious bigot. Just before the 1919 election, Massey declared – with what Kelly termed 'excessive vehemence' – that he 'had no connection with Howard Elliott or anyone connected with him'.[31] Massey saw the need to appeal to all parts of the electorate, rejecting the narrow view pressed on him in November 1920 by a Dunedin supporter.

> Just one or two more addresses like that of Archbishop O'Shea and Father Coffey and a few more of Father Kelly's articles in the *Tablet* and the position is secure. I am confident there will be a bitter sectarian fight at the next election and the 14% will see where they are. You never got their vote anyhow.[32]

It was in Massey's interests, however, to prevent a Catholic block vote for Labour, especially after Ward's defeat had removed the natural target of political anti-Catholicism. (As P. S. O'Connor has remarked, 'for what it was worth, the "Protestant vote" was Reform's already'.)[33] Massey's attitude to the Marriage Amendment Act therefore needs to be explored further.[34] While distancing himself from the Bill during its passage, Massey believed that the vital clause would prevent the 'cruel' allegation that a civil marriage was not a true one: 'The clause is intended to deal with mixed marriages, to

The Observer*'s caustic commentary on clerical reactions to the Marriage Amendment Act.* NZO

some an unpleasant duty but we have to do it'.[35] He denied that the measure owed anything to a PPA deputation which had interviewed him in June 1920, claiming that they had discussed the high cost of living, the meat supply and the price of hides (the price of whose hide? Kelly might well have asked).

While admitting during the debate that he had once been a member of the Orange Order, Massey made a ringing declaration of his belief in freedom of conscience: 'And, while I have been in Parliament 26 years, I challenge my fellow-members of Parliament, and anyone who knows me inside the House or out of it, to say whether I have been guilty of intolerance in word or deed during the whole of that time – or before it, for that matter.'[36] By referring the Catholic challenge to the clause to the Crown Law Office and by allowing a conscience vote on the Bill, Massey did all that could reasonably be expected of him.

While Catholic leaders agreed to differ on Massey's personal role in their reverses, they all saw the Irish issue as the driving force behind post-war sectarianism. Kelly convinced himself and his readers that Massey was as fierce a supporter of Ulster Protestant unionism as Kelly was of Irish Catholic nationalism. When Massey once praised

Carson over de Valera, Kelly declared, 'Massey is exactly where we always held he ought to be – at the head of the rank Orange bigots who hate everything Irish and Catholic'.[37] However, the historical orthodoxy that Massey 'found it difficult to discard his Orangeism' needs to be tested against his response to the enduring Irish question.[38]

Massey had kept stoically silent during the long and bitter fight for Irish home rule. There was widespread colonial support for the measure, which its friends maintained would merely extend to Ireland the freedom that made New Zealand so loyal and contented. Even when former Governor Lord Ranfurly told the Ulster Volunteers of Massey's alleged concern at the prospect of home rule being forced upon his native province, the Prime Minister made no comment other than that the entire issue was none of New Zealand's business.[39] When war in Europe caused Irish ranks to close against the foreign foe, Massey spoke feelingly at a patriotic meeting in Wellington:

> I am proud of being of Irish birth. . . . [A] fortnight ago the two great sections of the Irish people were looking at each other along the barrels of their rifles, but today they are standing side by side and shoulder to shoulder ready to fight for their country and their Empire. (Cheers).[40]

One year later Massey contributed to a debate on allegedly biased cable reports denigrating the Irish war effort. After urging that 'not the slightest notice' be taken of stories of Irishmen shirking their war duties, he concluded by asserting that, 'whatever has been the case in past years, Irishmen today stand united in defence of their country and of the Empire to which they belong'.[41] After 1916, the rise of revolutionary separatism in Ireland made it increasingly difficult to reconcile Irish national ambitions with imperial security. Massey continued to exercise restraint in his references to the Irish conflict, despite the weekly provocation offered by the *New Zealand Tablet* and constant needling by the Labour Party. He even found himself speaking up in the House for Irish home rule as against self-determination.[42]

Massey's political enemies were well aware of both his private sympathies and his short fuse. The Prime Minister's hatred of Bolshevism was such that Labour's espousal of Sinn Fein damned both doubly in his eyes. In October 1919 he was provoked into denouncing de Valera as 'a traitor and a disloyal man [who] has done more harm during the last two years than any other man in the Empire', and into grudging praise of Edward Carson (although he admitted that the Unionist leader had 'made mistakes').[43] During the 1919 election campaign Massey announced defiantly, 'I am coming back, and all the Bolshevists, Sinn Feiners and IWWs can't keep me out!'[44]

Massey was genuinely horrified by disloyalty and ever vigilant against those 'who would sell their immortal souls to see the Empire broken up and dismembered'.[45] He believed that the latter should be kept strong 'at any sacrifice and at any cost'.[46] This requirement, rather than the preservation of Protestant Ulster from Sinn Fein clutches, was his primary concern during the Anglo–Irish conflict. When the treaty was concluded, Massey immediately expressed the hope that 'the people who have been opposing the Government of the United Kingdom – of the Empire – will become loyal citizens of the new Dominion which is being set up'.[47]

Despite heavy pressure on him to get off the fence, Massey's silence on the Irish issue in New Zealand was accompanied by an equal circumspection abroad. When leaving for the Imperial Conference in London in mid-1921, he was lobbied by both the friends and enemies of Irish self-determination.[48] In the event, Massey had little to contribute apart from repeated pleas that nothing be done to weaken imperial unity. After elections for the newly created Parliament in Northern Ireland, he cabled his congratulations to Prime Minister Sir James Craig along with his 'earnest hope that the event would help to restore peace and harmony to the whole of Ireland'.[49] Massey chose not to attend the official opening of the Northern Ireland assembly, sending instead a stirring message:

> Ulster citizens have again proved their loyalty to King and country and given a guarantee that their Parliament will stand fast for those principles of freedom, liberty and righteousness upon which the Empire has been built up, and which have placed Britain in the front rank of the nations of the world.[50]

His finest hour came at the Imperial Conference in 1921. Once in London – for Massey, 'the Mecca of every British citizen'[51] – he was lionised by the press; ten cities and municipalities granted him their freedom, honorary doctorates were awarded by four universities. Boasting a leadership record longer than any other of those sitting around the conference table, Massey seemed to embody the tenacious qualities of the British race. Lloyd George requested that their photo be taken together outside No 10 Downing Street; Massey responded by inviting the Welshman to visit New Zealand. He referred to Lloyd George, Winston Churchill and Andrew Bonar Law as 'personal

Massey and Lloyd George – a Briton and a Celt – outside No 10 Downing Street. ATL

friends'.[52] In the *National Review*, Lord Milner described New Zealand's leader as 'the most staunch, the most sturdy, the most consistent of Imperial statesmen':

> In that he is, I believe, a true interpreter of the spirit of New Zealand. In no part of the British world does the fire of Imperial patriotism burn with a stronger or steadier flame than in that distant Dominion.[53]

In the fervour of his imperialism may be found Massey's essence. The British Empire reconciled his two identities as Ulsterman and New Zealander; it was echoed in his accent, a mixture of Irish brogue and colonial twang.[54] Escaping his narrow Ulster heritage, Massey came to embrace a broad imperial faith with a quasi-religious intensity. Although his bucolic appearance made him seem slow witted and occasionally a figure of fun, Massey's transparent sincerity struck a chord with most New Zealanders, who shared his views on the British Empire and on their place in it. He spoke emotionally on the links that bound the British people, bonds of sentiment 'as light as gossamer but as strong as steel'.[55] The visiting Prince of Wales was

The New Zealand Herald*'s view of the Massey–Lloyd George relationship.* NZH

'that blue-eyed, flaxen-haired Anglo-Saxon boy'; the empire over which he would rule was both 'a family of nations' and 'the greatest Empire the world has ever seen'.[56]

Massey nurtured an imperial vision all of his own: when 'the good British blood which flows in our veins' asserted itself, New Zealand would do for the South Pacific what Britain had done for the world. Hence the necessity of keeping New Zealand white; there must be no undesirable immigration to corrupt 'probably the purest Anglo-Saxon population in the British Empire', not even of those native races whose wartime loyalty he had applauded. He was prepared to concede, however, that 'the strain of Polynesian will be no detriment'.[57]

Massey believed the British people to be descended from the lost tribes of Israel – God's chosen people.[58] How else to explain Britain's miraculous deliverance from the clutches of her enemies during the late war. By divine will alone had the empire survived and triumphed, to continue its work for justice and world peace. For Massey, it was an empire like no other, greater than those of Rome, Greece and Germany, based on the principles of Calvary rather than Kaiserdom.[59] He held a dog-eat-dog view of geopolitics: should the Empire fall then all those lesser breeds without the law would imme-

Massey waving the Union Jack.
NZFL

diately devour their weaker neighbours, the world would be thrown into chaos, with wars and rumours of war spreading across the globe – a nightmarishly apocalyptic vision.[60]

Massey wanted the delicate bonds of empire reinforced by gun-metal. The war had taught them a bloody lesson in the cost of unpreparedness. While he gloried in New Zealand's response to the empire's call, those who did not return had left a sacred duty for all who remained to protect the empire from future danger. Massey described Viscount Jellicoe's appointment as Governor-General in mid-1920 as 'the highest possible compliment' to New Zealand's war effort. Their young soldiers had made history by deeds of heroism which would inspire others should war come again.[61]

Indeed, the war had ended too soon for Massey's liking. He seemed to relish the prospect of a future conflict in which Germany would be forced to admit its utter defeat. When an opportunity to refight the Gallipoli campaign arose during the Chanak crisis in September 1922, he at once cabled an offer of military assistance to London. (Of all the dominions only Newfoundland showed an equal willingness to commit troops to this renewed imperial adventure.)[62] Massey had earlier called for Gallipoli to be placed under permanent Allied control, regarding it as 'sacrilege' that any mere Turk should tread the soil that covered their British dead.[63]

Convinced that the next war would be fought in the Pacific, Massey told all his British audiences in 1921 that a strong navy meant life or death for the Empire: 'The very existence of Australia and New Zealand as British nations depended on the Empire being able to protect them in case of necessity.'[64] He was greatly alarmed by the prospect of Britain falling below Japan and the United States to the status of a third-rate naval power. Massey welcomed the idea of an alliance between Britain and the USA, regarding Americans as 'our cousins' (a 'British-speaking race') for whom immigration restrictions could be lifted.[65] Anglo-Saxon unity was to be their watchword.

> The Empire's enemies were beaten on the battlefield, but they have not ceased in their work. They are as keen today in their operations as ever they were, only their tactics have changed. Their methods are underground methods, as recent events in India, Ireland, Egypt, and even in the overseas Dominions and Dependencies show. . . . The sacrifices that were made in the great war cannot be forgotten and with these thoughts it behoves us to stand sternly and solidly against Bolshevism and disloyalty.[66]

The Prime Minister voiced those views on Empire Day 1922, a week after the conclusion of the Liston case. Was the bishop's Town Hall speech on his mind as he spoke? Did he identify Liston with this worldwide conspiracy to subvert and destroy the British Empire? Massey had given fair warning to potential seditionists during the preceding decade; regardless of rank, status or wealth, they would be brought to justice. 'New Zealanders, as British citizens, had to prove their loyalty whenever they had the opportunity', he declared in mid-October 1921.[67] Five months later, James Gunson's vigorous public protest gave Massey the chance to practice what he preached.

10

Why Prosecute?

From all the muddled Ministers, from Massey's merry men,
From pests like Parr and Nosworthy, and geniuses like Lee,
From Anderson – the statesman! – from Elliott's puppet, Bell,
From earthquakes and from lightning and terror on the sea,
May God defend New Zealand!

James Kelly's suggested new verse for 'God Defend New Zealand',
New Zealand Tablet, 2 March 1922

Massey's ultra-Britishness reflected an intolerance of dissent and an overweening pride in empire voiced by many other speakers in the New Zealand Parliament. The Reform Party's 1919 electoral campaign trumpeted loyalty to empire; its manifesto concluded with an assurance of Reform's 'consistent encouragement by educational and other means of practical patriotism, love of country, appreciation of British citizenship, pride in Britain's record in peace and war, determination to make New Zealand a model British community'.[1] Reform might almost have been running for electoral office in Britain itself.

The Liberal Party sang much the same song: 'In Imperial matters and loyalty there is no line of demarcation between Liberal and Reform', exclaimed Ward's successor, T. M. Wilford.[2] Responding to Labour Party provocation in late 1920, Massey and Wilford combined to pass a motion declaring 'the continued loyalty of this Dominion, sympathy with the Imperial Government in the difficulties with which it had to deal, and expressing the confident hope that the Empire would emerge from the troubles more solid and more powerful than ever before'.[3] Another of Ward's old lieutenants, Sir John

Findlay, praised Massey for voicing the true New Zealander's feelings for King and Empire. In July 1921, with Massey in his audience, Findlay boasted to the Royal Colonial Institute in London:

> The people of my native land feel for this country and its Empire a pride, a loyalty and a devotion as fervent and as ready to make sacrifices for these sentiments as you whose home has always been in England. I may remind you that in point of race we are more purely British than the people of Britain.[4]

Britain's victory in the Great War was also a New Zealand triumph; the dominion could now rightly claim its place as a partner (albeit a junior one) in the great imperial firm. It was suggested in Parliament that this new status be symbolised by the addition of another cross to the Union Jack; also that the Tasman Sea be renamed the Anzac Sea as a tribute to their patriot dead.[5] In this Anglo-Saxon heaven Irish self-determination had no place. The war had not been fought and won to precipitate the Empire's dissolution, but rather to stamp its imprint more firmly upon civilisation. Britain and the United States would now police the seas and run the world, keeping New Zealand safe from both the Prussian militarist and the Asiatic invader.

However, the post-war cables proved just as disturbing to the supporters of the Empire as to the adherents of Sinn Fein. The fruits of victory seemed to be endangered by the peace settlement, while British naval supremacy was threatened at a time when almost every part of the imperial body politic was hurting. Crippled by huge war debts, Britain now faced rising unemployment and protracted strikes by miners and railwaymen.[6] Egypt was a hotbed of discontent as native leaders demanded an end to the wartime protectorate and the creation of a sovereign state.[7] The news from South Africa was no more cheerful: Prime Minister J. C. Smuts was keeping General Hertzog's Nationalists at bay, but a revolt on the Rand in early 1922 showed how dangerous the forces of disorder were.[8]

India was in the worst state. The world conflict had added strength to calls for Indian self-government. In April 1919 General Dyer answered its advocates by slaughtering several hundred of them at Amritsar.[9] An appalled Secretary of State for India was moved to ask the House of Commons whether Britain was going to keep her hold on India 'by terrorism, racial humiliation and frightfulness'.[10] Despite the tragedy of Amritsar, M. K. Gandhi's repeated calls for a non-violent pursuit of Indian national ambitions failed to impress the authorities, who took more note of his de Valera-like warning that

*In this turn-of-the-century cartoon Queen Victoria is comforted by her other children while ungrateful Paddy stands apart. By 1920 most of the other Imperial children were in revolt as well.*NLI

India had to 'pass through a sea of blood' before independence would be secured.[11] On trial for sedition in March 1922, Gandhi pleaded guilty and took the blame for violent disorder at Madras and Bombay, later thanking the judge for his lenient sentence of six years' imprisonment.[12] (The *New Zealand Herald* paused in mid-pursuit of James Liston to give one small cheer: 'Perhaps the decision of the Government to lay this arch-agitator by the heels is the most reassuring feature of the Indian situation.')[13]

Despite these multifarious troubles, both the friends and enemies of empire identified the corrosive Irish issue as the crucial factor in its ills. Egyptian and Indian nationalists were taking up the cry of self-determination with the same 'unreasoning obstinacy' as the Irish, lamented the *Evening Post*.[14] Among the most persistent advocates of imperial reform in New Zealand were those Labour politicians who conducted what has been described as an 'Irish campaign' from 1919 to 1921. Their support of Sinn Fein during these critical years helped to cement an informal alliance between the Catholic Church and Labour.[15] Facing a Liberal Party without its long-time Catholic leader after Ward's defeat, Labour hoped to lure Catholic voters both by supporting Irish self-determination and by advertising its rival's failure to follow suit. While the Irish imbroglio demonstrated the evils of imperialism, questioning the sincerity of the Allied war aims in relation to Ireland also distracted attention from the Labour Party's dubious wartime record.[16]

Labour's 'Irish campaign' was sustained through motions and questions in Parliament, public speeches up and down the country, and the importation and publication of Sinn Fein literature. Harry Holland and Peter Fraser did most of the platform speaking, occasionally seconded by Paddy Webb and Michael Joseph Savage.[17] At the Labour Party conference in 1920, a resolution was passed praising the Irish struggle for self-government and condemning 'the military occupation of that country'.[18] The following year the party conference declared in favour of economic and political self-determination 'to end the exploitation of modern imperialism in South Africa, India, Egypt and Ireland'. Holland had earlier attempted to introduce a motion in the House along the lines of the British Labour Party's demand for the withdrawal from Ireland of 'the British army of occupation'.[19]

The ubiquitous P. J. O'Regan provided a vital personal link between Catholic and Labour groups, writing on the deteriorating Irish situation in both the *Maoriland Worker* and the *New Zealand Tablet*.[20] His friend James Kelly was delighted by Labour's attitude towards the Irish question. He had frequently condemned Ward's 'fainéant silence', declaring him 'almost as culpable as Mr Massey' for ignoring Irish self-determination.[21] Labour was now prepared to do what Ward's Liberals would not. After Peter Fraser delivered a lecture in Dunedin in February 1921, Kelly declared 'in the name of Ireland we thank him for his brave words'.

> Holland and Fraser could be always trusted to stand up and speak out for one of the small nations for which so many brave boys were sent to die. If we have not commented oftener on what they have done for the Irish cause it is not due to any lack of appreciation and gratitude. We are their debtors, as is every Irishman, and every man of Irish blood in New Zealand, and we do not forget it.[22]

Others felt differently about Labour's Irish policy. When questioned on his attitude towards Ireland during the 1919 election campaign, Reform candidate C. F. Bennett replied that he was 'standing for the loyal electorate of Auckland West and not for Cork or Tipperary'.[23] Vivian Potter, Gunson's nemesis in Roskill, declared that the British Government had been far too lenient on the 'murderous and rotten crowd' of Sinn Fein.[24] T. A. H. Field, member for Nelson, denounced the Labourites in Parliament as representing 'the Sinn Fein element – the irreconcilable Irish element – the pro-German element in New Zealand. This alien element is largely Bolshevist.'[25] Some local councils refused to allow the itinerant Labour lecturers to use their public halls. After Peter Fraser's meeting in Hawera in March 1921, the secretary of the local Political Reform League advised Massey of widespread local resentment at 'the base tactics adopted by the Labour Party in dealing with the Irish question'.[26]

The government made desultory efforts to stifle debate on Ireland both inside and outside Parliament. Replying to a question in the House about Holland's lectures, Massey warned that the Labour leader might find himself in trouble with the law if he continued them.[27] When the Speaker refused to allow a provocative motion from Harry Holland in 1920, Massey strongly supported his ruling.[28] Undeterred, the Labour Members moved an amendment during the address-in-reply debate in 1921 calling for 'the granting to the people in Ireland, India and Egypt [of] that full measure of self-determination which for all small nationalities the statesmen of Britain declared the recent war was fought'.[29]

Irish peace, when it eventually arrived, was to cause almost as much strife as Irish war. First reports of the Anglo–Irish Treaty signed in London gave the impression of a British surrender. Massey happily contradicted this view when announcing the treaty details in Parliament: an oath of allegiance to the King, no reversal of partition, naval facilities secured, Ireland to be a new dominion of the empire.[30] Liberal and Labour spokesmen were equally enthusiastic. At a Wellington meeting held to celebrate the agreement, Harry Holland declared that Irish affairs were henceforth a question for the people of Ireland. P. J. O'Regan assured the same audience that the treaty had been accepted 'by the appointed representatives of the Irish people'.[31]

There was a note of surprise in the *Tablet*'s acknowledgement that the treaty was being welcomed 'by practically all sections of the community'.[32] Even its longtime rival the *Otago Daily Times* hailed the agreement as a 'great achievement' which could prove to be 'the foundation for a strong, stable national system'.[33] Peace in Ireland would at last reconcile the Irish abroad to the British Empire and remove a major obstacle to Anglo–American harmony. Many New Zealanders had begun to share the fear that the Irish imbroglio signalled the start of the empire's break-up.[34] The *Auckland Star* set its face sternly against this possibility: 'Ireland must remain an integral part of the Empire, but it must have the right to govern itself, save always the right of the north-east province to self-determination'.[35] Editor T. W. Leys spelt out the limits to the march of the Irish nation:

> Beyond Dominion Home Rule neither the [British] government nor the people behind it are prepared to go. This is a hard fact. . . . How could any

> responsible party? It would mean the admission of the principle that any part of the United Kingdom that wished to do so could break away. . . . It would mean that Britain would be vulnerable in a place designed by nature to be part of her own system. She would still have to defend Ireland though Ireland would contribute nothing to that defence and might be plotting for her overthrow.[36]

Press and political commentators found it impossible to imagine how any Irish man or woman could desire to leave the empire. 'Which holds the promise of a greater destiny', asked one editor rhetorically, 'an Irish Republic thrown entirely on its own resources and not even commanding the allegiance of the whole of Ireland, or a self-governing Ireland that is a member of the greatest Commonwealth of free nations the world has ever seen?'[37] Catholic spokesmen had an entirely different view of what Providence had ordained for Ireland. Not only had 'the omnipotent hand of God made Ireland a nation', He had also made its people the greatest of missionary races: 'in the wake of the English flag the Irish spread the faith through the vastness of the Empire'.[38] The sun never set on the Irish race, boasted Kelly, while 'the one thing the sun never set on in the British Dominions is bigotry and dishonesty'. He dismissed the empire as 'a tottering, ruined thing only kept together by lies and trickery'.[39]

Cheering for the wrong side was a dangerous pastime in the hysterically patriotic atmosphere of post-war New Zealand. Wellington's coadjutor Archbishop, Thomas O'Shea, described the popular mood in the dominion as 'such a temper as I believe does not exist in England itself, even in war time'.[40] The war had imposed a repressive, smothering conformity on the home front, with a sharpened suspicion of dissidents and minorities. There was a widespread belief that pre-war subversion by the Empire's enemies had led to British unpreparedness for the world conflict. This illiberal climate intensified after the conclusion of peace, as the crash of empires and the rise of Bolshevism and Sinn Fein heightened the mood of insecurity and xenophobia.

How could the dominion best preserve its loyal virginity? Every citizen was to be closely questioned on his or her commitment to King and Empire. Member after Member stood up in Parliament to demand that disloyalists be rooted out and that the rising generation be kept free from their influence. In 1920 legislation was passed requiring all school teachers to take an oath of allegiance; some suggested that this should be extended to public servants and clergymen. Compulsory flag saluting and lessons in British history were introduced into the state schools in an effort to teach 'pride of race, pride of Empire, and love of country'.[41] Steps were also taken to prevent any contagion of sedition from abroad. No one would be allowed into New Zealand, Massey declared, 'unless they are going to be like ourselves, loyal to the British flag, loyal to the Empire, and loyal to our Monarch who reigns over us'.[42]

Slogans and symbols, songs and flags, became the vital signs of loyalty or disloyalty. Labour and Catholic functions (like St Patrick's Day) were of particular interest in this respect. Vigilant loyalists claimed to have spotted the 'rebel flag of Ireland' fluttering over several such gatherings,[43] while Labour leaders were criticised for a supposed inability to sing the national anthem.[44] The *New Zealand Tablet* mocked the various expedients taken to encourage patriotic fervour among New Zealanders; Kelly gleefully suggested a law requiring all underwear to be made from Union Jack bunting.[45]

Despite the frequent claim that the sedition law was rarely taken out of the legal arsenal, it became the government's favourite weapon against dissidents during the decade 1912–22. Labour strikers, anticonscriptionists and pacifists during the war, and Irish agitators after it, all served time for their seditious utterances. Under the war regulations, a magistrate alone decided whether the speaker's sentiments merited his or her incarceration. In late 1916 the wholesale jailing of Labour leaders for their agitation against conscription seemed to indicate a hardening attitude towards internal dissent.[46] However, the national government (a wartime coalition from 1915 to 1919) could not summon up the courage to take similarly stern action against Howard Elliott and James Kelly, the rival sectarian firebrands.[47]

Massey's post-war administration was reluctant to surrender the increased powers of surveillance, censorship and punishment it had assumed during the national crisis.[48] Responsibility for censorship was transferred from the military authorities to the Crown Law Office, while a strict ban was maintained on the importation of any literature deemed to encourage violence. In mid-1921 Harry Holland publicly argued the case with Sir Francis Bell, Acting Prime Minister during Massey's absence at the Imperial Conference. Bell ended their exchange by bluntly declaring, 'I will not be a member of a Government that sets free advocacy on murder'.[49]

Irish literature took up much of the Crown Law Office's time. Anything sympathetic to Sinn Fein was forbidden entry: pamphlets, badges, newspapers. In 1917 Massey announced that de Valera would not be allowed to enter New Zealand; three years later this ban was extended to include his very image.[50] Some preventive measures worked better than others. The compulsory oath of allegiance imposed on all arrivals was sufficient to deter the Sinn Fein spokesman Osmond Grattan Esmonde from touring New Zealand in mid-1921; however, his colleague Katherine Hughes had no such qualms about taking the oath. She spent two months spreading the Sinn Fein gospel and founding branches of the Irish Self-Determination League throughout the country.[51]

From 1917 to 1921 Kelly had several vigorous tussles with the Crown Law Office; his escapes from prosecution were narrow, frequent and remarkable, especially considering the fate of others slightly less clever than himself.[52] Immediately recognising the danger, Solicitor-General John Salmond had pressed for Kelly's arrest and trial after just nine *Tablet* issues from his pen. A further shot across Kelly's bows came in mid-1918 with the suppression of the *Green Ray*, a Dunedin monthly devoted to radical politics and Sinn Fein (only the difficulty in securing copies of this publication had prevented its earlier demise).[53] The editor and publisher were jailed for sedition for an article on the 1916 rising; two of their supporters were then convicted and fined for referring to the Easter rebels as 'that gallant band of heroes'.[54]

The successful prosecutor of the *Green Ray*, William Cunningham MacGregor, had succeeded Salmond as Solicitor-General in June 1920. A Scots-born Dunedinite, MacGregor had risen rapidly through the legal ranks. On his appointment the *New Zealand Truth* described him as 'a Tory to the backbone and an ardent Ber-ritish Imperialist'.[55] Twelve years earlier, MacGregor had revealed an uncompromising political credo in his pamphlet 'Ideals of Empire':

> We are all citizens of the British Empire. . . . Speaking for myself I am a Scot by birth and training, a New Zealander by adoption, but before all, and above all, and beyond all, I feel that I am a British subject – entitled to the rights, and bound by the duties, appertaining to the citizenship of that great and glorious Empire.[56]

For MacGregor, New Zealand was but one link in 'the great Imperial chain', part of a community of race and of religion bound together by sentiment and self-interest. He urged his readers to 'think Imperially', which meant supporting the cause of imperial federation. This would 'at once create a world power which could dictate terms to the other nations, and would ultimately in all probability ensure international peace, and possibly disarmament'. By uniting with 'our

William Cunningham MacGregor, Solicitor-General 1920–23.
NZ Truth

cousins' in the United States, the empire could 'crush any likely opposition'. New Zealanders were urged to do their bit by adopting universal military training and making a bigger contribution to the British navy. They must above all 'discourage jealousy and discord between the members of the English-speaking races of the world'.

> Everyone of us Britons – whether in Old England or New Zealand – has his own duty clear before him. That duty is for each of us to realise his individual responsibility to the Empire – that great inheritance which has been handed down to us from our forefathers.[57]

This vigilant guardian of empire was now in the right place. On assuming office he was immediately required to advise the Attorney-General on the legality of meetings held to raise funds for Irish self-determination. If this object was to be achieved by lawful means, he informed Bell, the meetings could not be prevented; however, 'if it could be shown otherwise' then action might be taken under the Crimes Act.[58] Police detectives and reporters were present at subse-

Sir Francis Bell, Attorney-General 1919–25. ATL

quent Irish meetings. MacGregor's determination to keep out publications which he felt 'reeked with sedition' was undermined by the increased radicalism of the British press on the Irish issue (much of the literature refused entry by his office was freely circulating in other British countries).[59] When the *Herald* report of Bishop Liston's speech arrived on his desk, William MacGregor was at last able to fix the local enemies of empire squarely in his sights.

Before committing himself to an opinion, MacGregor noted the absence of a verbatim account of Liston's alleged remarks. What he had before him was 'obviously a condensed report of a somewhat lengthy oration'.[60] He urged that every effort be made to obtain the shorthand notes of any reporter who might have attended the concert. On the assumption that Liston had been correctly reported, MacGregor found the remarks 'expressive of a seditious intention', firstly to raise discontent or disaffection amongst His Majesty's subjects, and secondly to promote feelings of ill-will and hostility between different classes of such subjects. While the bishop might disclaim such intention, liability depended neither on the truth of his statements nor on his motives. The key question was whether, considering the audience addressed, his words were calculated to have that effect.

MacGregor was convinced that a magistrate would commit the bishop for trial and that an average grand jury would find a true bill against him; it would then be up to the judge and jury, whose decision he felt unable to predict. He curtly dismissed Bell's reservations:

> I quite appreciate that in cases of alleged sedition a line is frequently drawn between laudation of sedition in the past and incitement of sedition in the present or future. In this case, however, I think the Bishop would rightly be held to have crossed that safety line by his statements regarding the present and the future: (1) That Ireland was 'determined to have the whole' of her freedom, and (2) that in order to achieve the desired result there 'would be many to fight and even die' – presumably 'murdered by foreign troops' i.e. the loyal soldiery of their 'foreign masters' of England![61]

Did this son of the manse relish the chance to put a disloyal Catholic bishop in his place? In Dunedin MacGregor had to endure the taunts regularly directed at his beloved Empire by the *Tablet*. After dissecting Liston's remarks, MacGregor concluded his opinion with a sweeping censure: 'In fact, when the speech as reported is carefully considered in its entirety, there is underlying it throughout an undercurrent of seditious disloyalty'. For this reason he considered that Liston had done further violence to the sedition law by remarks tending 'to incite His Majesty's subjects to attempt to procure otherwise than by lawful means the alteration of the Constitution and Government of the United Kingdom'.[62]

Sir Francis Bell had one last chance to influence proceedings before he left on a long-postponed trip to Europe. At a Cabinet meeting on Friday, 24 March, the Attorney-General was presented with a travelling rug and best wishes for his journey.[63] The ministers then discussed the Liston case, Massey producing MacGregor's opinion of the day before. No minute or other record of the meeting has survived, but it seems that the decision to prosecute the bishop was taken only after long discussion (Bell subsequently informed Bishop Cleary that the final vote was very close).[64] Later that afternoon Massey told an *Evening Post* reporter that the matter was 'not yet finally dealt with'. As there is no evidence of a further Cabinet meeting on Saturday, did Massey choose to delay the announcement of legal action until he was safely on the night train to Auckland?[65]

Just as Liston was arriving in Wellington for the official opening of St Mary of the Angels, the Prime Minister headed home to South

Ernest Page Lee, Minister of Justice 1920–23. ATL

Auckland to celebrate his sixty-sixth birthday. It seemed to many observers that the Cabinet was presenting its leader with a Catholic bishop's head on a platter. For over five years James Kelly had ransacked his dictionary for insults to hurl at 'the Limavaddy blusterer' and 'his Cabinet of bigots and bunglers'.[66] How far did Massey's men deserve these scornful epithets? Minister of Agriculture William Nosworthy was one who did; a prominent apologist for the PPA, he assured the Orange Lodge in April 1919 that he would never support a government containing either a Roman Catholic 'or anyone who had a drop of German blood in his veins'.[67] The *Auckland Star* roundly condemned his promotion, describing him as unfit for Cabinet rank: 'Nosworthy is a mediocre, narrow-minded man, who has lent whatever weight attaches to his position to the campaign of religious intolerance'.[68]

Ernest Page Lee, Minister of Justice and Acting Attorney-General in Bell's absence, was another marked down as hostile. Of English birth, the member for Oamaru had expressed sympathy for the PPA and called for the suppression of the *Tablet*. When Lee seemed in danger of losing his seat in the 1922 general election, Kelly commented gleefully, 'next to seeing Massey himself put out nothing could please me more'.[69] Minister of Education Christopher James Parr was 'the flag-flapping Minister' responsible for imposing loyalty lessons

Massey and his Cabinet, from left: W. Downie Stewart, G. J. Anderson, C. J. Parr, D. H. Guthrie, Sir Francis Bell, Massey, W. Nosworthy, J. G. Coates, Sir R. H. Rhodes, E. P. Lee, Sir Maui Pomare. AW News

on pupils and an oath of allegiance on their teachers.[70] Minister of Labour George James Anderson had also felt the stab of Kelly's pen. He and his colleagues were collectively abused in the *Tablet* a mere month before Liston's speech.

> The names of several other Ministers are often received with shouts of laughter, and all one can say of them is that they have merited Lord Bryce's terrible comment on the lack of manners and education of the men who pretend to govern this country.[71]

Once considered a special friend by Catholic leaders, Attorney-General Sir Francis Bell had fallen from grace after piloting the Marriage Amendment Bill through the Legislative Council. An atheist, Bell prided himself on a Gallio-like objectivity in religious matters, based presumably on his ability to scoff equally at all denominations.[72] Archbishop O'Shea heard a rumour that Bell was 'exasperated almost to madness' at the thought of Ireland breaking away from the Empire.[73] On the other hand, the Attorney-General later told Bishop Cleary that both he and Massey had opposed the decision to proceed against Liston but had been outvoted in Cabinet. While Bell's cautionary letter to Gunson and his advice to MacGregor speak to his own reluctance to see the bishop hauled into court, he cannot be taken as an infallible guide to Massey's attitude.[74] Bell sailed for Europe immediately after the intended prosecution was announced. In his absence, Massey might well have begun to listen more sympathetically to those Cabinet ministers who were less than friendly towards the Catholic Church.

There are, of course, several reasons apart from anti-Catholic animus to explain the government's decision to proceed. The Crown's legal expert had deemed the speech to be entirely beyond the pale. Liston's refusal to challenge the accuracy of the newspaper report gave no excuse for delay in moving against him. Over the past decade the government had vigorously pursued seditionists of humble rank; by hesitating now it would appear to be favouring Liston because of his social status. With the case declared to be *sub judice* a halt would be called to the furious press debate, which was turning nasty as apologists for the bishop began to speak up.[75]

The government had watched uneasily as the rival forces lined up behind mayor and bishop. As one Wellington daily lamented, 'religious dissension and racial antagonism raise their heads higher and begin already to walk with greater stature over the land'.[76] Public meetings of support for Gunson were arranged in Wellington and Christchurch; both were called off after the prosecution was announced.[77] What might have occurred had the Cabinet decided otherwise? From 1919 the threat of violence in Kelly's anti-conscription editorials had became increasingly explicit; the returned men, 'accustomed to the use of arms', would not stand for continued misgovernment, while the Irish people would fight their cause 'to the end' assisted by their cousins overseas.[78]

Kelly was even accused of seeking to foment sympathetic uprisings in the dominion should open war break out in Ireland.[79] While this probably exaggerates the *Tablet* editor's ambitions, he was desperate to involve the New Zealand Catholic community as deeply as possible in Erin's cause, once expressing the fear that 'the last Black and Tan will have been driven out of Ireland while we are dreaming and we shall have had no share in the deliverance'.[80] Had popular indignation at Liston's reported remarks spilt over into physical confrontation, then New Zealand Catholics might well have found themselves fighting much closer to home.

11

Not a Happy One

When constabulary duty's to be done,
A policeman's lot is not a happy one.

The Pirates of Penzance, W. S. Gilbert

The announcement of Liston's prosecution set legal wheels spinning furiously. On Monday, 27 March the case file landed on the desk of Police Commissioner Arthur Hobbins Wright. 'Will you kindly take the necessary action?' requested MacGregor, adding that 'the Auckland Crown Solicitor will assist the police there'.[1] In the top job for just eight weeks, the English-born Wright was well acquainted with the northern force, having spent the previous three years as superintendent in Auckland.[2] He passed the file on to Inspector Edwin Eales, instructing him to collect all the available evidence and submit it to the Crown Solicitor. Eales was told to treat the file as strictly confidential.[3]

Sir Francis Bell was far from happy with this. When handing over temporary charge of the Attorney-Generalship to E. P. Lee who was Minister of Justice, he seemed to doubt the objectivity of his legal confrère. Bell was especially concerned at the prospect of the Auckland police acting without proper guidance. On Tuesday afternoon, less than twenty-four hours before he sailed for Europe, he sent the Solicitor-General a detailed memorandum which he intended to shape the development of the case.

> 1. The Crown Law Office (and not the Police) must be responsible for the proceedings to be taken against Bishop Liston.
> 2. Of course, the Bishop must not be arrested. The proceedings must be by information and summons.

Far left: Police Commissioner Arthur Hobbins Wright.
Left: Inspector Edwin Eales.
NZO

3. The Crown Solicitor at Auckland should be employed, but under your direction – not that of the Police.
4. The Crown Solicitor should have copies of your opinion to the Government.
5. I think the information should be in a form to be directed by you.
6. No time should be lost in laying the information. Mr Massey is much concerned.[4]

Bell was anxious to prevent any sectarian bitterness affecting the course of justice. Was this also his way of reminding MacGregor of his responsibilities? Bell's experiences as Attorney-General over the previous four years had made him painfully aware of the powerful subterranean forces which threatened community peace. He also knew that the Auckland police force was deeply divided. At least two deputations had approached the Minister of Justice in 1916 to demand the removal of Catholic police officers from leading positions in Auckland, citing deep dissatisfaction on this score by both police and public there.[5] One historian has claimed that Auckland's Ulster-born policemen were prominent among those who established the PPA there in mid-1917.[6]

'Equality for all, special treatment for none', the PPA's catch-cry, was aimed directly at the Catholic Church. The charge that Catholics were exercising an illicit influence behind the scenes was made in 1901 by no less a figure than the Anglican Bishop of Christchurch.[7]

He received the enthusiastic support of the *Prohibitionist* which complained that:

> to an extent of which the ordinary citizen has no conception, official positions in this colony, from that of the Premier to that of the village policeman are influenced, almost dominated by the intrigues of the Roman Catholics, and in all sorts of unsuspected ways they make their influence felt.[8]

Henry Cleary, editor of the *New Zealand Tablet* from 1898 to 1910, responded by publishing a survey of employment in the Railways and the Post Office which showed not only that Catholics were employed in no more than their due numbers, but that they tended to occupy the lowest positions.[9] Such an exercise in refutation had a limited effect; no amount of disproof could remove so potent a weapon from the opponents of the Catholic Church. Moreover, Catholic over-representation in the Police Department could not be denied and was a factor in the several inquiries held into the state of the force. In 1898 a royal commission supplied ammunition to both sides: while it found no evidence of corrupt influence, it also revealed that despite numbering only fourteen per cent of the population, Catholics made up almost forty-two per cent of New Zealand's police force.[10]

P. J. O'Regan, as the member for Buller 1896–99, attempted to explain these figures to the New Zealand Parliament.[11] Had not the colony's earliest police recruits been drawn largely from the ranks of the Irish Constabulary? Possessing limited formal education, the immigrant Irishman was obliged to seek work that required little previous knowledge or trade skills. The Auckland press next took up the debate on the merits of the Catholic Irishman as policeman. In 1904 one correspondent claimed that Englishmen generally considered police work beneath them, while another chose to stress how well suited the Irish were for the role. ('But then the ideal policeman has always been an Irishman, and it cannot be denied that the members of "th'-foorce" are a very fine body of men.')[12] Constabulary duties would continue to attract New Zealand Catholics; in 1918 they made up a third of all ranks, while a quarter of the 1922 intake was Catholic.[13]

One consequence of this numerical strength was to raise Catholic expectations that one of their number, if suitably qualified, might rise eventually to become Police Commissioner. This day seemed to have arrived in March 1912 when John Cullen was the favourite candidate for the vacancy. Irish-born and Catholic, he had worked his way up from the beat.[14] Convinced that Cullen had been passed over for the position twice before, the Catholic hierarchy was delighted

The Auckland police force around 1916, with Cullen (second from right).

to receive Sir Joseph Ward's promise that its man would at last become commissioner. Bishop Grimes of Christchurch had just cabled Cullen his congratulations when news arrived of a plot to give the job to another man.[15]

Ward had recently been replaced as Prime Minister, and a faction in the new Cabinet was plumping for another candidate, H. W. Bishop, a Christchurch magistrate who had held the most recent commission of inquiry into the force.[16] Henry Cleary, since 1910 the Bishop of Auckland, had been assured by Ward that Cullen's appointment was 'settled and decided'. Now, however, a man who was not even a member of the force was to be preferred. Was Catholicism an insuperable obstacle to promotion in the public service, Cleary asked the ex-premier bluntly? Cullen's career had come to be regarded as 'a sort of test case'. If such a bar were proved to exist, Cleary continued,

> I would feel it my duty . . . as a citizen and patriot to exercise to the utmost whatever influence I may possess to drive from power any party that would, directly or indirectly, institute or continue religious tests in appointments to, or promotion in, the Public Service.[17]

Cleary repeated this threat to the incoming MacKenzie administration, warning the new Minister of Internal Affairs, G. W. Russell, that 'the conviction is now being greatly intensified that the profession of the Catholic faith is a clog upon promotion at any stage of progress in the Public Service, and that it is made or being made an absolute bar to the higher and highest offices therein'.[18] When announcing Cullen's appointment as Police Commissioner on 16 April 1912, Russell assured Cleary, 'you need not fear any bigotry from us'.[19]

Howard Elliott would have been fascinated to learn of the political muscle flexed by the Catholic bishops in nailing down this

William McIlveney. NZO

appointment. Yet, as Massey soon recognised, Cullen was by far the best candidate for the job. He served the Reform Government loyally during the social upheavals of 1912–13 and under the stresses of war, before retiring in late 1916. The national government then had no hesitation in selecting another Catholic candidate from the ranks as his successor.[20]

How was an ambitious Catholic policeman who did not enjoy the benefit of episcopal patronage to ensure that he rose to the level of his ability? This was the problem facing Sub-Inspector William Bernard McIlveney, one of the Catholic officers whose removal was so vociferously demanded by Auckland Orangemen. During a case in late 1916, when informed of the personal objections to him, McIlveney expressed surprise and regret rather than indignation, and treated the court to a denial of faith that would have done credit to St Peter.

> He hoped the Court would accept his assurance that he had not been in church for several years. He was not of a religious turn of mind, and his wife was a member of the Church of England. He added that he did not take part in religious questions, and so far as he knew enjoyed the confidence and respect of every member of the force and the Auckland public.[21]

It is difficult to assess the effect of such sectarian sparring on actual events. Howard Elliott and his friends got their wish soon afterwards when McIlveney was transferred to Wellington; but he went as a newly appointed inspector and was to become Police Commissioner within ten years. Who can say if his promotion was helped or hindered by his nominal Catholicism?[22]

The sectarian issue was one of many which troubled the New Zealand police in the decade before the Liston case. The force's loyalty was questioned during the industrial unrest of 1912–13; had it shown sufficient energy in pursuing the labour agitators?[23] Talk of forming a police trade union raised further doubts about its reliability.[24] The outbreak of war greatly increased its responsibilities. Despite exemption from conscription and a ban on voluntary enlistment, the force lost eighty-seven men and was obliged to recruit sixty temporary constables in the two years before the armistice.[25] Its workload had never been heavier; the enforcement of conscription from late 1916 involved regular hunts for shirkers, including a group of Irishmen who had taken to the Taranaki hills to avoid the call-up.[26]

As community harmony deteriorated, the police played a vital part in keeping peace on the home front. Recognising that 'not all the enemies of the country were in Germany and Northern France', the government gradually tightened up the war regulations against all forms of dissent.[27] An overworked constabulary was fully employed in attending public meetings and taking notes of the speeches made there.[28] The numerous court cases that ensued gave members of the force an opportunity to perfect their forensic skills. A typical police witness would give evidence of the circumstances of the speech in question, the audience's response to it, the demeanour of the speaker and so on. He was also expected to corroborate the accuracy of the newspaper report on which the charge was based. Magistrates proved very sympathetic towards such witnesses, who frequently displayed powers of hearing and recall which stretched the credulity of unbiased observers.[29]

Some policemen were better at this sort of thing than others. In Detective Sergeant Reginald Ward the Auckland force found an expert counter-seditionist. Ward acted as a troubleshooter; his transfer from Christchurch to Greymouth in early 1917 prompted the *New Zealand Truth* to wonder if there was not 'something doing' on the West Coast.[30] A year later he was a key witness against the Reverend J. G. Chapple, a Unitarian minister whose anti-war speeches earned him a twelve-month jail term. Ward's transfer to Auckland in 1920 may have been an indication of increased concern about unrest in the north.[31]

There could easily have been a Catholic priest or two sharing Chapple's cell. Several clergy were reported to the Defence Department during these years for sermons and activities deemed to be prejudicial to the war effort. After being alerted by the authorities in 1915,

Bishop Cleary was obliged to warn Father Westeinde of Tauranga to keep his disloyal opinions to himself.[32] Westeinde was soon in trouble again; a neighbouring priest was tipped off by Sergeant O'Grady that legal action was being contemplated against Westeinde 'for his seditious and offensive utterances'.[33] Dean Patrick Power of Hawera, an Irish priest who made no secret of his Sinn Fein views, was also the subject of several police investigations. Following an inquiry into Power's alleged anti-recruiting speeches, Inspector Wilson of Wanganui assured Commissioner Cullen that the dean was 'a most loyal subject'.[34]

Alarm bells rang loudly in Wellington in early 1918 when news reached the Attorney-General that a cousin of Archbishop Mannix, one Father O'Carroll, had just arrived in the country from Ireland. It was reported that the priest's behaviour and outspoken views on the journey out had 'disgusted even those of his own flock'. O'Carroll was allegedly planning to do in New Zealand 'what Dr Mannix has tried to do in Australia'. Despite exhaustive inquiries and a careful watch on the new arrival, the hopes and fears held of Father O'Carroll were not realised. (The man himself chose April Fool's Day to assure the Christchurch police of his loyalty.)[35]

At least one Catholic priest appeared in the dock on a charge of seditious utterance during the war. In February 1917 Father Roche, a visiting Australian, picked the wrong soldier to tell that he was 'a fool to go to the war'. He also expressed the opinion that the Germans were a more civilised people than the British.[36] Roche was immediately arrested when the Auckland police learnt of his outrageous views. As the Crown Solicitor, a prominent Catholic, J. A. Tole, chose not to appear, Chief Detective McMahon took the case for the prosecution, showing a touching concern for the accused. Roche denied any intentional disloyalty and claimed that what he had said 'was not an offence against the law in Australia'. After prompting by the magistrate, he added that the words on the charge sheet might not be completely accurate. McMahon also put in a good word for Roche; the soldier in whom he had confided had been in uniform. Taking account of Roche's expressions of regret and his refusal to attempt to justify the offensive remarks, the magistrate let him off with a £5 fine and a warning.[37]

Pressure on the police increased sharply from mid-1917 with the rise of institutional sectarianism. Howard Elliott ignored official advice to tone down his aggressive speeches, choosing instead to target elements in the Auckland force which displeased him. When launching

Another Voice: The Pope is the only man in Christendom who stands up for Peace.
Howard: What about me?

Howard Elliott throwing mud in early 1917.
NZO

the PPA in July 1917, he claimed that a child had been buried in the grounds of an Auckland Catholic institution 'at the expense of a local police officer'.[38] That this false allegation was part of a barrage of scurrilous nonsense did not save the police from the distasteful duty of digging up the St Mary's convent grounds. Another of Elliott's vicious charges was that a young nun who had accidentally drowned in the Wanganui River some years earlier had been pregnant; in October 1917 her soldier brother returned from the trenches and gave the Baptist minister a richly deserved public horsewhipping.[39]

Other violence directed at the PPA and its adherents was less pardonable. In February 1918 two Protestant ministers were assaulted after attending a meeting in Feilding. Later that year a Greymouth mob attacked the hall in which Elliott was speaking. He had to be hustled off to Christchurch for his own safety early the next morning. There is evidence that after this incident Elliott enjoyed police protection on his travels around the country.[40] The sins were not all on one side. In March 1921 after the Grey Lynn Catholic convent burned down in suspicious circumstances, Bishop Cleary asked the Minister of Justice to assign men to guard the twelve wooden convents that remained in Auckland.[41] He had earlier declared war against Elliottism, giving the authorities a clear message:

> I warn the Government that we are not going to take this filth-bombardment lying down. If there is not in this Dominion a Government strong enough or patriotic enough to abate this indecent and dangerous propaganda of (in effect) pro-German hatred and dissension and strife in and out of our army, we ourselves will see to our proper defence.[42]

Elliott was unimpressed by the efforts of the Auckland police to steer an even course between the sectarian shoals. After his public thrashing he insisted on lodging a private prosecution, not trusting the police to pursue the case with sufficient diligence. Although Elliott would not take the stand to defend his noisome charges, his assailant was duly convicted. The magistrate refused to impose a penalty, however, delivering instead a savage censure of the Baptist minister: 'Speaking as a man . . . I am satisfied that he deserved all he got, and a good deal more.'[43] The subsequent assaults in Feilding redoubled the PPA's fury; for the second time the country had faced the awful prospect of a Protestant minister 'being murdered in cold blood'.[44] An angry deputation interviewed the Minister of Justice, T. M. Wilford, and predicted (wrongly) that the Feilding assailants would not be caught because the police did not want to catch them.[45]

Aiming to demonstrate the force's overwhelmingly Protestant identity, Wilford produced a breakdown of its religious affiliation. When it revealed that Catholics made up a third of all ranks and occupied seven of the twenty top positions, Elliott remarked drily, 'not a bad percentage, 33% instead of 14%'.[46] The PPA was determined to cut Catholics back down to their proper size. Its 1919 electoral platform included a promise 'to secure just and equitable employment in the Public Departments'.[47] It was an article of faith with Elliott and his adherents that the Catholic hierarchy exercised an undue influence over the country's press and politicians, Post Office and police, Labour Party and trade unions. Had not Archbishop O'Shea threatened to call all Catholic public servants out on strike if conscription was applied to the priests and Marist Brothers?[48] For that matter, how had all those groups with a high Catholic representation – West Coast miners, clergy, religious teachers, policemen – secured special exemption from military service?

The loyalty and sectarian purity of the Auckland police force were thus under intense scrutiny during the Liston case. The first suggestion of a possible 'conspiracy of silence' by its Catholic members was made by none other than the local Crown Solicitor, Vincent Meredith, after reading the results of an internal police investigation into the events of St Patrick's Night.[49] This intriguing exercise had

Superintendent Charles Hendrey. NZO

been ordered by Superintendent Charles Hendrey, recently arrived from Christchurch to replace Arthur Wright as head of the Auckland force. On Monday, 20 March, Hendrey had sent Inspector Eales a cutting of Gunson's *Herald* statement, underlining the sentence, 'It is seditious and designedly calculated to cause disintegration of all that Britishers hold dear'. He noted on the copy, 'For careful inquiry and full report please'.[50]

After preliminary questioning revealed only three likely attenders among the entire Auckland force – Sergeant Fitzgerald, Detective McHugh and Constable Kelly – Eales decided to issue a circular. Every member of the force who had been present was ordered to send in a report detailing 'any utterances made by any of the speakers, especially that which is alleged to be seditious'.[51] The three men named proved to be of little value to the investigation. Fitzgerald immediately denied attending the concert, even though his colleague, Sergeant C. J. Halke, had seen him heading down Grey Street from the Town Hall just as the audience was dispersing. ('I said "Goodnight Fitz" and he replied.') The next day, when Liston's speech was the talk of the station, Halke mentioned the incident to his senior sergeant. Despite this circumstantial evidence, Fitzgerald would not be shaken from his story. Nor would McHugh or Kelly admit to being present or to knowing any policeman who was.[52]

Eales now called up his sedition expert. Reginald Ward was deputed to investigate every policeman, in both uniformed and detective branches, and to flush out those refusing to come forward. When he mentioned that the uniformed men had already been questioned, Ward

Far right: Detective Gourlay. Right: Detective Ward. NZO

was ordered to repeat the process.[53] By Tuesday, 28 March, he had come up with four more names: Detective Gourlay and Constables Thomas Collins, J. R. Allen and J. Skinner. The three constables had all visited the Town Hall when passing on their beats. As Eales told his superior: 'Detective Gourlay is the only member of the Auckland Police that admits being there while off duty, and he was not present during the time that Bishop Liston was speaking.'[54]

Gourlay was something of a puzzle. As the only off-duty policeman to make it to the Town Hall that evening he might be expected to have taken in the entire performance; but Gourlay claimed to have arrived just after Liston had finished his speech, thus missing the first half of the programme.[55] Constable Allen told an equally unhappy tale. He had been called into the auditorium around 8.15 p.m. to stop a woman shouting out while the singing was in progress. 'Finding that the woman had stopped making remark I left the hall. I was only there for about five minutes.'[56] Only two policemen would admit to hearing the bishop actually speak. Constable Collins was on duty in Grey Street when he succumbed to the temptation to pop into the Town Hall; he entered at 9.10 p.m. and left soon afterwards.

> When I entered the Hall, Bishop Liston was speaking, and as I was well away back I couldn't quite hear what he was saying. I heard him say the glorious 1916. I would say that he was alluding to the 1916 rebellion in Ireland. I only stayed a few minutes, and didn't hear very much except that the Bishop seemed by his manner to be strongly in favour of the rebellion that is going on in Ireland.[57]

If this last sentence was calculated to please his superiors, the rest of Collins's report must have disappointed. He was unsure of Liston's exact words and had not heard the crucial sentence concerning 'foreign murderers'. On his way out Collins may have passed Constable Skinner, who deserted his Queen Street post around 9.15 p.m., again for only a few minutes, 'to see how things were'. Skinner had a better excuse for his inability to recall the speech clearly: 'as there was a great amount of clapping and cheering going on, I could not very well hear Bishop Liston who was speaking at the time.' Nevertheless, he was able to shed some light on the most contentious of Liston's remarks and to confirm that the bishop had read from a list. While strong on the use of the word 'murdered', Skinner's repeated denial of a clear recollection compromised his worth as a witness.

> Bishop Liston also said that the British soldiers murdered many of the Irish. He also said that he held in his hand a list of the chief people who were murdered. The Bishop then went on to say how and when they were murdered. I then left the Hall. I heard nothing distinctly.[58]

The entire Auckland police force had now been closely questioned and had repeatedly denied knowledge of the Town Hall incident. Reginald Ward was more successful in his wider investigations. He secured from Gordon Stanbrook a written statement which the reporter described as 'a copy of what I wrote from my notes immediately after the meeting'.[59] This differed slightly from the declaration Stanbrook had made (on Gunson's request) before a justice of the peace. Ward had managed to tease out of Stanbrook a fuller version of Liston's critical sentence describing those who had been murdered; he scribbled the new sentence at the bottom of the reporter's statement.

> We must not forget the martyrs who died in the fighting in 1916 – that glorious Easter. I have here a list of 155 men and women who were proud to die for their country, some were shot, some were hung and some died on hunger strike – murdered by foreign troops.[60]

Ward next tried to secure corroboration of Stanbrook's report from the two *Auckland Star* reporters who had also attended the meeting. After learning the fate of Laurence O'Brien's shorthand notes, Ward decided not to waste time interviewing him: 'O'Brien is addicted to drink, is of the same faith as Bishop Liston and would not help us in the matter', he reported to Eales.[61] The other *Star* man in the audience was there merely as a spectator and had taken no notes. Nevertheless, Francis Edward Carson was able to confirm almost all of Stanbrook's account of the speech, which he considered to be 'a very good summary'. His major criticism was that it 'considerably minimised the bitter and libellous nature of the address'.[62] Despite this forthright opinion, Carson was reluctant to take part in any case against the bishop.[63] Astonishingly, Ward completely overlooked a portion of Carson's statement which dealt with Liston's key phrase:

> In referring to the 1916 Easter rebellion Bishop Liston did not say that 155 martyrs were murdered by foreign troops. He said that some were killed by hunger striking, some were shot, and some were hung, he gave figures in each instance. He referred to about 16 who were murdered by foreign troops.[64]

Here was a direct and unambiguous rebuttal of Stanbrook's version by an experienced reporter who could hardly be suspected of secretly sympathising with the bishop. His account of an enumerated list accorded with the fuller sentence Ward had extracted from Stanbrook. Nevertheless, the detective refused to be put off by this troubling new evidence – he was seeking corroboration rather than contradiction. Ward next found two of the ushers on St Patrick's Night. Stanley Albert Greenough, a clerk with the Department of Agriculture, had been standing at the front of the gallery while Liston was speaking. He had no difficulty hearing the bishop and recalled with uncanny accuracy his references to the 'snobs of Empire' and those ready 'to fight and even die' for Irish freedom. Unfortunately for Ward, Greenough's patience quickly ran out:

> At this time I thought the address was bitter and disloyal and I was sick of listening to it so I left and did not hear any more. His speech was applauded more than once by the audience. I heard no one dissent from his remarks.[65]

By contrast, Frank Baller, a cleaner for the city council, managed to stay for the entire speech, despite Liston's 'very bitter and sarcastic manner'. Standing at the back of the hall on the ground floor, Baller claimed to have heard the bishop 'distinctly', unlike Constables Collins and Skinner. His statement was almost identical to Greenough's in its verbatim recall of the offensive phrases, while shedding a little more light on Liston's enumeration of the patriot dead: 'I remember he gave the number of martyrs who were murdered by foreign troops in the glorious Easter of 1916 and their glorious deeds would ever live in the hearts of Irishmen.' Confirming the *Herald* report's accuracy, Baller added that 'if anything the newspaper has toned down the speech which appeared to me to be very bitter towards England'.[66]

Ward's report reveals that neither Baller nor Greenough were able to recall the speech in any detail until the detective had jogged their memories with a copy of the *Herald*: 'Both of them found it difficult to state what sentences they could remember but when shown the report they agree with the sentiment of it and with some of the actual words.'[67] Ward called them 'intelligent men' and was convinced of their value as witnesses to back up Stanbrook. The detective had done his work well, not least by identifying the three reporters whose combined skills should have enlightened the prosecution on both the speech and how it came to be misreported. After the government ordered the commencement of proceedings, Ward was told to place his services at the disposal of the Crown Solicitor.

Vincent Meredith was about to begin his biggest case. Born in Whangarei of English immigrant parents, the forty-five-year-old lawyer had only recently been appointed Crown Solicitor. A partner with Hesketh Richmond Clayton and Meredith, he had succeeded the veteran J. A. Tole some fifteen months before.[68] Three years' experience with the Crown Law Office during the war had taught Meredith much about sedition law. In May 1917 he had successfully prosecuted several trade unionists for organising a go-slow – a 'seditious strike' – in the coal mines.[69] He hardly needed the Solicitor-General to remind him of the importance of locating a shorthand note of Liston's speech.

Meredith moved quickly after receiving MacGregor's letter of Monday, 27 March. By Wednesday he had consulted with Superintendent Hendrey and assessed the case file. Impressed by the deafening silence in the ranks, he told the Solicitor-General of the circular's 'remarkable result that no Police Officer admits being there with the exception of one who arrived after Liston had spoken'.

> As it is known that a large percentage of the Police Force are Irish and Roman Catholics and that men not on duty invariably attend these meetings in large numbers, the result of the inquiry by the Inspector is somewhat surprising. Put frankly, I understand that we shall be faced by [a] conspiracy of silence.[70]

Having 'a very experienced man' like Ward to assist him was some consolation to Meredith: 'He is not a Catholic and can be relied on to do his utmost.'[71] (No doubt provoked by the thought of Auckland Catholic policemen evading their duty, MacGregor sent this letter on to Commissioner Wright, who returned it with the brief note, 'Det Sgt Ward will get this evidence if it is to be got.'[72]) Denied the usual complement of police witnesses to bolster his case, Meredith was

Crown Solicitor Vincent Meredith. NZ Truth

forced to dig deeper. Clearly he did not expect to receive any assistance from Catholic sources; he told MacGregor, 'the *Star* reporter with the significant name of O'Brien took shorthand notes but states that he has destroyed them and I understand his memory is now very hazy as to what was said'.[73]

Unlike Ward, Meredith did not allow his scepticism to dissuade him from interviewing O'Brien. Even apart from his Catholic faith there were strong reasons for suspecting the reporter's objectivity. He had taken a full shorthand note of the address and read it over on the morning after the concert. Yet he could not recall the bishop using the phrase on which all others were agreed: 'I heard him refer to the glorious Easter of 1916 and he referred to numbers who were murdered and hung, but I did not hear him say that they were murdered by foreign troops.'[74]

Although he later claimed to have interviewed 'all possible witnesses', there is no evidence that Meredith spoke to Frank Carson.[75] If he did question the *Star* reporter, one wonders why he failed to take more notice of his alternative reading of Liston's most offensive sentence. Did Meredith prefer to believe the witnesses who came forward in the week that followed, all of whom were prepared to stand by Stanbrook's version? Collectively they were an unimpressive lot; most were employed by one or other of the local authorities. Meredith asked each potential witness to recall the address unaided, only then allowing him to refresh his memory with a copy of the *Herald* report.

The members of the orchestra were all close enough to the stage to have heard the bishop clearly, but could they remember what he had said? Meredith interviewed three part-time musicians. James Todd, a driver by occupation, was sitting six rows from the stage. He remembered a reference to Easter 1916 and the murder of a number of Irish people. Once the report was shown to him he recalled several other phrases but was far from confident about it: 'I cannot say that the report is the actual words used.' He was also uncertain about the bishop's exact remarks on murder by foreign troops, 'but he said something similar to that'. Even had Todd's memory been clearer he was not keen to appear in court: his orchestra was conducted by a Catholic 'and I will lose my employment if I do so.'[76]

George Broadley, a gas-meter reader, also played in the orchestra. As an Englishman he found the speech 'disloyal and very offensive to my country'. He could not repeat the bishop's precise words but remembered 'snobs of Empire' and a reference to Irishmen being murdered by foreign troops. Prompted by Meredith, he confirmed the accuracy of most of the report.[77] Gregory Ratcliffe Smith, a storeman, was the third musician interviewed. He had listened to the speech with mounting anger: 'I felt that I would like to take to him for what he said,' he confessed to the Crown Solicitor. Smith was not required to give evidence.[78]

Cecil Gibson, another Department of Agriculture employee, had heard the speech clearly from the top gallery and thought it most disloyal. He did not make promising witness material either: 'I cannot remember what he said. I know he referred to murders by foreign troops (meaning English soldiers).' Prompted, Gibson repeated several other phrases but with no real conviction. 'I can remember that he said all that when I see the report of the speech, but cannot remember it unless I saw the speech.' He did recall that Liston had given totals of the various people murdered by foreign troops. Gibson was yet another reluctant witness; he had been with the department only briefly and his chief was a Catholic. 'I am afraid that if I give evidence I will suffer for it later on.'[79] Nor was auctioneer Percy Nicholls willing to appear. He thought the address 'very disloyal and offensive', but added 'I cannot remember the speech without I saw it in print'. He claimed to be leaving the country on 24 April and wanted nothing to do with the case.[80]

Towards the end of the week Meredith finally located two members of Liston's audience prepared to speak up in court. Robert Beswick was made of sterner stuff than the others: he had risen to his feet when the bishop spoke of 'snobs of the Empire' and had remained standing for the rest of the address.

> I am an Englishman and I objected to these disloyal remarks so I stood up as a protest. Those around me called out to me to sit down and I said I won't as a loyal subject sit down and listen to sedition.[81]

Beswick had his own peculiar version of the list. 'I heard him say that at the glorious Easter a number (156?) including three priests, martyrs, gave their lives in the cause of freedom, shot by foreign troops.'[82] When shown the report, he recalled several other offensive phrases. Beswick's evident rancour was offset by his willingness to appear for the prosecution. Graham Brook Bell, a draughtsman with the Auckland Harbour Board, also thought the speech 'very disloyal'. Indeed, he wanted to add another charge to the indictment; the *Herald* had not mentioned Liston's outrageous claim that Ireland had 'defeated' the British Empire. Bell was solid on most of the report but somewhat confused about the key phrase: 'I heard him refer to the glorious Easter of 1916 and heard him use the words murdered by foreign troops but I could not understand who he said was murdered.'[83]

On the evening of Tuesday, 4 April, exactly one week after he had taken over the case, Crown Solicitor Meredith left for Wellington to attend a sitting of the Court of Appeal. Following Bell's instructions, MacGregor had invited him down to discuss all the evidence he had gathered; accordingly, Meredith brought the draft informations with him. Bearing in mind the need for urgency – 'Mr Massey is much concerned' – he had worked swiftly. Was the price for this despatch to be paid when the case came to court? With no police witnesses to call upon, Meredith had assembled a motley group of usher, meter-reader and fourth violin. They were all, however, prepared to support the *Herald*'s version of Liston's remarks. The way was now clear for the Crown to pursue the case – and the bishop.

12

The Truth Shall Make You Free

And you shall know the truth, and the truth shall make you free.

John 8:32

On Sunday, 26 March, Bishop Liston helped to open St Mary of the Angels in Wellington.[1] As the procession of priests and prelates wound down Boulcott Street and up the steps to the church's main entrance, the *New Zealand Free Lance* photographer took a picture. A worried-looking James Liston can be glimpsed towards the rear of the line of clerics, just in front of the venerable Archbishop Redwood.[2] One female spectator among the huge crowd thought that Liston looked so sad she barely resisted the temptation to go up and hug him.[3] Bishop Liston completed the morning's ceremonies by celebrating Pontifical High Mass.

The dramatic news of Liston's impending prosecution probably added several hundred to the numbers thronging the church and its precincts. His very public appearance at the opening won him much sympathy. While Father Tom McCarthy, the renowned Marist missionary preacher, and Bishop Whyte of Dunedin both addressed the huge congregation, neither made even a veiled reference to Liston's plight. Not so the Wellington clergy. Later that afternoon some thirty priests met to express their sympathy with the beleaguered bishop 'in the unjustifiable attacks now being made upon him'.[4] When calling for three cheers for Liston, however, Father Gilbert allowed a note of ambivalence to creep into his statement.

> Whatever our private political opinions may be we agree that the attacks being made upon the Bishop arise out of religious animosity, engineering for political purposes. All that His Lordship said in his speech has been

> said – and far more – in England itself by leading English writers and statesmen.[5]

The bitter tone of the *Evening Post*, in both its editorial and its correspondence columns, had deeply offended Wellington Catholics. A requisition was also circulating, signed by several prominent citizens, asking Mayor R. A. Wright to convene a protest meeting against the speech.[6] The Catholic reply to this assault on faith and fatherland fluttered defiantly from the tower of St Mary of the Angels – an Irish tricolour.[7] A deputation of laymen considered calling on Liston to assure him of local Catholic sympathy and loyalty, but Patrick O'Regan discouraged anything that could evoke a reply from the bishop.[8] There was every chance of a belligerent Liston responding in terms that might deepen his predicament. While taking his lawyer's advice over the proposed demonstration, Liston must have contrasted this enthusiasm with the muted support offered him in Auckland.

O'Regan approved less of the speech's content than of the spirit behind it. After reading the *Herald* report, he had commented wryly that 'certain passages could have been modified with advantage'.[9] Despite this reservation, he attributed the press outcry largely to sectarian bias: 'Now that the words are published it is best to give bigotry no apology, but to stand by them'.[10] Following Liston's request for advice, O'Regan investigated the bishop's legal situation. Those war regulations that were still in force applied to seditious documents rather than to spoken words; any proceedings would have to be taken under the Crimes Act (1908) and before a judge and jury. While feeling that most lawyers would find Liston's remarks expressive of a seditious intention, O'Regan believed that only the final phrase, 'murdered by foreign troops', truly deserved this description. Moreover, to convict him the jury would have to be unanimous; one dissident could cause a disagreement, with the prospect of two more trials before the Crown cried halt.[11]

O'Regan held out no hope of acquittal, but was equally dismissive of the chances of the case coming to court. 'I shall be surprised if you are prosecuted', he assured Liston, predicting instead a government statement endorsing the strong public protest and promising future legislation if needed.[12] O'Regan's diary tells a slightly different tale.

> I doubt if proceedings will be taken, but still religious rancour is one of the assets of the present Government, and in view of the elections at the end of

John Callan. ATL

the year and the desire to draw herrings across the scent of their own rascally conduct, it would not surprise me if proceedings were taken.[13]

Liston was fortunate to be able so soon to consult such an experienced sedition lawyer, but O'Regan's sceptical approach did not encourage the bishop to take his predicament as seriously as he should have done. After the announcement of proceedings O'Regan seemed almost gleeful: 'Now we shall see and hear things.'[14] Like many of his fellow Catholics, he failed to recognise that the prosecution might stem less from political trickery than from a desire properly to test the legality of a very controversial speech. He had lengthy meetings with the bishop on Sunday and Monday, during which Liston asked him to act should the case come to court. O'Regan promised to consider the matter; had he accepted immediately Liston would have been spared the subsequent undignified scramble to find a lawyer.[15]

O'Regan may have hesitated because Liston wanted him to share the task with the Dunedin lawyer John Bartholomew Callan. Liston had known Callan since their school days and had frequently consulted him during his time in Dunedin. Despite his Irish heritage, Callan was conservative and loyal in politics; he had volunteered during the war, was wounded in action and rose to the rank of captain.[16]

Two such different horses might well have trouble pulling together. Perhaps aware of this, both lawyers were scrupulous to avoid the impression of pushing their individual political views on the bishop. On the train back to Auckland Liston wrote telling Callan of the new turn his troubles had taken.[17] Significantly, Liston complained to neither Callan nor O'Regan of any gross misrepresentation of his remarks by the *New Zealand Herald*.

On returning home, Liston at once followed O'Regan's advice to recruit a support committee composed of local lawyers and businessmen. In fact, the crowd of advisers who soon appeared presented him with an embarrassment of riches. And a quandary: who among them could be best trusted to preserve his episcopal dignity while furthering what he described to O'Regan as 'our cause'?[18] Many of them were friends of Bishop Cleary and had acquiesced in his policy of inoffensive Irishism, while the men Liston most wanted to advise him were out of easy reach.

This raised a more fundamental question: was Liston going to fight or apologise? His correspondence after proceedings were announced reflected the fury of his co-religionists. Fifty Dargaville parishioners forwarded a resolution of support 'in this campaign of calumny and villification [*sic*] which has broken out against Your Lordship nominally, but against the Catholic Church in reality'.[19] Sister Mary Dominic, of Invercargill, commented bitterly: 'It seems to be a mere matter of politics and the approaching election is to be propelled Masseywards by the petty persecution of a Catholic Bishop.'[20]

Not everyone was so upset at the decision to proceed. Father W. J. Forde told Liston of the pride he felt at seeing his Bishop square off against their common foe, 'the enemies of church and country'.[21] Father Jack Riordan blamed the PPA for the Cabinet's decision: 'More than likely Massey's lord and master [Elliott] is behind the guns because it is a bishop and they want big game to frighten other lesser dignitaries who are a continual source of annoyance.'[22] Not all of Liston's clergy were so supportive; at least two refused to join their brethren in expressing sympathy for his plight. Liston also told Whyte of some 'candid criticisms' that had come his way since the speech.[23]

The Auckland priests may have been encouraged to rally around Liston by the cable which soon arrived from Bishop Cleary in Ireland: 'In the present circumstances and always you have my kindliest wishes, fraternal affection and full confidence.'[24] One of the senior Auckland clergy, Dean Harry Holbrook, had cabled his absent chief on Thursday,

31 March, telling of Liston's predicament.[25] Cleary's prompt reply effectively placed a protective mantle around his young colleague. Liston was extremely grateful for this backing, especially as Cleary had given it when only the most hostile version of his remarks was publicly available. The contents of the cable were made known privately among the clergy, but Liston chose not to publish it until after the case was over.[26] While personally thanking all those who spoke up on his behalf, Liston did not need his ecclesiastical superior to fight his battles for him.

Some Catholic priests were not entirely unhappy at the turn of events: persecution was good for the church, so the more of it the better! It passed their understanding how the events of recent years had failed to arouse New Zealand Catholics to an acceptable level of fury. Instead, they saw apathy, indifference, and even irritation with the constantly rehearsed wrongs of Ireland. Father Farragher of Ormond hoped that the case would 'stiffen the backbone of our people and be the means of a closer and more solid organisation in the future.'[27] He was scathingly critical of lay inaction: 'What has the Catholic Federation done? What is it doing? Then look at the Self-Determination for Ireland League; it seems to be asleep and dying. From none of the large centres have we seen or heard of a resolution or protest regarding this matter . . . How low some of our people can cringe!' Father Michael Edge of Te Awamutu relished the thought of the coming combat:

> No one can deny that our prestige has fallen greatly during the past few years. We seem to go down every time – Scholarships, Ne Temere condemnation, railway concessions. Is it that God is abandoning us for some unrepented sin? Herein lies our first consideration. For the rest I would like to see the Gunsonian element fought to a finish. The fight, if undertaken, will either make or break us. Hence the necessity for utmost precaution and capable generalship.[28]

Immediately after his return to Auckland, Liston had conferred with Edge on his choice of legal counsel. The priest responded by praising P. J. O'Regan as both lawyer and practical Catholic, 'but it must be admitted that he has not (probably only through lack of opportunity) established a great reputation. In fighting I consider it necessary to put your forces in the hands of a commander whom the enemy fears.'[29] In the absence of the regular diocesan lawyer, Robert McVeagh (away in Europe for much of 1922), Liston turned to one of his St Benedict's parishioners, John Laurence Conlan. Born in Christchurch and educated at St Patrick's College, Wellington, Conlan had been based in Auckland only since 1916.[30] During the war he earned an unenviable reputation as the military representative on the First Auckland Military Service Board; Captain (later Major) Conlan was notorious for his stern questioning of those seeking exemption.[31] He had attended the St Patrick's Night concert and was probably one of those who urged silence on Liston after Gunson's statement.

The prospect of attempting any sort of defence receded after John Callan's opinion arrived from Dunedin. Liston's letter had come at a sad time for Callan; after a prolonged illness, his mother was in the last week of her life. While he knew that James Liston (of all people) would not expect him to leave her bedside, there is every reason to suspect that Callan was grateful for so convincing an excuse to avoid involvement in the case. He had been in a quandary since reading the paper on Monday: how to convey sympathy for the bishop without expressing an opinion on his Town Hall views? To comment without invitation would be impertinent, but once Liston requested his professional advice he had to bite the bullet. In the course of a long letter profuse in condolences ('the whole business must be inexpressibly painful to you'), the lawyer maintained a diplomatic silence on the speech itself.[32]

Callan reviewed the legal position largely as O'Regan had done earlier. In an unintended reflection on the bishop's advisers, he assumed from Liston's public silence that the press report represented a fair summary of his remarks. Callan approached the problem carefully; while counsel would normally dictate his client's policy such a course was clearly out of place here. However, a lawyer was not obliged to appear should a policy with which he disagreed be chosen. Callan then outlined four possible lines for Liston to follow. The first was to own up and take what was coming to him: 'Yes. I said the words and they represent my considered opinions. According to the law of this country that constitutes an offence and I am prepared to take the consequences.' Obviously, Callan added glumly, counsel could be of little use in this case.

The second course – to argue that the speech did not on the face of it imply any seditious intention – was even less palatable to the Dunedin lawyer. He believed the speech to be clearly seditious as it encouraged Irish readers to pursue complete independence by unlawful means, while in New Zealand its natural consequence would be to promote ill will and hostility between different classes. Callan claimed to know no one less likely to break the law than his former classmate.

> But I am endeavouring to give a candid opinion on the legal position as I see it, and the fact remains that, in my opinion, these are the natural consequences of the speech. I apprehend that as a matter of law, in this and in other offences, a man is deemed to intend the consequences that would naturally follow his words at the time and in the circumstances in which the words were used – at least, unless and until he clearly establishes the contrary.[33]

While arguments might exist against his opinion, Callan felt that a lawyer out of sympathy with the line chosen by his client would be 'only a drag and hindrance to his chief and to other counsel who may enthusiastically believe in the defence' (probably an allusion to O'Regan, who was well known for his aggressive Irish advocacy). Callan could not have been plainer: if it was to be argued that the language did not *prima facie* import a seditious intention then he would respectfully decline the brief.

Callan's third possibility was to attempt to persuade the jury that these natural consequences were not necessarily intended – that Liston had no seditious intention, even if his actual words suggested otherwise. Against this defence could be cited the nature of the occasion, the fact that a speaker would surely prepare his remarks in advance, and Liston's eloquent silence when the speech was commented on. Callan held out no hope of an acquittal, believing that a disagreement was the best a jury would deliver. Indeed, he seemed to discount the value of legal argument over the merits or otherwise of Liston's remarks. 'In matters of this sort the average juror will, after all is said, be influenced . . . by his preconceived views on the Irish question, rather than by what transpires in the court.'[34]

Callan painted Liston's case as very black: 'one of those unfortunate positions in which no course is free from grave objections'. The bishop had to choose the least of several evils. Callan advised him – the fourth option – to plead guilty while denying any seditious intention. His plea would be merely an admission that a jury was more likely to draw a contrary inference from his speech. This course had the merit of avoiding a trial and the risk – if he was found guilty – of a two-year jail sentence. The judge might even let him off with a fine (which Callan had no doubt Liston would pay). For the rest, all he had to offer was the mitigating circumstance that equally seditious language had been used throughout the Empire on the Irish question and allowed to pass unnoticed.

'The writing of this letter has given me much trouble', Callan confessed to Liston. He probably suspected that his views would conflict with those of the bishop's other advisers, as well as Liston's own inclinations. He cannot be accused of minimising his friend's dilemma; indeed, at times Callan sounded more like a prosecuting counsel, his judgement on the speech recalling Solicitor-General MacGregor in its harshness. He seemed to regard Liston's silence as a practical admission of guilt. However, his negativity may have offset O'Regan's breezy confidence that the affair would end in smoke. Callan clearly had no stomach for a fight; rather, he wanted Liston to throw himself on the mercy of the court – and the sooner the better.

> Ever since I first read the report of the speech I have hoped that Your Lordship's decision would be to disavow any intention of stirring up strife or of inciting anyone to fight for a Republic. It would be possible to do so even now. I mean in court.[35]

The difficulty experienced by all the bishop's advisers in constructing a convincing defence was complicated by uncertainty over the government's determination to prosecute. This left them susceptible to offers of a compromise. After the opening of St Mary of the Angels, Dean J. R. Holley had promised to keep an ear cocked for news of Liston's case. A week later he told the bishop of rumours circulating in the capital that Massey would 'go no further in the matter'. Holley also consulted O'Regan, who had not heard the stories but could easily believe them. 'He still thinks they will not prosecute', Holley reassured Liston.

> Another rumour is that Massey had lost control of the Bigots and recognising they were doing the country a lot of harm by their sectarian strife, he thought to silence them (and us I suppose) by declaring a case under judgement. That later on when things have quietened down, he will simply and quietly withdraw it.[36]

Such a belief was strengthened by the fact that no summons had yet been served on Liston. The bishop was also comforted by rumours of Sir Francis Bell's reservations about the intended prosecution. The Attorney-General's cautionary letter to Gunson came to assume a significance out of all proportion to its true worth, despite O'Regan's warning that Bell's agreement was not necessary for legal action to be instituted.[37] Viewing the affair as a sordid political stunt further obscured a true appreciation of the bishop's plight. One correspondent suggested a mass meeting of Auckland Catholics at which Liston could deny any disloyal intent and explain that Ireland's full freedom did not involve imperial disruption.

> You could then explain the figure of speech called metonymy and show that

Michael Sheahan. NZO

> your references to the Empire were in reality to be applied not to its citizens in general, but to various placemen who have given the Empire bad grace in the eyes of the world. Of course there would be much quibbling in all this, but it would be good enough for the knaves.[38]

Here was the seed of an idea which would grow. Callan had already urged Liston to end his public silence by clarifying his views on the loyalty issue, a message reinforced by his local legal advisers. One of the bishop's confidants was Michael Joseph Sheahan, the uncle of Monsignor Ormond (Liston's closest friend among the Auckland clergy).[39] Sheahan's distress at recent events was compounded by his friendship with both Massey and Gunson. Once the prosecution was announced he quickly approached two of his business colleagues, Eliot Davis and Oliver Nicholson, who were prominent Auckland supporters of the Reform Party.[40] On Saturday, 1 April, Sheahan brought Liston what purported to be their offer of a compromise solution. The bishop wrote at once to tell O'Regan of the 'new situation':

> Massey and his chief advisers here (Nicholson and Davis) conveyed to me yesterday that they do not want to go on with the case – too much ill-will, no good for the political situation etc – + would be glad of an honourable settlement. What could or would I do? I sent them word, unofficially, that if they wanted a settlement I was open to one also. I offered, if they would withdraw the charge, to make immediately afterwards a statement. My idea was to touch on two points – the question of loyalty to N.Z. + forgiveness for the past, reconciliation etc. I would not withdraw one word of my convictions, but had no particular desire at present to ram them down anyone's throat.[41]

It was next suggested to Liston that he make his public statement before the charge against him was withdrawn. Turning once more to O'Regan for advice, Liston cited Callan's gloomy view of his legal position. Would such a course be 'dignified, fair to our cause, advisable'?[42] In reply, O'Regan encouraged him to take the overtures seriously, urging that several people be involved in drawing up the statement, which should be published in the *New Zealand Tablet* before being handed to the secular press. O'Regan decided against going to Auckland to assist in the process. Had he done so he might have probed the genuineness of the supposed offer and exposed the naive expectations of it harboured by Liston's friends.[43] He had just sent the *Auckland Star* a fiery letter in reply to the editor's taunt that colonial Irishmen had done nothing towards inducing Ireland to accept the treaty – 'Not that I care much for the editorial censure, but my real object is to assist in creating a more friendly atmosphere in the northern city for the Bishop.'[44]

Liston also asked Callan whether he approved the idea of a public statement expressing his desire to bury the hatchet. Callan's cabled answer – 'Yes' – arrived on Wednesday, 5 April, just as Liston was completing the final draft of his message to the Prime Minister.[45] In a long letter of the same date, Callan warmly endorsed the idea even if (as it turned out) the promise of withdrawal was an empty one. Such a message of forgiveness and reconciliation would 'take the sting out of a prosecution, even if it were persisted in'. Rather than lose face by revealing his real views to those who did not know him, the sooner it was done and the less by way of a bargain the more dignified Liston would appear. Callan shared Liston's disbelief that the government was really out for a bishop's blood. He interpreted a recent paragraph in the *Otago Daily Times* stressing the police role in the impending prosecution as 'intended to prepare the public gently for the back-down that Your Lordship's letter tells me is in course of arrangement'.[46]

While the Crown might dread the prospect of one obstinate juror repeatedly wrecking its case, Callan felt that any sort of trial would be a disaster for Liston, especially if an attempt was made to justify his remarks. Unaware that Robert McVeagh was out of the country, Callan urged Liston to consult the Auckland lawyer over the terms of his proposed statement. The bishop's latest letter delighted Callan: he had feared that his earlier advice would offend everyone in Auckland, but Liston soothed his worries on this score. Moreover, he was taking Callan's advice by ending his public silence. The lawyer ended on an optimistic note, hoping soon to hear that 'this nine days' wonder has finally and definitely faded'. Sympathy for Liston's plight did not blind him to Massey's predicament.

> We should not close our eyes to the fact that Gunson, by his forcing tactics, has got the Government into the position that, unless something is settled along the lines of Your Lordship's letter, they must push the thing, to their own considerable embarrassment, but to Your Lordship's considerable embarrassment also, whatever the final issue.[47]

Liston's statement emerged along the lines described earlier to O'Regan. Handed to the Press Association on the morning of Thursday, 6 April, it was ostensibly an open letter to the Prime Minister; however, its contents were published up and down the country well before Massey received it. This deliberate adoption of Gunsonian methods was intended partly as revenge and also (Liston told O'Regan) 'to make Massey toe the line'.[48] Among Liston's private papers on the case is a note describing how it came to be conceived. If, as Callan implied, Massey needed help to escape the straitjacket applied by Mayor Gunson, it was not going to come from Bishop Liston.

> After the Government had decided to take these proceedings against me I decided to address the public by means of a letter to the Premier (letter read) . . . I made no reference whatever to the pending charge of sedition for the reason that it was then *sub judice*. I retracted nothing & apologised for nothing of what I had said. I had nothing to retract, nothing to apologise for.[49]

13

Loyal At Last?

BISHOP LISTON

LETTER TO THE PREMIER
MISUNDERSTANDING REGRETTED
Auckland, This Day.

Bishop Liston, in a letter to the Premier, says: I yield place to no one in love for this beautiful country of New Zealand, in which I was born, and loyalty to the King. In so far as any reported remarks of mine should have led those who do not know me, I quite frankly regret my share in the misunderstanding, and I trust, when the people of New Zealand come to know me better, they will think of me as my friends do.

I speak in that matter as a citizen of New Zealand no less than a Catholic bishop. The Church is mother of my faith in things eternal; New Zealand is my country, protectress of my liberty, and of my fortunes on earth. I could not utter one syllable that would belie either my Church or my country, and when I assert, as I now solemnly do, that the teachings of the Church are in thorough harmony with the interests of my country, New Zealand, I know in the depths of my soul that I speak the truth. That Catholics in New Zealand have carried out this obligation of loving their country, their generous part in her children's toil and sacrifice is honourable proof. Loyalty, however, does not preclude me or anyone else from striving for betterment of any part of the Empire.

What I said, and what I say now with all sincerity, is this: In spite of an all-too-unhappy past, Irish people at home and abroad, and their sympathisers, are both willing and eager to hold out the hand of friendship. The very first to strike this note were the bishops of Ireland to a man, and one amongst them who was often denounced as an out-and-out extremist has hailed the Treaty which binds his country to the Empire as a very gift of God.[1]

By reporting only a third of his letter to Massey, the Press Association did James Liston a further injustice. Its peculiar selection of sentences rendered his message almost impossible to decipher. Worse still, while most newspapers carried the same brief report, only a few of them published the letter's full text in a later issue. Dean Holley immediately complained to Liston: 'Last night's *Post* gave a garbled, truncated, nonsensical extract from your letter – sent by Press Ass. It was very misleading and caused much wonder by its interpolated, disconnected, nonconsequential jumble.'[2]

To be fair, the confusion was only partly cleared when the complete letter became available. Liston had followed O'Regan's advice to involve several people in its composition (various drafts in different hands survive among Liston's papers).[3] While the tone was considerably softened during the process of composition, the letter's overall impression is of muddle; it touched on several issues without illuminating any of them – least of all the one that might have been expected.

The letter was intended to answer all those critics who had lectured the bishop on his responsibilities. Liston addressed himself not to the press or to local politicians, but to his fellow New Zealanders. His clergy had taken some of the fire aimed at their chief; he repaid them by declaring that they would 'cordially agree' with the views he now expressed. Massey was used merely as a channel of communication.

> I feel that I owe a duty to my fellow-countrymen to make a statement at the present moment regarding my recent speech, and it seems to me that the most fitting way to approach them is through you, Sir, as head of the Government in New Zealand.[4]

Liston flatly denied the charges of disloyalty and of disturbing the peace. 'Those who know me set down that description of me as incredible, and for my own part I cannot accept it for one minute.' But what was he loyal to? Not to England or the Empire, but to his native land. Liston's fierce patriotism was strictly local, with New Zealand rather than the British navy cast as the protectress of his liberty. Shifting ground slightly from his position on St Patrick's Night, he asserted his right to speak as a New Zealand citizen rather than as a prince of the Catholic Church. Amid copious references to 'my country', Liston declared a personal loyalty to the King, his reply to those who had interpreted the speech as a repudiation of the British Crown.

He expressed regret not for his speech but for 'his share in the misunderstanding', some of the blame for which he clearly attributed to the newspapers. However, the press assault had at least awoken him to the danger posed to his flock. Whatever private expectations he harboured of the letter to Massey, Liston also intended to clarify Catholic attitudes towards 'the institutions of the country'.

> The Catholic Church lays on her children a solemn obligation to love their home, and to honour their parents. Like to that, is the command she gives to them to love their country and to honour their King. To no one, be he priest or layman, does she leave this a matter of free thought or free choice. Patriotism is not a mere opinion which a man may hold today and discard tomorrow: it is a duty, and a solemn one.[5]

Liston's claim to be 'striving for the betterment of the Empire' recalled the wording of section 118(2) of the Crimes Act, which protected those who spoke to this effect. Was there a deliberate attempt to seek shelter behind this legal barrier?[6] Liston also buttressed his case by citing several eminent critics of the British government's policies in Ireland:

> In this respect, I find myself in the distinguished company of His Majesty The King, Mr Lloyd George, Mr Asquith, General Smuts, the Anglican Bishops, the Nonconformist leaders, and the greater number of the representative newspapers of the Empire in calling for a change in the hitherto bitter relations between England and Ireland.[7]

The bishop clearly opposed any further violence in Ireland and was not hankering for an Irish republic; rather, he rejoiced in the Anglo–Irish accord and looked forward to 'a perfect and a lasting friendship' between England and Ireland. 'I dwelt on this point in my speech, and intended it to give, and it really did give the key to that speech, but it has been almost completely overlooked in all the subsequent criticism of myself.'[8] Here was the closest Liston came to a complaint: the press had ignored the main thrust of his remarks in favour of its own sensational interpretation. This solitary reference to his speech neither explained nor corrected it, still less apologised for it.

While Liston would not deny the unhappy facts of Anglo–Irish history, he believed that the Irish (both at home and abroad) were willing to look to the future. In this forgiving pose, Liston aligned himself with the Australian and Irish hierarchies, and particularly with Bishop Fogarty of Killaloe (the 'out-and-out extremist' of his letter).[9] It was an ironic twist: Fogarty, the most passionate Sinn Fein bishop, had become the treaty's warmest supporter, and Liston was now sheltering behind his skirts. By granting the Irish Free State the status of a dominion, the treaty allowed Liston to raise one weak cheer for the Empire. His letter concluded with the confident prediction that the Irish clouds would soon disappear:

> Ireland's friends desire nothing better than that the obstacles should vanish as speedily as possible and leave the way open to complete reconciliation between North and South, the Free State and England. This will give us in the words of the now famous Treaty the union, under His Majesty the King, of Ireland with the Commonwealth of Nations known as the British Empire.[10]

First reaction to the open letter came from the *Auckland Star*, whose editor felt that it would be read 'with very general interest and approval'.[11] While the legal situation precluded detailed comment, Leys applauded Liston's breaking of a silence which many had found difficult to comprehend. The long-time champion of home rule saw the issue primarily in an Irish context. With Ireland teetering on the verge of civil war, the leaders of north and south had been forced to overcome their mutual antipathy in an attempt to restore peace on the border. In these circumstances, Leys insisted, the fledgling Irish Free State needed the unqualified support of all overseas Irishmen.

The *Star* acknowledged that Liston had done a service to both his Church and to the community: 'His letter makes it clear and unmistakable on which side the Catholic Church and Irish people range themselves'.[12] The *New Zealand Herald* was much less gracious about what it termed Liston's 'somewhat belated expression of regret for his speech', although it grudgingly approved his love of country, loyalty to King and 'most admirable wishes for the healing of Irish sores and the reconciliation of Ireland with the Empire'.[13] If Liston had taken offence at the criticism he had received, editor Hackett trusted that he would realise, 'in his calmer judgement, that there was in it nothing of personal enmity or religious or racial malice'. The community had spoken more in sorrow than in anger and was now relieved that the affront had been withdrawn.

Hackett noted that the bishop had not explained his St Patrick's Night speech. 'What he fails to do no one else will attempt to do because the difficulty of reconciling the authorship of the speech to the Irish of Auckland with that of the letter to the Prime Minister of New Zealand is well nigh insuperable.' He could not resist taking a final swipe at Liston:

> It is not easy to perceive how wounds are to be assuaged by such words as Bishop Liston used in his speech, but the people of Auckland will not be

'Strange Bedfellows.' The New Zealand Herald*'s view of the Irish situation in February 1922.* NZH

ungenerous and they will accept the explicit assurances of the letter in the spirit in which they are given. The Bishop who writes as a New Zealander is a very much better citizen than the Bishop who spoke as an Irishman.[14]

The Dunedin *Evening Star* also accepted Liston's loyalty as he now chose to define it. However, its editor struggled to square his 'innocuous sentiments' under the threat of prosecution with the outburst that had provoked so much resentment, recalling how little Liston had done to prevent the interpretation he now regretted. The bishop's professed loyalty to Empire contrasted with his glorification of the Dublin rebels, while 'the whole tone of the bitter and gibing address was most ill-judged to assist the reconciliation which we are now assured he has most at heart'.[15] Nor did Liston's praise of the Anglo–Irish Treaty as 'the very gift of God' sit easily with the prospect of endless strife he had seemed to welcome in his earlier speech.

In a barbed reference to the Labour Party's leaders, the *Evening Star* remarked: 'we have become used to the geographical love which other disturbers of the peace are accustomed to profess for New Zealand while they work for the disintegration of the Empire'.[16] Given Liston's professions of Catholic loyalty to King and country, the *Star* saw no good reason why the national anthem ('by which the King is honoured') should not be played at all future St Patrick's Day celebrations. Indeed, the entertainment offered at such gatherings might be better restricted to musical items alone. Despite such harsh observations, the *Star* did not appear anxious to see Liston in the dock. 'Whether the Government proceeds or does not proceed with its prosecution . . . is a matter of small importance to the general community.'[17]

Several editors did Liston a favour by exaggerating the degree of his penitence, the *Dominion* even calling his letter to Massey 'an explanation of the offending speech'.[18] There were divided opinions on the bishop's sense of timing. While applauding his 'admirable and worthy' sentiments, the *Waikato Times* regretted that he did not break his silence when first challenged, 'and that other organisations so promptly ranged themselves on his side and in effect endorsed his sentiments as published'.[19] By contrast, the *Oamaru Mail* was effusive on Liston's '*amende honorable*': 'He has done the right thing in the right way and has made full atonement.'[20] It commended him for not speaking out during the height of the press fury, 'for to have done so would have only had the effect of adding fresh fuel to the fire'. Deeming any detailed comment upon the letter as 'an outrage upon journalistic propriety', the *Mail* urged Liston to prove his loyalty by helping the local Irish to 'banish recollections of the wretched past'.[21]

Liston had no fiercer critic that the editor of the *Taranaki Daily News*, who had earlier demanded an unreserved apology and a complete withdrawal of the bishop's 'bitter words'. Instead, Liston had merely expressed regret that some people considered his remarks disloyal, 'thus studiously avoiding the real point in question'.[22] Annoyed by the letter's 'ambiguous language', the *Daily News* editor saw no way in which Liston's 'explicit and definite' words could have been misunderstood. He laid before his readers the awful prospect of sectarian strife on an Irish or Australian scale, unaware how awkwardly these professions of concern for the Empire sat with his dismissive attitude towards Irish troubles.

> We do not want the alleged wrongs of a country 13,000 miles away to be obtruded and made capital of in this fair Dominion, which has troubles enough of its own, nor do we want the Mother Country, to which the great bulk of us are proud to own allegiance, defamed. Let this sort of thing end, or else religious and political conditions here will become as bad as they are in Australia and elsewhere.[23]

Liston found an unexpected sympathiser in the *Otago Daily Times*. It saw the letter as evidence that a summons had yet to be issued, as it would otherwise have been 'wholly irregular' for Liston to have written to Massey. 'Moreover, the receipt and publication of the letter may well decide the Government to abandon any idea of the prosecution.'[24] The *Times* editor praised Liston's emphatic personal loyalty to the Crown and his declaration of Catholic teaching on patriotism, but was less willing to accept that the speech had been 'misunderstood'. Citing Liston's panegyric to the 1916 rebels, he concluded drily, 'that the Empire, including New Zealand, so dear to Bishop Liston, survived the ordeal of the war was not the fault of those who participated in his "glorious Easter".' Despite finding his apologia 'strangely deficient', the editor was prepared to let Liston off the hook. 'Even if it is closed now the incident will not be without a salutary effect.'

> Where, prompted by an honest desire to overcome the causes of differences in Ireland and to promote the welfare and peace of that country, Irish people hold out, as he says, the hand of friendship it is not to be spurned. For this reason, it is to be hoped that the Government will accept Bishop Liston's statement, inadequate though it is in its expressions of regret for what he said, and cancel the instructions which have been issued for his prosecution.[25]

This forgiving line was not to the taste of several readers of the *Otago Daily Times*. R. Ferguson immediately let the editor know how unhappy he was at the paper's three-week silence on the case, in contrast to most of the other leading dailies. Tardy in condemnation, the editor was now the first to advocate a withdrawal of legal proceedings.

> Until this morning I do not remember seeing one editorial word of comment on the question. At this belated hour you, making use of the Bishop's letter to the Premier, avail yourself of the opportunity to quote a few of the Bishop's St Patrick's Day remarks in order to criticise them adversely. But your main object in writing on the question appears to be to try and influence the Government not to prosecute the Bishop.[26]

Ferguson insisted that, as the Crown Law Office had found a case to answer, the courts should weigh that case on its merits: 'Government or any outside interference with the course of the law is wrong and should not be tolerated under any circumstances.' 'Loyal Protestant' was also surprised at the stance of the *Otago Daily Times*: 'you should be the last to use your influence to prevent justice being carried out'.[27] The errant editor had plenty to say in his own defence. He had seen no especial need to join other newspapers in condemning Liston's original utterance:

> The passage in the speech which our contemporaries justly condemned was of a class that a local publication has made familiar to us. We have repeatedly in the past expressed in fairly emphatic terms our views regarding the anti-British character of the propaganda which has been carried on in this quarter. As a consequence the *Daily Times* has become an object of constant attack from it and hardly a week passes in which persons connected with the production of the *Daily Times* are not personally and violently assailed by it.[28]

The *Daily Times* editor mentioned this 'childish and foolish' behaviour merely to remove any doubts about his paper's attitude towards the speech; he would ignore such provocation in the interests of peace in both Ireland and New Zealand. In his view, Liston's 'perfervid expressions of loyalty to the Crown' and his 'abjectly humiliating' apology had removed the principal reason for taking action against him. A trial would only arouse more sectarian strife. As the law had yet to be set in motion there was nothing to prevent the government from cancelling its instructions to proceed.

> Is it not, however, the case that a public service may be effected . . . if, now that the Bishop has wrapped himself in a penitent sheet and expressed regret for what he said, the Government adopts the conclusion that his profession of loyalty should be accepted?[29]

One wonders whether the mock sympathy of the *Otago Daily Times* was harder for Dunedin Catholics to bear than its previous hostility. Few of those southerners who had rushed to praise his speech would offer Liston their opinion of his letter to Massey, while the *New Zealand Tablet* made no reference to it whatever. Kelly's first editorial on the case was written on Thursday 23 March after reading Gunson's protest and the chorus of press approval it received. Entitled 'March Madness', it took a detached view of the developing controversy. After St Patrick's Day 'to the great amusement of the public one Mayor, several editors of daylies [*sic*], a host of those anonymous writers who are ashamed of their names, and a few Council-of-Churches people stood on their heads and made a deal of pother in the foolish manner habitual to them'.[30]

While Kelly took the opportunity to refight the sectarian battles of recent years (Sinn Fein violence, Howard Elliott, the Marriage Amendment Act), he would publish nothing specific on the address

Dr James Kelly, New Zealand Tablet *editor.*

itself. Even before the announcement of proceedings he seemed wary of any direct reference to the speech, offering as an excuse the lengthy accounts of various St Patrick's Day celebrations that were passing across his desk. He remarked, without apparent irony, that 'as most are fully or partially published in local papers there is no good reason why we should publish them again'.[31] This unusual display of reticence contrasted with the lavish space he devoted to similar events in Melbourne.

Kelly may well have been heeding the threat of legal action contained in Gunson's statement. (Bishop Whyte had also asked J. B. Callan to warn the *Tablet* editor to curb his comments on the affair.)[32] Once legal proceedings were announced, Kelly sarcastically regretted his inability to discuss the case further:

> Everybody knows what the newspapers told us that his Lordship said, and everybody also knows what the *Tablet* had to say on the matter, and we are sorry to disappoint them. We have been advised that, as a summons might be issued between the time of writing and our date of publication, the prop-

er policy to adopt is that of Mr Asquith. Wait and see. While professing our extreme regret for the natural chagrin of people who would not be sorry to see us put ourselves within reach of the law, by criticising a case *sub judice*, our native Scots canniness dictates a policy of silence.[33]

Had Kelly chosen to speak out, no amount of cautioning from Callan and Whyte would have silenced him; for the moment, however, he preferred to let Liston stew in his own juice. As we have seen, Kelly fell out with his old friend during the long interregnum after Michael Verdon's death.[34] The new bishop had further disappointed Kelly after going north; he complained in early 1922 that Liston had 'done nothing to help us since he got the chance'.[35] When the case first broke, Kelly had to exercise all his self-control to keep out of the fray. (Did he hope to hit the jackpot with a conviction? What a weapon to use against his local enemies!) As events gathered pace Kelly pursued a policy of masterly inactivity, refusing even to launch a fighting fund for Liston's defence.[36]

Kelly preferred to publish Liston's haughty reply to Gunson rather than his open letter to the Prime Minister. In private, he made no secret of his disapproval of the *démarche* to Massey.

> Liston used to be a friend of mine but he has developed into a snob pure and simple since he got a little authority – dignity he will never have. His crawl to Massey was the most awful thing [that] ever happened here. It just illustrated the difference between being pig-headed and courageous, for he lost his head completely. He also lost the respect of clergy and laity throughout New Zealand and it was a common saying that he ought to get gaol for writing such a letter instead of sticking to his guns.[37]

Was Kelly behind some of the messages Liston now received urging him not to retreat before his enemies? On the day the open letter appeared Bishop Whyte wrote to Liston inquiring about the state of his 'little affair'.[38] Liston replied two days later: 'I should like to think that the statement of mine pleases you. So far as I can gather it has done our own people a service and has been well received by others.'[39] Rather than give an opinion on the letter, Whyte begged his colleague to resist even the appearance of a climb-down.[40] Other clerical friends were less diplomatic. 'Your letter to the Premier was not received favourably here', James Kennedy told Liston bluntly.[41] Dean Regnault advised him to avoid such veiled apologies in future, while P. J. O'Regan remained silent about the letter in his correspondence with the bishop.[42]

By contrast, Callan was predictably warm in his praise of Liston's action: 'I don't think, My Lord, you need entertain any doubt as to either the prudence or the dignity of the step you have now taken.' To Callan even the Press Association's version 'read well – very well'.[43] Dean Holley disagreed strongly, believing that the abbreviated report of the letter did Liston a great injury:

> But oh! how different the text, the reality!! It is just what is wanted at the present time; there is no back-down, no retraction, but ample explanation. If it does no other good and if the matter ever goes before a jury, it will have done the signal service to you and the Catholic community of forming a favourable and sympathetic atmosphere upon which a good lawyer can work with wonderful effect. I congratulate you, my dear Lord, upon this masterly exposition!![44]

After an initial nervousness about the letter's reception, Liston soon came to see it as a stroke of genius. 'I am told the statement has won me big sympathy here', he informed a disapproving O'Regan.[45] To Whyte he enthused that 'our own people are very pleased as it puts them on side and rather ties up the others'.[46] Several Auckland Catholics had written to him expressing their approval. A typical lay response came from Vincent Ryder, secretary of the Auckland Merchant Service Guild. As a Catholic he had come under considerable pressure from his Protestant colleagues to explain both Liston's speech and his silence; Ryder's rather lame defence was that 'the moment was not opportune for you to reply to the tirade of abuse'. The letter to Massey had come along just in time.

> It affords me a considerable amount of pleasure in reading your letter as published in the Press, particularly as it gives the lie direct to the frequent utterances of bigoted societies and individuals whose sole aim is the besmirching of our grand and glorious religion . . . I consider your letter a diplomatic victory of immense importance to every Catholic throughout the country.[47]

Buoyed up by this positive reaction, Liston and his friends grew ever more confident that legal proceedings would be abandoned. He had completed his part of the supposed bargain, all that remained was for Massey to do the same. Callan concluded, 'I await with great interest news from Your Lordship and from the public print of the further development – or rather, arrested development of the affair'.[48] There was a shock in store for them all. Late on Friday afternoon, 7 April, the day after the bishop's letter had appeared in the local papers, a policeman arrived at the door of St Benedict's presbytery to serve a summons on James Michael Liston.

14

A More or Less Trivial Incident

A prosecution of any Catholic Bishop or other Catholic ecclesiastic would create difficulties for the Administration which no Administration in this Dominion would lightly face.

Bishop Cleary to Archbishop Cattaneo, 13 February 1921[1]

The Prime Minister received Liston's letter on Thursday 6 April. Besieged by reporters demanding an immediate response, he stalled for time. 'The assurance of loyalty to the King and the expression of regret contained in this letter are gratifying to the Government, but the letter has not yet been placed before the Cabinet. In the meantime the decision that the Bishop shall be prosecuted for his recent speech stands.'[2] Massey was in no hurry to have his colleagues pronounce on the letter, nor was he going to let Liston dictate the pace at which his case would be considered. After a Cabinet meeting on Friday morning, he again informed the press that the letter was still to be discussed.[3]

Massey had every reason to receive the letter coolly. Its prior release to the press was part of an alleged deal of which it is likely he knew nothing; the attempt to force his hand probably only irritated Massey.[4] Nor was the press alone in spotting the letter's weaknesses; the bishop's loyal sentiments were severely circumscribed, his expression of regret much qualified. In the copy sent to Massey the reference to the King was merely a scribbled addition to a typewritten text. Alongside the claim to yield to none in his love for New Zealand, Liston had first added 'and my respect for the King', then replaced the words 'respect for' with 'loyalty to'.[5] That this

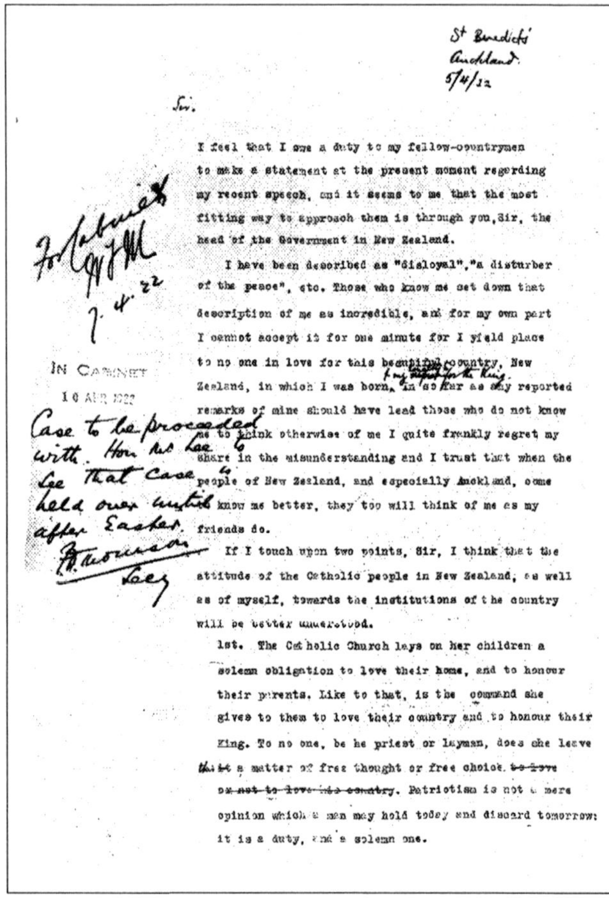

St Benedict's
Auckland.
5/4/22

Sir,

I feel that I owe a duty to my fellow-countrymen to make a statement at the present moment regarding my recent speech, and it seems to me that the most fitting way to approach them is through you, Sir, the head of the Government in New Zealand.

I have been described as "disloyal", "a disturber of the peace", etc. Those who know me set down that description of me as incredible, and for my own part I cannot accept it for one minute for I yield place to no one in love for this beautiful country, New Zealand, in which I was born, & my respect for the King. In so far as any reported remarks of mine should have lead those who do not know me to think otherwise of me I quite frankly regret my share in the misunderstanding and I trust that when the people of New Zealand, and especially Auckland, come to know me better, they too will think of me as my friends do.

If I touch upon two points, Sir, I think that the attitude of the Catholic people in New Zealand, as well as of myself, towards the institutions of the country will be better understood.

1st. The Catholic Church lays on her children a solemn obligation to love their home, and to honour their parents. Like to that, is the command she gives to them to love their country and to honour their King. To no one, be he priest or layman, does she leave this a matter of free thought or free choice. ~~to love or not to love his country~~. Patriotism is not a mere opinion which a man may hold today and discard tomorrow: it is a duty, and a solemn one.

Page one of Liston's letter to Massey. NA

late alteration – almost an afterthought – did not merit a retyped text would not have escaped Massey's notice.

The letter appeared to be a highly calculated production. Liston's friends valued it largely for its hopeful effect on a jury, while even the least cynical reader might have seen it as a ploy. This was also the Solicitor-General's verdict when discussing it with Massey on Friday morning. Later that afternoon MacGregor sent the Prime Minister his written opinion.

> Since we met this forenoon, I have re-read the Bishop's letter to you. I feel bound to say it does not appeal to me as frank or candid. It is noteworthy, however, that it does not (1) deny the accuracy of the newspaper report of the Bishop's speech, nor either (2) withdraw nor (3) apologise for the terms of that speech as reported. In fact as an apologia it is quite futile. It is neither a retraction of, nor an apology for, the seditious words originally used.[6]

Solicitor-General W. C. MacGregor. ATL

By now MacGregor had studied the letter closely enough to read between the lines. 'The whole epistle appears to me a laboured attempt to bring the offending speech within clause 118(2) of the Crimes Act 1908. It has in my opinion been carefully prepared under advice, and published as the groundwork for an address to the jury of public opinion.' He suggested that Massey simply acknowledge it without comment. MacGregor seemed determined that the case should reach court, but was well aware that the final result could not be predicted. He repeated Lord Kenyon's aphorism that 'a man may publish whatever a jury of his countrymen thinks is not blameable'.[7]

MacGregor then outlined the degree of calculation that he believed had gone into the letter. Presented by a clever lawyer, it could enable Liston to avoid explaining in the witness box exactly what he had meant on St Patrick's Night. MacGregor must have regarded O'Regan's recent letter in the *Auckland Star* as a further appeal to public opinion on the bishop's behalf. Did he go on to discuss the details of the prosecution case with Massey? Only the day before he and Vincent Meredith had pored over all the evidence that the latter had been able to gather. While MacGregor seemed satisfied with its strength, legal circles in Wellington soon buzzed with rumours of Meredith's pessimism about the case.[8] One wonders if the Auckland Crown Solicitor had the nerve to share his doubts with his zealous chief. MacGregor was almost as severe on Liston's letter to Massey as he had been when condemning the Town Hall speech.

It is likely that Sir Francis Bell's absence became critical at this stage. Having from the outset discouraged the idea of a prosecution, he would almost certainly have alerted Massey to the fragility of the Crown's case. Despite MacGregor's urging, Meredith had been unable to secure a shorthand report of the speech, and his witnesses were a rather undistinguished crew whose testimony was confused and contradictory. Although MacGregor made no mention of it in his letter, Massey must now have agreed to the serving of a summons on Liston. Meredith promptly sent Detective Sergeant Ward a telegram to this effect and the summons was served late on Friday afternoon.[9]

This moved the case onto a different plane. After vigorous cranking, the machinery of the law had finally shuddered into action; it would require an equal effort to halt it. There is no evidence that the Cabinet gave any serious consideration to Liston's letter at its next meeting on Monday, 10 April; the key debate had already occurred over the decision to commence proceedings. MacGregor's hostile opinion must have counted strongly against the letter, while the ministers may also have been reacting to public rumours that the case would soon be dropped. That very morning several dailies carried a paragraph suggesting the imminent withdrawal of proceedings.

> There were many rumours current in the city today that, following Bishop Liston's letter to the Prime Minister, the proceedings authorised against him on a charge of seditious utterances would be stopped . . . No confirmation of the rumour could be obtained. Though it may be within the power of the Government to stop proceedings, such power is used only on very rare occasions, and when there are special circumstances; for example, if information upon which the charge is based is found to be incorrect in essential particulars, so that, even if the case went for trial, there would be no likelihood of a conviction being obtained.[10]

Had Liston chosen publicly to challenge the *New Zealand Herald*'s version of his remarks – adding an unambiguous declaration of love for King and country – he might have caused the authorities to hesitate before launching the prosecution in earnest. As it was, his letter probably reinforced the Cabinet's decision to proceed. Rather than abandon the case, Massey decided merely to delay proceedings for a fortnight, after being alerted to the danger of making the bishop too complete an Easter sacrifice.[11] Liston thus not only avoided having to face his accusers on Holy Thursday, but was spared the task of defending the Easter rising exactly six years after it had taken place.

Denied the opportunity to play either Jesus Christ or Patrick Pearse (both brought to trial and death by their enemies), Liston must have been alarmed by the distressing news which continued to come out of Ireland.[12] Fierce fighting raged in Belfast, with the IRA launching raids across the border into Northern Ireland, while in the south the drift towards civil war seemed unstoppable. Worst of all was the continued confusion over the constitutional situation. Following Dail Eireann's ratification of the treaty, a provisional government had been set up under the chairmanship of Michael Collins to oversee the establishment of the Irish Free State. While the Irish people were due to vote on the treaty in June, it seemed increasingly unlikely that the Republican diehards would accept their verdict.[13]

The New Zealand press tended to attribute the strife in Ireland exclusively to divisions over the treaty. Wellington's *Evening Post* confessed to 'a kind of ironic satisfaction' that the old devils remained to plague even a native government: 'British *amour propre* may find some not altogether illegitimate consolation in seeing the Dail Eireann confronted by the same ghosts who for centuries have haunted Dublin Castle.'[14] There seemed to be no doubt about who was responsible. The *New Zealand Herald* had welcomed de Valera's fall from power: 'his disappearance is a matter of the liveliest satisfaction'.[15] The former President's campaign against the Irish Free State made his name synonymous with the Republic. He was blamed for all the excesses of the anti-treatyites, dubbed 'the de Valera irreconcilables' by the *New Zealand Free Lance*.[16]

Unfortunately, de Valera not only refused to go away, but seemed to be successfully smothering the nascent Irish Free State. Although he aligned himself with the Republican forces only after the outbreak of civil war, de Valera had only himself to blame if no one noticed this fact. What the *Evening Post* called his 'relentless vendetta' was marked by frequent bloodcurdling predictions of fratricidal strife, which de Valera himself seemed most bent on causing.[17] In late February 1922, he told a Cork audience that he and his followers 'would not allow any foreign Government to rule in Ireland'. Irish freedom could be secured 'only by bloodshed', with Irish Republicans marching over the dead bodies of their own brothers. 'You must wade through Irish blood', he was reported as declaring at Killarney three weeks later.[18]

The press was obliged to reverse its Irish stereotypes; no longer a cowardly leader of assassins, Michael Collins became the brave pilot

'To Spite His Face.' The Observer*'s graphic representation of Irish strife.* NZO

of the Empire's newest dominion, while de Valera was transformed from mild-mannered professor into bloodthirsty extremist.[19] Easter once more threatened to bring a crisis in Irish politics. The hasty agreement in late March between Collins and Craig on measures to restore order (which the *New Zealand Herald* dubbed 'another paper peace in Ireland') was overshadowed by rumours that the Republicans were planning a repeat Easter rising.[20] While Collins worried about an attempted 'coup d'état', and the IRA leaders spoke of a 'military dictatorship', the New Zealand press raged at how the Irish Free State was allowing itself to be destabilised.[21]

Lloyd George had lost interest in Ireland after the treaty was signed, handing over responsibility to a committee headed by Winston Churchill. Collins and Churchill now became the key players in the Anglo–Irish relationship.[22] During the negotiations the Englishman had developed a grudging respect for his Irish opponent, and now wanted to help him in the onerous task of implementing the treaty. However, as the danger of renewed conflict increased, Churchill declared bluntly at Dundee: 'if Irishmen choose to cut off their own noses to spite their faces we cannot prevent them and will not try to do so . . . Nothing in the nature of a republic in Ireland will be accepted in Britain. I believe the Irish nation is now in a position where it ought to look forward and not brood over the past'.[23]

Churchill regarded Easter 1922 as 'the most critical' period in the Irish Free State's short life: it must 'assert itself or perish', he warned Collins on 12 April.[24] Two days later, Republican forces occupied the Four Courts, the imposing law buildings in the centre of Dublin. Here was a brazen challenge to the fledgling state, one which surely lit the fuse of civil war.[25] Press reaction was predictably hostile, not least at the farthest edge of Empire. The *Evening Post* urged Collins to 'grasp the nettle' and deal firmly with the wreckers, while the *New Zealand Herald* wondered whether the provisional government could recapture the public buildings 'which the Republican wild men have seized by a coup no doubt deliberately planned to recall the rebellion of another Easter'.[26] During this period of tension and uncertainty both Collins and Churchill were obliged briefly to consider the troubles of one James Michael Liston.

Bishop Cleary had moved swiftly on receiving Harry Holbrook's panic cable: 'Olympus charged sedition reference Easter Week; get Dail intercede London.'[27] He fired off a supportive message to Liston 'so that people shall know you are not standing alone'.[28] Writing more fully to his coadjutor on 5 April, Cleary seemed more concerned with the style of Holbrook's message than its actual content:

> The wording of the cable was decidedly indiscreet – in plain English, and asking me to 'get the Provisional Government to intercede.' I took steps in that direction without a moment's delay, and put cable and my pressing request thereon into the hands of the Prov. Govt., and got a promise that whatever could be done in the matter would be cheerfully done. But (as I was told) if proceedings were ordered or initiated, the matter would be one of great difficulty, added to which the N.Z. Govt. might resent either pressure or interference.[29]

Cleary had gone over to Ireland in late 1921 to spend Christmas with his relatives. Had he remained in London, he might have used his considerable influence with the British authorities on Liston's behalf. His services as a propagandist in the Allied cause had earned him a splendid wartime reputation for patriotism.[30] As it was, Cleary had to rely on Michael Collins, who promptly wrote to Churchill on 8 April.[31] (There is every possibility that Cleary drafted this letter: his hand can be detected in the minimising of Liston's offence and the reference to the effect on the Irish overseas.)

> Representations have been made with regard to the proposed prosecution by the Government of New Zealand of Monsignor Liston, Coadjutor Bishop of Auckland for disparaging references to British troops in Ireland made by him in a speech about a fortnight ago.

> It has been pointed out to me that the effect of a conviction upon the large Irish population of Australia and New Zealand would be injurious to the promotion of that spirit of friendship which we are endeavouring to foster between our peoples.
>
> It would be a great pity at the present moment if a more or less trivial incident were given an importance which it does not deserve, and I fear that the prosecution of Monsignor Liston would have this result. I sincerely hope in consideration of all the circumstances and seeing that general amnesty as between Ireland and England is the order of the day, that you will use your influence with the New Zealand Government to have the prosecution withdrawn if this can be done.[32]

On his appointment as Colonial Secretary a year earlier, Churchill had promoted the idea of closer consultation among the constituent parts of the Empire on their individual difficulties, while 'sharing with the Mother Country the responsibility for dealing with great and dominant questions'.[33] (It was even suggested that the dominion premiers might lend a hand in ending the Irish imbroglio.)[34] Churchill was thus well placed to urge the New Zealand authorities not to rock the Anglo–Irish boat by prosecuting a prominent spokesman for the Irish abroad. During the House of Commons debate on the treaty, he even showed some appreciation of Liston's perspective.

> Ireland was not a daughter but the parent of a race scattered all over the world, and in their treatment of the Irish problem they must be guided by an intense desire to penetrate the true spirit of the Irish heart, and by understanding it to lay aside once and for all the ghosts of medieval hatreds that had survived to this hour.[35]

'No newspaper seen by me has professed to give, so far, anything purporting to be your exact words', Cleary complained to Liston, summing up the quandary of those trying to influence the case from afar.[36] The letter from Collins caused a mild panic in the Colonial Office, where an exhaustive search produced nothing more than the brief New Zealand Press Association announcement of the intended prosecution. Despite complete ignorance of the affair, Churchill's advisers presented their chief with various options: Collins might be told that public opinion in New Zealand appeared entirely to support the government; or that it was not a matter in which the Colonial Secretary felt it appropriate to become involved. Alternatively, Churchill could simply convey the view from Dublin in a private cable to New Zealand's Governor-General. One anonymous adviser minuted tartly: 'if the policy of letting bygones be bygones and of fostering a spirit of friendship between the two peoples had been observed by Monsignor Liston he

Viscount Jellicoe, New Zealand's Governor-General 1920–24. 'Jellyfish' was the Maoriland Worker*'s pet name for him.* AWN

would not have made the offending speech'. Churchill decided upon the last course and cabled the Irish message to Wellington without further comment.[37]

Viscount Jellicoe of Scapa had become Governor-General around the same time as Liston arrived in Auckland as a freshly consecrated bishop. He was warmly acclaimed as 'the victor of Jutland', New Zealand's saviour from the German fleet.[38] There was, however, considerable debate about the winner and loser of that particular sea battle. Some suggested that Jellicoe had missed the chance to destroy the enemy fleet by turning away, against orders, from a further engagement. (The *Post* hardly flattered him with its comment that 'sometimes it requires real heroism to adopt the unbrilliant plan'.)[39] Dr James Kelly referred to the Governor-General as 'the man who did not win the Battle of Jutland', while 'Jellyfish' was the *Maoriland Worker*'s pet name for him.[40] Massey preferred to hail the appointment as a further recognition of New Zealand's elevated status within the empire.[41]

Jellicoe received Churchill's 'cypher telegram' on 13 April, passing it on at once to Massey. Two days later the Prime Minister replied with a note (written in shorthand). 'Feeling is very high at present and my opinion is the case must go on. I shall be glad if you will inform Mr Churchill to this effect.'[42] Jellicoe then sent the substance of this reply to London.

> As the case is now before the courts my Prime Minister is of the opinion that any attempt to withdraw it now would do more harm than good and that it must go on. I may add that utterances such as that of Bishop Liston do infinite harm in New Zealand to the spirit of friendship referred to by the Head of the Irish Provisional Government.[43]

Jellicoe expanded on this reply five days later in his regular quarterly report to the Colonial Office. He had difficulty in reconciling the mild-mannered prelate of repute with the fire-breathing orator of the Auckland Town Hall.

> The matter has given rise to very considerable feeling throughout the Dominion. It is probable that the Bishop said more than he intended, being impelled thereto by the presence of several members of Hibernian organisations. I am informed by the Mayor of Auckland that Bishop Liston is ordinarily a quiet inoffensive man.[44]

Jellicoe also revealed the Prime Minister's opinion of Liston's attempted apologia: 'Mr Massey informed me that he did not consider that the Bishop's letter of explanation was in any sense satisfactory.' He recalled Archbishop Redwood's earlier speech 'on somewhat similar but less offensive lines'. Unaware that he was echoing its own sentiments, Jellicoe concluded with a sideswipe at the Colonial Office: 'There can be no doubt that the delivery of such speeches does infinite harm to the good relations between people of British and Irish descent in New Zealand.'[45] Churchill must have been amused when later approving this reply for transmission to Michael Collins.

Despite the advice of several newspaper editors and the pleas of his Auckland supporters, Massey refused to accept Liston's peace offer. Indeed, it is more likely that the Bishop's open letter stiffened his resolve to see the case through. Quite apart from what it left unsaid, the letter suggested that Liston had no substantial defence to offer to the charges levelled against him. Not even a plea from his old friend Winston Churchill to consider the wider imperial interest could now change Massey's mind.

15

An Easter Sacrifice

On this beautiful day when Our Lord Himself was brought before Judges and accused by false witnesses surely you to whom he has granted a share in His humiliation will be most abundantly blessed and guarded by Him. May the Easter joy be very perfect after your share in the Sacred Passion.

Sister Mary Gertrude to Liston, 12 April 1922[1]

The arrival of a summons caused pandemonium in the Liston camp. A telegram was immediately despatched to P. J. O'Regan urging him to come north by the next available train. Accordingly, the lawyer went into his Wellington office prepared to catch the Saturday afternoon express. Shortly after 10 a.m. a message arrived from John Conlan telling him not to come. Convinced that this meant the case had been abandoned, he sent Liston his congratulations. 'Have all along felt certain the threat of proceedings was mere camouflage', O'Regan noted complacently in his diary.[2]

What had caused the change of mind overnight? When the bishop's advisers gathered at St Benedict's presbytery on Friday evening to discuss the disturbing new development, they knew from the *Auckland Star* that Liston's letter had yet to be considered by the Cabinet. How, then, to explain the serving of a summons? Seizing on the fact that it had come while the Auckland Crown Solicitor was away in Wellington, Liston's friends soon convinced themselves that a malevolent police force was attempting to scupper the imminent compromise solution – a nice balance to Vincent Meredith's suspicions of a conspiracy of silence in Liston's favour among the Auckland constabulary.[3]

While Detective Sergeant Ward's reputation as a zealot encouraged a belief in his hostility, his soldier brother having recently died of war wounds, the fact that Meredith had simply sent his instructions from Wellington seems to have eluded Liston's advisers.[4]

Michael Sheahan was perhaps most bewildered by the arrival of the summons, especially as Oliver Nicholson and Eliot Davis assured him that they had urged the government to drop proceedings. He now decided on a personal appeal to Massey hoping that it might tip the delicate balance towards Liston. Sheahan composed his plea on Saturday morning (possibly with Liston's assistance, as the only surviving copy of the letter is among the bishop's papers).

> In the midst of your numerous and onerous duties I beg respectfully to intrude. As the head of our Dominion, and in memory of an acquaintance of other days, I make an appeal to you. In view of the statement sent to you and widely published by Dr Liston I earnestly request you not to proceed further in a matter which cannot possibly produce, no matter in which way it ends, other than mischievous results . . . In view of the times present and to come the rulers of States require the assistance and the support of the most conservative of our institutions viz. the Churches, and in the ecclesiastical leader under review you have, believe me, one whose support is desirable. The King at Belfast said we should 'Forgive and forget.' Let us do so.[5]

The dispatch of this letter seemed to calm the nerves of Liston's entourage and O'Regan was told to stay in Wellington. On Saturday afternoon the bishop wrote confidently to his counterpart in Dunedin telling of Cleary's supportive cable but not of the summons he had just received: 'The whole affair is doing our Catholics here immense good – I can feel it in the air.'[6] He declared himself 'ready for anything'. In another letter to Whyte four days later, Liston mentioned the summons only in passing – it 'duly came' – preferring instead to speculate on why the government decided to postpone proceedings.

> I understand my statement is being considered by Cabinet these days and it looks as if there is a tussle going on between the Diehards and the more sensible amongst them. I am very hopeful the proceedings will be withdrawn. So far as I can gather my statement has completely changed public opinion here and, unless a violent change takes place, even a picked jury would not convict.[7]

The delay had in fact a quite different explanation. Sheahan had pointed out to Massey the unfortunate timing of the legal action: 'The summons issued is made operative on Holy Thursday in Holy Week, a period held in deep reverence and solemnity by many

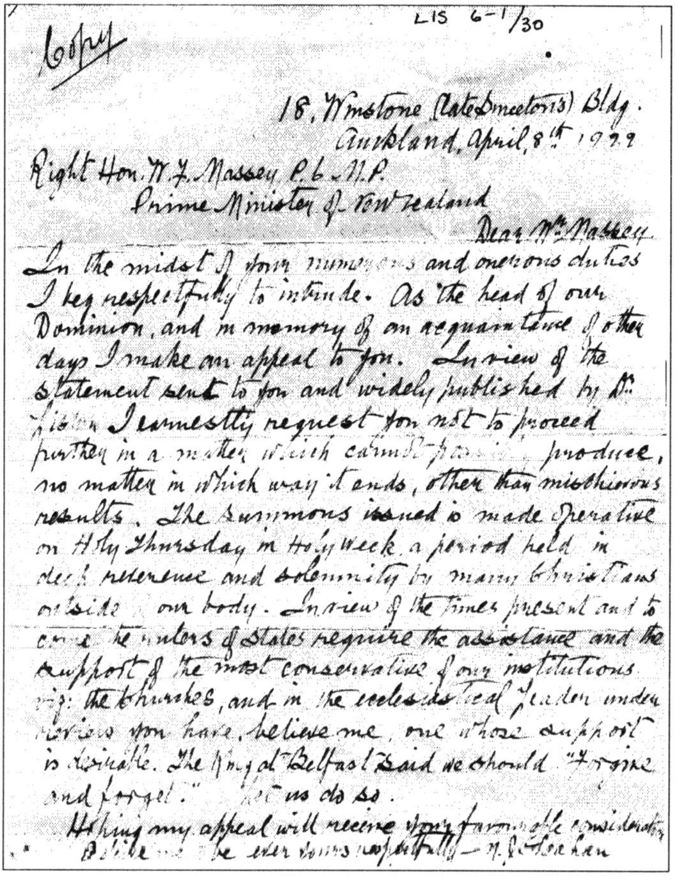

Copy

LIS 6-1/30

18, Winstone (late Smeeton's) Bldg.
Auckland, April 8th 1922

Right Hon. W. F. Massey P.C. M.P.
Prime Minister of New Zealand

Dear Mr Massey

In the midst of your numerous and onerous duties I beg respectfully to intrude. As the head of our Dominion, and in memory of an acquaintance of other days I make an appeal to you. In view of the statement sent to you and widely published by Dr Liston I earnestly request you not to proceed further in a matter which cannot [illegible] produce, no matter in which way it ends, other than mischievous results. The summons issued is made operative on Holy Thursday in Holy Week a period held in deep reverence and solemnity by many Christians outside our body. In view of the times present and to come the rulers of states require the assistance and the support of the most conservative of our institutions viz: the Churches, and in the ecclesiastical leader under review you have, believe me, one whose support is desirable. The King at Belfast said we should "Forgive and forget." Let us do so.

Hoping my appeal will receive your favourable consideration

Believe me to be ever yours respectfully — M. J. Sheahan

The only surviving copy of Michael Sheahan's letter to Massey. ACDA

Christians outside of our body.'[8] Several Catholics had already drawn the parallel. Sister Mary Baptist of Dunedin confided to Liston: 'I picture you closely associated with our persecuted Saviour when He was knocked about from Herod to Pilate.'[9] Sister Mary Lynch of Te Aroha assured Liston that 'with the dawn of Easter morn your clouds and crosses will vanish and your Gethsemane will be transformed to Thabor'.[10] In the circumstances, the government's decision to postpone the case for a fortnight was a wise one.

The Crown's request for a delay completely fooled the Liston camp. Aware of the various pressures on the authorities to withdraw the proceedings, his advisers misread the signs available. The tussle in the Cabinet had been over the initial decision to prosecute; Liston's letter to Massey was seen as insufficiently convincing to prompt a reconsideration. Press rumours of a withdrawal, perhaps fuelled by knowledge of the approach from Churchill, were equally misleading. Indeed, the bishop's friends failed to take a proper measure of the case from the start. Everything seemed to them to indicate a happy ending: Gunson's extravagant language, Bell's supposed opposition, their own deep scepticism about government intentions, the reassurances of several legal pundits, the numerous appeals to Massey, Bishop Cleary's long-distance influence. Liston drew comfort when the summons was slow in arriving; once it came he found excuses to minimise its significance.

Not that Liston's legal advisers in Auckland should be left with all the blame; O'Regan was equally guilty of misjudging the seriousness of the situation. The Wellington lawyer now looms larger in this story; not only do his diaries and letters enable us to follow events as they unfolded, but he becomes steadily more central to the case – despite the best efforts of several of his colleagues and fellow Catholics. After the affair was over, he confided to a friend:

> Personally I had something to contend with below the surface inasmuch as, although the Bishop decided from the outset in favour of engaging me, he had a host of voluntary advisers who were of [the] opinion that, on account of my well known anti-imperialist views and also for the reason that I am President of the Self-Determination for Ireland League, I would be likely rather to prejudice the jury.[11]

This was only half the story. O'Regan had not accepted the case when first offered it and had refused to act as anyone's junior. He was especially unwilling to defer to J. B. Callan. While he had immediately advised Liston to seek non-Irish Catholic counsel, as time went on O'Regan discovered that he was reputed to be conducting the bishop's defence but had none of the responsibility. Callan also was avoiding involvement in the case, leaving Liston dependent on his local advisers, many of whom favoured conciliation – an impulse that had culminated in the open letter to Massey.

O'Regan believed that he was central to Liston's defence plans; when the letter to Massey revealed how peripheral his influence actually was, he began to consider withdrawing entirely from the case. On Tuesday, 11 April, Dean Holley called into his office with the news that the case, far from being abandoned, was scheduled for a preliminary hearing in two days' time. O'Regan revealed his frustration when confiding in his diary later that evening: 'I have yet hopes that if the case goes on some other counsel will have the work rather than I. There are really so many people proffering advice that one is apt to become irritated and annoyed.'[12]

The Wellington lawyer had bid too high too soon, wanting not merely to shape the defence but to control it. Unwilling to stomach the degree of compromise demanded by a team approach, he had now to wait until the case came back his way – in effect until Liston had exhausted all other legal options. Distance from Auckland also limited O'Regan's involvement – doubly frustrating once he had changed his mind about the worth of an outsider as counsel. As a disagreement was the best result to be anticipated in court, it would matter little who actually addressed the jury.[13] O'Regan had no doubts about his ability to defend the truth of Liston's reported remarks. A later diary entry contradicts his declared disinclination to act: 'Were the case placed unreservedly in my hands and were his Lordship to evince enough "ginger" to follow my advice, the Government would be tried first!'[14]

After learning that proceedings were continuing, O'Regan wrote to Liston on 11 April to explain his earlier message of congratulations. He mentioned that Vincent Meredith had visited Wellington during the week and was said to be 'strongly against the proceedings'.[15] Expressing no surprise at this report ('as I know Mr Meredith very well'), O'Regan did little to disturb the sense of complacency in Auckland: 'I may state that there appears to be here a consensus of opinion that the matter will not be proceeded with and that it would be inadvisable to do so.' In the interim, O'Regan advised Liston to plead not guilty and to reserve his defence, as the magistrate would almost certainly find a case to be answered in the Supreme Court.

The letter to Massey strained O'Regan's powers of diplomacy to their limit: 'I did not really understand the full purpose of your last letter to me until I saw your letter in the press. It did not occur to me that the suggestion was that you should make a statement by way of a letter to the Premier.'[16] O'Regan seemed to view it as a private communication which Massey had released to the press. He made no comment at all on its contents. Sensing O'Regan's disapproval, Liston responded on 12 April, explaining that an open letter had seemed to be the best way of securing publicity, offsetting adverse press comment and forcing Massey's hand. It had won him great public sympathy in Auckland 'and the prevailing opinion is that the proceedings ought not to go on'. He saw the Crown's decision to postpone the case as a very hopeful sign: 'I feel sure the Government will withdraw altogether.'[17]

Liston no longer attempted to justify the letter as part of a deal to end the affair, citing instead a host of tactical benefits: bigots confounded, Catholics cheered, public opinion swayed in his favour. Even the arch-pessimist Callan professed himself delighted with it. The Dunedin lawyer was proving a most elusive recruit for the defence. Although his mother was now dead and buried, there were sheaves of briefs which prevented him from coming north. Bishop Whyte found it impossible even to get Callan on the telephone.[18] With O'Regan also keeping his distance (albeit for quite opposite reasons), Liston had little choice but to continue relying on John Conlan.

Conlan represented Liston in court on 13 April, when a fortnight's remand was granted at the Crown's request. Later that day he told O'Regan of the latest rumours rife in Auckland: 'I have heard that Cutten will preside on the Bench and also that he thinks the case should be dropped, but I am afraid he would not be strong enough to throw the case out on the question of "intent".'[19] Conlan, the only Catholic lawyer who seems to have actually heard the St Patrick's Night speech, had few clues on how best to defend his bishop. He mentioned possible lines of defence to O'Regan almost as an afterthought, 'in case the proceedings are not withdrawn'. *R.* v. *Burns* (1886) dealt with seditious intent and might be useful; indeed, O'Regan had himself relied on this case when defending Harry Holland in 1914.[20]

Conlan was wholly unoriginal in his approach. He began by adopting Callan's line completely, before promising to follow O'Regan's instructions in the magistrates' court: 'To my mind it would be useless to deny that the words were used and it accordingly would convey a dishonest defence to suggest that the witnesses were mistaken.' He would ask no questions, but merely ensure that the witnesses were out of court and that each gave his own statement as to what took place. 'I feel that as I shall not be handling the higher Court proceedings that my policy at the lower Court should be dictated by Counsel.' Conlan's passive approach owed something to his belief in the accuracy of the *New Zealand Herald* report; fortunately for the defence, he chose to keep this opinion to himself.

Conlan then broke the news to O'Regan that all of Liston's other advisers were agreed on the need for an outsider as leading counsel. The reasoning behind this preference was plausible enough.

> Meredith is certain to stop any Catholic getting on the jury and I am rather afraid that no matter how fine a defence Catholic counsel could put up that the jury will be an antagonistic one or at any rate that the majority will enter the jury box with preconceived ideas difficult to shake unless coming from one of themselves.[21]

Not only did this self-denying ordinance preclude O'Regan from taking the case, but his services were now required merely to help recruit the best Protestant lawyer available. In what would soon become a who's who of the legal confraternity, Conlan sought his opinion of Skerrett, Findlay, Myers, Martin and Earl. Or did O'Regan know anyone else he deemed suitable for the task? Conlan realised that the quest would not be to O'Regan's taste: 'I trust you will take my suggestion regarding leading counsel as actuated solely by a desire to render the best help possible – unfortunately racial and religious prejudices will be a large factor in the case if it goes before a jury.'[22]

Conlan's belief in an apologetic defence was bolstered by the fear that he might end up conducting the case unaided (he preferred not to think of it actually coming to trial). He knew nothing of the potential Crown witnesses, had interviewed none of the newspaper reporters, and had no idea of who might be taking the case for the Crown. 'We can take it as quite definite that if the case is not withdrawn before the 24th that we must go on,' he concluded blithely to O'Regan. After finishing this letter, Conlan left Auckland on a two-week holiday, leaving his episcopal client to stew.

Replying on 17 April, O'Regan urged Conlan to let the prosecution lay all its cards on the table in the magistrates' court. He agreed that they should not attempt a dishonest defence, accepting Conlan's implication that the *Herald* had fairly summarised Liston's remarks: 'It is useless questioning the accuracy of the press report, unless it is in fact inaccurate in a vital respect, and I gather from you that it is not so.'[23] He could imagine only one reason for Conlan to break his silence in court. Although critical of the letter to Massey, O'Regan appreciated its potential value as a public relations exercise. Had not it been written after an approach by influential supporters of the government, ostensibly with Massey's knowledge? In such circumstances, he deemed the continuation of proceedings to be a gross breach of faith. He suggested that Conlan put Liston in the witness-box to lay bare the whole affair and then ask the magistrate to dismiss the case. Massey might deny that he was privy to the overtures made by his friends, but the exposé would be powerful propaganda; Catholic stocks would surely rise in the jury market, O'Regan thought.[24]

While others believed that Liston's mere appearance in court would damage his dignity, O'Regan felt that the bishop could best protect his reputation by marching proudly into prison. Liston would be better off behind bars than under caution or paying a fine. O'Regan advocated a policy of 'no beg pardons'. The government would be increasingly embarrassed as public opinion shrank from treating Liston as a criminal. 'If I were in the Bishop's place I would prefer imprisonment to being bound over,' he told Conlan, 'because the bigots would be as implacable in one case as the other, and the Bishop's friends would be rallied better by imprisonment than anything else.'[25] O'Regan then attempted to disengage himself from the case, citing his distance from Auckland as the major obstacle. Local counsel could more readily confer with the Bishop, while he was also due to take a brief holiday on the West Coast. The real reason became clear as he went on to complain that the letter to Massey had been sent without being submitted to him first.

All this left Liston in a vulnerable position. At the outset he had firmly opposed being represented by anyone whose heart was not really with him. He had no thought of retraction and was even planning to repeat his remarks. Now, one month later, the ordeal of a trial still lay before him. While many local Protestant lawyers were willing to murmur reassuringly in his ear, none would tackle the job of defending him in court; their Catholic counterparts were even less eager. The best prospect his advisers could offer was a series of hung juries and the possibility of three court appearances before the Crown gave up and entered a *nolle prosequi*. His friends were urging him to accept a two-year jail term if convicted, both his active lawyers were off on holiday, while his preferred counsel, J. B. Callan, could not be persuaded to come north. To cap it all, he was now in danger of losing O'Regan's services completely.

Liston peppered O'Regan with nervous letters in the week leading up to his first court appearance.[26] Conlan had left him confused on his exact role in the approaching legal drama. Would he be examined and cross-examined? Would O'Regan come up to speak for him? His Auckland friends were trying to persuade J. C. Martin to appear should the case go on to the Supreme Court; failing Martin, what did O'Regan think of Skerrett? On 25 April Liston informed O'Regan of Martin's refusal, adding the ex-judge's consoling comment as a postscript: 'Possibly the speech is beyond the pale, though to judge from the cuttings a big blaze has come from a very, very small fire.'[27] Aware that O'Regan was sour about the letter to Massey, Liston promised to explain when they met how hurriedly the statement had to be considered and drafted. He begged O'Regan to approach either Findlay or Skerrett on his behalf: 'I think we simply must have an outsider and that is the opinion of all friends here. No doubt his mere presence will tell.'[28]

Charles Skerrett, a future Chief Justice but not to O'Regan's taste.
NZFL

To drive this point home, Liston sent O'Regan two letters in which Callan had presented the argument for an outsider at length.[29] Callan approved of J. C. Martin, or anyone with similarly Protestant virtues: 'I thoroughly agree that it is very desirable that the defending counsel should not be Irish – or at any rate not be identified with the Church or with Irish national aspirations.' Not that whoever was selected could do much by way of defence. They might give evidence on the whole of the speech, Callan continued, 'assuming that the omitted portions would be helpful – not damaging – to the defence'. He also urged silence in the magistrates' court, preferring Liston to reserve his debut in the witness-box for a Supreme Court audience. 'In fact, from some points of view there is much to be said for the idea of Your Lordship conducting the defence yourself, without the intervention of counsel in Court. But on the other hand this might leave the suggestion that no counsel can be found to undertake it.'[30] Callan seemed unaware that his insistence on an outsider was bringing Liston very close to this embarrassing position.

O'Regan refused to approach Charles Perrin Skerrett, ostensibly on the grounds that the New Zealand Welfare League (founded and led by Skerrett) had congratulated Gunson on his response to Liston's speech. Over the previous three years, O'Regan and Skerrett had fought several wordy battles in the Wellington press on Labour issues.[31] O'Regan's diary reveals the depth of his scorn for the future Chief Justice: 'Poor Skerrett, a conceited little Jingo snob! He has been

Sir John Findlay, who had represented the Catholic church in earlier legal battles, but chose not to touch the Liston case. NZ Truth

ambitious to enter politics for years, but dreads to address a popular audience where he might be heckled by mere ordinary people. Bank clerks, law clerks, retired shopkeepers and land agents are his heart's delight.'[32]

O'Regan had scarcely more respect for Sir John Findlay, formerly Minister of Justice and Attorney-General in Ward's government. After Findlay made a public profession of faith in Masseyism on his return from England in late 1921, O'Regan ascribed it to his ambition to represent New Zealand at the forthcoming Washington Conference: 'Verily Findlay is a humbug, and it is most remarkable and appropriate that he should have written *Humbugs and Homilies*, which has been described as a text-book on humbug.'[33] Findlay was almost as experienced as O'Regan in defending alleged seditionists. For Liston, O'Regan cryptically estimated the capacities of Skerrett and Findlay as 'about equal'. Nevertheless, he swallowed his pride and interviewed Findlay on 27 April; much to O'Regan's surprise – and after taking two days to consider the matter – Findlay declined the brief.[34]

Also on 27 April another remand for the Liston case was granted; it was now to be heard on Monday, 1 May. The day that all the bishop's men had agreed would never arrive was now less than a week away. O'Regan hastened to reassure Liston about his coming ordeal: 'If Meredith acts – and I think he will – I do not think you will find him rancorous.' While disapproving strongly of his Tory politics, O'Regan absolved the Crown Solicitor from any suspicion of religious bigotry. Similarly, the presiding magistrate, J. W. Poynton, was 'a very fair man and will not be in any way hostile to you'.[35] Bishop Whyte had a more sobering message for Liston: 'I am in the dark about the possible penalties upon conviction. Anything in the nature of a climb-down would be disastrous. You would be injured forever. Even imposing silence on you would be a terrible penalty which you could not safely accept.'[36]

A week before his day in court Liston wrote a long letter to his absent chief, Henry Cleary. He was full of gratitude for Cleary's cable of support: 'It has given me real courage and our priests and people are immensely delighted.'

> When I wrote to you last mail, I thought and we all thought that the business would end in smoke. Apparently however Massey did not care to ignore Gunson and so decided there should be a prosecution for sedition. I have really said nothing worth talking about – merely what has been said much more emphatically by yourself almost since you first held a pen, by all the prominent leaders in England and elsewhere.[37]

Liston did not burden Cleary with the details of his continuing search for senior counsel, preferring to cite the legion of Protestant lawyers who had offered him sympathy. 'The President and Vice President of the Law Society, Russell, Singer, Nicholson, Hesketh and others, to my certain knowledge, reckon it a political stunt of a particularly mean type.'[38] He had engaged O'Regan as the acknowledged expert on Irish affairs, Callan was sending sound advice, while Conlan was doing 'minor but important local work'. Popular feeling had swung his way after he published an open letter to the Prime Minister: 'So strongly did my letter tell that many of the Government's biggest supporters in Auckland urged them to withdraw.'[39] Had Liston forgotten the original reason for this manoeuvre, or was he deliberately misrepresenting it? On the eve of his greatest test, he was full of fight and hope. Like his hero Oliver Plunkett, the Archbishop of Armagh executed for sedition in 1681, he was prepared to suffer for his faith and fatherland.[40]

> The whole business is of course an anxiety, but I'm not afraid of the ordeal and I feel much good will come of it. I ain't done nothing to be ashamed of . . . Our people are now deeply touched and have opened their eyes. Every day made them realise that it was the Church more than the Bishop that was being attacked and by the time the trial is over I am sure their Faith and dormant Catholic spirit will have been thoroughly roused . . . I am confident the whole incident will do us good in the long run, painful as it is for the time being, because it will raise instead of crushing our people.[41]

16

Bishop in the Dock

> The Grand Jury returned true bills in the following cases: A. W. Page, alleged murder; J. M. Liston, alleged sedition; F. W. Hargreaves, alleged assault; R. A. Carlysle, alleged forgery; C. J. Williams, alleged carnal knowledge, horse-stealing and false pretences; G. G. Farland, alleged attempted rape; Barney Elias, alleged selling indecent pictures; William Knox, alleged breaking and entering with intent to commit a crime; Sydney Hinton, alleged book-making.
>
> *New Zealand Herald*, 10 May 1922

Liston's trial began in the Auckland Magistrates' Court on the morning of Monday, 1 May. Twice disappointed by prior adjournments, the general public either had become used to meeting in the common court on the ground floor or had no knowledge of the more respectable court upstairs; as a result, many spectators missed the opening acts of the drama and filtered in only to find the public gallery already full. The rest of the courtroom was packed to overflowing. One reporter noted the numerous ladies who 'graced the proceedings throughout with extremely grave and anxious faces'.[1] The mood was of suppressed nervous excitement. Just before the luncheon adjournment, a burst of laughter from the crowd at the rear of the court drew the magistrate's ire. 'This is not a picture show', Poynton declared sternly. 'If there's any more of that you'll go out – the whole lot of you!'[2]

The restrained nature of proceedings seemed to disappoint several press observers. Potential friction between the rival supporters was whimsically alluded to by the *New Zealand Observer*: 'The leaders of

THE SEDITION CHARGE AGAINST BISHOP LISTON.
Sketches from the Magistrates' Court sitting.

The Observer *cartoonist, William Blomfield, covered both of Liston's court appearances. NZO* both Irish factions were absent, but most of the people were undoubtedly one side or the other, and the clerk of the Court had supplied blotters edged with green.'[3] Save for an attempt at oratory by Frank Baller, there was no pugnacious speechifying, no dramatic cross-examination and no verbal fireworks. The prosecution went about its work without unnecessary flourish. 'Detective Sergeant Ward flitted backwards and forwards, supplying tit-bits and looking generally well pleased with everything in his important case.' Vincent Meredith spoke throughout in a quiet voice.[4] Indeed, Poynton and Meredith seemed so subdued that Liston received 'the unmistakable impression that they were sorry to have anything to do with the business'.[5]

It is more likely that the magistrate and Crown prosecutor were feeling sorry for Liston rather than for themselves. The coadjutor Bishop of Auckland cut a pathetic figure as he entered the court accompanied by Dean Jeremiah Cahill, 'whose cheery countenance and twinkling eyes contrasted with His Lordship's sad and strained demeanour'.[6] Liston stood in the dock with head bowed while the clerk of the court read out the lengthy information. 'The Bishop seemed to feel his position keenly and only lifted his eyes when he stood to boldly deny the charge.'[7] He then took his seat alongside Conlan at the solicitor's table. The *Observer* cartoonist drew the accused, hunched over in his chair, downcast and sombre. (Two days later, when writing to Bishop Whyte, Liston had no complaints: 'I was treated with perfect consideration – a special room, a seat alongside counsel, and every mark of courtesy.')[8]

Meredith rose to outline the case for the Crown.[9] Advancing the dubious claim that sedition trials were rarely witnessed in New Zealand, he emphasised the circumstances in which the speech was made: on St Patrick's Night, during a public concert in the Town Hall, before 'what was probably a mixed audience'. 'Prior to this the grave question of the settlement of the Irish difficulty was in the melting pot, and was exercising the public mind considerably, not only here, but in all other parts of the Empire. So much so that it was looked upon as the burning question.' The Crown prosecutor maintained that Liston's high office aggravated his offence; his eminent position in the church and his reputation as a man of 'culture, learning and experience' gave his words an added weight and bearing.

The prosecution would rely mainly on the evidence of the *New Zealand Herald* staff reporter, Gordon Leith Stanbrook, with other members of the audience adding their recollections of the evening's events. While unable to recall everything the bishop had said, they

Vincent Meredith. ATL

could testify to those portions of the speech that had impressed their memories. Stanbrook now took the stand to explain how he came to produce his report.[10] He described his memory as 'pretty fair', but was unable to recite the speech off-hand. Over Conlan's objection, he was allowed to use his notes to refresh his memory. After faltering over a phrase on the dismemberment of Ireland, Stanbrook continued, 'He also referred to several defeats of England.' When Conlan demanded to know the precise words Liston had used, Stanbrook replied lamely, 'I don't remember the actual words.' A small chink had appeared in the Crown's armour.

Meredith tried to steer his key witness through the shoals. Liston had said much more than the *Herald* had reported; were the portions omitted by Stanbrook of importance? 'No, it was mainly eulogistic of Ireland. It would not qualify in any way the statements I have given.' Meredith: 'Your memory is quite clear on the phrases you have given verbatim?' Stanbrook: 'Absolutely.' When Meredith began to cite phrases from the report and ask Stanbrook whether or not they were verbatim, Conlan objected to his leading the witness. Stanbrook was then invited to pick out the verbatim parts unaided. The Crown prosecutor led him gently towards the key phrase.

> Stanbrook: 'I have here a list of 155 men and women of whom some were shot.' He gave the actual figures but I only took the total.
> Meredith: Did he say how others met their death?
> Stanbrook: He gave the method by which others died, which I cannot

Liston sits uncomfortably as the prosecution case unfolds. NZO

> remember, and then said that some died on hunger strike. The phrase covering all these methods of death then used was that these people were murdered by foreign troops. . . .
>
> Stanbrook: The words 'that glorious Easter' of 1916 I took to mean the rebellion in Dublin of Easter Monday 1916 and the troops I took to refer to the troops who came in from the Curragh and in the next few days from England to quell the rebellion . . . On the day this speech was made news was being cabled from England to New Zealand about the Irish question. I took the 'foreign masters' to refer to the British Government.[11]

Conlan again objected that the interpretation of the phrases was not a matter for the witness, but Poynton overruled him. The defence lawyer repeatedly turned down the opportunity to cross-examine Stanbrook or any of the clutch of witnesses Meredith now produced to corroborate his evidence. Frank Baller, Robert Beswick, George Broadley, Graham Bell and Stanley Greenough all gave testimony along the lines of their earlier depositions. Baller discussed the *Star* and *Herald* reports as if they were mutually supportive rather than the same text. Greenough could endorse what was said only up to the time he 'had heard enough' and went outside. (Meredith: 'How do you mean "had heard enough"?' Greenough: 'I was full up of it.')[12] Beswick's memory had by now sufficiently improved to testify (with Bell) that Liston had boasted of the Irish 'beating that great Empire'.[13] The two returned soldiers, Broadley and Beswick, gave their evidence with an enthusiasm that drew laughter from some quarters. Bishop Liston was not amused, telling Whyte later: 'Two witnesses were very poor. Two others had their story off parrot-like. One could see they had been coached – yet the fact remains that all four will swear to the use of certain expressions.'[14]

The defence now took centre-stage. Conlan had repeatedly promised to stay silent before the magistrate and to reserve Liston's defence for the Supreme Court. It is not clear when he decided to attempt some special pleading of his own; he later claimed that Liston wanted him to speak up if the magistrate seemed inclined to listen.[15] Poynton was an enigma to both sides, neither Meredith nor Conlan having any idea how he would act in the case. (He had the eccentric habit of bringing his dog with him when presiding on the bench, but it is not recorded if the animal was in court on this occasion.) 'Although a very decent, likeable magistrate [he] is very erratic', Conlan confided to O'Regan.[16] Despite Poynton having ruled against him more than once during the morning, Conlan judged the magistrate sufficiently receptive to entertain a direct appeal to dismiss the case.

He began uncertainly. If the magistrate was satisfied that a *prima facie* case had been made out, then Conlan 'did not wish to take up the time of the Court'. Poynton replied drily that, if the defence counsel wished to address the court, he was free to do so. Conlan then practically invited those assembled to weep for the accused: 'He was very deeply moved – as were many others in the community – that one who was so personally loved and who filled so high an office should be placed in such a position.' He also claimed a little of their sympathy for himself. When first approached to defend Liston he was extremely diffident because of the position he had recently filled in the community. (As the *Observer* noted, Conlan was 'well known as the advocate who prosecuted conscientious objectors during the war.')[17]

There followed a clumsy attempt to shelter Liston behind Conlan's own conspicuous loyalty. Strong as his feelings for the British Empire were, Conlan insisted that the bishop fully shared them. Confident in this knowledge, Conlan could detect no seditious intent when perusing Liston's reported speech. The *Auckland Star* presented Conlan's remarks slightly differently: 'He had undertaken the defence with diffidence, and only after having been convinced of the defendant's loyalty.'[18] The lawyer's confused offering almost deserved this sort of treatment; he had at least managed to avoid blurting out his agreement with the wording of the information.

Conlan next produced a string of mitigating circumstances calculated to influence a vacillating magistrate. He recalled the case of

Conlan attempts to read from Hugh Martin's Ireland in Insurrection. NZO

R. v. *Burns* (1886), where the accused (John Burns, later a member of the British Cabinet) allegedly climbed the parapet of the Carlton Club, waved a red flag, and made a speech which was followed by serious riots.[19] These circumstances were infinitely worse than in Liston's case, where there was not the slightest disturbance during or after the concert; yet Burns had been found not guilty. Conlan read several quotations from the judgement, indicating the very wide latitude permitted by the British authorities in public discussion of political issues. A conviction in that case would have been a great tragedy, he continued, 'because it might have turned Burns and a large number of his followers into disloyal members of the Empire'. Conlan's message could not have been more transparent.

According to Conlan, the right to free speech existed 'because those who ruled our destiny considered it much better that men should speak their own minds and not bottle their views up'. He cited the British Home Secretary's reply when challenged to punish those making seditious utterances in Hyde Park: so long as there was no breach of the peace, or direct advocacy of violence, there was no need to take any notice of them. Hyde Park was widely regarded as the safety-valve of London, Conlan added:

> May I also suggest that on a night like this, 17 March, speakers might possibly say words which they would not use at other times or on other occasions. I submit it might be regarded as a safety valve of the Irish to speak their own minds and get it over.[20]

On St Patrick's Night one expected frankness on matters Irish, and Liston had spoken with 'a close knowledge of Irish affairs' not possessed by his critics. Conlan attempted to enlighten the latter by reading out the preface to a just published account of recent life in Ireland, when Meredith objected and Poynton ruled the extract irrelevant. Conceding reluctantly, Conlan maintained that reading the preface might give the magistrate some idea of Liston's state of mind when making his address.

The book in question was *Ireland in Insurrection*, an exposé by *Daily Mail* journalist, Hugh Martin, of the depredations committed by the Black and Tans in Ireland over the previous eighteen months. The celebrated war correspondent Sir Philip Gibbs had contributed a vigorous preface attributing the violence by Irish nationalists to 'the continued betrayal of their legitimate hopes [and] the wilful disregard of their national pride'. Severity towards the 1916 rebels had 'made martyrs of them', Gibbs claimed, while the British regime in post-war Ireland recalled that of the Germans in Belgium.

> To every country in the world went day by day lurid details of English reprisals, cruelties, blackguardism. Not only in America was this stirring public opinion against us, but in Australia, Canada, South Africa, France, Italy, and other countries, our own relatives, and our warmest friends, were disturbed and distressed and filled with a sense of amazement and indignation that England, the champion of small peoples, the friend of liberty, pledged to the self-determination of peoples, should adopt a Prussian policy in Ireland.[21]

This was the closest Conlan came to identifying the infamous Black and Tans as those 'foreign murderers' whom Liston had excoriated. Foiled in his attempt to lay this testimony before the court, Conlan was briefly at a loss. He made a desultory effort to invoke the protection of section 118(2) of the Crimes Act: might not Liston have been acting responsibly by pointing out defects in the Anglo–Irish relationship? 'If the magistrate was going to hold that the words were used – he was not admitting they were – did it not appeal to him that in making a frank statement the bishop's intention was to bring about the solidarity of the Empire? It might be said it was a very high duty to speak what was in his mind and not bottle it up.' Conlan had earlier asked Meredith to enter the bishop's letter to Massey as evidence, but the Crown prosecutor did not have the original and refused to put in a copy.[22] Conlan decided against mentioning the letter himself, possibly because this would have been too radical a departure from O'Regan's instructions.

The rest of Conlan's defence showed signs of hasty preparation. He cited the bishop's sacred office as a guarantee that he would uphold the law rather than break it. 'One could rest assured he would not say any words with the intention of causing strife.' He also saw Liston's reference to his parents – 'of infinite pathos' – as colouring his later expressions. 'Notwithstanding how inadvisable the statements might be', Conlan insisted that the Crown's case did not support a charge of sedition. 'People could have strong and diverse views and express them, and there was no reason why they should be bad friends over it.' While Liston's remarks might be considered 'indiscreet and unpalatable', they had not incited anyone to violence. As for their alleged effect on excitable Irish readers, Conlan was confident that no one in Ireland would take any notice of the speech.[23] He ended his brief exercise in apologetics with a shameless appeal to expediency.

> A great many Irish people disagreed with [Liston's] reported statements, but if the case went on those people would stand solidly behind His Lordship in this matter. If the case were dismissed it would save quite a lot of trouble and strife. He knew that was not an element to be considered by the Court, but he mentioned it in the hope that the wide distress that would be occasioned should the matter go further would be averted.[24]

Meredith began his reply by reminding everyone that this was not a trial, merely a process to decide whether or not the case should go before a judge and jury. The issue was very simple. The evidence given had not been challenged, nor was it necessary for the Crown to prove that violence had resulted from the words used. There could be no doubt under the authorities that the words constituted a seditious intention. No one wanted to compromise the right of free speech in New Zealand, but this was hardly a case of dispassionate criticism. The words 'murdered by foreign troops' could not be considered a fair reference to events in Dublin during Easter 1916. As the question was one of fact, it was not the court's function to usurp the duty of a jury. Unless the magistrate was convinced that twelve reasonable men would not find the words seditious then the case must proceed.

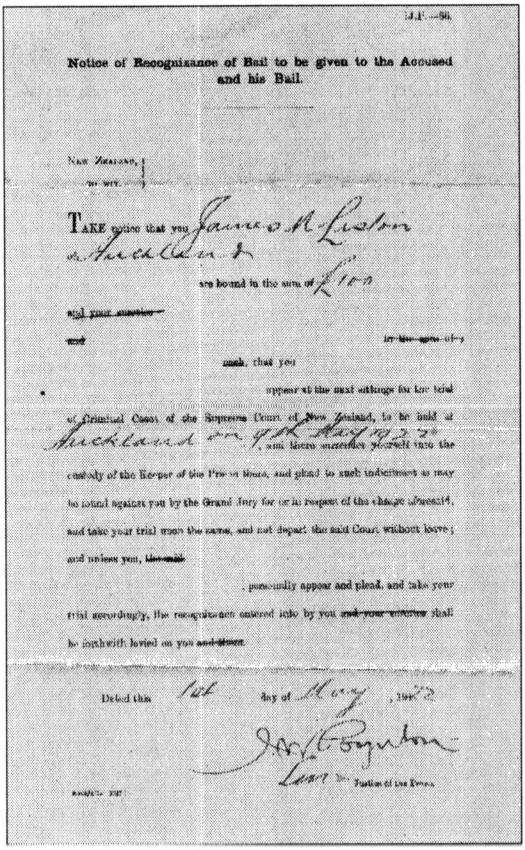

Notice of Recognizance of Bail to be given to the Accused and his Bail.

New Zealand,
to wit.

Take notice that you James M. Liston of Auckland are bound in the sum of £100 ~~and your sureties~~ ~~and~~ ~~in the sum of~~ each, that you appear at the next sittings for the trial of Criminal Cases of the Supreme Court of New Zealand, to be held at Auckland on 9th May 1922, and there surrender yourself into the custody of the Keeper of the Prison there, and plead to such indictment as may be found against you by the Grand Jury for or in respect of the charge aforesaid, and take your trial upon the same, and not depart the said Court without leave; and unless you, ~~the said~~ punctually appear and plead, and take your trial accordingly, the recognizance entered into by you ~~and your sureties~~ shall be forthwith levied on you ~~and them~~.

Dated this 1st day of May, 1922.

J. W. Poynton
Justice of the Peace.

Notice of Recognizance of Bail.
ACDA

The Crown prosecutor was scathing about Conlan's suggestion that St Patrick's Day be reserved as a safety-valve for the Irish. This, he claimed, 'would simply mean granting a dispensation to Irish people to cause a lot of trouble by saying all sorts of things'. Conlan immediately interjected that his reference to the occasion of the speech was intended merely to explain any excess of feeling that might have been shown. Poynton ended the argument by committing Liston for trial at the next sitting of the Supreme Court in Auckland. Bail was fixed at £100. For all his presumed sympathy, Poynton was emphatic: 'Following the authorities on the offence of sedition it appears to me that in four respects at least the speech is seditious. . . . It would be improper for me to comment or attempt to analyse the speech. It might prejudice the case in the higher Court.'[25]

How close had he come to making the opposite decision? Liston and his lawyer were convinced that Poynton was keen to halt proceedings. The bishop later confided to Whyte: 'My counsel spoke on the spur of the moment, for it looked for a minute or two as if the magistrate just wanted some kind of excuse for dismissing the case. He has since said in confidence that if I had made a statement disclaiming any seditious intent and if a few witnesses had been called to say the same, he would have dismissed the case.'[26] Conlan expanded on this theme when explaining his performance in court to an unimpressed O'Regan:

> Mr Poynton told me this morning that if I had gone further and put Dr Liston in the box and got from him a denial of any seditious intent, together with evidence from two or three more men who know the bishop and his sentiments, [and] could not conceive of him using these words with seditious intent – that then he, Mr Poynton, would have dismissed the case as he felt sure that no jury would convict.[27]

Poynton seemed belatedly eager to assist the defence, if only with good advice. He found Liston's letter to Massey unconvincing on the question of intent, as it had contained no specific denial. He told Conlan that a visiting Indian lawyer, Dr Manilal, also used very seditious words, but instead of prosecuting the police had hurried him out of the country. For that matter, should not the frequent (and unpunished) seditious utterances in the *Maoriland Worker* and *New Zealand Truth* be collected for use in the Supreme Court?[28] Poynton's desire to see Liston in the witness-box denying any seditious intention was later to be matched by his counterpart in the higher court. On both occasions Liston was accorded every courtesy by the authorities. Is it possible that the sympathy shown by the two judges owed something to inspiration received from a higher quarter?[29]

In telling all this to O'Regan, Conlan was on the back foot. He dismissed his performance in court as 'some remarks just on general lines' which 'I trust have done no harm'.[30] There was really nothing to be worried about, according to Conlan. Several lawyers had assured him that, however seditious the words might be, no jury would believe that the bishop had uttered them with any seditious intent. Nevertheless, Conlan had been doing his homework. He had recruited Alfred Hall Skelton for the defence.[31] Just before the latter's own Town Hall speech on the Irish question in late 1921, Liston had 'put him on the mat' over what he was going to say.[32] Hall Skelton's statement would be obtained and sent to O'Regan. Conlan also promised to secure other evidence refuting seditious intent, and enclosed several newspaper reports to show how the press had inflamed public opinion over the affair.

Conlan had not yet discovered from Liston which parts of the prosecution evidence he disagreed with. Clearly desperate for another lawyer to come to his rescue, his hurry-up to O'Regan was not very subtle. As the Auckland criminal sessions began in a week, 'we must go now to have everything ready'.[33] The charge sheet contained only fourteen cases and, with two judges sitting, they would soon be completed. Conlan repeated Liston's request that O'Regan approach either Skerrett, Gray or Myers on his behalf. If O'Regan thought none of these men suitable, perhaps A. H. Johnstone, an Auckland lawyer, might do.[34]

Despite his disgust at Conlan's contribution to the lower court proceedings, O'Regan's reproof on 4 May was unusually gentle. Repeating his belief that silence would have been the better policy, he was more critical of Poynton's attempt to run with the hare and hunt with the hounds: 'Of course, we are all wise after the event, but a hint might have been given you from the right quarter beforehand. One cannot be expected to know everything by intuition.'[35] O'Regan continued to question the Auckland insistence on an outsider as leading counsel, even while playing his part in the search for one. He ruled out Michael Myers as unlikely to be *persona grata* to a jury and 'shrank from approaching' his old enemy Skerrett. Later that day he interviewed Alexander Gray about acting for the bishop, receiving a prompt but courteous rebuff. O'Regan noted wryly in his diary, 'The fact is that none of the legal big guns are willing to take the bishop on!'[36]

Were they intimidated by the prospect of having to face the redoubtable William MacGregor in open court? The Liston camp believed that the Solicitor-General was planning to take over the case for the Crown, and Callan felt sure that this would mean 'a peculiarly bitter and unpleasant cross-examination'.[37] While it is unlikely that this course was ever contemplated, a similar confusion reigned in the Crown Law Office over who was going to defend Liston. Meredith sent MacGregor a confident account of events in the magistrates' court: 'The evidence on the depositions came out very well. There was no cross-examination, so that on the face of it there is a clear case.' He was unsure of the identity of his future opponent: 'I understand some leading counsel is to be imported from somewhere, but Mr Conlan informed me that it was not yet decided who and did not care to indicate who it would probably be.'[38]

A fierce argument now began over who should defend the bishop and how they ought to do it. After Conlan's abject performance,

Patrick O'Regan. ATL

Liston received bundles of letters urging a change of lawyer. H. H. Cornish of Wellington pleaded with him to ensure that he was 'vigorously, skilfully and successfully defended'.[39] Frank Gill of Morrinsville approached the matter delicately: 'As things are some of your well wishers feel that you may be handicapped in the fight by reason of the particular counsel who happens to be in charge of the case on your side.'[40] One of Liston's relatives blurted out what many were feeling.

> We are all disgusted . . . You mention that he spoke on the spur of the moment so perhaps we should excuse him, but I'd hope you have someone more competent for the 15th . . . Imagine an usher being called to give evidence and allowed to say what he thought or didn't, and the floor not being swept with him before he left. I'm too annoyed to write coherently. I'm like poor Margaret Priest who said she was trying to make the mission (with murder in her heart). There are people down here who have never even met you imploring me to write and beg you not to spare expense. They would sell all they've got to help you. I suppose you are pestered to death with people suggesting things and doing nothing. I very nearly went up to Auckland, so you've been spared the humiliation of an over-wrought creature standing up in Court and telling the magistrate and all what she thought of them.[41]

The clerical verdict was equally severe on Conlan. James Kelly told O'Regan that Conlan's remarks had 'excited in most quarters intense disgust. Why on earth did he get a man who is notorious all over the country for his jingoism to defend him?'[42] Dean Regnault was almost as harsh when writing to Liston: 'All here hope that before the Supreme Court your solicitor will be a man who will defend your cause without bringing in veiled apologies or extenuating circumstances.'[43] Father James Kennedy was aware of the choice now facing the bishop: 'Our friend, Mr Conlan, seems to belong to a different school of politics to us. O'Regan would be much more at home in defending an unpopular issue.' Kennedy wanted Liston to 'fight the matter out on the merits of your statements, and to substantiate same.'[44] Regnault also advocated attack as the best means of defence:

> Every word you uttered was a statement of facts. The rebellion of 1916 was due to Carson's rebellion against the British Crown, and treason to Ireland; the murderers of the Pearses and Skeffington and others were, in the eyes of the Irish, foreigners in the true sense of the word and the present Treaty is only a small portion of that independence for which the Irish have longed for hundreds of years and for which so many Irish Patriots bled and died.[45]

With his options rapidly narrowing, Liston was fortunate still to have O'Regan to fall back upon. Fuming at the treatment he had received from the 'well-meaning numbskulls' who surrounded Liston, the Wellington lawyer had almost exhausted his (limited) resources of patience and tact.[46] At least the humiliating procession around his rivals' legal offices was now over. When he caught the night train to Auckland on Friday, 5 May, O'Regan must have felt that once more the case was his for the asking. On arrival at the Central Hotel, he found that both Conlan and Liston had been telephoning for him. By Saturday evening, the combined legal expertise of Catholic Auckland was closeted in St Benedict's presbytery.[47] Despite this wealth of talent, nothing had yet been decided about senior counsel. J. J. Sullivan continued to press for an outsider – 'we must have a leader who is regarded by the public as not one of us' – and it was agreed that Liston should phone Wellington in an effort to contact Skerrett.[48]

While the bishop left to do this, O'Regan laid his grievances before the gathering. He was reputed to be organising Liston's defence, yet several steps had been taken of which he strongly disapproved. He wanted his position clarified as soon as possible. O'Regan was careful to show no ill feeling and convinced himself that he had the sympathy of all present. Conlan, who was meeting O'Regan for the first time, took the implied criticism well and seemed very keen on his taking charge. As they dispersed, O'Regan was confident that the bishop and his entourage (with the possible exception of Sullivan) were secretly hoping that Skerrett would refuse the brief.

The conference resumed on Sunday afternoon. It turned out that Skerrett was away on a shooting holiday and nobody knew quite where to find him. When Sullivan suggested sending an urgent telegram to Skerrett's confidential clerk, O'Regan decided to put his foot down. He recorded the details in his diary.

> I respectfully but firmly pointed out to the bishop that I had endured a good deal without complaint, but that I proposed asking definitely my position, seeing that the public had learned, I knew not how, that I was his counsel. I had the name without the responsibility of acting for him, and already two thing[s] had been done to which I objected – the one without consulting me, the other in spite of my instructions. Of course I referred to the letter to Massey, and secondly – more objectionable still – Conlan's address in the Lower Court in face of my instructions that he was merely to plead Not Guilty and reserve defence. The bishop then and there . . . stated that he would henceforth have no adviser but me – that I had complete charge of the case.[49]

Nine days before the case came to trial Liston had finally found his lawyer – the very man he had asked some six weeks earlier. On Tuesday, 9 May, O'Regan lunched with Liston and Conlan. He instructed Conlan (who was to be his junior counsel) to secure the jury list when it became available and distribute it to various friends for scrutiny and report.[50] All three men were aware that, as they were speaking, the grand jury was deliberating on whether to send the Liston case on to the Supreme Court.

In addressing the assembled jurors at the opening of the Auckland criminal sessions, Mr Justice Stringer conceded that they would all be familiar with the case. 'It had been fully ventilated in the public papers to an extent that it would be affectation on his part to suppose that they did not all know as much about it as he did himself.'[51] After citing the definition of sedition from the Crimes Act, Stringer read out passages from the speech, drawing particular attention to the portion commencing, 'We must not forget the martyrs who died in the fighting of 1916 – that glorious Easter.' Of course, he reminded the jurors, the allegations in that passage had to be read in the context of the whole of the speech.

> If the speech had been the idle vapouring of a street orator it might be said that it would have no effect on reasonable and sensible people, but it was

> important that it was made by a person in the position of the bishop, who had great influence over the congregation over which he presided. The grand jury had only to determine whether the words were reasonably susceptible of the interpretation alleged, and if they were they would find a true bill.[52]

Although it took the grand jury some four hours to find a true bill against him, this last legal hurdle to Liston's trial was duly cleared.[53] Meanwhile, O'Regan was being congratulated on having charge of the case and enjoyed confirming the fact. He was about to receive his reward for keeping cool under extreme provocation. On Tuesday afternoon he paid Liston a farewell visit before returning to Wellington. Just as O'Regan was leaving to catch his train, Liston told him of a memorial notice that he had received from Ireland on the very afternoon of St Patrick's Day. O'Regan's subsequent diary entry reveals his growing excitement as he realised the significance of what Liston was saying:

> It was from this he had spoken about the Dublin Rising and the number of people who had died for Ireland then and since. Conlan was of opinion that the document was of great importance. I questioned the bishop further and found that the document . . . contained the words he had used, and that it would show that he had used the words, 'murdered by foreign troops', only when referring to the lives taken by the Black and Tans.[54]

O'Regan could scarcely believe that neither Liston nor Conlan had previously mentioned any such document. He went straight to Conlan's office in Queen Street to inspect it. Although the Auckland lawyer had no more understood its value as evidence than had his client, Conlan now enthusiastically agreed on its importance (without explaining why he had not used it earlier). In the circumstances, O'Regan saw it as providential that Liston had kept the paper. Privately, he was jubilant: 'Had I been aware of its existence I would almost certainly have blown the case out in the Magistrate's Court, but doubtless it is all for the best.'[55] He caught the evening train to Wellington in high spirits.

17

Let Me Carry Your Cross for Ireland, Lord!

Let me carry Your Cross for Ireland, Lord!
Let me suffer the pain and shame;
I bow my head to their rage and hate,
And I take on myself the blame.
Let them do with my body whate'er they will,
My spirit I offer to You,
That the faithful few who heard her call
May be spared to Roisin Dhu.

Thomas Ashe, 1884–1917[1]

O'Regan returned to Auckland on Saturday 13 May and spent the next few days organising Liston's defence. He and his Auckland friends pored over the jury list. There were also lengthy rehearsals with the bishop and his witnesses, going over the details of their evidence. O'Regan swore everyone to secrecy on the nature of the defence he planned to present. With the crucial new evidence of the memorial notice in his possession, he felt confident of undermining the jury's trust in the *Herald* report.[2]

When he met Vincent Meredith on Monday morning, one wonders whether O'Regan appreciated how much he had in common with his legal adversary. Both men had risen by talent rather than by the advantages of birth. They each found the law relatively late in life; Meredith following an apprenticeship in the Customs Department,

Inside the Supreme Court.
AWN

O'Regan after his political career was cut short by defeat at the polls.[3] They may even have attended the same lectures at Victoria University College. Sedition law was no mystery to either lawyer. After his admission to the bar, O'Regan made something of a specialty of defending sedition cases, while Meredith spent three formative years at the Crown Law Office. At forty-five, Meredith was O'Regan's junior by some eight years.

On his arrival in 1917, Meredith had made an immediate impact on the Auckland legal scene, winning thirteen straight acquittals in the Supreme Court. ('Of course, I was fortunate in that I was engaged to appear for so many innocent people!')[4] In 1921 he was appointed Crown Solicitor for the Auckland provincial area, commencing what would be a record thirty-one-year tenure. Meredith brought several qualities to the position. An accomplished courtroom performer, he had remarkable histrionic talents. His strong baritone voice was heard in amateur theatrical performances throughout New Zealand, although (it is said) he soon gave up the stage when Gilbert and Sullivan clashed with murder.[5]

The *New Zealand Truth* described the new appointee as 'the essence of fairness',[6] a quality reflected in Meredith's own view of his role. 'I learnt the lesson that the job of the representative of the Crown was not to try to get a verdict but only to see that justice was done . . . also that an accused person should not be condemned unless the permitted admissible evidence clearly justified his conviction.'[7]

Meredith's major concern when meeting O'Regan was to ensure that there would be no mud-throwing during the trial, 'as he had many Catholic friends and didn't want to lose them'. Promising him 'a fair deal', O'Regan noted that his opposite looked more like a man who had to defend a hopeless case than a Crown prosecutor eager for his quarry.[8] O'Regan was mistaking nervousness for pessimism. All eyes would soon be upon Meredith. Prime Minister Massey, Solicitor-General MacGregor and Mayor Gunson were known to be 'much concerned' with the case – not to mention every newspaper editor and lawyer in the country. Despite such intense pressure, the Crown prosecutor had every reason to be confident as he approached the biggest case of his life. He had interviewed all the Crown witnesses personally (unwilling to delegate anything owing to 'the sectarian influence at work') and had checked the resultant informations with MacGregor.[9] Liston's lawyer had put up no contest in the magistrates' court, while both Poynton and Stringer were on record as supporting the Crown's case. If O'Regan's substitution for Conlan promised a tighter tussle in court, Meredith was well prepared for it. The conversation between the two lawyers was cut short by a summons to confer with Mr Justice Stringer.

Thomas Walter Stringer had only recently been appointed a resident judge for the Auckland district. During his seven-year presidency of the Arbitration Court the sixty-seven year-old had earned a reputation as a 'straight goer' with a nice sense of humour on the bench.[10] His determination to avoid any suspicion of sectarian influence over proceedings was immediately apparent. Stringer assured O'Regan that the bishop would not be treated as a criminal. To spare him any unnecessary indignity, Liston would not be searched or placed in the cells below the dock; after registering his plea, he could sit at his counsel's table. Stringer seemed genuinely sensitive to the predicament of the accused, while Meredith offered no complaint at this special treatment.[11]

The same delicacy was then shown in the selection of jurors. O'Regan had strong objections to several names on the jury list, which included one of Mayor Gunson's nephews and the brother of an Auckland city councillor. He resented having to waste any of his six challenges on them. At Stringer's prompting, Meredith agreed to reject any of those whom O'Regan deemed especially unacceptable.

Thomas Stringer. ATL

The judge then asked O'Regan if he was putting Liston in the witness-box, and when this was confirmed added, 'It will be most satisfactory if His Lordship will give in evidence that he had no seditious intent'.[12] This very favourable hint made the defence lawyer wonder whether Stringer might withdraw the case from the jury if the chance presented itself. O'Regan's confidence grew as the day progressed. Conlan had quizzed him several times about his proposed address to the jury. Although he had as yet prepared nothing in writing, O'Regan knew exactly what he was going to say. Before retiring to bed early on Monday evening ('the best preparation for the fray'), he confided the secret to his diary:

> I am certain that no other counsel would take the line I contemplate – of insisting that the bishop rightly called the Black and Tans murderers and that he was amply entitled to use the term 'that glorious Easter' in reference to the 1916 rising in Dublin.[13]

O'Regan scrupulously noted the details of the next few days in his journal. 'There is much suppressed excitement, and though I did not sleep heavily the last three nights, I am not really nervous. . . . A light breakfast and then in my room until it was time to walk to the Court. Found it crowded.'[14] The Auckland Supreme Court was crammed to overflowing, while the gallery was filled almost entirely with women. As his name was called, James Liston walked in briskly from a side door and stood in the dock with head bowed while the lengthy charge was read over. Once he had pleaded not guilty, Liston was permitted by the judge to take a seat beside his counsel.

There followed the lengthy business of empanelling the jury, in O'Regan's view a crucial process. He had been given varying information about some of the jurors and was forced to use all six of his permitted challenges without excluding any of the men whom he described as 'the very worst'. By waiting until each man was about to sit down before calling out 'challenge!', O'Regan had the satisfaction of seeing Meredith stand aside several whom he had marked down as hostile. The Crown prosecutor rejected sixteen men in all, including several Catholics. The fact that this produced an all-Protestant jury did not seem to discomfit Liston's defence. Thomas Henry Chapman – 'a man of means', O'Regan noted – was chosen as foreman. The other eleven good men and true were David Amos, Eustace Cavaye, William Richardson, Theophilus Hollis, Robert Holmes, William Simmond, Alfred Goodwin, Frederick Jupp, Lionel Hodder, William Nicholson, and Guy Pearce.[15]

Meredith then opened at some length, largely repeating what he had said in the magistrates' court.[16] He presented the sedition clauses of the Crimes Act as a rarely used but necessary accompaniment to every civilised government: 'Fortunately, we in New Zealand were not yet divided into camps hostile to one another – Pray God that that condition might never arise here – and that fact made it all the more imperative to punish seditious utterances, so that the present fortunate position might not be altered.' (His allusion to Ireland was obvious.) While every citizen was permitted to write and speak without censorship, the right of free speech did not cover malignity or licence. It would be for the jurors to decide whether Liston had crossed this clear line of demarcation.

To assist their deliberations, Meredith dwelt on the circumstances of the speech and the speaker, before subjecting the address itself to searching analysis. It had been delivered to an Irish audience on St Patrick's Night at a time of great turmoil in Ireland. Passions were also running high on the issue here in New Zealand. Meredith denied any direct concern with the Irish question, remarking merely that the jury might like to consider it – a neat trick to associate the speech with actual violence, even if half the world away. With similar sleight of hand, he noted that the concert programme did not include the

The jury, 'Twelve good men and true'. NZ Observer

national anthem: 'It was possibly a matter of no great moment, but he simply wished to draw it to the attention of the jury so that it might gain some idea of the atmosphere of the gathering.'

Liston represented, or would be taken to represent, the views of his fellow Catholics. His rank and education presumed a skill with words and a knowledge of their meaning and import. Liston had cited his position in the church as giving him a special right to speak, well knowing the importance that his remarks would assume on a matter of public interest. 'His speech could not be compared with the words of any irresponsible, illiterate member of the community.' Meredith tried to reduce O'Regan's freedom of manoeuvre by anticipating the arguments the defence counsel might put forward (Conlan's earlier performance having given no hint that any stronger defence was available). The speech could not be dismissed as a chance or haphazard affair, as it was advertised on the programme; Liston had surely prepared his remarks carefully beforehand.

Meredith asked the jury to consider the speech 'in a broad, fair and generous spirit, and not be captious or lay stress upon any particular sentence to which exception could be taken'. This request was the easier for him to make, knowing that the *Herald* report read consistently badly for Liston: Meredith was eating his cake and having it too. 'He would suggest that underlying the speech was a vein of hostility and bitterness towards the British Government, and that particular sentences to which strong exception could be taken were not isolated instances, but fitted in with the whole tone and colour of the speech.'[17]

The jury would have to decide whether Liston's reference to his parents being driven from Ireland was fair criticism of constituted authority. 'It was an allegation that the British Government cruelly oppressed and drove out the Irish people from their own land to hand it over to the snobs of the Empire, presumably the landed aristocracy.' To Meredith this constituted an abuse of freedom of speech, while the prediction that many would fight and die to achieve full Irish freedom was a clear call for further bloodshed. Such a sanction of armed violence was not permissible in any country. Liston's praise of de Valera as the man best fitted to prevent Ireland being duped by England was equally reprehensible, implying as it did that the English authorities would stoop to trickery to rob the Irish of what they had gained. 'That showed the temper and feeling behind the speech', Meredith concluded primly.

He next tackled 'that glorious Easter', Liston's description of 'the revolution in Dublin in 1916 when armed men for some days held possession of the city and wrought irreparable damage to buildings and caused large loss of human life'. The bishop not only glorified this rebellion, but also claimed that certain Irish men and women were 'murdered by foreign troops'.

> That referred to the loyal soldiers of the British Empire who were called in to restore order and take charge of Dublin, so that the city might be safe to live in. They were referred to as foreigners, and in the same breath as murderers . . . There were many men here who were comrades in the Great War with the soldiers who were branded thus and would reasonably resent this description.[18]

Meredith now called upon his first witness, Gordon Stanbrook, to explain the genesis of his report. 'I took a longhand note of what I wanted from his speech and I wrote up the story from my notes immediately on getting back to the office.' His original notes had then gone into the waste-paper basket. Stanbrook read through his report, mentioning several portions of the speech which he had omitted to record. 'I didn't take the whole of the speech – I had no need of it.' Meredith at once had him assure the court that nothing he had left out would have qualified Liston's other remarks: 'I had no other desire than to get a correct report of what was said.'

Stanbrook claimed as verbatim all the key phrases singled out by

Stanbrook in the box. NZO

the Crown prosecutor. Was this Meredith's way of getting around the lack of a shorthand record? The reporter's interpretation also fitted the Crown's needs perfectly. 'I took the reference to "foreign troops" to mean British troops who were brought in to repress the rebellion on the evening it broke out. The reference to "foreign masters" I couldn't take to mean anything but the British Government.' As Meredith completed the examination of his chief witness, he must have felt quietly satisfied. Stanbrook had come across as an honest, competent journalist, frank and thoughtful in his answers to both counsel and the bench. However, the true test of his worth was to come.

O'Regan began his cross-examination by getting Stanbrook to estimate that Liston had spoken for about twenty-five minutes. 'And yet your report took only three minutes to read. I know that because I timed you.' What did the witness mean by saying he had taken 'only what he wanted'? Stanbrook defended this phrase as indicating those parts of the speech he considered to be of public interest. 'You did not take a shorthand note?' 'That was not necessary. The speech was only incidental to the concert.' Stanbrook was then made to confess his inability to write in shorthand. Was it not risky to say that any part of a speech was verbatim when it had been taken down in longhand? Stanbrook did not think so. 'Well I am going to show you presently that your report was not accurate', O'Regan replied sharply.[19]

Perhaps shaken by this aggressive handling, Stanbrook admitted that his present evidence might well differ from what he had said in the magistrates' court. When informed that a key passage in the indictment had not appeared in his report (concerning the bishop's 'little Irish mother' and the wrongs that she and her generation had suffered), Stanbrook dismissed this as 'sob stuff' which was not published in a paper like the *Herald*. 'Unless you are reporting a Rotary Club meeting', came the instant retort. O'Regan next attempted to get Stanbrook to agree that the phrase 'plenty to fight and even die' should have read 'men in Ireland and women too to fight and even die'. When Stringer queried the point of this distinction, O'Regan insisted that the addition of women made an important difference. Stringer then asked the witness whether Liston might have said 'men and women'. Possibly he did, Stanbrook replied, although he did not remember it that way. 'I wouldn't like to be positive on the point', he added weakly.

O'Regan moved on to the critical part of the indictment. 'Do you say your report about the glorious Easter of 1916 correctly reports what the bishop said?' 'I think so.' 'Do you still think the 155 people referred to by the bishop died during the Easter of 1916?' 'On consideration I think the reference also concerned people who died afterwards.' 'Would it not be inaccurate to say that people who died on hunger strike were murdered?' 'It is not for me to say.' When Stringer remarked that it did not follow that Liston had not said such a thing, O'Regan promised to call evidence to refute this claim.

He next fired a series of rapid questions at the hapless reporter, designed to reveal either bias or gross ignorance of Irish affairs. Stanbrook admitted knowing that the Black and Tans were an auxiliary police force and not British regular troops; also that several women and priests had been killed in Ireland. (O'Regan took the chance to educate the judge and jury: 'Canon Magner was shot by Black and Tans when administering the last sacraments, and Father Griffin was taken from his presbytery to a lonely mountain and murdered.')[20] The witness recalled Liston reading from a document and enumerating the various categories of those who had died.

> Q: I put it to you that the words used were, 'I have here a list of 155 men and women who, during and since 1916, have died for Ireland. Sixteen were

executed by shooting in 1916, 52 were killed while fighting during Easter Week, seven died on hunger strike (including Terence MacSwiney, the Lord Mayor of Cork), eight were executed by hanging, twelve by shooting and 57 including three priests were murdered by foreign troops.'
A: That is not my recollection of it.
Q: Will you deny that those were the words used?
A: I couldn't very well deny it when I have no notes to support me and I am relying entirely on my memory.
Q: I put it to you that the Bishop used the term 'murdered' only in regard to the outrages committed by the Black and Tans?
A: No. That is not my recollection of it.[21]

O'Regan made more progress when he turned to discuss the abbreviated nature of the report. At first Stanbrook was prepared to admit only that it was 'a close condensation'. O'Regan added, 'So condensed as not to give a fair impression?' 'It conveyed the impression I got from the bishop. I am prepared to admit it is possible that in many respects my impressions may be incorrect.' O'Regan then took a calculated risk by asking the reporter why the *Auckland Star* had published an identical account of the speech. Stanbrook told the court that Laurence O'Brien had covered the concert for the *Star* – they had been but a few seats apart – and had also attended the magistrates' court, but was not called to give evidence. He was convinced that the *Star*'s report was a direct crib of his own, although with a different introduction. O'Regan concluded his cross-examination by asking about the bishop's demeanour and the reception his remarks had received. Stanbrook recalled that Liston had spoken in a calm, unemotional manner; while there had been no disturbance in the audience, 'there was some very wild applause'.

O'Regan's ploy took Meredith by surprise. While the defence needed to explain how both Auckland papers had come up with identical versions of the speech, the Crown prosecutor was hardly expecting his opponent to make capital out of O'Brien's failure to appear as a prosecution witness. Meredith counter-attacked by asking Stanbrook if he knew what had become of the *Star* reporter's notes. When O'Regan objected that this was hearsay, Meredith replied that it depended on whether the defence proposed to elaborate on why O'Brien was not called to testify. Or why, for that matter, the *Star* had used Stanbrook's account in preference to that of its own man. On Stringer's ruling this question inadmissible, Meredith reluctantly changed tack.

Now the defence of misquotation was out of the bag, Meredith made Stanbrook confirm that the words 'murdered by foreign troops' had actually been used. 'We do not deny it', O'Regan replied, at which Stringer intervened: 'The point is that the words referred only to those people killed by the Black and Tans, who we know carried on reprisals and a great many people lost their lives.' Meredith then asked Stanbrook: 'Was reference made to the Black and Tans?' 'No.' This drew another sally from the judge: 'You must realise that the reference "murdered by foreign troops" can hardly have applied to those who were hanged or died on hunger strike?' Stanbrook: 'It would be straining it a bit.' Stringer: 'Is it not then possible that the words referred only to a section of the 155 who died?' Stanbrook: 'It is possible, but it did not seem so to me at the time.' With this exchange Stanbrook's involvement in the case ended. (O'Regan later noted in his diary, 'Everybody appeared to feel that we had scored when the reporter stood down.')[22]

As Frank Baller entered the witness-box, the tension in the crowded courtroom visibly relaxed. The council cleaner proceeded to tell his story as if he had rehearsed it well and in a voice that reminded O'Regan of a practised street preacher.[23] He was employed as an usher in the Town Hall, and his attention had been drawn first by the claim that foreign masters had driven Liston's parents from Ireland. He recalled the bishop's prediction that many would fight and die for Ireland's whole freedom, his praise of de Valera, and his enumeration of those Irish men and women 'murdered by foreign troops'. The *New Zealand Herald* report seemed 'fairly accurate' to Baller, although he admitted to having 'refreshed his memory' since by reading the newspapers. Conlan then conducted a meandering cross-examination which at times threatened to degenerate into farce. On the bishop's lament for his exiled parents, Baller's immediate reaction was: 'Well, you have not got much to grumble about. If you had stayed in Ireland you might never have become a Bishop. (Laughter.)'

Conlan asked Baller how Liston had delivered the address. 'If I could have delivered it in the same way I should have thought myself very eloquent.' The court had no sooner recovered its composure when Baller had everyone laughing again. 'When he referred to murder by foreign troops, I felt like interjecting but thought discretion the better part of valour.' The witness concluded by confusing himself over the list of those who had died. 'Referring to the rebellion [Liston] gave the number and said some were shot, some were hung [*sic*], and some died on hunger strike. He simply said they were murdered by foreign troops.' Baller had taken great umbrage at this phrase being applied to men who were merely doing their duty.

Frank Baller in the stand. NZO

Robert Moffat Beswick now had his turn in the limelight.[24] One wonders what the customs clerk was doing attending the St Patrick's Night concert at all. He had risen to his feet after Liston criticised the 'snobs of the Empire', initially intending to ask the bishop a question but settling instead for a dramatic exit when the address concluded. He now gave an almost word-perfect recitation of the indictment, adding the provocative claim that Liston had boasted of Ireland 'beating' the British Empire. O'Regan must have smiled when Beswick declared that 'these statements I am giving are just as they come to my mind'. O'Regan began his cross-examination with relish: the witness had entered the box sporting a returned soldier's badge. ('Obviously this man was brimming over with hatred of the bishop, and I took good care to make him show it to the full.')[25] Beswick soon faltered under pressure. While sticking by his belief that 'plenty' (not 'men and women') were said to be willing to fight for complete Irish freedom, he claimed that Liston had spoken for no more than fifteen minutes. His attempt at correcting the bishop's version of Irish history was less than convincing:

> I have read history. Four million people were not evicted from the country in fifty years. They could have stayed if they chose. The bishop was romancing when he said his people were driven out. They were not driven from the country.

> Q: Four millions could have stayed even after they had been driven out of their farms?
> A: Yes.[26]

Beswick recalled the list as an enumeration of various categories of Irish dead (including three priests), all of whom were 'murdered by foreign troops'. After Stringer got him to agree that this description scarcely applied to those who had perished by hunger strike, Beswick made a crucial admission on the wording of the list: 'It is quite probable that I have omitted the word "some" which would make it read "some murdered by foreign troops".' O'Regan immediately took the opportunity to read out the defence's version of Liston's controversial sentence, after which Beswick concluded lamely, 'He certainly gave some statistics. I believe he gave some such enumeration as Mr O'Regan gives.' As the witness made his forlorn departure, Stringer adjourned the proceedings for lunch.

On resumption at 2.15 p.m. the procession of Crown witnesses continued. George Broadley, a meter reader from Onehunga, made a less than impressive showing.[27] He stumbled over the reference to Liston's parents being driven from their land 'so that it could be used as a cattle ranch for foreign snobs'. His version of the list was absurdly abbreviated: 'that glorious Easter rebellion where so many of our countrymen had given their lives murdered by foreign troops'. He concluded by endorsing the *Herald* report as 'pretty accurate'. On O'Regan's reminding him that he had used the words 'hounded out of Ireland' during his lower court evidence, Broadley admitted his error. He also corrected his reference to 'foreign snobs', adding that, 'I took the words as I heard them and interpreted them as I could only interpret them'. After recalling that everyone on the list was said to have been murdered by foreign troops, Broadley immediately contradicted himself, before ending with a half-hearted plea of amnesia:

> There was evidently a great deal said that I don't recollect . . . I have a very bad memory but I can remember what I stated here. There are things that struck me and they remain fixed in my memory.[28]

Graham Brook Bell next entered the witness-box, with his own memory greatly improved since his first interview with Meredith. He went through the indictment in a manner that persuaded O'Regan of his sympathy with the accused.[29] His evidence on the list established many of the points the defence wished to make well before O'Regan rose to cross-examine him. Bell at once withdrew the suggestion that

Left to right: Robert Beswick, George Broadley, Stanley Greenough. NZO

Liston had used the word 'martyrs' when referring to the Irish dead. 'He spoke of them as though they were martyrs.' Ignoring Bell's claim that the bishop had boasted of an Irish victory over the empire, O'Regan was more concerned to tease a fuller description of the list out of him. Bell admitted that Liston had referred to various classes of Irish victims, not merely those killed in 1916, and that only some of these had been 'murdered by foreign troops'. When O'Regan read out the defence version of the list, Bell agreed that 'something like that was said'.

The final Crown witness was another clerk-turned-usher, Stanley Albert Greenough. O'Regan thought him 'a youthful looking person full of bias' and deemed his evidence to be valueless.[30] Greenough also had bridled at Liston's reference to cattle ranches and empire snobs. When the bishop went on to predict that complete Irish freedom would be gained by those willing to fight and die for it, the usher's patience ran out completely: 'I did not hear anything after that. I had heard enough and walked out. I did not wish to stay and hear any more.' O'Regan did not bother with a cross-examination.

In opening for the defence, O'Regan cheekily asked Stringer to rule that there was no case to answer.[31] To support the serious charge of sedition, he said, all that had been presented was the longhand note of a reporter, who had admitted to taking down only as much as he wanted, supplemented by the hazy recollections of several witnesses who were 'brimming over with bias and who broke down in important details'. O'Regan recalled later:

> I did this knowing well that it would most probably be refused, but then I didn't mind giving the Judge a chance to rule against me in something of comparatively small importance. His Honour ruled against me in the course

> of a neat little speech during which he conceded that the Crown's evidence was by no means free from serious discrepancies.[32]

Stringer replied that the proof of the words used was a matter of evidence: 'He supposed that the best evidence which could be procured had been procured. If it had infirmities it was for the defence to point them out to the jury.' He could not withdraw the case when there was direct evidence that Liston had used words which might be deemed to convey a seditious intention. Even had no reporter been present at the concert, seditious words could have been proved by those who heard them.

> In this case there was something a little better than that. There was a person, and a skilled person, present taking notes though not in shorthand. He could not but recognise that there were very serious discrepancies in the evidence as to what the bishop actually said. That was a matter for the jury and not for the bench.[33]

The judge then invited the defence to open its case. O'Regan began with what he later described as a few 'incisive remarks'.[34] The jury had to satisfy itself that the admittedly brief *Herald* report was also accurate. Unlike Stanbrook, Liston had preserved his notes and they would be put in as evidence. The bishop would also take the witness stand to state exactly what he had said and to explain the intent behind the words he had used. After hearing him, O'Regan predicted, the jury would have no difficulty in ruling out any seditious intention and in agreeing that the address, properly reported, was not capable of that interpretation.

O'Regan now attempted to settle a few old scores. As the whole speech needed to be considered in its proper setting, was it not very unfair of the press to have isolated a portion of Liston's alleged remarks and made drastic comment upon it? Such behaviour made this the type of case which put the jury system to its severest test. They had to dismiss from their minds not only such reports and press criticism, but also the innuendo conveyed by the 'vulgar' cartoon which the *Herald* had published on the incident.[35] The jurors were not bound by any view they might have expressed earlier which was founded on this biased commentary. Nor was it important whether they agreed or disagreed with any part of the speech. Their primary duty was to prevent interference with 'the British right to free expression of opinion'.[36]

O'Regan then outlined the evidence which Liston proposed to give. The bishop had been asked to speak only a week before the concert and had done so with reluctance. He rarely spoke from the public platform and was a member of neither the concert committee nor the Irish Self-Determination League. The document he had read from the Town Hall stage had been received in the mail on the very afternoon of the concert. It listed those people killed during the disturbances in Ireland and had been printed there in connection with religious observances (the recipients being asked to pray for the souls of the dead). The bishop had counted the names in the various sections, marked the number in the margin, and quoted the headings which stated the manner of their death. 'It had to be remembered that the document was printed in Ireland where feelings ran high.' The final category, referring to those killed in 1920–21 and including the names of three priests and two women, was headed 'murdered by British troops'. The bishop had substituted the word 'foreign' for 'British' because he knew that this part referred to the Black and Tans:

> We make no apologies and do not desire to deny our opinion that their victims were murdered. But it is unfair and untrue to suggest that because we believe they were murdered we say that they were murdered by British troops or by the people of England.[37]

It was doubly wrong, O'Regan insisted, to suggest that the bishop used these words to describe those killed during the 1916 rebellion. The *Herald* had misrepresented Liston, while the Press Association had telegraphed the lie throughout the country. 'It was most fortunate in a way that these proceedings were instituted for it stopped newspapers and politicians from making fools of themselves by saying things which he [Liston] did not say.' O'Regan then briefly explained Liston's silence after the report had appeared; why he had not immediately contradicted it, and why he had written to Massey affirming his personal loyalty and that of his church. After a rapid summary of the indictment, indicating where its accuracy would be challenged by the defence, O'Regan turned to his client. 'Will you go forward, your Lordship?'[38]

18

Rex v. *Liston*

It is hard to find the twelve good men and true, so hard that a Catholic would rather risk facing the judge than a packed jury of bigots. If even ten just men could not be found in Sodom and Gomorrah what hope is there of finding twelve in Massey's Murderland.

New Zealand Tablet, 15 December 1921

James Liston rose quickly from his seat, entered the witness-box and took the oath. A sketch by the *Observer* cartoonist captures the bishop's defiantly jutting chin and coolly levelled eyes.[1] The abashed, hangdog look of the magistrates' court has been replaced by a pugnacious stance, no doubt reflecting the change in his counsel. Liston gave his evidence in a forthright, confident manner which delighted O'Regan. He well remembered the night of the concert. It was the first public meeting he had addressed in Auckland and he accepted the invitation reluctantly. The notes he prepared for the occasion were then produced. He was born in Dunedin of Irish parents who had emigrated to New Zealand in the 1860s. The indictment correctly stated his comments on their being driven from their native land: 'He was referring to the eviction of his parents and the three and three-quarter million evicted with them. He was recalling what eviction meant in Ireland.'[2]

Meredith immediately interjected that this evidence was barely relevant; the words should speak for themselves. Stringer replied that it was a question of intent and Liston was entitled to explain his own intent to the jury. Encouraged by this ruling, O'Regan then led his

Liston defiant. NZO

client through the speech phrase by phrase. The 'foreign masters' he had criticised were English and Irish landlords 'who did not live in Ireland being in that sense foreigners'. His claim that Ireland had received merely an instalment of freedom was a statement of historical fact. He was referring to the Anglo–Irish Treaty, 'in my opinion the gift of God because it gave political freedom to Ireland'.[3] By 'determined to have the whole of it' he meant the peaceful union of the two Irish parliaments. He had not mentioned force and was considering Ireland in terms of New Zealand, whose relations with Great Britain were changing by friendly agreement. The phrase about there being plenty to fight and die was not accurately reported: 'I did not intend that anyone should understand from that passage that I was advocating recourse to physical force.'

Liston defended his comparison of Irish and British problems as a means of reassuring his Town Hall audience. The recent Craig–Collins conference and de Valera's statements in Paris supported his prediction that Ireland's troubles would be overcome.[4] 'I did not have any seditious intention or any idea of encouraging disorder.' His reference to the man who had stood by Ireland was correctly reported: 'Everybody knew that de Valera did not agree with the form the

Treaty was taking. I thought in view of past history that it was well for Ireland that there should be a man to be keenly on the watch to see that she got all she was entitled to.' Liston now came to the critical part of his evidence:

> The words in the indictment do not set out correctly what I did say. The report is inaccurate, misleading and hopelessly bungled. I think it was taken down by a man who, however honest, was as competent to report this lecture on Irish affairs as I would be to report a lecture on engineering.[5]

Liston was able to reinforce this aggressive line by producing both his original notes and the list from which he had quoted. The jury was told again of the latter document's arrival in the mail and of how he had incorporated its contents into his address: 'I employed very largely and almost exactly the subheadings of the list.' He then read out the complete sentence, by now familiar to everyone in court from O'Regan's repeated questions. Liston denied describing the Easter Week dead as having been murdered, a term he intended to refer exclusively to those killed by the Black and Tans 'while the policy of reprisals was in full swing'. He admitted that it would have been better to call them Black and Tans instead of 'foreign troops', but was confident that his audience knew whom he meant. 'I used the word "murdered" because it was commonly used by leading statesmen and Anglican clergy in England when speaking of the "Black and Tan" reprisals.'

> I used the term 'that glorious Easter' parenthetically. It was a common phrase used in reference to that insurrection. At the time of the rising in 1916 most Irish people thought it was a mad enterprise, but after these men had died for Ireland it was felt they had passed beyond the realm of criticism . . . Many thought they were foolish, but when they did the glorious thing they could only be referred to in one way, namely, as heroes.[6]

His address had concluded with an appeal for the audience to forgive the wrongs of the past. He spoke without any show of feeling and there was no sign of disorder in the hall. 'I never had any seditious intention nor any intention of encouraging the use of force. I say that most emphatically.' When he read the *New Zealand Herald* on Saturday morning, he felt 'grossly misrepresented' and resolved to take action 'fairly quickly'. Gunson's public protest changed his mind, while his lawyers advised silence in face of the threatened legal action: 'Otherwise I would have given the public of Auckland at once the explanation I am giving them today in this unhappy position.' Once criminal proceedings were announced, he wrote a public letter to the Prime Minister assuring him of Catholic loyalty.

O'Regan had mixed feelings as he sat down following his examination of the bishop. Although Liston responded well to almost every question, the jury did not seem convinced by his attempts to explain 'that glorious Easter'. O'Regan's careful coaching had broken down as the bishop forgot several points his counsel had been expecting him to mention. While Conlan was very depressed by this failure, O'Regan hoped that Liston would recall these arguments when under cross-examination.[7]

'Nothing makes the handling of a cross-examination so easy as a little bit of luck – in favour of your side, of course', wrote Vincent Meredith some forty-two years after the case.[8] Unfortunately for him, the largest piece of good fortune had already gone to the defence with the belated discovery of the key Irish document. Meredith may have been surprised by the alacrity with which Liston now proceeded to disavow his remarks as reported: 'I would not care to be responsible for them. They could very well be criticised. I agree they would be improper for any prominent man to make.' The Crown prosecutor turned to Liston's stubborn silence after his speech had been published. Had he not owed it to the public and to his co-religionists to disavow the report? Were not the papers in a turmoil over it? If the mayor was deemed unworthy of notice, why had he not unburdened himself in his letter to the Prime Minister? In response, Liston stuck closely to his script, citing legal advice to justify his silence and scorning the press tumult. He defended his letter to Massey: 'I retracted nothing, because I had nothing to retract.'

There remained one card for the prosecution to play. O'Regan's unease steadily grew as Liston was asked about the Irish rebellion of 1916. It was a masterful exercise by Meredith, a series of simple questions, their drift apparent and easily followed by the jury.

> Q: The term 'glorious Easter' was used in connection with Easter of 1916?
> A: Yes.
> Q: It was the occasion of an insurrection in Dublin in which there was considerable damage to property and loss of life?
> A: Yes.
> Q: It was ultimately quelled by bringing in troops from England?
> A: Yes.
> Q: In what respect do you suggest it was glorious?
> A: Because of the manner in which a few young men of the highest probity of life and against all odds tried to do something for their country.

> Q: Men of the rebel party?
> A: I was thinking of the men who did something for Ireland – Irishmen on the Irish side – members of the party in rebellion.
> Q: In using those words did you support them?
> A: I admired them.
> Q: When you used those words did you support and advocate their action?
> A: Must I answer that question, Your Honour?[9]

Mr Justice Stringer considered it to be hardly a proper question: the witness was being asked if he supported rebellion! Meredith replied that intent was under consideration; he was merely asking Liston to explain what was in his mind when using those words, just as he had explained himself over the other phrases. Stringer would not budge: 'If the witness objects to answering he is entitled to do so, and he has objected.' Meredith had to move on. He focused on Liston's choice of 'foreign' over 'British' as a less offensive term to describe the Black and Tans. Liston was agreeing that these men were in fact British and properly enlisted in the Royal Irish Constabulary, when Stringer intervened decisively: 'It is notorious that when reprisals were in progress the Black and Tans committed murders. Everybody knows that.' Meredith gave up in exasperation at this point and the case was adjourned for the day.[10]

The close of proceedings could not have come too soon for Conlan and O'Regan. Meredith's late sally had thrown the defence into confusion, well reflected by Liston's hesitant replies. O'Regan grumbled later in his diary.

> He never fired off a single [one] of the verbal missives I had given him. My poor junior was terribly depressed as the Court adjourned for the day and was anxious that we should recall the Bishop the next morning, but I emphatically turned the suggestion down, unless he could in the meantime show me anything to justify further evidence in some other connection from His Lordship.[11]

A conference hastily convened in St Benedict's presbytery at which it was agreed that Liston would not be recalled. O'Regan declared his intention of dealing with the troublesome phrase, 'that glorious Easter' in his closing address. This meant dispensing with the evidence of concert organisers Philip Dee, James Coleman and Mary McIlhone (secretary of the St Patrick's Night concert committee), and calling only three defence witnesses. O'Regan then returned to the Central Hotel for dinner and another early night, despite everything still 'in good spirits'.[12]

Dean Jeremiah Cahill. NZO

The case resumed at 10 o'clock the next morning, when Dean Jeremiah Cahill entered the witness-box. O'Regan was confident that the priest's evidence would corroborate the defence version of Liston's actual words. Cahill began by describing the delivery and reception of the speech, which he considered to be one 'appropriate to an Irish audience'. The bishop had read out a list of those who had died for Ireland during and since 1916, mentioning the number and manner of their death. The last category, including three priests, comprised those killed by foreign troops ('I would not be sure whether he said killed or murdered'). Cahill believed this to be a reference to the Black and Tans. At O'Regan's prompting, the witness could recall nothing to support Mayor Gunson's assertion that Liston had 'sneered' at the British, or to justify the *Herald* cartoon of him trampling the Union Jack into the Town Hall stage.[13]

In reply, Meredith attempted to discount the worth of Cahill's testimony by questioning his memory: how had he failed to hear the word on which all other witnesses were agreed? Also, as Liston had not mentioned the Black and Tans by name, how had Cahill known who these 'murderers' were? 'I inferred that was what he meant.' Stringer quickly came to Cahill's aid: 'You knew three priests had been killed by the Black and Tans, and you took the reference to apply to them?' 'Yes.' Meredith would not be put off this time.

Q: Would you consider 'foreign murderers' a fair reference to British troops?
A: I know the Bishop so well that I could not conceive he would so refer to the regulars. When I heard that expression I deemed he was referring to the Black and Tans.
Q: Would you say it was an accurate description of them?
A: I don't care to express my opinion on that.[14]

The next defence witness had impressive credentials: lawyer, Anglican, and president of the Auckland branch of the Irish Self-Determination League – Alfred Hall Skelton was all of these at once. Several newspapers had reported his recent adventures in Paris as one of New Zealand's representatives at the Irish Race Convention (the story of his heroic stand for the Irish Free State against de Valera's Republic lost nothing in the telling).[15] As his evidence unfolded, it became clear that he was concerned not with Liston's Town Hall speech, but with one he had delivered there himself on the Irish question some seven months earlier. A worried Bishop Liston had subsequently quizzed him about his future lectures, and Hall Skelton was busily describing this exchange when Meredith objected.[16]

O'Regan had expected trouble over Hall Skelton's evidence, but felt it worth a fight to show the bishop's views on the divisive Irish issue in a New Zealand context. While conceding there were different opinions on the question of admissibility, O'Regan claimed that the weight of the authorities was in his favour. He cited *R.* v. *Hardy* (1886) and *R.* v. *Horne Tooke* (1794) as sedition cases in which writings by the accused from years before were admitted as evidence. Surely, he contended, for someone charged with sedition any evidence was relevant that revealed that person's ordinary views upon the very issue on which he was charged; it was an anomaly to the usual rule.[17] Affecting surprise at this argument, Meredith insisted that, even apart from the time factor – a person might completely change his views in seven months – the evidence had to be connected in some way with the action alleged against the accused.

Stringer: Mr O'Regan says they are connected in that they are views on the matters dealt with in the speech.
Meredith: There can be no connection between the speech and a discussion on Irish questions seven months before.
Stringer: The question of date does not seem important. Supposing the statements had been made three days before the speech, would not they be relevant?
Meredith: It is an extremely dangerous class of evidence to admit unless the statements have direct reference to the particular speech.[18]

O'Regan then quoted a passage from Powell on *Evidence* regarding the relaxation of the rules permitted in this particular type of case. Perhaps swayed by the defence counsel's persistence, and despite 'very serious doubts' about its admissibility, Stringer agreed to allow the evidence. An increasingly resigned Crown prosecutor insisted that his objection be noted.[19]

Hall Skelton then told the court how he had reassured Liston by promising to cite only the writings of Protestant historians and to avoid any friction 'other than that ignorant people might cause'. Eager to prevent dissension arising between different sections of the community, the bishop had warned him to be careful 'owing to the want of knowledge of the people of New Zealand of Irish history and Irish grievances'.

Hall Skelton did well under cross-examination. He reminded Meredith that both Protestant and Catholic delegates had attended the Irish Convention in Paris. There had been no trouble over his Town Hall speech. Liston's summons to him was cleverly explained away.

> Q: You rather got into hot water yourself over that speech?
> A: I do not think so.
> Q: Was there not some unfavourable comment?
> A: No. Who by? I thought the PPA might say something, but the speech did not cause any trouble among the people of the town.
> Q: Anyhow the Bishop sent for you because he thought you were getting over the edge?
> A: No. He thought I was Irish and that I might say something that would not be wise.
> Q: He advised you to be careful?
> A: He told me to be very careful of what I said, as the Irish were only a small section of the people of New Zealand, and to have regard to the ignorance of the people of New Zealand on the Irish question.[20]

The last defence witness was James Joseph O'Brien, an Auckland timber merchant whom O'Regan described as 'a very much respected business man'.[21] He had neither heard the speech nor attended the concert, but had come along to give the bishop a character reference. He knew from personal contact that Liston was loyal to the Empire – 'as loyal as I am, and I yield in loyalty to no other citizen in the country'. O'Brien also described Liston as a strong supporter of the treaty, in common with the rest of the Catholic hierarchy. While the judge had again over-ruled Meredith's objection to O'Brien's testimony, he now informed O'Regan that his witness was not permitted to deliver a eulogy on bishops generally. 'That is beyond all limits', Stringer declared, before solving the problem in his own way.

O'Regan on his feet. NZO

Stringer: From your conversation with the Bishop do you think from the views he expressed that he would be likely to give utterance to seditious opinions?
O'Brien: No.
Stringer: Very well, you are entitled to say that.
O'Brien: I would just like to mention . . .
Stringer: I am afraid we cannot hear a witness make voluntary statements, Mr O'Brien.[22]

All present now had to listen to O'Regan for one hour and twenty minutes (he would have spoken longer but for the sudden illness of a juryman, perhaps overcome by the stifling atmosphere in the crowded courtroom).[23] O'Regan felt that he was listened to 'with great attention' throughout his address. He began with some general observations on sedition law. By its very nature difficult to define, sedition hinged on the question of intent: what were the bishop's intentions when speaking on St Patrick's Night? The jury could divine this both from the language he had used and from the evidence presented in court. The consequences of the utterances and the circumstances surrounding the use of the words had also to be considered.[24]

The jury might not share Liston's views, but this was not necessary. Providing he refrained from using improper language or from advocating violence, every man was entitled to his own opinion on public questions and even to persuade others to share it. O'Regan repeated his warning against pre-judgement based on the 'coarse and unnecessary criticism' by press and local bodies. 'Needless to say, religious bigotry has taken full advantage of its opportunity', he added caustically. The evidence presented during the trial was cause enough to alter any hasty opinion the jurors might have already formed. He asked for nothing but fair play for the accused, 'even though he happened to be a Bishop'. O'Regan recapitulated the reasons for Liston's silence in the face of the public outcry – 'whereat, no doubt, his Worship the Mayor, like Pilate of old, has wondered exceedingly'. He charged Gunson with disregarding every principle of fairness:

> Had he really desired to hear the Bishop, he could have anticipated the post by sending the letter on Saturday direct to his Lordship and making a statement in the press on Monday to the effect that he had asked the Bishop for an explanation and hoped the public would reserve judgement in the meantime. Such a course would have deprived many people of a great deal of prominence, but would have prevented the storm which has since arisen.[25]

O'Regan then attempted to demolish the Crown's case. Its witnesses had been so severely shaken in cross-examination as to persuade the jury that Liston had referred solely to the Black and Tans as 'murderers'. The twenty-two minutes of the bishop's speech left unreported by Stanbrook would surely explain and qualify the three minutes he had managed to write down. Even as it stood, unexplained by evidence, the speech did not bear the damaging inferences which the Crown sought to draw. O'Regan contended that Liston had simply told the truth about Ireland. The landlords who depopulated the country were literally the masters of the people; as most of them were absentees they deserved to be called 'foreign masters'. It was 'an indisputable historical fact – a deplorable fact – but one which belongs to the past'.

> You will remember, gentlemen, that he was speaking to an Irish audience on a subject on which the Irish heart feels deeply. It may be difficult for you who are not Irish to understand that feeling. Shakespeare says, 'He jests at scars, that never felt a wound.' I ask the jury, to put yourselves in our place – for I am proud to be of Irish extraction myself – and not only to make allowances, but to feel some sympathy for the sentiment of deep indignation with which they recall the evictions which

> drove such immense numbers of Irish people from their country and which accounts in no small measure for the abiding affection which many of their descendants still cherish for the land of their ancestors who suffered such cruel and inexcusable wrongs.[26]

So much for the arguments in favour of an outsider as defence counsel! The Dominion President of the Irish Self-Determination League was well equipped with the fact and fiction needed to explain Irish politics to his uncomprehending audience. The 'whole freedom' that Ireland was determined to have was simply a united parliament. (Did not the treaty provide for the ultimate inclusion of Ulster in the Irish Free State?) This hope was shared by the vast majority of the people of Ireland, O'Regan argued. Liston's commendation of de Valera was also well within the limits of free speech. While the bishop should have made it clear that he was referring to the government rather than to the people of England, his Irish audience well understood what he meant. To illustrate the necessity for vigilance against British political trickery, O'Regan gleefully cited Dr Addison, until recently Lloyd George's Cabinet colleague, denouncing the latter as 'a prevaricator and an expert in duplicity'.[27]

O'Regan chose his words carefully when speaking of those 'murdered by foreign troops': 'I concede at once that the indictment would be fully justified if the Bishop really spoke as the press reports him.' Having offered this sop to Liston's critics, O'Regan went onto the offensive: 'Here let me state that we cannot recede from our contention that the men and women included in that category were in fact murdered.' Anticipating Vincent Meredith's concentration on the phrase 'that glorious Easter', O'Regan reminded the jury that Liston had used it parenthetically. He then instructed his listeners on the meaning of Easter 1916:

> It has been well said by an English publicist that, though the rising occurred in Ireland, it was not an Irish rising. In other words, those connected with it were a small number of young men – Sir Philip Gibbs has described them as 'dreamers and patriots' – in the city of Dublin. Brave and courageous as they were, I concede that the British Government was bound to employ force to subdue them, and I freely admit it would be unjust to brand all the soldiers who opposed them as murderers.[28]

Rather than deal with the rising directly, O'Regan chose to adopt the historical method. He produced all his favourite moments like so many rabbits out of a hat, with the aim of showing how illegal acts in the past were frequently accounted glorious by posterity. He cited Milton's justification of the beheading of King Charles I, Monmouth's

A Republican cartoon shows Michael Collins forcing the Anglo–Irish Treaty on an unwilling people, backed up by the threat of renewed violence. NLI

rebellion, the anti-slavery crusade of John Brown, and the Eureka Stockade. 'The littoral of history is strewn with the wreck of such enterprises . . . Condemned by their contemporaries, such men soon pass into the martyrdom of a nation, and in the process of time they become almost deified.'

> It were idle for me to deny – and I do not pretend to deny that the people of Ireland, and indeed, the Irish race everywhere, hold in reverence the men who have fought and bled in the cause of nationality. Just as they revere the memory of Robert Emmet, who engaged in a forlorn hope, so they cherish the memories of the young men who died during Easter 1916. Emphatically, however, I must insist that no Irishman regards the soldiers employed against them as murderers. In quite a different category, however, do they regard the atrocities committed by the Black and Tans, and we claim the right freely to denounce them and to characterise them as the Bishop did.[29]

With tongue firmly in cheek, O'Regan recalled that among those most deeply involved in the Easter rising was Michael Collins, subsequently Commander-in-Chief of the IRA and now a Minister of the Crown in the Irish Free State government. O'Regan presented Collins as one who might in future help to reconcile the two nations: 'Indeed, I submit that it requires no effort of imagination, should Mr Collins ever visit New Zealand, to picture him dining at the Auckland Club in company with his Worship the Mayor and my friend, the Crown Prosecutor. (Laughter.)'[30]

O'Regan next called up two of his pet historical personalities in Liston's defence. Sir George Grey had repeatedly introduced a bill into the New Zealand Parliament to make the governorship an elective office: John Dunmore Lang, a Presbyterian minister and Australian politician, was a tireless advocate of an Australian republic:

> But no-one questioned the loyalty of Dr Lang, no charge of sedition was ever preferred against him, and no opponent ever suggested that his principles disqualified him from taking the oath of allegiance as a member of the Legislature . . . I recall this fact because in these days of reiterated protestations of loyalty I have no doubt that were one to propose an elective Governor or a republic for New Zealand, he would be accused by many, and not merely by religious sectaries, of sedition and disloyalty.[31]

Such political questions aroused the fiercest passions, O'Regan declared, warming to his theme. 'Hence it is that men who profess unpopular opinions or principles not properly understood are often exposed to unfair attack by opponents who make a cheap parade of loyalty to the established order of things by levelling lying accusations of disloyalty and sedition against brave and upright citizens. Thus it has been in every age and in every country.' (O'Regan's friends would surely have had no difficulty in recognising the Catholic lawyer in this description of a man persecuted for his principles.)[32]

> 'We have no king but Caesar,' shouted the Scribes and Pharisees of Jerusalem long ago, and again they said to Pilate, 'If thou release Him thou art not Caesar's friend.' Yet they hated Caesar and all that his government stood for. They affected loyalty to Caesar because they desired to have Him declared guilty whom they accused of stirring up sedition! There, gentlemen, we have the first historic instance of the use of malignant lip-loyalty to destroy the innocent, and history is replete with such cases.[33]

O'Regan lauded the jury system as the only real safeguard for those daring to speak their convictions in the teeth of unpopularity: 'It is revered among us as the corrective, not merely of popular tumult, but of regal tyranny and of official persecution in the name of law and order.'

> It is your high office, gentlemen, not alone to ensure the punishment of wrongdoers, but to protect the innocent and to preserve the liberty of fellow-citizens from unscrupulous enemies who, under a pretence of zeal for the Throne and Constitution, would destroy the liberty they affect to honour.
>
> Bearing all this in mind, it is your duty to resolve any doubt in favour of freedom of speech. I feel assured, however, that your deliberations

> will not reach the stage of weighing any doubt, because you can have no doubt. Having heard the Bishop's evidence, you must have been impressed by his frankness, his simplicity of manner, and his transparent truthfulness, and accordingly I appeal with confidence to you, gentlemen, to find a verdict of Not Guilty.[34]

Meredith had the unenviable task of following this barrage of argument and rhetoric. The morning session was all but over. Were he to reply at any length his address would be interrupted by the luncheon adjournment. He settled instead for brevity and directness, declaring at the outset that he would be making no historical references. (O'Regan later judged his half-hour speech to be 'clever and telling, not less so because it was brief'.)[35] Meredith began by yet again defining the crime of sedition for the long-suffering jurors, before making a brave attempt to rehabilitate his chief witness in their eyes.

Liston had characterised Stanbrook as an incapable reporter. Meredith preferred to accept the judgement of the *Herald*'s editor and sub-editor. Was not the *Auckland Star* management also prepared to reproduce his copy on such an important matter? Stanbrook, a skilled and practised journalist, was the only one who took an actual note of the speech and his version was supported by several Crown witnesses. Even the defence had objected to only two small elements of his report.[36] Given these facts, Meredith insisted, 'Stanbrook's evidence must be accepted. It must stand absolutely.'

Meredith saw Liston's silence as suggestive of guilt. Despite the nationwide outcry over the speech, no denial was made until the case came to court. Why had the bishop not repudiated the report at once? He may have been acting on legal advice in ignoring Mayor Gunson, but in writing to Massey he neither retracted nor explained any misreport: 'If he had done so there probably would have been none of these unpleasant proceedings.' Liston had prepared his speech in advance and had delivered it calmly; the jury was thus entitled to attribute full responsibility to him for every word spoken. The tone and spirit of the whole speech had also to be considered.

> It was just possible a man may in a chance expression say something he did not mean, but when you get the whole tone of the speech agreeing with some particular expression a man tries to explain away, then there was reason to believe that that phrase was not accidental.[37]

Hostility to England pervaded the entire address, Meredith maintained, citing the references to foreign masters, 'duped by England', the men and women prepared to die, 'that glorious Easter' and those 'murdered by foreign troops':

> The 'glorious Easter' was a reference to an armed rebellion against authority in Ireland during England's darkest hours of the Great War. Liston said he had referred to the bravery of young Irishmen facing certain death against odds that were overwhelming, but when pressed to state whether or not he approved that rebellion he claimed privilege not to answer. The inference was obvious, that he approved of the action of the rebels in endeavouring to set up a republic in Ireland.[38]

Meredith ended by examining the final, most wounding phrase. O'Regan had suggested that, because the bishop was not referrring to regular British troops, this was not a seditious utterance. However, Liston had merely altered a phrase from a document which did in fact refer to British troops. Even had he meant the Black and Tans alone, surely these were British men, properly enlisted in the Royal Irish Constabulary, who were merely doing their duty. Most of them had served in the Great War. 'He submitted that Liston had no right to use such a phrase to describe them. He might have discussed them heatedly and criticised them and their policy of reprisal, but the use of that phrase was beyond the privilege allowed by law.'[39]

When Liston spoke of men and women ready to fight and die that God's desires might be realised, he was referring to the present state of Ireland. Meredith urged the jury to consider these remarks in the light of his earlier glorification of Irish rebellion: 'Those plain words could have only one meaning – that there were in Ireland people prepared for armed violence to get what they wanted. No other construction could be given to the words.' With this final salvo, Vincent Meredith resumed his seat and the judge adjourned the proceedings for lunch. As the court dispersed, Liston walked across the room to thank the Crown prosecutor for his fairness in handling the case.[40]

Mr Justice Stringer began his summing-up at 2.20 p.m.[41] His announced intention was to assist towards a just verdict by pointing out to the jurors the various factors that should govern their decision. He urged them to rid their minds of preconceived views on the case. An atmosphere of hostility had developed towards the bishop because of publicity which might well have been avoided. If the mayor had simply awaited a reply to his query, then public feeling might not have arisen. He considered it 'almost equally unfortunate' that the bishop had refrained from comment, even after Gunson's protest was published. Stringer absolved Liston from blame as he had acted under legal advice, but an explanation 'showing that the mean-

Stringer and Irishman. NZFL

ing of vital passages had been altered by omissions in the report' would probabably have prevented proceedings from being initiated.

Stringer defined sedition as disloyalty in action, adding that the term was not applicable 'to foolish utterances on various subjects, political, religious, or racial'. The Crown had contended that Liston's words were calculated to stir up strife among the people and to set one class against another; the jury had to be convinced that the language used was intended to have that effect. Then there was the conflict of evidence over the speech, a large part of which had not been taken down. 'This was apt to be misleading', Stringer warned, as the speaker's full meaning could be lost. The lack of the complete shorthand note customary in such cases had also to be considered, even though both sides agreed that the report was fairly accurate.[42]

As Stringer began to analyse the report itself, it soon became clear that he had done some research on the Irish background. The first paragraph, whatever might be thought of its good taste, was not seditious in his view. It referred to events some forty or fifty years past. Liston had merely recalled the circumstances which brought his parents to New Zealand:

> There were in Ireland a great many evictions of farmers from their holdings by the landlords, most of whom were absentees, some English, some Irish. There could be no doubt these were historical facts, of which anybody could read for themselves. It seemed to him rather far-fetched to suggest that the mere mention of it to an audience mostly of Irishmen involved a seditious intention.[43]

The whole freedom desired by Irish men and women was political unity between north and south. 'That did not suggest they were going to bring it about by invading Ulster, but by using all legitimate means to induce Ulster to come in, forming a united party representing a united Irish nation.' Stringer felt that many Englishmen 'of the highest position' would agree with Liston on Ireland's centuries of oppression. While his praise of de Valera could have been expressed in terms slightly less offensive to English people, the fact remained that British and Irish politicians were striving to get the better of each other. 'There was nothing very wrong in suggesting that it was well to have a man who would be a strong critic of any bargain.'

Then came what the judge declared as 'the crucial part of the charge'. Liston had admitted praising the insurgents of Easter 1916, in what Stringer called 'an insane and wicked rebellion'. However, he added quickly, these 'so-called Irish rebellions' had to be considered in a different light from ordinary ones:

> There had been a great many rebellions in Ireland, and it was reasonable to suppose that Irishmen considered those who died in fruitless rebellions were entitled to respect, because they died not for themselves, but in the endeavour to free Ireland from what was considered oppression.[44]

Drawing the jury's attention to the St Patrick's Night concert programme, he singled out two of the songs performed by the Catholic school children. 'A Nation Once Again' and 'God Save Ireland' both revealed the degree of homage traditionally paid by the Irish to their patriot dead.[45] Seen in this light, the words at issue probably conveyed a different meaning to an audience of Irishmen than they would to a jury of Englishmen. Such songs revealed both the context of Liston's speech and the peculiar views of his Irish audience: 'For the children to be singing these hymns together would probably prove much more effective in stirring their feelings than the words of any single individual.' Clearly, the dead rebels were looked upon as martyrs by the Irish:

> That was borne out by what the bishop said. He admitted that the rebellion was foolish and fore-doomed to failure, yet the people who died in

> it were, in the eyes of the Irish people, and the Irish Catholics in particular, more or less patriots. That was the difference in the point of view from an Englishman.[46]

As it stood in the indictment, the sentence involving the list of Irish dead could be regarded as 'exceedingly provocative and calculated to cause disaffection and ill-will'. However, if the defence version was to be accepted, it put quite a different complexion on the matter. Stringer had made his choice: the Crown's evidence had not disproved Liston's definite testimony, 'and it seemed to him that the words were spoken as stated by the Bishop'.

> There was no doubt that these people killed by the Black and Tans were in law murdered. That was recognised by the British Government itself. It arose from the policy of reprisals which took place and afterwards had to receive a certain amount of sanction from the State itself.[47]

Stringer then quoted from a speech by Winston Churchill justifying these murders as retaliation for the killings of policemen and soldiers and referring to 'official reprisals' conducted under martial law. This proved that murders had been committed on both sides – 'that was freely admitted', added the judge. If the jury was to accept Liston's version of events,

> it was no more inciting to disaffection and strife than many speeches made in the British parliament drawing attention to the murders of Irishmen, nor if a gathering of Englishmen met to discuss the murder of policemen by Irishmen. That was a most important point to consider.[48]

Had the Crown proved that these words were used, or was Bishop Liston's version to be believed? They had the bishop's 'direct and positive' testimony, supported by those witnesses who remembered the enumerated categories he had given.

The jury had then to decide whether he had spoken with seditious intent. They were obliged to consider the occasion of the speech.

> It was St Patrick's Day. It was a gathering of Irishmen, and if a few Englishmen strayed in they would be very few. The speech was made to Irishmen, and if the jury were to look at these things in a fair, broad, and liberal spirit they must not criticise them too closely. They might think that some of the things would have been better left unsaid, that some were more provocative than they might be; they might think it far better in New Zealand, where Englishmen and Irishmen dwell together in amity, that the memory of these wrongs or supposed wrongs should fall into oblivion, and that it was unfortunate that such an address should be made.[49]

However, Stringer insisted, they must go much further than that before deciding that the bishop intended to stir up strife. Had not Liston 'breathed a word of peace' at the conclusion of his address by asking his audience to forgive? Then there was his impressive demeanour in the witness-box to be considered. Not long before the concert he had taken steps, 'so far as could be judged in good faith', to prevent others from using inflammatory language on the Irish issue. Despite this sympathetic summary, Stringer could not resist chiding Liston for his last words; instead of echoing the King's wise exhortation at the opening of the Northern Irish Parliament to 'forgive and forget', he had urged his people 'to remember and forgive'.[50]

After a final reminder that a bishop stood no better nor worse in the eyes of the law than any other person, the judge directed the jury to go and consider its verdict. His address had lasted almost an hour and left the defence with no room for complaint, while Meredith and his friends seemed to find it very disappointing. O'Regan was sure that the defence policy of 'no beg pardons' had assisted Stringer in summing up so strongly in Liston's favour.[51]

When the jury filed out at 3.15 p.m. the general expectation was for a long retirement. After barely half an hour a whisper ran around the courtroom that a verdict had been agreed upon. The Liston camp felt sure that this would mean acquittal, but had to wait for confirmation until the judge could be located. Stringer, equally confident of a lengthy break in proceedings, had retired to the bar of the Grand Hotel with his colleague A. L. Herdman for some mid-afternoon refreshment. There was a further delay of thirty minutes before the judge ascended the bench and Liston once more stepped into the dock.[52]

Registrar: Gentlemen of the jury, have you agreed upon your verdict?
Foreman: We have.
Registrar: How say you, gentlemen, do you find the prisoner guilty or not guilty?
Foreman: Not guilty.
Registrar: The prisoner is discharged.
Foreman: Your Honour, we desire to present a rider to our verdict. We consider that Dr Liston was guilty of a grave indiscretion in using words capable of an interpretation so calculated as to give offence to a large number of the public of New Zealand, and we hold that he must bear the responsibility, in part at least, for the unenviable notoriety that has followed his utterance.
Stringer: Thank you, gentlemen. That is a very sensible rider.[53]

19

Verdict

> The trial has yielded some lessons to New Zealanders. It has shown the Papal hierarchs that they are not above the law of the State. It has given them warning to keep a watch upon their lips, and it has heartened Protestants to know that we have a Government which will not allow rabid Empire wreckers to carry on their vicious propaganda without restriction.
>
> *New Zealand Sentinel*, 1 June 1922

As the verdict was read out, the packed gallery burst into frantic applause and cheering. The registrar announced 'the prisoner is discharged' and Liston quickly left the dock. O'Regan tried vainly to stop the tumult by raising his hand. Once it had abated, Stringer solemnly declared that the courtroom was not a theatre and threatened to have the disturbers removed by the police. A huge crowd then gathered outside the Supreme Court hoping to catch a sight of the bishop, but Liston left by a side door and took a taxi back home. His two lawyers decided to wait inside for the multitude to disperse. When O'Regan was incautious enough to go out for a look, he barely escaped being 'hoisted' by 'the boys'.[1]

After emerging eventually, O'Regan and Conlan met several jurymen in the street. 'They readily owned that they were dry and we made for the nearest hotel.'[2] O'Regan learnt from them the details of what had transpired in the jury room. None of the twelve jurors had been in favour of a conviction. On first meeting they had all been surprised to discover not a single Catholic among their number. The rider was tacked on to the verdict in an effort to please a couple of them 'who had friends who were very unfriendly to the Bishop'.[3] As the bar of the National Hotel filled with noisy well-wishers, the lawyers moved on to St Benedict's presbytery. There they found another celebration in full swing; messages of congratulations were pouring in as rapidly as the champagne was poured out. O'Regan took his first sip for several years; he later put a disturbed night's sleep down to its effects, but the excitement of the previous two days was probably more to blame.

In keeping with its role throughout the affair, the Auckland press was first to pass judgement upon the verdict. The *Star* had predicted that an acquittal would not change public feeling about the bishop's speech. It modified this view only slightly when confronted with the trial evidence, gathering crumbs of comfort from the judge's impartiality and the jury's rider: 'In arriving at its verdict the jury must have been influenced by the able and broad-minded summing-up of his Honor.' Stringer had impressed most by commenting upon the tricky Irish question 'with knowledge and in a liberal spirit'. The *Star* believed that Liston and his friends had learnt their lesson: 'They will, we trust, manage to combine with their deep love for Ireland a better appreciation of what is due to their British citizenship and the community in which they live.'[4]

The *New Zealand Herald* was no more generous in its reaction, attributing the verdict largely to the judge's direction that sedition was not to be applied to foolish utterances. Editor Hackett also hugged the rider for consolation:

> The jury found Bishop Liston not guilty of sedition, but guilty of a grave indiscretion. As sedition is a legal offence, but indiscretion, even of a character offensive to the great majority of loyal citizens, is merely a social error, the bishop was acquitted, to face as a citizen the 'unenviable notoriety' – to quote the jury's rider – which has attached to his utterance. The community will take no exception to either the verdict or the rider.[5]

Though deeming it uncharitable to dwell upon Liston's 'grave indiscretion', the *Herald* could not resist firing a few parting salvoes: 'Even with the emphasis laid on words and phrases which Bishop Liston offers as furnishing the keys to his speech it must be said that portions of his address were an inexcusable affront to the loyalty of Auckland and the patriotism of New Zealand.' Hackett also challenged the implied criticism of Mayor Gunson contained in the jury's rider, insisting that Liston had got no more than he deserved: 'That his first folly entailed the unpleasant experience of a charge of sedition is due entirely to his own taciturnity.'

Despite these strictures, the *Herald* was not unwilling to see the hatchet buried. 'The incident is happily now over and the feeling it excited is best forgotten. For his indiscretion Bishop Liston has been severely punished, and no friend of public peace will desire to add to his embarrassment.' By urging the municipal authority to withdraw its bar on the hire of public facilities, the paper offered something more than soft words: 'Under the circumstances the City Council can scarcely avoid reconsidering its decision to refuse the use of the Town Hall and the Domain to certain organisations on conditions which may now appear to the public to be unnecessarily humiliating.'[6]

Newspapers outside Auckland expressed no great surprise or dissent at the verdict. The Christchurch *Star* felt that it would be welcomed by all 'who do not allow their reason to be ruled by their prejudices'.[7] Several editors even found cause to cheer. The *Evening Post* saw the result as 'redounding to the credit of the administration of justice in this country'.[8] Liston should count himself fortunate to have been the recipient of 'British justice by a British jury', opined the *Dannevirke Evening News*.[9] Dunedin's *Evening Star* believed that the twelve good men and true had done well enough to silence the rumblings of discontent heard over the results of recent jury trials: 'Decisions have been in the last twelve months which have not raised the jury system in the public eyes; but the verdict given on this occasion . . . precisely meets the public needs of the case.'[10]

Much of this press satisfaction stemmed from the sting in the verdict's tail. Several editors overstated the strength of the rider, ignoring its careful balance of blame. According to the *Northern Advocate*, it did credit to the common sense and fair mindedness of its framers, with Stringer's endorsement redoubling its worth.[11] While some press commentators felt that there was little more to be said, others chose to analyse the trial. The *New Zealand Times* gave a consistently upbeat assessment of proceedings: conducted without fear or favour, the prosecution searching, the defence vigorous, both lawyers avoiding the temptation to indulge in patriotic declamation; Stringer had summed up with exhaustive impartiality, while the jury pondered hard on its verdict.[12]

For the *Times*, the trial had disentangled the web of words woven by Liston and put all his contentious phrases into their proper perspective. He had used 'a commonplace of discussion' when complaining of his parents' treatment; likewise his reference to the Easter rebellion was a matter of feeling, not of sedition – 'a view of the unfortunate episode of 1916 now universally accepted' – while the term 'foreign murderers' applied only to the Black and Tans.[13] O'Regan's part in the proceedings weighed little with the *New Zealand Times*. Rather, Liston's own explanation, supported by competent witnesses, had provided the jury with a compelling alternative to the Crown's case. Even the unsympathetic *Evening Post* agreed that the defence had won this crucial point; those murders attributed to 'foreign troops' were of Irishmen killed during 1920–21 'The distinction is, of course, absolutely vital', the *Post* conceded.[14]

There was general relief at the way the case had been conducted. Stringer's 'just and judicial' performance came in for special praise from the *Southland Daily News*. He had kept a fair balance between two sides moved by strong emotions, thus defusing a potential sectarian explosion: 'His entire attitude was exemplary and discouraged in every way the feeling that a Catholic Bishop was on trial for an offence that involved religious bigotry.'[15] A change of venue from Auckland might have been in order, were not most major centres similarly affected. The *Evening Post* had feared that passion and prejudice, running amok in the jury-box, could have resulted in a miscarriage of justice.

> That, in circumstances of exceptional difficulty, British justice has once more shown itself to be as prompt, as impartial, and, we may even say, as generous in this country as in the land of its origin, must be attributed to the jury's subordination of patriotic prejudice to common sense and fair-play, and to the admirable guidance which they received from the Judge.[16]

Indeed, the *Post* seemed to think that Stringer had been slightly more than fair to the bishop, noting what it called 'his readiness to mitigate the harshness of the rules of evidence where they threatened to operate adversely to the accused'. By allowing Hall Skelton's testimony, despite his serious doubts about its admissibility, Stringer had gone beyond the strict interpretation of the law. However, the *Post* was willing to be equally generous in its own judgement: 'But on this and other points the public is glad to see that the ruling, where there was room for doubt, was against exclusion, and in favour of the accused.'[17]

Had Liston ever been in danger? The Dunedin *Evening Star* believed so, stressing the time taken by the jury to reach a verdict.[18] Others were unhappy that the case had come to trial at all. The government had turned 'a mole hill into a mountain' from the very beginning, said the *Balclutha Free Press*. Although the *Herald* reporter had adopted a superior tone in defence of his version of events – 'as befitted a member of the "Fourth Estate"' – the case rested on the flimsiest evidence of seditious intent and a clearly inadequate summary of the bishop's speech.[19]

It remained for the press only to apportion blame for the affair, previously laid almost entirely at Liston's door. The rider encouraged some critics further to censure him for both his speech and his subsequent silence. Indeed, the delayed explanation was now seen as the main cause of the proceedings. The *Dominion* maintained that Liston's failure to withdraw his offensive remarks fully justified the government's decision to prosecute, while the *Evening Star* sarcastically regretted that Liston had not acted on his initial indignation at being 'grossly misrepresented'.

> It was a pity, for his own sake, that he did not point out the misrepresentations of which he has since complained, either immediately following publication of the report or in his later letter to the Government. The advice which caused him not to take that course must have been as unwisely given as his own counsel to his compatriots, when he bade them put their faith in Mr De Valera as the protector of Ireland.[21]

Once again the *New Zealand Times* found excuses for the beleaguered bishop, claiming that he would have given a 'spontaneous explanation' but for the threat of legal action contained in Gunson's public statement: 'Realising that he had been unfortunate enough in his address to cause misunderstanding, he was about to publish an explanation to make his attitude clear.' The *Times* saw Liston's letter to Massey as a selfless act, designed to clear the Catholic name of any imputation of disloyalty to King and country. 'By this publication he arrested the progress of public judgement, impelled by the misunderstanding of his address, which was becoming more hostile to his people.'[22]

Other papers gave some ground on this point. Gunson's prompt rebuke and the criticism that followed had 'complicated' matters, conceded the *Evening Post*.[23] While admitting Gunson's error of judgement, the *Auckland Star* felt that Liston was 'much more to blame' in not at once publishing 'what he has since claimed was the correct version of his remarks'. He had not behaved like an innocent man.[24] Had Liston's right to free speech been infringed? The *Carterton Daily News* rejected the very idea: 'In all British communities free speech is enjoyed to the fullest extent compatible with order and good citizenship.' It read a lesson in the bitter sectarian strife which scarred the Australian Commonwealth: 'It should be the aim of everyone to most carefully avoid in this country anything likely to create even a faint approach to the conditions prevailing in another part of the Empire through the fomenting of combined political and sectarian differences.'[25]

Liston's real offence, according to the *Wairarapa Age*, was in 'counselling his hearers to remember the wrongs of Ireland when most wise men were counselling them to forget'. Peace in Ireland and in New Zealand could be ensured only by tolerance and good will.[26] The Christchurch *Press* also condemned any attempt to keep the Irish question alive in New Zealand: 'We say 'from any quarter' because there are people who have shown themselves disposed to stir up trouble from a standpoint the opposite of that of Dr Liston.'[27] Its city rival, the *Sun*, lamented that the treaty had not sufficed 'to put a stop to the defamatory tirades of Irish colonials'.[28] Only the *Lyttelton Times* was willing to admit that Liston had told some painful truths.

> To an extent, however, while we completely deplore the references to murders of Irish people by 'foreign' troops, we cannot deny the truth of part of the reverend doctor's remarks. Irish people were driven from Ireland by British misrule, and the reprisals sanctioned by the British Government and executed by the 'Black and Tans' are not inaptly or recklessly described by the word 'murder'.[29]

What other lessons could be learnt from the case? The *New Zealand Times* suggested a rather prosaic one: if speakers on sensitive topics were to hand copies of their text to the press it would 'supply a written check to the impetuosity of strong feeling'.[30] The Christchurch *Sun* felt that Liston's experience would be instructive for 'those Irishmen who are forever trailing their coats in this community'. Perhaps they would now 'realise that Mannix outbursts will not be tolerated in New Zealand'.[31]

Few doubts were raised about the value of the trial. The *New Zealand Times* thought it better for the sake of public order and amity to have the whole matter thrashed out. How otherwise could the cloud over Liston have been so completely dispelled? 'For the rest, the outcome of the case is happy. Dr Liston has had a public opportunity of declaring his complete lack of seditious intent and his loyalty to the Crown and Empire, and New Zealanders of every shade of opinion will congratulate him on having done so.'[32] The *Southland Daily News* was more impressed by the protests of loyal Catholics than by anything Liston had to say:

> The Liston incident may be considered closed, with little honour to the Bishop, but with no discredit to his co-religionists. They have disavowed

> responsibility for such gratuitous remarks as were contained in the speech, and, if his own explanations have failed to extenuate his offence against good taste, it is significant that the sharpest criticism comes from within his own camp.[33]

The *Otago Daily Times* had good local reason to welcome Liston's loyal effusions in court and in the press. With one cold eye on the *New Zealand Tablet*, it noted that 'there are representatives of his Church in New Zealand who speak and write in flagrantly disloyal terms, and it is gratifying to know that Bishop Liston dissociates himself from them and protests that he yields to no one in his loyalty to the Crown'.[34] Well might James Kelly have preferred to see Liston behind bars than giving such lethal ammunition to his bitter foe! Kelly devoted an entire issue of the *New Zealand Tablet* to the case.[35] It was his final answer to the enemies of faith and fatherland: Orangemen, local body politicians, press editors, and so-called 'prominent Catholics.' 'Here was a chance of showing what they could do in the way of a real, true-blue No Popery stunt and at it they went ventre-à-terre, pitching common sense, charity, justice, and similar considerations to the winds.'

Kelly wanted to see the real sedition-mongers in the dock. Had not Massey publicly praised 'the rebel Carson who plotted with the Kaiser', while the Mayor of Auckland had allowed the PPA to peddle its poison from the Town Hall stage for five years. 'Mr Gunson, Mr Massey, the Council of Churches and Mr North did not denounce treason in their friends when it was real treason and real rebellion. All this shows the utter hypocrisy of such people, who are just as contemptible as our daily papers.' Kelly found it 'almost pitiful' to read the newspapers after the verdict: 'They fall back on the jury's rider and ride it to death.'

> And the truth is that it was the Mayor of Auckland, and the wild parsons, and the headstrong editors, from Auckland to the Bluff, who left no stone unturned to cause bitterness and ill-feeling, who did not make such inquiries as ordinary prudence would suggest, who acted in the matter from first to last like a group of Bedlamites.[36]

If the authorities were sincere, Kelly continued, why had no action been taken against the PPA for stirring up ill feeling between classes during the war? Why was a PPA paper allowed to warn its readers that Catholic soldiers might stab their comrades in the back?[37] Had not Massey caused bitter feelings when he raised a professed bigot, William Nosworthy, to Cabinet rank?

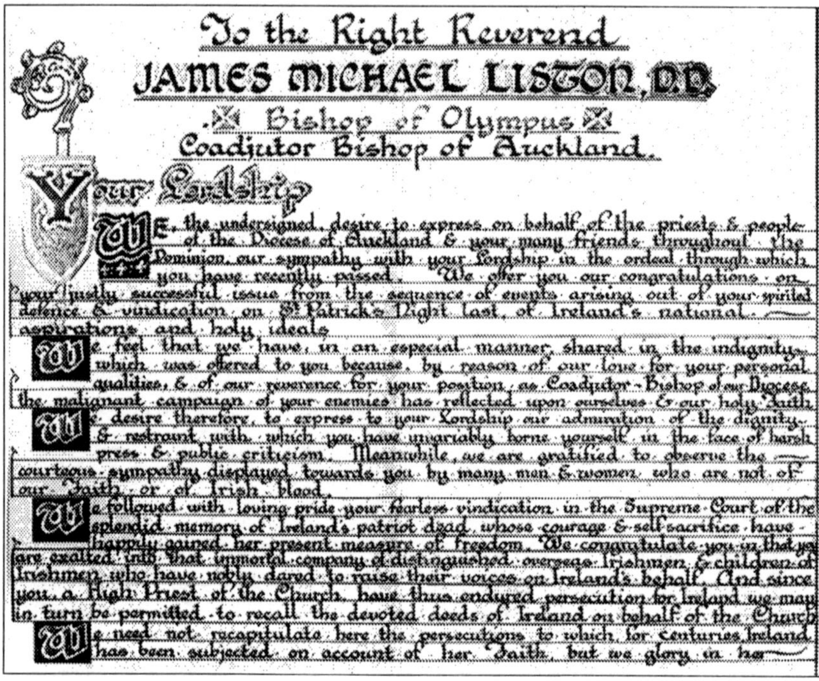
To the Right Reverend
JAMES MICHAEL LISTON, D.D.
Bishop of Olympus
Coadjutor Bishop of Auckland.

Your Lordship

We, the undersigned, desire to express on behalf of the priests & people of the Diocese of Auckland & your many friends throughout the Dominion, our sympathy with your Lordship in the ordeal through which you have recently passed. We offer you our congratulations on your justly successful issue from the sequence of events arising out of your spirited defence & vindication on St Patrick's Night last, of Ireland's national aspirations and holy ideals.

We feel that we have, in an especial manner, shared in the indignity which was offered to you because, by reason of our love for your personal qualities, & of our reverence for your position as Coadjutor-Bishop of our Diocese, the malignant campaign of your enemies has reflected upon ourselves & our holy Faith.

We desire therefore, to express to your Lordship our admiration of the dignity & restraint with which you have invariably borne yourself in the face of harsh press & public criticism. Meanwhile, we are gratified to observe the courteous sympathy displayed towards you by many men & women who are not of our Faith or of Irish blood.

We followed with loving pride your fearless vindication in the Supreme Court of the splendid memory of Ireland's patriot dead, whose courage & self sacrifice have happily gained her present measure of freedom. We congratulate you in that you are exalted into that immortal company of distinguished overseas Irishmen & children of Irishmen who have nobly dared to raise their voices on Ireland's behalf. And since you, a High Priest of the Church, have thus endured persecution for Ireland we may in turn be permitted to recall the devoted deeds of Ireland on behalf of the Church.

We need not recapitulate here the persecutions to which for centuries Ireland has been subjected on account of her Faith, but we glory in her

This page and opposite: testimonial to Liston. ACDA

In his editorial, entitled 'Much Ado About Nothing', Kelly did not analyse the trial too closely; it had been an ordeal for Liston, but 'he has now the consolation of seeing his enemies, and the enemies of every Catholic among us, defeated and their attack on him converted into a triumph in which we all participate'. Gunson had been repaid for his impudence by an episcopal snub and a magisterial rebuke: 'He only requires a small amount of self-respect to inspire him to resign from the Mayoralty of Auckland.' In Kelly's view, he and his abetters were the only guilty ones: 'If they are not ashamed and discomfited now it is because they are incapable of seeing how foolish they were and too thick-skinned to feel their disgrace.'[38]

Kelly had already written to praise O'Regan for his brilliant advocacy: 'I must congratulate you on your great victory and no less on your able and fearless conduct of the case. There were current comments on the desirable change of tone after your arrival on the scene of action.'[39] He also gave the lawyer credit for Liston's dignified performance in the box. Kelly's views were reproduced in the correspondence columns of the Dunedin *Evening Star* (albeit under his friend John Robinson's name). Robinson ridiculed the press for 'lashing itself into a fury' over the case: 'If there was no strife among

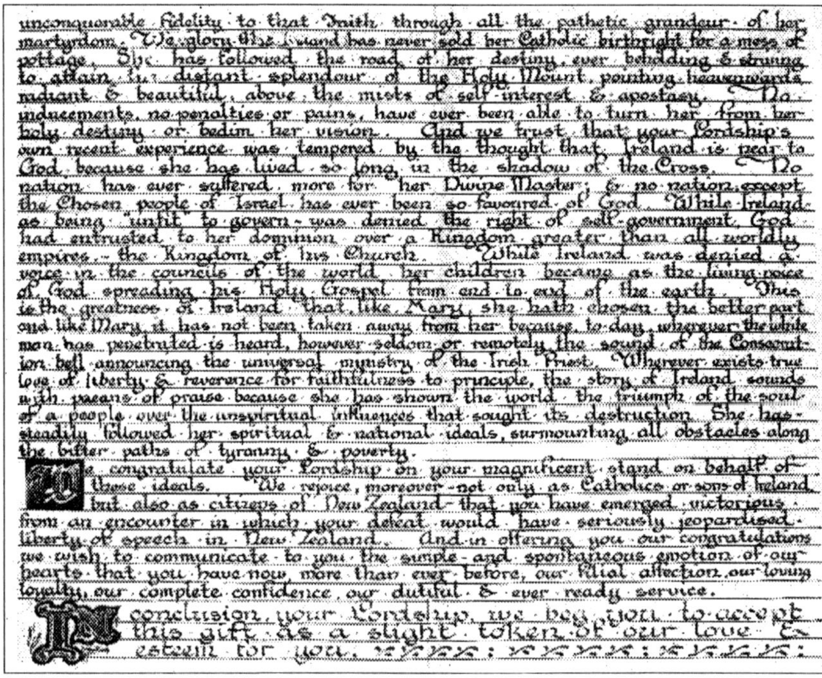

unconquerable fidelity to that Faith through all the pathetic grandeur of her martyrdom. We glory that Ireland has never sold her Catholic birthright for a mess of pottage. She has followed the road of her destiny, ever beholding & striving to attain the distant splendour of the Holy Mount, pointing heavenwards radiant & beautiful, above the mists of self-interest & apostasy. No inducements, no penalties or pains, have ever been able to turn her from her holy destiny or bedim her vision. And we trust that your Lordship's own recent experience was tempered by the thought that Ireland is near to God because she has lived so long in the shadow of the Cross. No nation has ever suffered more for her Divine Master; & no nation except the Chosen people of Israel has ever been so favoured of God. While Ireland as being "unfit" to govern – was denied the right of self-government, God had entrusted to her dominion over a Kingdom greater than all worldly empires – the Kingdom of his Church. While Ireland was denied a voice in the councils of the world her children became as the living voice of God spreading his Holy Gospel from end to end of the earth. This is the greatness of Ireland that, like Mary, she hath chosen the better part and like Mary it has not been taken away from her because, to-day, wherever the white man has penetrated is heard, however seldom or remotely the sound of the Consecration bell announcing the universal ministry of the Irish Priest. Wherever exists true love of liberty & reverence for faithfulness to principle, the story of Ireland sounds with paeans of praise because she has shown the world the triumph of the soul of a people over the unspiritual influences that sought its destruction. She has steadily followed her spiritual & national ideals, surmounting all obstacles along the bitter paths of tyranny & poverty.

We congratulate your Lordship on your magnificent stand on behalf of these ideals. We rejoice, moreover – not only as Catholics or sons of Ireland but also as citizens of New Zealand – that you have emerged victorious from an encounter in which your defeat would have seriously jeopardised liberty of speech in New Zealand. And in offering you our congratulations we wish to communicate to you the simple and spontaneous emotion of our hearts that you have now, more than ever before, our filial affection, our loving loyalty, our complete confidence, our dutiful & ever ready service.

In conclusion, your Lordship, we beg you to accept this gift as a slight token of our love & esteem for you.

the people over the matter it was certainly not the fault of the newspapers, for they spared no pains to sow the seeds of hatred and intolerance throughout the country.'[40]

Back in Auckland, Liston's mailbox was bulging with congratulatory messages on what Mary McKeefry (mother of a future archbishop) described as 'your victory over bigotry'.[41] Liston's view of the whole affair is revealed in his handwritten draft of the testimonial presented to him shortly after the trial.[42] He had, at least in his own mind, 'endured persecution for Ireland'. His Town Hall speech was a 'spirited defence and vindication of Ireland's national aspirations and holy ideals'. Auckland Catholics were deemed to have shared in the indignity offered to him: 'The malignant campaign of your enemies has reflected upon ourselves and our holy Faith.' The testimonial expressed admiration for the 'dignity and restraint with which you have invariably borne yourself in the face of harsh press and public criticism'.

> We followed with loving pride your fearless vindication in the Supreme Court of the splendid memory of Ireland's patriot dead, whose courage and self-sacrifice have happily gained her present measure of freedom. We congratulate you in that you are exalted into that immortal company of distin-

> guished overseas Irishmen and children of Ireland who have nobly dared to raise their voices on Ireland's behalf.[43]

Liston also received a more tangible expression of his flock's devotion in the form of a huge cheque.[44] To twist the knife, application was made to the Auckland City Council to use the Town Hall for the presentation ceremony. The belligerent wording of the testimonial reflected the mood in the Liston camp. Someone was going to pay for the embarrassment and humiliation he had suffered; hunted would now become hunter.[45] Liston was at first prepared to let Gunson off lightly. He sent the mayor a private note which was intended to lay the ground for a public reconciliation: after Gunson had responded in similarly soothing terms, he hoped, the city council would then expunge its hostile resolutions.

> Now that my fellow-citizens of Auckland are fully acquainted with all the facts of the case I desire to say to Your Worship that so far as I am concerned the incident is closed. I beg to express the hope that all of us may, even though we look at many questions from different angles, learn to respect the views of one another and live together in peace and amity. The country that we all love and the City that is so dear to us are big enough for all of us and worth the best we can give them. May they both prosper and be the better for our having passed this way.[46]

Gunson would have none of this. In his stand against the speech he had acted as Auckland's chief citizen with the solid backing of his council. Liston had snubbed them both by keeping a disloyal silence, for which he had received a deserved rebuke from judge and jury. Now, the very people behind the St Patrick's Night concert were planning once more to invade the Town Hall to praise their leader and pay his defence costs. Gunson's answer was to insist that Liston not only deny the accuracy of the press report on which the council had acted, but also add 'an expression of loyalty to the King and Empire'.[47] In the absence of such assurances, the Town Hall would not be available for hire. Liston's fury at receiving this demand is evident in the memorandum he immediately wrote on the incident:

> I thought the Mayor's objections absolutely puerile, if not insulting. I told Conlan to let the Mayor know that he could hang himself if he had a mind to do so – that I had been generous and could and would do no more – that it was up to him (the Mayor) to do now what he should have done immediately after the verdict, viz. apologise to the Bishop.[48]

The next few weeks saw an exchange of increasingly angry letters. Liston maintained that, as the mayor and council had condemned him on the strength of a newspaper report, so could they absolve him. Gunson presented the rider as justifying the council's action, but was prepared to compromise as long as the proposed Town Hall presentation was called off. Liston then shifted his focus to the Council's condemnatory resolutions of 23 March: 'You accused me of a grave crime. The jury acquitted me. Yet up to the present you preserve the record of your accusation in the Council's books. Is this fair play?'[49] He concluded this letter with a barely veiled threat of legal action, writing soon afterwards to Bishop Whyte:

> I am having a very happy time since my return toasting Gunson by letters . . . He evidently sees that he is in a corner and wants to get out – at my expense. So I have given him a dirty right and an uppercut in the shape of two letters, which you will see later on in the *Month*. Our people have applied for the Town Hall in order to have a demonstration for this criminal – but so far the request has been denied. That can't continue. I am pressing Gunson hard, first to grant the Hall unconditionally and secondly to expunge the famous City Council resolutions.[50]

His fun was ended on 3 July when Gunson closed the correspondence, citing the threat of proceedings and Liston's alleged determination to settle the matter entirely on his own terms. The bishop was now forced to act through intermediaries. On 27 July Tom Bloodworth's motion to have the offensive resolutions rescinded found no support among his fellow city councillors. Liston again gave Whyte the gossip: 'The Mayor had rounded up Councillors, threatened to resign etc, and squared the papers.' There now seemed to be no alternative to legal action: 'Our people are savage with Gunson, who has really proved a bungler.'[51] When Liston attempted to interest O'Regan in a resumption of the conflict, the Wellington lawyer warned his erstwhile client how fickle juries could be in libel cases: 'I can only hope you will again be fortunate enough to have the case tried before Mr Justice Stringer.'[52]

The next few months were occupied with lengthy legal manoeuvres which exasperated Liston almost to breaking-point. 'The lawyers seem to spend much time in sending polite notes to each other', he complained to Whyte.[53] Did this frustration induce him to accept the services of T. W. Leys as a go-between?[54] By late November a compromise had been painfully worked out; Liston sent Gunson a letter intended largely for public consumption, but containing no denials or declarations of loyalty; he merely withdrew the threat of legal proceedings and expressed his desire to do nothing to 'accentuate or re-open old differences'. The city council then passed a motion rescinding the resolutions of 23 March. There was no discussion, although Councillors Bennett, Knight and Paterson refused the bitter cup and registered their vigorous objection.[55]

Recalling the sectarian carnage of three years earlier, many observers rejoiced that the ghost of St Patrick's Night would not now be around to spook the electors in December. The *Observer* cartoonist had sketched the bishop trumpeting his disloyal sentiments to an expiring PPA, which rose from its deathbed on hearing the blast.[56] In fact, Howard Elliott was out of circulation for almost the entire period between speech and trial, undergoing two major operations for an eye abscess. The *New Zealand Sentinel* complained bitterly at the suggestion, allegedly spread by Catholics, that he was suffering from cancer of the tongue brought on by all the lies he had told.[57] For whatever reason, the PPA did not play much of a role in the Liston affair, although it claimed great credit for the case actually coming to trial. In mid-July Elliott boasted to a Napier audience that 'the people of New Zealand ought to be proud of having a Government with the backbone to prosecute a bishop for sedition. If there had been no PPA the Government would never have had the courage to do it.'[58]

Press predictions regarding the general election were to be only partly fulfilled. For at least some of those involved in the Liston case, the end of 1922 was a time for settling scores. Bishop Cleary would later criticise the *Month*'s 'party-political attitude' in the lead-up to the poll (despite the explicit instructions he had sent from Europe).[59] However, the journal made only two oblique attacks on the Reform Party and was infinitely more discreet than its southern counterpart; the *New Zealand Tablet* bluntly advised its readers to 'vote for Labour and to get all your friends and relations to do the same'.[60] Although Liston denied any direct responsibility for the *Month*'s editorial content, he would hardly have disagreed with the views expressed in the November issue:

> It is fitting to point out that the record of the present Government – including its passage of the Marriage Amendment Act – its educational legislation and administration – its attitude in regard to Bishop Liston – its general tendency to show anti-Catholic bias – is not calculated to inspire enthusiasm in Catholic voters who have any regard for the status of Catholics as citizens.[61]

While there was little open advocacy of the Labour cause, or even direct criticism of Massey and his party, considerable activity went on behind the scenes. Liston's private correspondence betrays his deep involvement in the drive to unseat Massey's government.[62] O'Regan, Liston and Kelly busily plotted the downfall of Reform candidates and their replacement by Labour men. Specific electorates were targeted, such as Gisborne, where the sitting Reform member, W. D. Lysnar, was described by O'Regan as 'a cloven-footed bigot'.[63] Liston set his clergy to work to get all the Gisborne Catholics on the electoral roll; Dean Lane assured him on 11 November, 'We will leave no stone unturned to get Lysnar out. If we could only succeed in getting an organised Catholic vote throughout New Zealand we would deliver a staggering blow to the Massey Government and his PPA supporters at the election.'[64] O'Regan also let Liston know how 'wise and expedient' it would be for him to support the Labour member for Auckland Central, W. E. Parry. He stressed the Labour Party's commitment to proportional representation, but showed an awareness of the principal motivation of his episcopal ally by adding that 'the main thing after all is to beat the Massey candidate'.[65]

Despite O'Regan's confidence that the electoral dice would go against Reform, Massey's government was returned by the narrowest of margins and Massey clung onto office with the support of three independent members.[66] However, the Labour Party doubled its representation in the House, coming back seventeen-strong. Kelly led the cheering in the *Tablet*. 'Labour has gained a great victory, securing nearly twice as many seats as it had before . . . The Labour gains are the more wonderful when we consider what money and the unscrupulous agents of money tried to do against the candidates.'[67] Liston wired in triumph to O'Regan, 'Sursum Corda' (Lift up your heart), receiving the immediate reply 'Dignum et Iustum Est' (It is right and fitting).[68] The bishop wrote more fully on 9 December:

> It's really a fine victory and I think our people may well claim a big share in it. I am immensely proud of the Auck[land] Catholics – they worked solidly for Labour and didn't need any coaxin' neither! Yesterday you could tell every Catholic in the streets by the smile they didn't attempt to hide. I am satisfied that 'Liston's Lapse'(!) and your own action and speech have created a new spirit amongst us . . . The Labour people here are very grateful for our strong support. They recognise the fact and I only hope they won't forget.[69]

The losses suffered by the PPA brought an especial joy: five of the nine candidates it had endorsed in Auckland were beaten; other major reverses occurred in Balclutha, Christchurch and Oamaru.[70] Before the poll, O'Regan had noted that the PPA was much less in evidence; afterwards, he described it as suffering a 'crushing rout'.[71]

An example of the PPA's propaganda from the 1919 election. NZ Truth

The PPA's decline can be explained partly by the removal of the Irish issue from New Zealand's political agenda. It was not mentioned during the election campaign, nor was there any reference to the Liston case. Labour spokesmen had earlier defended the bishop's right to free speech rather than the truth of his remarks about Ireland. With the elections in view, there was no point in drawing attention needlessly to Labour's dubious record on the loyalty issue.[72]

The major sectarian incident of the campaign came one week after the results had been announced: another controversial public speech by Bishop Liston. At a Catholic function, after gloating over Massey's reverses, he declared: 'Thanks be to God, the Labour people, our friends, are coming into their own – a fair share in the Government of the country.'[73] In a replay of events nine months earlier, the *New Zealand Herald* opened its columns to a flood of correspondence denouncing the bishop.[74] Strong complaint came from within the Labour camp itself; O'Regan heard directly from one Westport critic:

> Wish Bishop Liston would not put his spoke in as he appears to have done, it surely will cause trouble. Already we have a lot of people saying 'I told you so' and enquiring what sort of a bargain has been made between Labour and the Catholics, and it will be hard to persuade them that there is none.[75]

Truth's view of E. P. Lee. NZ Truth

What might be termed Liston's one victory whoop was not to go unpunished, but for the moment his vindication was complete. The sedition case had stiffened Catholic spines; perceived bigots (overt and covert) had been taught a lesson; the Mayor of Auckland and his council had eaten humble pie; Gunson was still out of Parliament while Labour strength there had doubled. There was jubilation in Catholic ranks at the downfall of E. P. Lee in the general election: the defeated member for Oamaru was identified as a bitter anti-Catholic and a vigorous apologist for the PPA. As Minister of Justice and acting Attorney-General he had played a part in the proceedings against Liston. Catholics were able to savour even sweeter revenge six months later. After a by-election was ordered for Oamaru in April 1923, Massey went south to help revive the career of his former colleague. The *New Zealand Free Lance* described how the Prime Minister 'worked almost his toe nails off' for Lee – all to no avail. Catholic delight at Lee's second reversal was sweetened by the belief that a block vote by the local Dominican nuns had tipped the electoral balance against him.[76]

20
Aftermath

Police may evoke the little-used sedition law to prosecute Maori activists who have threatened overseas investment in New Zealand. They are reviewing cases dating back to the First World War . . . The Prime Minister, Mr Bolger, accused the activists of advocating anarchy and declared: 'If they pursue it they will find themselves rapidly looking at the world from behind bars.'

New Zealand Herald, 12 May 1995

Six years after his triumphant acquittal, James Liston was obliged to relive the whole affair. By then Henry Cleary had completely changed his mind on his coadjutor's fitness to succeed him as Bishop of Auckland. The gulf between the two men had grown steadily since Cleary's return from Europe in mid-1923. While such disagreements were not unusual between an elderly incumbent and a youthful prelate-in-waiting, a major factor in Cleary's disenchantment was Liston's habit of making incautious political utterances.[1] In late 1928, Cleary resurrected the sedition case as part of a campaign to persuade Rome to replace Liston as his intended successor. He supplied the Cardinals of Propaganda Fide with a summary of events that James Gunson could easily have endorsed:

> [Liston] made what was admitted on all hands to have been a singularly ill-timed and indiscreet political public speech. (He is, by the way, a native of New Zealand, not of Ireland.) The most vehement parts of that speech were published throughout Australia, New Zealand, and the British Empire at large, and they created a great sensation and aroused much bitter feeling. As a result he was criminally prosecuted for sedition. Through the brilliancy of his lawyer and action with the jury, he narrowly escaped a verdict of

Cleary repudiates the 'political' bishops, including Liston, on his return to New Zealand in mid-1923. The Observer *contrasts this with his outspoken support for prohibition.*
NZO

'Guilty', and the jury added a rider to their acquittal condemning in strong terms the impropriety of the words on which the charge of sedition was based.[2]

That Cleary had taken an entirely different view of the matter six years earlier is shown by the account he had presented to the Vatican authorities then. Blaming a false report for the entire controversy, he declared: 'Monsignor Liston proved before the courts that his speech was lawful and true; thus all turned out well and without any harm to the church.'[3] In his formal refutation of Cleary's later allegations, Liston was also able to cite the supportive letters that his bishop had sent him from Europe. The passing years had not altered Liston's positive view of the case:

> The speech that I really made on St Patrick's Day was in point of fact a very mild affair and I am satisfied that the greatest surprise about the whole incident received by those who heard it was that any notice should have been taken of it.
>
> The outcry against me on the occasion was simply a plan to put Mr Gunson . . . into Parliament and to further the cause of the Reform Party,

> under Mr Massey, then in power and notoriously anti-Catholic. The passions of bigotry were deliberately inflamed.[4]

Nor had time softened Liston's wrath towards his Catholic critics: 'The few Catholics in Auckland who criticised me were and are of no standing whatever in Catholic social, business or intelligent [*sic*] circles. They have never done anything for the Church by word or deed. Indeed one felt that one must be right when these took the other view.' He fondly recalled the loyalty and affection shown him by bishops, priests and laity alike. 'The conviction of our people was and remains that the whole thing was an act of pure bigotry. The majority of our Catholic people [is] persuaded that the incident did us much-needed good by welding us together in the day of stress.'[5]

Appealed to by Rome for an objective assessment of the Auckland imbroglio, Bishop Brodie of Christchurch strongly supported Liston and attributed most of the trouble between the two men to Cleary's chronic ill health. His verdict on the sedition case was unambiguous: it was an unfortunate incident ('the outcome of hysterical bigotry') long since forgotten. Liston was now revered by Catholics and respected by non-Catholics, while 'his prosecutors admit the mistake in formulating the charge of sedition'. Brodie preferred to lay the blame elsewhere. 'Bishop Liston was made to suffer for the hero-worship won by other members of the Hierarchy of Australasia who had ventured into the political or semi-political sphere, and thereby gained for themselves fame and unbounded popularity.'[6]

This barb was aimed at Archbishop Mannix of Melbourne (and possibly also at Wellington's Francis Redwood) and referred particularly to his advocacy of advanced Irish nationalism. Brodie had begun his own episcopate by arguing with the Christchurch *Press* over the 1916 rising. Born of Irish parents and possessing a full share of Hibernian piety, he could still see the danger posed to Catholic interests by too close an association with Irish political extremism.[7] In mid-1920 he begged the rectors of two Irish seminaries to keep their young priests quiet on political issues when en route to New Zealand.

> While I yield to no-one in my love of Ireland and my advocacy of Ireland's just and legitimate claims, I have realised that the greatest and the real work of the priesthood is the work for our Holy Faith and for souls, and I do not consider it a sacrifice of our principles to use discretion in our utterances on such questions as . . . the situation in Ireland so that our standing as priests will not be endangered.[8]

The Catholic Church in New Zealand could not help but follow the rhythm of Irish politics. It was the child of an Irish mother, the farthest outpost of that 'Spiritual Empire' which accompanied the British flag throughout its nineteenth-century expansion. Shaped in an Irish mould, staffed by Irish men and women, it shared the axiomatic belief that Irish and Catholic concerns were inseparable. 'Ireland's cause is vitally connected with our Catholic interests', was James Kelly's constant refrain.[9]

The price of such fidelity had to be paid once separatism replaced constitutionalism as the dominant political force in Ireland. Where home rule had reconciled Irish national ambitions with imperial security, Sinn Fein posed loyalty to Ireland and the empire as alternatives.[10] The post-war drive for Irish self-determination completed the polarisation of colonial opinion on the issue. As violence in Ireland made distinctions between varieties of Irish nationalism increasingly irrelevant, the deep clerical involvement in the rise of Sinn Fein seemed to confirm suspicions of Catholic disloyalty to Britain.

However Catholic leaders chose to handle the increasingly thorny issue of Irish politics, their task was complicated by the dilemma of minority status in an overwhelmingly Protestant country. From 1917 Daniel Mannix and James Kelly presented an aggressive alternative to the conciliatory policies hitherto adopted in Australia and New Zealand. The Sinn Fein formula – no compromise, self-reliance, separatism – was offered as a solution to the problems faced by Catholics. Kelly went to war against the enemies of Catholicism and Ireland 'which is the same thing', he asserted.[11] By exploiting troubles over conscription and sectarianism, he hoped to awaken the Catholic community to a sense of its duty to Ireland and the church. He also demonstrated how what Liston called their 'sacred traditions of sorrow' could be enlisted to aid Ireland in her present difficulties. Kelly wrote of this obligation on Catholics in much the same terms as used by Massey when urging New Zealanders to do their duty by the British Empire.[12]

The move towards Sinn Fein followed a trend of opinion in expatriate Irish communities elsewhere. Kelly, however, brought an unreserved commitment to the new political credo, together with a personal bitterness that expressed itself in torrents of Anglophobia. In 1922 Liston suffered for Kelly's outrageous provocation; as several newspapers were quick to point out, his Town Hall speech read like a typical *Tablet* editorial. Bishop Cleary bluntly informed Rome: 'the antipathy stirred up by the *New Zealand Tablet* was the main reason for the proceedings against Monsignor Liston.'[13]

Liston's worst offence was his apparent refusal to accept the Anglo–Irish Treaty as a solution to the ancient quarrel between England and Ireland. In fact, the signing of the settlement had performed the miracle of uniting New Zealand public opinion on the Irish issue – they were all Free Staters now. Kelly even believed that the treaty would 'put an end to the bigotry that has been raging during the past five years'.[14] The *Tablet*'s belated publication of the Irish Declaration of Independence of 1916 was an empty gesture, barely concealing the editor's wholehearted acceptance of the compromise forged in London.[15]

While no New Zealand bishop was willing to follow Archbishop Mannix's republican line, Liston's regard for de Valera survived his court appearance. After the death of Arthur Griffith on 12 August 1922, the *Month* described the anti-Treatyites as 'gallant, chivalrous men'.[16] This admiration was tempered when news arrived ten days later of the assassination of Michael Collins; his killers were then denounced as rebels 'in the truest sense of the word'.[17] The outbreak of civil war in Ireland (June 1922 to May 1923) was deeply embarrassing to New Zealand Catholics, who had now to witness the heroes of the Irish revolution turn their guns upon each other. Liston deplored the 'open exultation' with which some of the daily press reported events in Ireland, but the violence of the civil war made the depredations of the Black and Tans seem almost minor by comparison.[18]

Bishops Cleary, Brodie and O'Shea had the added misfortune to experience the fratricidal conflict at close quarters. Indeed, Brodie was almost caught in the crossfire; he lost all his luggage when his Dublin hotel was destroyed during the fighting, later receiving compensation from the Free State Government.[19] Cleary kept Liston informed of the activities of 'de Valera's organised gangs of robbers and assassins', his contempt for the fallen leader accurately reflecting clerical opinion in Ireland.[20] Irish delegates no longer found a welcome in New Zealand. The approach of two republican emissaries in 1925 prompted Brodie to remark sharply: 'I leave the affairs of Ireland to the Irish in Ireland.'[21] When Archbishop Mannix paid his first-ever visit to New Zealand (for Francis Redwood's golden jubilee in 1924), he was surprised to find his host begging him to keep off the Irish issue in his public utterances.[22]

One wonders what might have occurred had Liston's day in court been delayed for a month or so. By the end of June two events had deeply affected public opinion. First came the IRA's assassination of Field Marshal Sir Henry Wilson, war hero and controversial Irish

The Free Lance*'s reaction to news of the assassination of Sir Henry Wilson.* NZFL

politician; six days later the Provisional Irish Government ordered an attack on the Four Courts, thus launching the Irish civil war.[23] The passions aroused by these events could easily have invaded the courtroom in the manner feared by some pressmen. If, in addition, O'Regan had failed to find the crucial Irish document from which Liston quoted, the jury might well have deemed his description of British troops to be a seditious utterance. Once convicted, the bishop faced possibly two years in jail. Would this have led to violent protests by an exasperated Catholic community? Such action had been threatened often enough during the past six years by the *New Zealand Tablet*, while at least one group of Auckland laymen offered to aid Liston in terms that suggested a willingness physically to defend his person.[24]

A more likely sequel to Liston's conviction would have been a split in Catholic ranks even wider than that revealed by the newspaper correspondence columns. Several prominent Catholic laymen in Melbourne had repudiated Archbishop Mannix because of his speeches on Ireland and the war. P. J. O'Regan was convinced that Liston had only narrowly escaped similar handling by 'Catholic jingoes'.[25] While Kelly was wont to dismiss the latter as social climbers whose material success had robbed them of true Catholic instincts, sadly for the *Tablet* editor there were almost certainly more loyal Catholics than disloyal ones.[26]

Although it passed Kelly's understanding, patriotic Irishmen could combine their love for Ireland with a due respect for the empire and its head. Father John O'Connell reconciled his attendance and fiery speech at the Irish Race Convention in Melbourne with an appearance on the Prince of Wales' platform in Wanganui.[27] The Catholic dilemma was well expressed by another Irish priest, Dean Harry Holbrook: 'We, Catholics, yield to none in the true spirit of loyalty to our King and country. But this PPA has raised a smoke-screen of spurious loyalty simply to try and get one on to the Catholic body.'[28] The note truly representative of New Zealand Catholicism was struck in Liston's public letter to Massey: loyal and patriotic – but to New Zealand, to the King, and only then, grudgingly, to the Empire.

In these years Irish Catholics found themselves increasingly the victims of a narrowing definition of loyalty. The frequent paeans to empire masked a British patriotism intolerant of any rival. 'British' New Zealanders would not allow the Irish to enjoy a similar dual allegiance, insisting that a loyal New Zealander had to be a loyal Briton. Nor, despite his colonial birth, were Liston's expressions of pride and love for New Zealand found acceptable. That such declarations rang hollow to many listeners is perhaps understandable in view of the tactics adopted by Mannix and Kelly. The former coupled his professions of loyalty to Australia with the charge that imperial apologists were indifferent to Australian interests, while Kelly touted 'New Zealand First' as 'a call that ought to be heard widely'.[29] He wanted the anthem sung in the classrooms to be 'God Defend New Zealand', and the New Zealand flag to be saluted by pupils rather than the Union Jack. (He drew the line at local control of the Catholic Church.)[30]

Despite this hostile climate, the Catholic community stood up briefly to be counted for Ireland, under Kelly's able generalship. Besides orchestrating an impressive number of resolutions and meetings, he despatched some £6000 to aid the Sinn Fein cause – no mean achievement.[31] The fighting mood of the Catholic body was reflected in the flood of letters sent to Liston after his speech, and in his lawyer's refusal to apologise for or withdraw the epithet 'murderers'. A white-hot fury was felt by New Zealand Catholics at press silence over the crimes of the Black and Tans. Why was it that only they could see blood seeping from under the Irish door? The arguments over the phrase 'that glorious Easter' revealed a gulf in perception between Catholics and their fellow-New Zealanders; though a tribute to Kelly's success in influencing his readers, this also indicated his failure to persuade the wider community of the legitimacy of Sinn Fein claims.

These rival traditions were never better illustrated than during the Easter of 1922, exactly half-way between Liston's speech and trial. On 24 April the Catholic community solemnly remembered those who had died in the Dublin rising six years earlier. The next day saw the seventh anniversary of the landings on Gallipoli, Anzac Day, the event that most New Zealanders regarded as truly 'glorious'. The country proceeded to indulge in an orgy of patriotism. What was previously a half-holiday had recently been made a 'holy day'. The Anzac Day Amendment Act, passed in January 1922, meant that 25 April would be observed as if it were a Sunday, with all shops, pubs and places of work and amusement closed for business.[32] In Auckland, some 2000 returned soldiers marched up Queen Street, pausing at the Cenotaph, where over 500 wreaths were laid, before packing out the Town Hall for a service of commemoration. This year also saw the first widespread sale of artificial poppies to raise funds for unemployed war veterans. The 43,000 flowers allotted to Auckland quickly sold out, the last ones reportedly fetching five shillings and more.[33]

The speeches and editorials on what Auckland's Anglican Archbishop called 'this sacred day' reveal a redemptive interpretation to match anything that James Kelly had to offer. 'The fields had taken unto their sacred embrace the bodies of the men who gave up their young lives that their Empire might live', declared the *New Zealand Herald*.[34] (Kelly described the 1916 rebels as 'brave men who gladly laid down their lives to regenerate Ireland'.)[35] Divine sanction was claimed for both causes, but whose side was the Almighty really on? While the *Tablet* mocked the British 'pretence of a God-given mission to lead the universe', Liston made explicit a claim frequently heard in Irish Catholic circles (but left unreported by the *New Zealand Herald*): 'Above all Ireland has been a builder of Empire, not for self, but for others; not for filthy lucre, but for God's cause, honour and freedom.'[36]

The champions of both sides also refused to concede that their heroes might legitimately be seen as 'murderers' by the victims of their excesses. In a vain attempt to rehabilitate the Black and Tans,

Adding insult to injury? The new Irish stamps symbolised the victory of Gael over Gall.

the *New Zealand Sentinel* once reminded its readers: 'They were the men who saved you from Germany. . . . Why believe ill of them?'[37] However, Kelly's complaints against the 'suborned hireling press' were not altogether groundless.[38] Offers of military and financial aid for Ulster unionist resistance made by New Zealand sympathisers in 1911 and 1922 were largely ignored by the newspapers. It is unlikely that such a discreet silence would have ensued had Liston or O'Regan made a similar offer to assist the IRA.[39] While Prince Edward thrilled his New Zealand audiences in 1920 by describing the country as 'unrepentantly British', Kelly was weekly listing the many good reasons for British penitence. The Prince's farewell message was unequivocal in its praise:

> New Zealand is one of the greatest monuments of British civilisation in the world, and I have felt, from end to end of the Dominion, that there is nowhere the British people are more set in British traditions or more true to British form. I have found the strength of your loyalty to the Empire and its Sovereign as keen and bracing as mountain air, and I hope that you will never weaken in your devotion to British unity and British ideals.[40]

In the flush of pride at New Zealand's war effort, it was suggested that an extra cross be added to the Union Jack. Yet this very symbol of empire was itself currently in danger of dismemberment. As

Archbishop Liston celebrates mass in 1954.
Zealandia

a result of the creation of the Irish Free State, the College of Heralds was considering removing the Cross of St Patrick from the Union Jack. The *New Zealand Herald* wondered whether this would mean also the abolition of the title 'United Kingdom' and the removal of the harp from the Royal Standard and Coat of Arms.[41] Another symbolic blow to imperial unity came with the news that several Irish regiments were being disbanded, including the Royal Irish Fusiliers and the Connaught Rangers. A final insult came in April 1922 with the appearance of the first Irish stamps, fifteen denominations of current British issues with the King's head heavily overprinted in black Gaelic characters.[42]

James Liston destroyed almost all his personal papers, perhaps sharing Daniel Mannix's desire to prevent posterity from attempting to analyse his soul. That he chose to keep every scrap of correspondence relating to the sedition case indicates how important the episode was in his life. On Liston's arrival in Auckland as a stranger in 1920, Bishop Cleary boasted of possessing the key to the hearts of his flock and offered to share it with his new coadjutor; two years later Liston earned the love and respect of Auckland Catholics all by himself.[43]

Liston cuts his jubilee cake. Zealandia

In December 1929, he became Auckland's seventh – and arguably its greatest – bishop. He would rule the diocese in imperious style for over forty years. When organising the Catholic centennial celebrations in 1938, he arranged for Eamon de Valera (Ireland's Prime Minister since 1932) to send a supportive message: 'Motherland is deeply proud.'[44] Ten years later, with de Valera briefly out of office, Liston hosted him royally on his visit to New Zealand.

In 1968 Liston showed his ability both to forgive and to forget by accepting the award of a CMG. Had he forgotten too completely? When suspending two priests for their opposition to the Vietnam war, there was no sign that he recalled his own stand against the tyranny of a great power over a small nation some forty-six years earlier.[45] Liston was also present in 1968 to celebrate the centenary of the Auckland Supreme Court, the scene of his humiliation and his triumph. Four years earlier, Prime Minister Keith Holyoake, Governor-General Sir Bernard Fergusson, and the Mayor of Auckland, Dove-Myer Robinson, had joined Liston for dinner in honour of the diamond jubilee of his ordination. When he finally stepped down from office

Prime Minister Keith Holyoake and Governor-General Sir Bernard Fergusson help Liston to celebrate the sixtieth anniversary of his ordination. NZH

in 1970, Liston paid a formal farewell call on the mayor, who described his resignation as 'a great loss to Auckland'.[46]

He had made his peace with James Gunson much earlier. One morning in 1926, noticing the ex-mayor walking along Mountain Road, Liston crossed and struck up a conversation. As legend has it, they became firm friends; they co-operated in relief work during the Second World War and later shared duties on various civic bodies.[47] Nevertheless, in 1929 Liston related with some relish Gunson's repeated failure to secure a seat in Parliament.[48] Despite Kelly's sneer that he had now earned his place there, Gunson surprisingly rejected several invitations to stand in the 1922 general election. While *New Zealand Truth* attributed his reluctance to fall-out from the sedition case, a more likely explanation was the painful memory of his crushing rejection three years earlier. The award of a knighthood just before his retirement as mayor in 1925 came as some consolation to Gunson, but regrets over his truncated political career may well have troubled him until his death in 1963.[49]

Little is known of the others involved in the case. Detective Sergeant

Reginald Ward rose to become superintendent in Auckland before retiring in 1945. Laurence O'Brien's employment with the *Auckland Star* ended soon after the trial was over. When George Broadley, the gas-meter reader, was refused entry to an Onehunga house because of his testimony in the case, the Auckland Gas Company promptly cut off the supply.[50] O'Regan's brave and successful defence won him plaudits throughout the country. Wherever he went for the next year or so there was an audience in presbytery, pub and parlour to hear him tell how the deed was done. (He arranged for his closing address to be specially printed as a pamphlet.) Wider recognition of his abilities came more slowly; he had to await the election of the first Labour government for an appointment as judge of the Arbitration Court.[51] The Crown Solicitor also came through with honour; Meredith lost no friends by his conduct in court, while his sole press critic was beneath contempt. Both Solicitor-General and Minister of Justice endorsed his performance by approving his request for a special payment of forty-four guineas in recognition of the arduous nature of the case.[52]

All the participants seemed to draw some consolation from the affair. Disappointed by the initial response of Auckland Catholics, Liston was delighted with the strong support he received as his ordeal went on. From the government's point of view, the trial had defused a potentially explosive incident; the legal smack on the wrist administered by the verdict's rider was a warning to Catholic leaders who might be tempted in future. The loudest cheers for legal action came from the PPA. However, despite boasting four members on the Liston jury, it was unable to secure a conviction.[53] Indeed, it is likely that the effect of the case hastened the decline of Elliott's organisation as press condemnation of the speech was frequently spiced with hard words for the PPA. The sight of a Catholic prelate in the dock probably shocked more New Zealanders than it pleased. In the event, the bishop had not escaped the law, while it could even be argued (from his letter to Massey and his evidence in court) that his loyalty had been proven.

Most Catholics regarded the prosecution as yet another example of establishment bigotry, an artificial fury whipped up by the anti-Irish press and exploited by those with hidden political agenda. However, Gunson's denunciation of the speech voiced an indignation shared by twenty-two of the twenty-three newspapers whose editorials were collected by the Crown Law Office.[54] The speech as reported touched a nerve in the New Zealand community which had little to do with religious bigotry, just as the cheering for Sinn Fein by

Redwood, Kelly and Liston alienated many who did not naturally regard the Pope as the source of all evil.

This is not to minimise the sectarian conflict which scarred New Zealand life in these years. Australian Catholics frequently expressed their horror at the degree of anti-Catholic animus witnessed across the Tasman.[55] New Zealand was the only part of the British Empire in which the Catholic clergy (and even a bishop) were called up for military service. It was also the first to pass legislation against the supposed effect of the papal decree against mixed marriages, *Ne Temere*. Nowhere else was a Catholic prelate forced to defend his political opinions from the dock. Yet, once over, the sedition case was soon consigned to the dustbin of history, meriting little more than a footnote in the textbooks. To be fair, those most involved have been the least willing to remember. On his appointment to the bench in 1937, Patrick O'Regan chose not to mention the affair in his contributed profile to the *New Zealand Law Journal*, while Sir Vincent Meredith's autobiography contains no clue that he had once prosecuted a bishop. For his part, Liston lived until 1976 and did not care to be reminded of this early blemish in his episcopal career.[56]

Why should the case be remembered? Circumstances would appear to have changed utterly over the last seventy-five years. New Zealand and Australia had, until recently, Irish Catholic leaders, both enthusiastic republicans who preferred to emphasise the Asian rather than the British identity of their respective countries. (Jim Bolger's National Party, Reform's spiritual heir, has even considered removing loyalty to the Queen from its list of principles.)[57] However, the echoes of 1922 are very strong, not least in Anglo–Irish relations. British politicians are once more steeling themselves to sit down with men they regard as murderers, while Sinn Fein leader Gerry Adams has undergone a Michael Collins-like transformation. At home the similarities are equally striking. In mid-1995, issues of the *New Zealand Herald* (recently taken over by an Irish Catholic) teemed with references to sedition and the Crown Law Office, while correpondents clamoured for Maori radicals to be prosecuted for their public utterances.[58]

The Maori–Irish relationship has tantalised several writers over the past century. Most have been captured by the romanticism well expressed in the much-quoted remark attributed to an Irish soldier in the Anglo–Maori War: 'Begorra, it's a murder to shoot them. Sure they are our own people, with their potatoes and fish, and children. Who knows but they are Irishmen, with faces a little darkened by the sun, who escaped during the persecutions of Cromwell.'[59] Donald

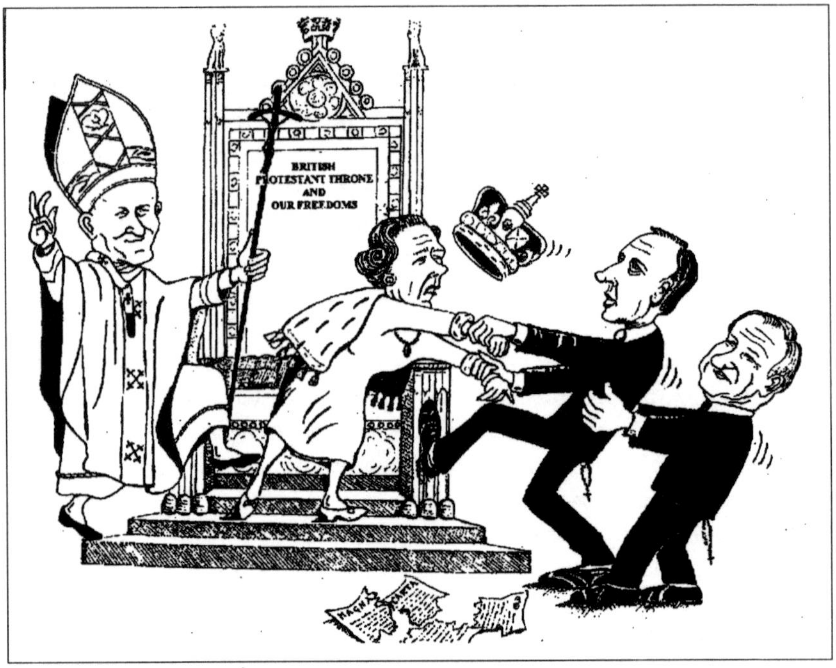

A recent cartoon shows that old fears have not entirely disappeared. The Prime Minister of New Zealand (Jim Bolger) and the former Prime Minister of Australia (Paul Keating) combine to dethrone the Queen, with the encouragement and assistance of the Pope. Commonwealth Chronicle

Akenson in *Half the World From Home* recently reminded us of the folklore suggesting a close Maori–Irish Catholic relationship based on intermarriage. However, the fact remains that Irish soldiers killed Maori during the land wars and subsequently settled on their lands, as Keremeta Ngahuripuke ruefully recalled in his open letter to Liston.[60] His lack of sympathy with Irish national aspirations was echoed by Dr Maui Pomare in Parliament:

> We ask for no self-determination for the Maoris. That was attended to in 1840, and that bond, the Treaty of Waitangi, is more than a scrap of paper to us . . . For eighty years we have been under British rule, and, as one of those who represent the subject race, I say we don't want a better government than the British government.[61]

What really links Irish Catholic and Maori is a sad history of dispossession and defeat, with the consequent loss of their language and their land. From this came a sense of powerlessness, of being invisible and excluded, a permanent minority with their cultural and spiritual identity under threat (although, it must be added, Maori matched Irish Catholic in a stubborn resistance to imperialism). The 'privations and wrongs' experienced by Maori last century have been handed down the generations; mixed with a sense of present injus-

St Patrick's Day, 1972. Exactly fifty years after Liston's speech supporters of Irish nationalism march up Queen Street, led by a Catholic priest. Even the 'Black and Tans' have not been forgotten. NZH

tice, this has produced a heady cocktail of grievance. Now, as then, frustration and anger at the apathy and ignorance of the majority bring an overwhelming desire to provoke some reaction from the perceived oppressor, however hostile. (Did not James Kelly similarly relish every opportunity to mock and challenge the symbols of his enemies, to trample on their flag and chip away at their sacred monuments?)

Perhaps the lasting message of the Liston case is the need to view the wilder actions and utterances of an alienated minority in the light of history. Also, as one perceptive editor suggested in 1922, to treat with responsible parties only, rejecting the extremists and those who pander to them for their own purposes.[62] Historians have a duty to look more closely into the darker corners of our past. There is a lesson in Patrick O'Farrell's critique of his Australian colleagues: 'Historians [who] took – still take – an English view of appearances, accept English priorities, reflect Protestant value-judgements. The sub-world of Irish Catholics had no real existence for historians who wrote from and about the walled gardens of the establishment.'[63] It is essential that the diversity and divisions of Pakeha culture be explored. Only thus can we overcome what Akenson has called a 'collective erasure of memory' regarding the sectarian dimension of our past.

Appendix 1

Crimes Act 1908, ss 118–119

118. (1) A seditious intention is an intention –

(a) To bring into hatred or contempt, or to incite disaffection against, the person of His Majesty or the Government or Constitution of the United Kingdom or of any part thereof, or either House of the Imperial Parliament, or the Government or Constitution of New Zealand, or the Parliament thereof, or the administration of justice; or
(b) To incite His Majesty's subjects to attempt to procure otherwise than by lawful means the alteration of any matter affecting the Constitution, laws, or Government of the United Kingdom or of New Zealand; or
(c) To raise discontent or disaffection amongst His Majesty's subjects; or
(d) To promote feelings of ill-will and hostility between different classes of such subjects.

(2) No one shall be deemed to have a seditious intention only because he intends in good faith –

(e) To show that His Majesty has been misled or mistaken in his measure; or
(f) To point out errors or defects in the Government or Constitution of the United Kingdom or any part thereof, or of New Zealand, or in the administration of justice, or to incite His Majesty's subjects to attempt to procure by lawful means the alteration of any matter affecting the Constitution, laws, or Government of the United Kingdom or of New Zealand; or
(g) To point out, in order to their removal, matters producing or having a tendency to produce feelings of hatred and ill-will between different classes of His Majesty's subjects.

(3) Seditious words are words expressive of a seditious intention.

(4) A seditious libel is a libel expressive of a seditious intention.

(5) A seditious conspiracy is an agreement between two or more persons to carry into execution a seditious intention.

119. Everyone is liable to two years' imprisonment who speaks any seditious words, or publishes any seditious libel, or is a party to any seditious conspiracy.

Appendix 2
Liston's Letter to Massey

Sir,

I feel that I owe a duty to my fellow-countrymen to make a statement at the present moment regarding my recent speech, and it seems to me that the most fitting way to approach them is through you, Sir, the head of the Government in New Zealand.

I have been described as 'disloyal,' 'a disturber of the peace,' etc. Those who know me set down that description of me as incredible, and for my own part I cannot accept it for one minute, for I yield place to no one in love for this beautiful country, New Zealand, in which I was born and my loyalty to the King. In so far as any reported remarks of mine should have led those who do not know me to think otherwise of me I quite frankly regret my share in the misunderstanding, and I trust that when the people of New Zealand, and especially of Auckland, come to know me better, they too will think of me as my friends do.

If I touch upon two points, Sir, I think that the attitude of the Catholic people in New Zealand, as well as of myself, toward the institutions of the country will be better understood.

First, the Catholic Church lays on her children a solemn obligation to love their home, and to honour their parents. Like to that, is the command she gives to them to love their country and to honour their King. To no one, be he priest or layman, does she leave this a matter of free thought or free choice. Patriotism is not a mere opinion which a man may hold today and discard tomorrow; it is a duty; and a solemn one.

I speak in that matter as a citizen of New Zealand, no less than a Catholic Bishop. The Church is the mother of my faith in things eternal; New Zealand is my country, the protectress of my liberty and of my fortunes on earth. I could not utter one syllable that would belie either my Church or my country, and when I assert, as I now solemnly do, that the teachings of the Church are in thorough harmony with the interests of my country, New Zealand, I know in the depths of my soul that I speak the truth.

That Catholics in New Zealand have carried out this obligation of loving their country, their generous part in her children's toil and sacrifice is honourable proof. During the past eighty years their work of hand and brain, their sweat and blood, have played no mean or grudging part in the building up of this fair young land.

Loyalty, however, does not preclude me or anyone else from striving for the betterment of any part of the Empire, and, in this respect, I find myself in the distinguished company of His Majesty the King, Mr Lloyd George, Mr Asquith, General Smuts, the Anglican Bishops, the Nonconformist leaders, and the greater number of the representative newspapers of the Empire in calling for a change in the hitherto bitter relations between England and Ireland. I rejoice that much has been done in that direction, and I pray that in a short time the promise which more recent events have borne will mature into a perfect and a lasting friendship between the two countries.

This brings me, Sir, to my second point. I dwelt on this point in my speech, and intended it to give, and it really did give, the key to that speech, but it has been almost completely overlooked in all the subsequent criticism of myself. What I said, and what I say now, with all sincerity is this - in spite of the all too unhappy past, Irish people at home and abroad and their sympathisers are both willing and eager to hold out the hand of friendship. The very first to strike this note were the Bishops of Ireland to a man and the one among them who was often denounced as the out-and-out extremist has hailed the treaty which binds his country to the Empire as the very gift of God.

With his views I am in hearty agreement. The most noteworthy of the Australian Bishops have proclaimed - and I re-echo their sentiments from my heart - that there is imperative need of reconciliation and friendship between hitherto conflicting classes and countries. Like ourselves Ireland has now her future in her own hands. It would be idle to deny the existence of difficulties, but it would also be the act of despair to think that these difficulties cannot be overcome. Ireland's friends desire nothing better than that the obstacles should vanish as speedily as possible and leave the way open to complete reconciliation between North and South, the Free State and England. This will give us, in the words of the now famous treaty, the union, under His Majesty the King, of Ireland with the Commonwealth of Nations known as the British Empire.

May I conclude by saying that I feel satisfied that my clergy who in their loyalty to me have expressed their sympathy with me, will cordially agree with the views I have expressed in this communication.

James M. Liston
(*NZH*, 7 April 1922)

Appendix 3

'A Nation Once Again'

When boyhood's fire was in my blood,
I read of ancient freemen,
For Greece and Rome who bravely stood,
Three hundred men and three men.
And then I prayed I yet might see
Our fetters rent in twain,
And Ireland long a province, be
A nation once again.

Chorus:
A nation once again,
A nation once again!
And Ireland, long a province, be
A nation once again!

And, from that time, through wildest woe,
That hope has shone, a far light;
Nor could love's brightest summer glow
Outshine that solemn starlight:
It seemed to watch above my head
In forum, field and fane;
Its angel voice sang round my bed,
'A nation once again.'

Chorus

It whispered, too, that freedom's ark
And service high and holy,
Would be profaned by feelings dark
And passions vain or lowly:
For freedom comes from God's right hand,
And needs a godly train;
And righteous men must make our land
A nation once again.

Chorus

So, as I grew from boy to man,
I bent me to that bidding -

My spirit of each selfish plan
And cruel passion ridding;
For, thus I hoped some day to aid -
Oh! can such hope be vain?
When my dear country shall be made
A nation once again.

Chorus

Thomas Davis (1814-1845)

'God Save Ireland'

High upon the gallows tree swung the noble-hearted three,
By the vengeful tyrant stricken in their bloom;
But they met him face to face, with the courage of their race,
And they went with souls undaunted to their doom.

Chorus:
'God save Ireland!' said the heroes;
'God save Ireland!' said they all.
'Whether on the scaffold high
Or the battlefield we die,
O, what matter when for Ireland dear we fall!'

Girt around with cruel foes, still their courage proudly rose,
For they thought of hearts that loved them far and near;
Of the millions true and brave o'er the ocean's swelling wave,
And the friends in holy Ireland ever dear.

Chorus

Climbed they up the ragged stair, rang their voices out in prayer,
Then with England's fatal cord around them cast,
Close beside the gallows tree kissed like brothers lovingly
True to home and faith and freedom to the last.

Chorus

Never till the latest day shall the memory pass away
Of the gallant lives thus given for our land;
But on the cause must go, amid joy or weal or woe,
Till we make this Isle a Nation free and grand.

Chorus

T.D. Sullivan (1827-1914)

Notes

1
That Fatal Occasion of Temptation

1. T. Jones, *Whitehall Diary: III. Ireland 1919–1925*. London, 1971. D. G. Boyce, *Englishmen and Irish Troubles: British Public Opinion and the Making of Irish Policy, 1918–1922*. Cambridge, Mass., 1972, p.92. *EP*, 12 October 1920. *Tablet*, 1 December 1921.
2. S. Lawlor, *Britain and Ireland 1914–1923*. Dublin, 1983, Ch. 6.
3. Archbishop Duhig of Brisbane. *Tablet*, 15 April 1920.
4. P. J. O'Farrell, *The Catholic Church and Community: An Australian History*. Sydney, 1985, p.232. See also his *The Irish in Australia*. Sydney, 1986, pp.236–38. C. Macintyre, 'The Adelaide Irish and the Politics of St Patrick's Day, 1900–1918', in R. Phelan (ed.), *Irish-Australian Studies: Papers Delivered at the Seventh Irish-Australian Conference*. Sydney, 1994, pp.182–196. The *New Zealand Tablet* (8 January 1897) insisted that 'everything unrefined should be mercilessly eliminated from the sports and concert programme.'
5. Bishop Lenihan's Diary, 14 March 1896, Lenihan Papers, Auckland Catholic Diocesan Archive [ACDA]. *Tablet*, 8 January, 19 March 1897.
6. R. M. Sweetman, 'New Zealand Catholicism, War, Politics and the Irish Issue, 1912–1922,' PhD thesis, University of Cambridge, 1991. ['New Zealand Catholicism'] Chs 9 and 11. See also Sweetman, 'New Zealand Catholicism and the Irish Issue, 1914–1922', in W. J. Shiel and D. Wood (eds), *The Churches, Ireland and the Irish*. Oxford, 1989, pp.375–384.
7. *Tablet*, 3 April, 1 May 1919 (Perth); 8 April 1920 (Melbourne); 23 June 1921 (Adelaide). For Tasmania, see R. P. Davis, 'Tasmania and the Irish Revolution, 1916–22,' *Tasmanian Historical Research Association (Papers and Proceedings)*, 21, 2 (1974), pp.69–88. For Melbourne, see M. Gilchrist, *Daniel Mannix: Priest and Patriot*. Melbourne, 1982, Chs 3 and 4.
8. Sweetman, 'New Zealand Catholicism', Chs 8 and 11.
9. *Tablet*, 24 March 1921. *ES*, Dunedin, 18 March 1921.
10. Sweetman, 'New Zealand Catholicism', pp.295–96. Fr H. Holbrook to Archbishop Cattaneo, 30 May 1929, Cleary Papers, ACDA.
11. *Tablet*, 21 July 1921.
12. *NZH*, 17 March 1922.
13. *Tablet* editor James Kelly called it 'the Irish National Anthem', and urged his readers to insist on its being played at every Irish gathering. He published the words and music to this end. *Tablet*, 27 June 1918, 17 February and 10 March 1921.
14. P. Galvin, *Irish Songs of Resistance*. London, 1962, pp.11–13.
15. See Ch. 8.
16. 'The Little Irish Mother' was composed by an Irish-Australian priest, Fr P. J. Hartigan, who wrote under the name 'John O'Brien'. The poem appears in *Around the Boree Log*. Sydney, 1944, pp.6–9. See F. Mecham, *'John O'Brien' and the Boree Log. A biography of Patrick Hartigan, 'John O'Brien'*. Sydney, 1981.
17. *NZH*, 18 March 1922.
18. Notes of Evidence: *His Majesty the King* v. *James Michael Liston*, 16–17 May 1922. High Court, Auckland. [Notes of Evidence] p.21.
19. Liston Defence Notes, 6-1/43, Liston Papers, ACDA.
20. Liston to Cleary, 24 April 1922, Brodie Papers, Christchurch Catholic Diocesan Archives [CCDA]. It seems that Cleary gave this letter to Brodie in Rome. None of the

other letters Liston sent to Cleary during this period have survived.

21. Liston to O'Regan, 21 March 1922, O'Regan Papers, Alexander Turnbull Library, Wellington [ATL]. Cleary was inclined to give his deputy the benefit of the doubt, believing that his controversial remarks had been delivered on the spur of the moment. Cleary to Liston, 6 June 1922, Liston Papers, ACDA. On the source of Liston's inspiration, see the panegyric by Bishop Fogarty (Killaloe) on Bishop O'Dwyer (Limerick), cited in *Tablet*, 7 December 1917: 'God made her [Ireland] a nation, and while grass grows and water runs, there will be men in Ireland to dare and die for her.'

22. 'His clear voice . . . rendered the words audible to those in the furthest part of the large building.' *NZH*, 26 April 1920, on the Prince of Wales, speaking at his civic reception in the Auckland Town Hall.

23. 'His struggle to overcome a stammer had left him with an odd intonation in his public speaking and often in his private conversations, so that his voice became one of the most widely mimicked by his students and later his priests.' E. R. Simmons, *In Cruce Salus: A History of the Diocese of Auckland 1848–1980*. Auckland, 1982, p.224. For Liston's nasal operation and voice lessons, see Liston to Cleary, 31 May 1920, Cleary Papers, ACDA.

24. This version of Liston's speech is a composite of press reports and his own notes. See notes 6-1, Liston Papers, ACDA.

25. *NZH*, 10 December 1921. Sir Edwin Mitchelson, one-time mayor of Auckland (1903–5), was the first to protest. *NZPD*, Vol 194, p.123.

26. Notes of Evidence, p.23.

27. *AS*, 18 March 1922. Archbishops Mannix (Melbourne) and Kelly (Sydney) both cabled Liston on 9 January 1922 advising against a public thanksgiving after Dail Eireann's narrow vote in favour of ratifying the treaty. Bishop Cleary repeated this advice from Dublin three days later. Cleary to Liston, 12 January 1922, Liston Papers, ACDA.

28. *NZH*, 6 and 23 January 1922. *EP*, 25 October 1921, 16 February 1922.

29. See Ch. 11. The RSA had marched that very day to protest against increased unemployment in their ranks. *NZH*, 17 March 1922.

30. *Tablet*, 25 April 1918.

31. *NZH*, 18 March 1922. Statement of Gordon Leith Stanbrook, 23 March 1922, Police File 22/477, National Archives, Wellington [NA].

32. Report of Detective Sergeant Reginald Ward, 24 March 1922, Police File 22/477, NA.

2
Murdered By Foreign Troops

1. *NZH*, 18 March 1922.
2. *NZO*, 27 May 1922.
3. Robert Mundie Hackett, born in Scotland, was the *Herald*'s editor from 1917 to 1942. *Who's Who in New Zealand and the Western Pacific, 1925*. Masterton, 1924, p.92.
4. *NZO*, 2 April 1910. *NZH*, 11 April, 28 October 1910, 28 October 1913. The rising was 'destructive, not constructive; the craving for loot, and not the love of freedom, evidently sustained its instigators and inflamed its dupes'. *NZH*, 2 May 1916. R. P. Davis, 'The Irish–Catholic Question and New Zealand Society 1868–1922', PhD thesis, University of Otago, 1968. Sweetman, 'New Zealand Catholicism', pp.100–101.
5. *Tablet*, 18 September 1919.
6. *Tablet*, 15 January 1920.
7. *Tablet*, 8 May 1919.
8. *Tablet*, 3 March 1921.
9. *Tablet*, 30 June 1921.
10. H. S. Moores, 'The Rise of the Protestant Political Association: Sectarianism in New Zealand during World War One', MA thesis, University of Auckland, 1966.
11. *NZH*, 7 and 11 January 1921. *EP*, 14 February, 1 July 1921.
12. *Tablet*, 16 February 1922.
13. *NZH*, 18 March 1922. See Appendix 1 for details of the Crimes Act 1908.
14. *Tablet*, 19 January, 2 March 1922.
15. *NZS*, 1 April 1922.
16. *Tablet*, 30 March 1922. *NZO*, 25 March 1922.

17. *NZO*, 25 March 1922.
18. *AS*, 18 March 1922. Liston to Propaganda Fide, undated [1929?], Liston Papers 6-3, ACDA.
19. Report of Detective Sergeant Reginald Ward, 24 March 1922; Statement of Laurence O'Brien, 31 March 1922, Police File 22/477, NA.
20. Thomson Wilson Leys, part-proprietor of the *Auckland Star*, was born in England. A stalwart of the Liberal Party, Leys had edited the *Star* since 1872. *Who's Who in New Zealand and the Western Pacific, 1908*. Wellington, 1908, p.96.
21. Report of Detective Sergeant Reginald Ward, 24 March 1922; Statement of Laurence O'Brien, 31 March 1922, Police File 22/477, NA. *NZS*, 1 July 1922.
22. Over the past decade, the New Zealand government had used the sedition laws to crush socialist, radical and pacifist protest. The proceedings against R. Semple, F. R. Cooke, J. Thorn, P. Fraser and T. Brindle were published by the *Maoriland Worker* as *1916 Sedition Trials* (Wellington, 1917).
23. Statement of Laurence O'Brien, 31 March 1922, Police File 22/477, NA.
24. *AS*, 18 March 1922. Bishop Cleary once praised the *Star* as 'the foremost champion of Irish home rule' in the country. Cleary to Hagan, 6 January 1914, Hagan Papers, Irish College Rome [ICR].
25. *AS*, 18 March 1922.
26. Ibid. For de Valera's own version of his remarks see M. Moynihan (ed.), *Speeches and Statements by Eamon de Valera 1917–1973*. Dublin, 1980, pp.97–104.
27. Sweetman, 'New Zealand Catholicism, War', pp.100–101.
28. *AS*, 18 March 1922.
29. *NZT*, 12 December 1921. O'Regan was careful to stress that the Irish people alone could pronounce on the treaty's true value.
30. See Ch. 1, note 28.
31. *Tablet*, 23 March 1922.

3
A Protestant With Backbone

1. The HMS *Renown* carried the Prince of Wales and his entourage on their world tour in 1920. *EP*, Wellington, 12 February 1921.
2. *NZH*, 26 June 1917.
3. *Tablet*, 15 December 1921. *NZH*, 3 December 1921. Jellicoe to Churchill, 24 April 1922, File 25684, Colonial Office [CO] Papers 209/312, Public Record Office, London [PRO].
4. This letter has not survived in Liston's papers, nor was it published in the newspapers.
5. Gunson and Wilson were close friends, their families holidaying together on Waiheke Island. Interview (22 April 1995) with Mrs Jean Goldie, daughter of F. W. Wilson. See also A. Caughey, *An Auckland Network*. Auckland, 1988. pp.17–18. I am indebted to Helen Milne for this reference.
6. *NZH*, 20 March 1922.
7. *Month*, 15 June 1922. Liston even claimed (wrongly) that the *NZ Herald* was run by Gunson's uncle. Liston to Propaganda Fide, undated [1929?], Liston Papers 6-3, ACDA.
8. *NZH*, 28 October 1921.
9. G. W. A. Bush, *Decently and in Order: The Centennial History of the Auckland City Council*. Auckland, 1971. pp.487–88. *NZH*, 7 March 1919, 9 and 25 February 1921.
10. *NZO*, 24 April 1915.
11. *EP*, 11 August 1915.
12. *NZFL*, 4 February 1916.
13. *NZH*, 27 July 1917.
14. *NZH*, 29 and 30 November 1918. The *NZO* called Auckland 'the most insanitary city in the Southern hemisphere'. (Cited in *NZ Herald*, 11 December 1918.) See also G. Rice, *Black November: The 1918 Influenza Epidemic in New Zealand*. Wellington, 1988, pp.29–30.
15. *NZH*, 2/4 December 1918.
16. *NZH*, 3 and 11 December 1918. Cleary urged his audience to 'rejoice that we have in our midst men prepared to take a firm stand, and take proper steps to do their duty and protect the people they represent'.
17. *NZH*, 4 and 11 December 1918.
18. *NZFL*, 17 August 1912. *NZH*, 18 July 1914.
19. Mitchelson (1846–1934) was mayor

from 1903 to 1905, Myers (1867–1926) succeeded him to 1909, while Parr (1869–1941) served from 1911 to 1915. All three men had distinguished parliamentary careers. As Minister of Education in 1920, Parr introduced compulsory loyalty lessons into the primary schools, including regular saluting of the Union Jack and an oath of allegiance to be taken by every teacher – measures that reflected the hysterical post-war fears of the enemy within.

20. *NZH*, 1 March, 1 October 1919. *NZFL*, 1 October 1919.

21. *NZH*, 3 June 1919. *NZFL*, 1 October 1919.

22. On Gunson's USA trip see *NZH*, 1 July 1919, 22 September 1919, 12 November 1919. On his health problems see *NZFL*, 1 October 1919 and *NZH*, 1 July, 9 December 1919.

23. Gunson was among the victims of a speculating ring which had cornered all the tickets for sailings months in advance. *NZH*, 25 October 1919. *New Zealand Truth*, 13 December 1919.

24. *NZH*, 17 December 1919. Vivian Harold Potter, born in Auckland, served two years in the Boer War, three years in the First World War. As chief executive of the Waihi Miner's Union, he strongly opposed the strike there in 1912. *Who's Who in New Zealand and the Western Pacific, 1925*. Masterton, 1924, p.180.

25. *NZH*, 10, 11 and 16 December 1919. 'Gunson is too big a man to keep out of any Cabinet', trumpeted all the mayor's men. Massey's response can be read in his cable to Potter (*NZH*, 26 November 1919) clearing up 'some misapprehension' which others had fostered: 'I desire to repeat that you are the official Government candidate.'

26. *NZH*, 4 and 18 December 1919.

27. *EP*, 28 May 1915, 25 August 1916. *Truth*, 14 July 1917.

28. *NZH*, 7 March 1917. A. F. Donoghue to Liston, 24 March 1922, Liston Papers, ACDA.

29. Such as the need to inspect Catholic convents, to end free train travel to school for Catholic pupils and teachers, and to stop Catholic priests from impugning the validity of legal marriages. Potter became an apologist for the PPA in parliament. *NZH*, 16 October 1919, 24 March 1921, 25 May 1922. *NZS*, 1 March, 2 October, 1 December 1922.

30. *New Zealand Methodist Times*, 1 April 1922. Several of Gunson's more prominent supporters were Catholic, notably P. J. Nerheny and M. J. Sheahan. See also Cleary to Gunson, 3 August 1922, Liston Papers, ACDA.

31. 'The Papal Delegate and the Mayor'. Auckland, 1916. See Moores, 'The Rise of the Protestant Political Association'.

32. *NZH*, 16 March 1917.

33. Mahoney to Cleary, 18 October 1917, Cleary Papers, ACDA.

34. *Tablet*, 1 February 1917, 5 May 1921. The correspondent was probably M. J. Sheahan.

35. *NZH*, 16 April 1921.

36. 'He seemed to emanate unseen arrows one of which entered the heart of every one person who saw him.' *NZFL*, 28 April 1922.

37. *NZH*, 26 April 1920.

38. Ibid. The royal party was equally impressed. In a record of the visit published later it was noted, 'There is no need for propaganda in New Zealand; the country is overwhelmingly enthusiastic for Empire.' Auckland was also accorded the honour of a short poem praising its loyalty, reproduced at the head of this chapter. *EP*, 12 February 1921.

39. On the award of a CMG, *NZH*, 3 January 1922; *NZFL*, 11 January 1922. The royal reaction was revealed in the *NZH*, 8 March 1922.

40. Alfred Hall Skelton was a New Zealander, the son of Irish Protestant immigrants, who ran unsuccessfully for the Auckland mayoralty in 1912 before securing a seat on the city council (1913–21). *NZH*, 14 July, 10 October 1921. On his selection as Auckland's delegate to the Irish Race Convention, see *NZH*, 10 and 31 October 1921. The farewell ceremony at the Town Hall was reported in the *NZH*, 1 December 1921.

41. *NZH*, 1 December 1921.

42. *NZH*, 7 December 1921.

43. Ibid. The *NZS* (2 January 1922) thundered, 'Is it not time that Auckland found

a Mayor that Protestants can trust and respect?'

44. *Truth*, 8 October 1921, 21 January 1922.

45. Several Australian Mayors had insisted on guarantees of loyalty before granting permission for St Patrick's Day marches to proceed through their city streets. In default of convincing promises to this effect Gunson's counterpart in Melbourne had attempted (unsuccessfully) to ban the 1922 procession. See Ch.1, note 8. Also M. Gilchrist, *Daniel Mannix*, pp.104–5.

46. *NZH*, 20 March 1922.

47. *Methodist Times*, 1 April 1922.

48. *Auckland Star*, 20 March 1922.

4
Studied Insults

1. *NZH*, 20 March 1922
2. *Month*, 15 June 1922.
3. *NZH*, 20 March 1922.
4. Gunson to Bell, 20 March 1922, Police File 22/477, NA.
5. Gunson to Massey, 20 March 1922, Police File 22/477, NA.
6. *AS*, 21 March 1922.
7. Ibid. Virgo was Field Secretary for the British National Council of the YMCA. *NZH*, 26 September 1916.
8. *AS*, 21 March 1922.
9. Ibid., 21 March 1922. Bishop C. E. Locke, head of the American Methodist Episcopal Church in the Philippines, had come to take part in the New Zealand Methodist Centenary Conference. He expressed great admiration for the 'British' people of New Zealand: 'But for the pacifist and pro-German element [in the USA], we should have been with you [in the war] long before.' *NZH*, 21 February 1922.
10. *AS*, 22 March 1922. The Catholic hospital board member was Michael John Coyle (1865–1940), a coachbuilder who became the first Mayor of Mt Albert. He served on the Auckland City Council from 1925 to 1935.
11. *NZH*, 23 March 1922.
12. Ibid.
13. Ibid.
14. Ibid. O'Meara attended the Irish Race Convention in Melbourne in 1919 (along with Dr James Kelly and M. J. Sheahan). *Tablet*, 30 October, 6 November 1919.
15. *AS*, 22 March 1922. The Welfare League was a post-war creation which aimed to combat an alleged growth of Bolshevism in the dominion. Its manifesto declared opposition to 'anyone who was a disloyalist, revolutionist and Socialist, or whose endeavour was to tear down the pillars of civilisation or break up the Empire'. See *EP*, 12 and 15 December 1919, 26 November 1920.
16. *NZH*, 24 March 1922. Recent incidents involving Wellington students had raised fears of the contagion of revolutionary sentiments among the rising generation. *NZS* (2 January 1922) declared Victoria University College to be 'under suspicion'.
17. *NZH*, 24 March 1922. For Entrican's involvement see *NZH*, 17 June 1920, for Massey see *NZPD*, Vol 206, p.14. British–Israelism was based upon an extremely literal interpretation of the Bible. See *Church Gazette*, Auckland, 1 November 1934, 1 January 1936. Also J. Mountain, *The Triumph of British–Israel*. London, 1930.
18. *NZ Methodist Times*, 1 April 1922.
19. *New Zealand Baptist*, June 1920. John James North (1871–1951), born in England, was ordained to the Baptist ministry in 1895. In 1922 he was based in Christchurch as editor of the *New Zealand Baptist*. A. H. McLintock, *An Encyclopedia of New Zealand*: Volume 2. Wellington, 1966, p.693.
20. *LT*, 21 March 1922.
21. North presumably meant the impressionable working classes, whose proclivity to Romanism was a sad but inescapable fact. See his book, *Roman Catholicism 'Roots and Fruits'*. Napier, 1922.
22. Carrington may have wished to keep the door open for future Catholic participation on the Council.
23. *Sun*, Christchurch, 21 March 1922.
24. *AS*, 21 March 1922.
25. *NZH*, 23 March 1922. *NZS*, 1 June 1922.
26. *EP*, 23 March 1922.

27. *NZH*, 24 March 1922.
28. On Rua's own trial for sedition, see J. Binney, G. Chaplin and C. Wallace, *The Prophet Rua Kenana and His Community at Maungapohatu*. Wellington, 1979, pp. 122–126.
29. For the background to this letter, see the *NZO*, 1 April 1922. Bishop Cleary ordered that Liston's Maori critics be excluded from his own welcome home function in mid-1923. Cleary to Liston, 21 January 1923, Liston Papers, ACDA.
30. Liston's letter was published in the *NZH* on 23 March 1922. See Ch. 7.
31. *MDT*, 20 March 1922. *Press*, Christchurch, 21 March 1922.
32. Bell to Gunson, 22 March 1922, File 732, CLO.
33. Gunson to Bell, 20 March 1922, Police File 22/477, NA.
34. *Tablet*, 26 April, 3 May 1917. *NZH*, 5 May 1921.
35. *NZH*, 3 December 1921. Patrick Joseph Nerheney (1858–1921) was an Irishman who served on the Auckland City Council from 1908 until his death. In 1920 he was appointed to the Legislative Council. G. H. Scholefield, *A Dictionary of New Zealand Biography*, Vol. 2, Wellington, 1940, p.118.
36. *NZH*, 7 December 1921.
37. *NZH*, 24 March 1922.
38. Ibid.
39. *NZO*, 1 April 1922.
40. See Ch. 3.
41. *NZH*, 7 and 16 December 1921.
42. *NZH*, 24 March 1922.
43. Ibid.
44. Councillor M. J. Savage, the future Prime Minister, would have spoken in Liston's favour but was away in Wellington for several weeks. B. G. Gustafson, *From the Cradle to the Grave: A Biography of Michael Joseph Savage*. Auckland, 1986, pp.122–123. A prominent Auckland Labour leader, the English-born Bloodworth claimed a natural sympathy with those whose loyalty was unfairly traduced. *NZH*, 3 May 1921, 11 July 1922.
45. A reference to P. J. Nerheny, whose Irish patriotism and devout Catholicism had not diminished his loyalty to Empire. *Tablet*, 15 December 1921. Even Massey eulogised him, *NZPD*, Vol 192, p.811.
46. *NZH*, 24 March 1922.
47. Ibid.
48. Ibid.
49. *NZH*, 25 March 1922.

5
Horribly Vulgar and Unspeakably Low

1. *Pahiatua Herald*, 21 March 1922.
2. *LT*, 21 March 1922. *ODT*, 21 March 1922.
3. *MDT*, 20–24 March 1922.
4. *Franklin Times*, 21 March 1922.
5. *Sun*, 21 March 1922.
6. *Dannevirke Evening News*, 24 March 1922.
7. *WC*, 20 March 1922. *Wairarapa Age*, 20 March 1922.
8. *Northern Advocate*, 20 March 1922.
9. *WC*, 20 March 1922.
10. *Coromandel County News*, 24 March 1922.
11. *EP*, 20 March 1922.
12. *Press*, 21 March 1922.
13. *MDT*, 20 March 1922.
14. *MDT*, 21 March 1922.
15. *MDT*, 22 March 1922. The editor would not, however, concede the point over Gunson's choice of terminology: 'The question of whether the Bishop has forfeited his right to the privileges of Britishers is one for the authorities to consider.'
16. *Southland Daily News*, 21 March 1922.
17. *Dannevirke Evening News*, 24 March 1922.
18. *Northern Advocate*, 20 March 1922. *Press*, 21 March 1922. *NZT*, 23 March 1922.
19. *Timaru Herald*, 22 March 1922.
20. *WC*, 20 March 1922.
21. *Rotorua Chronicle*, 21 March 1922. The editor answered his own question; most of the 'studious insults and overt threats' which had greeted England's every effort at reconciliation had come from 'high places'.
22. *SDN*, 21 March 1922.
23. *Star*, Christchurch, 22 March 1922.
24. *NZT*, 23 March 1922.
25. *NZT*, 23 March 1922.

26. *Press,* 21 March 1922. *WT*, 21 March 1922.
27. *Dominion* (21 March 1922) linked this fact with the alleged co-operation by Sinn Fein with German submarine commanders in the south of Ireland.
28. *Dominion*, 21 March 1922.
29. *Pahiatua Herald*, 21 March 1922.
30. *Dannevirke Evening News*, 24 March 1922.
31. *WC*, 20 March 1922.
32. *Wairarapa Age*, 20 March 1922.
33. *EP*, 20 March 1922.
34. *Press,* 21 March 1922. *Star*, Christchurch, 22 March 1922.
35. *WT* 21 March 1922. *MDT*, 22 March 1922.
36. *NZT*, 23 March 1922.
37. *EP*, 20 March 1922.
38. *AS* (21 March 1922) continued: 'To what extent this wicked rejection of peace and frenzied wooing of war may be due to diseased vanity that sees in a Republic the only means of accomplishing personal ambition, and how far it springs from a perverted and desperate nationalism, can only be surmised, but there is no doubt about the revolting reality – that de Valera is a monomaniac, who in his violence seeks to destroy the best opportunity of peace ever given to his long-suffering country.'
39. *EP*, 20 March 1922. *WC* (20 March 1922) agreed that he had adopted 'a queer way of showing his affection'.
40. *Press*, 21 March 1922.
41. *Gisborne Times*, 21 March 1922.
42. *Rotorua Chronicle*, 21 March 1922.
43. *EP*, 20 March 1922.
44. *Sun*, Christchurch, 21 March 1922.
45. *King Country Chronicle*, 23 March 1922. *Gisborne Times*, 21 March 1922.
46. *Franklin Times*, 21 March 1922.
47. *EP*, 20 March 1922.
48. *Sun*, Christchurch, 21 March 1922.
49. *Rotorua Chronicle*, 21 March 1922.

6
Disgusted

1. *NZO*, 1 April 1922.
2. *AS*, 21 March 1922.
3. *NZH*, 23 March 1922. For Bishop Whyte's speech see *AS*, 20 March 1922.
4. *NZH*, 21 March 1922.
5. *NZH*, 23 March 1922.
6. *NZH*, 18 March 1922.
7. *NZH*, 22 March 1922.
8. Ibid.
9. Ibid.
10. *NZH*, 21 March 1922.
11. *AS*, 22 March 1922. J. L. Kelly agreed that Irish Catholics were in a 'house of bondage': however, 'the "foreign" Power that has them in thrall is not Britain, but ecclesiastical Rome'. Kelly, a former editor of the *NZ Times*, wrote frequently in the daily press on quasi-religious themes. *NZFL*, 29 February 1908, 18 July 1913, 10 October 1914.
12. *NZH*, 21 March 1922.
13. *Taranaki Daily News*, 21 March 1922.
14. Ibid. One can sympathise with 'Returned Soldier' in his complaint against the Taranaki Catholic clergy, surrounded as he was by recent arrivals from Ireland: 'There are English priests to be had without importing Sinn Fein priests to stir up strife and bad feeling.' He suggested that Irish priests be classified as undesirable immigrants.
15. *LT*, 21 March 1922.
16. *ODT*, 21 March 1922.
17. *MDT*, 21 March 1922. *Waipawa Mail*, 22 March 1922.
18. *Taranaki Daily News*, 21 March 1922.
19. *ODT*, 21 March 1922.
20. *Hawke's Bay Tribune*, 23 March 1922.
21. This from 'Henry Tudor' in the *Franklin Times*, 24 March 1922.
22. *Dannevirke Evening News*, 24 March 1922. *Franklin Times*, 24 March 1922. According to the *SDN* (21 March 1922) three-quarters of New Zealand's Catholics would probably resent Liston's remarks.
23. *AS*, 18 March 1922. Mayor Gunson did not forget those who had applauded the Bishop; the preventive measures approved by the Auckland City Council were aimed at both offending parties.
24. *NZH*, 23 March 1922. See Ch. 7.
25. *NZH*, 24 March 1922.
26. *AS*, 21 March 1922.
27. *AS*, 22 March 1922.
28. *AS*, 21 March 1922. Of the 24 letters published by the Auckland dailies in the

week following the speech, at least fourteen were written by Catholics, of which only three favoured Liston. The *Herald* published 17 letters, seven by Protestants and ten by Catholics, while the *Star* featured four Catholic and two Protestant correspondents (plus one of uncertain religious allegiance).

29. *AS*, 20 March 1922. Napier continued: 'a Pact of Peace has been signed between the two countries, and a greater measure of Home Rule than ever Parnell or Redmond dreamed of has been obtained by Ireland.'

30. Ibid.

31. Napier's son had served in the war with distinction, suffering both wounding and gassing and reaching the rank of lieutenant: *NZH*, 30 October 1918. Napier had just returned from a tour of the United Kingdom; he assured the Auckland Victoria League of his deep conviction that 'the greatest asset this Empire possesses is the Prince of Wales'.

32. *AS*, 20 March 1922.

33. Ibid.

34. Dean Darby had had a clash of wills with Bishop Cleary and came off worst.

35. *AS*, 22 March 1922. *NZH*, 23 March 1922.

36. *AS*, 22 March 1922. In 1911, Darby made an eloquent plea for Irish home rule at a public meeting in Auckland. *Tablet*, 15 June 1911.

37. Ibid. George Graham agreed with Napier that the British Empire was 'as much the treasured heritage of Catholic as well as of Protestant'.

38. *NZH*, 21 March 1922. 'C.C.C.' described the endeavour to depict England as Ireland's implacable foe as 'not only ludicrous but sinful'.

39. *NZH*, 22 March 1922.

40. Ibid.

41. *EP*, 21 March 1922.

42. *EP*, 22 March 1922.

43. *EP*, 25 March 1922.

44. One wonders what William Massey and Howard Elliott thought of this novel suggestion. Both firmly opposed the continuation of a British representative to the Vatican. *NZS*, 1 November 1922. *NZH*, 1 August 1921.

45. *EP*, 25 March 1922.

46. Ibid.

47. *NZH*, 23 March 1922.

48. *NZH*, 25 March 1922.

49. 'Cut It Out' in the *NZH*, 25 March 1922.

7
I Weighed All My Words Carefully

1. T. Bracken, *Musings in Maoriland*. Dunedin, 1890, pp.175–176.

2. *Month*, 15 June 1922.

3. Liston to Propaganda Fide, undated [1929?], Liston Papers 6-3, ACDA.

4. Liston to Cleary, 24 April 1922, Brodie Papers, CCDA.

5. *NZH*, 21 March 1922. *AS*, 21 March 1922.

6. Liston to O'Regan, 21 March 1922, O'Regan Papers, ATL.

7. *NZH*, 23 March 1922.

8. Liston to J. A. Lee, 24 March 1922, Lee Papers, Auckland Public Library. See note 62 below.

9. *Tablet*, 25 May 1922. Fr James Kennedy (Hokitika) wrote to say how well the letter was received in the Christchurch diocese. Kennedy to Liston, 24 March 1922, Liston Papers, ACDA.

10. Fr John O'Hara to Liston, 26 March 1922, Liston Papers, ACDA.

11. The clergy telegrams are in Liston Papers 6-2, ACDA.

12. Fr Paul Cullen to Liston, 23 March 1922, Liston Papers, ACDA.

13. Fr Xavier O'Brien to Liston, 20 March 1922, Liston Papers, ACDA.

14. Fr Thomas Hayden to Liston, 5 May 1922, Liston Papers, ACDA.

15. W. H. Watson to Liston, undated, Liston Papers, ACDA.

16. J. P. O'Sullivan to Liston, 23 March 1922. W. H. Mulcahy to Liston, 23 March 1922. Liston Papers, ACDA.

17. Fr Farragher to Liston, 21 March 1922, Liston Papers, ACDA.

18. Fr Lynch to Liston, 21 March 1922, Liston Papers, ACDA.

19. Fr Lane to Liston, 24 March 1922, Liston Papers, ACDA.

20. Fr Lynch to Liston, 21 March 1922,

Liston Papers, ACDA.
21. J. P. Walls to Liston, 26 March 1922, Liston Papers, ACDA. Fr James Kennedy was singular in remembering Gunson as 'our one-time friend', recalling his generous reception of the Apostolic Delegate six years earlier. Kennedy to Liston, 24 March 1922, Liston Papers, ACDA.
22. J. P. O'Sullivan to Liston, 21 March 1922, Liston Papers, ACDA. Kelly also invented language to abuse his enemies – 'the Brutish Empire', 'John Cow' – while the daily newspapers were 'Day Lies'.
23. Bishop Whyte to Liston, 22 March 1922, Liston Papers, ACDA.
24. E. de M. to Liston, 21 March 1922, Liston Papers, ACDA.
25. Fr J. Riordan to Liston, 24 March 1922, Liston Papers, ACDA.
26. Joan O'Leary to Liston, 23 March 1922, Liston Papers, ACDA.
27. Kennedy to Liston, 24 March 1922, Liston Papers, ACDA. Chief Justice Sir Robert Stout was regarded by Catholics as their bitter enemy. See R. P. Davis, *Irish Issues in New Zealand Politics*; also *NZS*, 2 January 1922.
28. Fr Lane to Liston, 24 March 1922, Liston Papers, ACDA.
29. Ibid.
30. O'Sullivan to Liston, 23 March 1922, Liston Papers, ACDA.
31. Fr Patrick Lagan to Liston, 22 March 1922, Liston Papers, ACDA.
32. Te Kuiti Irish Self-Determination League to Liston, 18 March 1922, Liston Papers, ACDA.
33. Sr Mary Stephena to Liston, 26 March 1922, Liston Papers, ACDA.
34. Bryan Flannery to Liston, 26 March 1922, Liston Papers, ACDA.
35. O'Leary to Liston, 23 March 1922, Liston Papers, ACDA.
36. O'Sullivan to Liston, 23 March 1922, Liston Papers, ACDA.
37. Mulcahy to Liston, 23 March 1922, Liston Papers, ACDA.
38. Liston Papers 6-2, ACDA.
39. *Hawke's Bay Tribune*, 23 March 1922.
40. Peter Dowd to Liston, 28 March 1922, Liston Papers, ACDA. 'Uncle is in a terrible state over the matter', Sister Mary Antonia told Liston on 2 April. 'His letter to the press would not be published. I hope he gets it printed in some other paper.'
41. Fr Michael Edge to Liston, 24 March 1922, Liston Papers, ACDA. The letter survives among Liston's papers.
42. *NZH*, 17 March 1922.
43. Mulcahy to Liston, 23 March 1922, Liston Papers, ACDA.
44. Liston to Cleary, 24 April 1922, Brodie Papers, CCDA.
45. *NZH*, 25 March 1922.
46. *AS*, 21 March 1922. A shoneen was an unpatriotic Irishman, one who aped the manners and fashions of the English.
47. Liston to Cleary, 24 April 1922, Brodie Papers, CCDA.
48. Lynch to Liston, 21 March 1922, Liston Papers, ACDA. Fr George Colgan (Coromandel) predicted that the affair would do much good 'to Catholics and Irishmen who for years past have settled down into the game of cowardly silence'. Fr Colgan to Liston, 21 March 1922, Liston Papers, ACDA.
49. O'Leary to Liston, 23 March 1922, Liston Papers, ACDA. Walls assured Liston that 'for every supporter PPA Gunson may have in his city you have hundreds of warm true friends in this part of New Zealand'. J. P. Walls to Liston, 26 March 1922, Liston Papers, ACDA.
50. *ODT*, 22 March 1922. Liston had delivered the substance of a *Tablet* editorial from the Town Hall stage. His audience, both inside and outside the auditorium, was more used to hearing the exquisitely loyal phrases of Bishop Henry Cleary.
51. *NZH*, 25 March 1922. The writer was 'Mercutio' in his regular Saturday column 'Local Gossip'.
52. Kelly believed that shoneens possessed 'the souls of huxters and the mental stature of apes'. *Tablet*, 18 December 1919.
53. *Tablet*, 31 January 1918.
54. Sweetman, 'New Zealand Catholicism', Ch. 7. O'Sullivan told Liston of the many Catholics he had met since arriving from Ireland who showed little understanding of or sympathy for Irish troubles: They had asked him, 'Why don't the Irish agree among themselves? Why do they give a chance to the British Press to say nasty things of them?' J. P. O'Sullivan

to Liston, 23 March 1922, Liston Papers, ACDA.

55. Twomey to Cleary, 1 October 1920, Cleary Papers, ACDA. Twomey also complained to M. J. Sheahan that Kelly 'makes the paper a dirty gutter snipe . . . his work is doing great injury to poor Catholics who have to earn their living from the people whom he insults'. Twomey to Sheahan, 29 March 1920, cited in P. S. O'Connor, '"Protestants", Catholics and the New Zealand Government, 1916–1918', in G. A. Wood and P. S. O'Connor (eds), *W. P. Morrell: a Tribute*, Dunedin, 1973, pp.189–90. The *Tablet* (10 April 1919) dismissed Twomey as 'out of touch with Ireland'.

56. It must be said that Twomey and his kind proved better prophets of Ireland's bloody future after Sinn Fein won the 1918 election. *Tablet*, 10 April 1919.

57. Michael Joseph Sheahan (1856–1935) was born in Ireland and came to New Zealand when a child. An estate agent and justice of the peace, he knew and served every Catholic Bishop of Auckland from Pompallier to Liston. Sheahan struck up a friendship with the Irish nationalist leader John Dillon during the latter's visit to New Zealand in 1889 and they kept up a regular correspondence. Sheahan file, Dillon Papers, Trinity College, Dublin [TCD]. F. S. L. Lyons, *John Dillon. A Biography*. London, 1968.

58. Sheahan to Dillon, 15 November 1918, Dillon Papers, TCD. On Sheahan and Cleary see Sweetman, 'New Zealand Catholicism', pp.295–296. Kelly's rebuke is in *Tablet*, 15 April 1920.

59. *Month*, 15 August 1923.

60. Sheahan to John Dillon, 20 January 1899, Dillon Papers, TCD.

61. *NZH*, 24 March 1922.

62. J. A. Lee to Liston, 24 March 1922, Liston Papers, ACDA. Lee was the Labour candidate for the district encompassing Liston's parish. He promised Liston that he would oppose any hostile motion to come before the Auckland RSA: 'In a party like ours, a fighting party, we have a loyalty which prompts us to defend our members even when they err. How much sooner should we defend to the best of our capacity those who have merely offended by stating the truth.'

63. R. P. Davis, 'The New Zealand Labour Party's "Irish Campaign", 1916–1921', *Political Science*, 19, 2 (1967), pp.13–23.

64. P. Hickey to Liston, 21 March 1922, Liston Papers, ACDA.

65. *Maoriland Worker*, 29 March 1922.

66. 'Did Irish soldiers murder innocent and unarmed Irish women, children, and old men who were shot in cold blood during the past four years in Ireland?' *Grey River Argus*, 27 March 1922. The copy was sent to the Crown Law Office by J. Lowden and seen by the Solicitor-General on 3 April 1922. File 732, CLO.

67. *AS*, 24 March 1922. The clergy's resolution was more subtly phrased than that of the of Irish National Association, whose sneer that Liston's shoneen Irish critics voiced 'no opinion other than that of their own' brought a predictable response from J. F Walsh in the *King Country Chronicle* (23 March 1922): 'What other opinion should a man express than his own?'

68. Fr Riordan to Liston, 24 March 1922, Liston Papers, ACDA.

69. Fr Kennedy to Liston, 24 March 1922, Liston papers, ACDA.

70. *NZH*, 23 March 1922.

71. *NZH*, 25 March 1922.

72. Archbishop O'Shea (Wellington), and Bishops Brodie (Christchurch) and Cleary (Auckland) were all either in Europe or en route there for the Eucharistic Congress due to be held in Rome during May.

73. O'Regan's diary for 1922 is among his papers in the ATL. See also R. M. Sweetman, 'Patrick Joseph O'Regan: A Life of Advocacy', *Turnbull Library Record*, 21 (2), October 1988. pp.93–97.

74. O'Regan Diary, 25 March 1922, O'Regan Papers, ATL.

75. *EP*, 25 March 1922.

8
Sacred Traditions of Sorrow

1. E. O'Malley, *On Another Man's Wound*. Dublin, 1979, p.38.

2. Notes of Evidence, p.21. W. H. Mulcahy to Liston, 23 March 1922, Liston

Papers, ACDA. Fr T. J. Cahill to Brodie, 5 August 1921, Brodie Papers, CCDA.

3. Liston Defence Notes 6-1, ACDA. See also R. Dudley Edwards and T. D. Williams (eds), *The Great Famine: Studies in Irish History 1845–52*. Dublin, 1956. Joel Mokyr, *Why Ireland Starved*. London, 1983.

4. Liston preserved among his papers a record of the notorious 'coffin-ships' to Quebec, when disease on board led to the deaths of 17,000 of the 100,000 emigrants. Liston Defence Notes 6-1, ACDA.

5. J. S. Donnelly, 'The Irish Agricultural Depression of 1859–64', *Irish Economic and Social History*, 111 (1976), pp.33–54.

6. Liston drew freely on the writings of Michael Mulhall (1836–1900), especially his *Dictionary of Statistics* (Dublin, 1883). 'According to Mulhall's statistics, nearly 4,000,000 people were evicted in Ireland in fifty years, and nothing is more familiar in Irish families than the constant references of the old people to these evictions.' Liston Defence Notes 6-1/43, ACDA. Liston's attitude towards his parents' eviction contrasts sharply with that of Archbishop Duhig. T. P. Boland, *Archbishop Duhig*. Queensland, 1986, pp.20–21. On his mother as 'exile', see Liston to Cleary, 19 March 1919, Cleary Papers, ACDA.

7. W. E. Vaughan, *Landlords and Tenants in Ireland 1848–1904*. Studies in *Irish Economic and Social History* 2, Dundalk, 1984. pp.8–13. That such types existed was proved by the massive clearances in the immediate post-Famine years, with sporadic renewals in the early 1860s and 1880s.

8. 'The *national* spirit of Ireland manifested itself in the days of the Land League. The people looked upon the landlords as the agents who had taken away their liberties, and they hit at the agent whom they recognised as the common enemy. Were it not for this the killing of landlords would have been murder.' Liston Defence Notes 6-1/5, ACDA.

9. Thomas Bartlett, '"What Ish My Nation?": Themes in Irish History 1550–1850', in T. Bartlett, C. Curtin, R. O'Dwyer, G. O'Tuathaigh (eds), *Irish Studies: A General Introduction*. Dublin, 1988, p.56. Statistics show some 90,000 evictions from 1847 to 1880, far short of Liston's 3.8 million; rentals reveal only a modest average rise (20 percent from 1851 to 1878), while agricultural statistics refute the version of a countryside seething with violence between landlord and tenant. Vaughan, *Landlords and Tenants*, pp.14–17. See also W. E. Vaughan, 'An assessment of the economic performance of Irish landlords, 1851–81', in F. S. L. Lyons and R. A. J. Hawkins (eds), *Ireland under the Union*. Oxford, 1980, pp.173–199.

10. It would seem that while Liston's paternal relatives were among their number, his mother's people were not. His father's family had flourished by the 1920s, while he could find no trace of his mother's people in 1903. Liston to Cleary, 19 March 1919, Cleary Papers, ACDA. Biographical material on the Liston family sent to Fr E. R. Simmons (archivist), 1 April 1985.

11. Improved transport facilities helped the Irish economy to integrate more fully into an industrialised British state. In 1845 potatoes, grain and livestock each accounted for one-third of the value of Irish agricultural output; by 1914 the livestock sector contributed three-quarters of the total value. Joseph Lee, *The Modernisation of Irish Society 1848–1918*. Dublin, 1973, pp.10–11. Vaughan, *Landlords and Tenants*, p.14.

12. D. Fitzpatrick, *Irish Emigration 1801–1921. Studies in Irish Economic and Social History* 1, Dundalk, 1984, p.1.

13. Ibid., pp.3–13. C. Curtin, R. O'Dwyer, G. O'Tuathaigh, 'Emigration and Exile,' in Bartlett *et al.*, (eds), *Irish Studies*, pp.63–5.

14. Fitzpatrick, *Irish Emigration*, p.16. Kelly summed up this view in the *Tablet*, 28 October 1920, 26 May 1921. Irish politicians took to citing the emigration statistics as a bald indictment of British misgovernment. Kelly attributed the halving of the Irish population to 'the beneficent British administration, or as some people prefer to call it, exploitation'. *Tablet*, 14 July 1921.

15. Fitzpatrick, *Irish Emigration*, p.17. D. H. Akenson, *The Irish Diaspora: a Primer*, Belfast, 1993. For a stimulating

discussion of these issues, see C. Brady (ed.), *Interpreting Irish History: the Debate on Historical Revisionism 1938–1994*. Dublin, 1994.
16. Ibid., p.30.
17. Ibid., p.13.
18. Oliver MacDonagh, 'The Irish in Victoria, 1851–91: A Demographic Essay,' in *Historical Studies* VIII, Dublin, 1971, pp.67–92. Fitzpatrick, *Irish Emigration*, p.21.
19. P. J. O'Farrell, 'Emigrant attitudes and behaviour as a source for Irish history', in *Historical Studies* X, Dublin, 1976, p.112. Liston to Cleary, 19 March 1919, Cleary Papers, ACDA.
20. *Tablet*, 30 August 1900.
21. Indeed, by leaving Ireland in the early 1860s, James Liston and the thousands who accompanied him may have postponed the explosion of rural discontent that took place two decades later during the Irish land war. Fitzpatrick, *Irish Immigration*, p.41.
22. P. Quinlivan and P. Rose, *The Fenians in England 1865–1972*. London, 1982. See also K. Amos, *The Fenians in Australia 1865–1880*. Sydney, 1988.
23. *NZO*, 8 April 1922. David McGill, *The Lion and the Wolfhound: The Irish Rebellion on the New Zealand Goldfields*. Wellington, 1990. (See also my review in the *New Zealand Listener*, 21 January 1991, p.82.)
24. Fitzpatrick, *Irish Emigration*, p.35.
25. P. R. May, *The West Coast Gold Rushes*. Christchurch, 1962, p.284.
26. Liston to Cleary, 19 March 1919, Cleary Papers, ACDA. It is not clear exactly when Mary arrived in New Zealand. She may have been in the colony for some years; it is also possible that she came out to marry James.
27. *Tablet*, 30 August 1900.
28. F. Tod, *Pubs Galore: A History of Dunedin Hotels 1848–1984*. Dunedin, 1984, p.20.
29. B. F. Cadogan, 'Lace Curtain Catholics: The Catholic Bourgeoisie of the Diocese of Dunedin, 1900–1920', BA research essay, University of Otago, 1984.
30. D. H. Akenson, *Half the World from Home: Perspectives on the Irish in New Zealand 1860–1950*. Wellington, 1990, Ch. 6.
31. *Tablet*, 30 August 1900, 17 July 1902.
32. B. F. Cadogan, 'The bar-room church of early Dunedin,' in *Tablet*, 13 March 1985. The 1921 census revealed that 27.6 percent of licensees were Catholic. New Zealand Census Returns 1921, part VII.
33. Liston's birth certificate gives the place of birth as George Street, Dunedin.
34. Fr M. Walsh baptised Liston on 19 June 1881. A copy of his baptismal certificate is held in the archives of St Patrick's College, Manly, Australia. On Liston's links with St Joseph's, see *Tablet*, 15 July 1920, and *Zealandia*, 13 February 1936.
35. On Bishop Moran (1823–1895) see Hugh Laracy, 'The life and context of Bishop Patrick Moran', MA thesis, Victoria University of Wellington, 1964.
36. *Tablet*, 19 and 26 October 1927. Patrick Lynch (1858–1927) can be traced through his correspondence with Patrick Vincent Dwyer (Bishop of Maitland 1897–1931) preserved in the Catholic diocesan archives of Maitland [MCDA].
37. K. T. Livingstone, *The Emergence of an Australian Catholic Priesthood 1835–1915*. Sydney, 1977. Lynch to Dwyer, 19 March 1890, Dwyer Papers, MCDA. Lynch to Verdon, 25 January 1893, Verdon Papers, St Patrick's College, Manly.
38. Moran to Verdon, 26 January 1893, Verdon Papers, St Patrick's College, Manly.
39. *NZH*, 28 April 1970. On who paid the bill, see Moran to Verdon, 26 January 1893, Verdon Papers, St Patrick's College, Manly.
40. *Catholic Press* (Sydney), 30 March 1922. *Manly*, 1, 1 (October 1916), p.147. St Patrick's College Register, Book A, 1888–95. I am indebted to Dr Kevin Walsh (Sydney) for information on Liston's years at Manly.
41. Lynch to Verdon, 25 January 1893, Verdon Papers, St Patrick's College, Manly. This was a reference to the two other Dunedin students, Thomas Cotter and Patrick O'Neill, with whom Liston had come across.
42. The New Zealand students were a success story for St Patrick's College. Their rate of ordination was higher than that of their Australian contemporaries; they numbered three of the first five seminarians to

go on to Rome for further training; Brodie and Liston became the first colonial-born bishops to come out of Manly. (In recognition of this achievement fifty ex-Manly priests presented Liston with his pectoral cross and chain. *Tablet*, 26 August 1920). Livingstone, *The Emergence of an Australian Catholic Priesthood*, pp.131–132.

43. Verdon to Murphy, 4 February 1897, Murphy Papers, St Patrick's College, Manly.

44. On Lynch's qualities, see Bishop Grimes (Christchurch) to Archbishop Redwood, 16 June 1895; Bishop Luck (Auckland) to Archbishop Redwood, 8 July 1895, Redwood Papers, Wellington Catholic Archdiocesan Archives [WCAA]. Burke and O'Neill, who had come out to New Zealand together in 1882, were long time pastors of Invercargill and Milton respectively. O'Neill claimed Burke as his 'oldest friend' (*Tablet*, 25 May 1916). On Burke's terna vote, see Grimes to Redwood, 29 June 1895, and O'Neill to Redwood, 7 July 1895, Redwood Papers, WCAA.

45. Burke to Coffey, 13 May 1920, Cleary Papers, ACDA. (Coffey sent this letter on to Cleary.) On Lynch's joining the Redemptorists, see S. J. Boland, *Faith of our Fathers*. Armidale, 1982, pp.77–78. Liston later recalled Lynch's devotion to Moran in a note of 12 December 1973, Liston Papers, ACDA.

46. Verdon was its second president (1870–79), while Lynch was also a student there (1879–82). See *Holy Cross College, Clonliffe Dublin: College History and Centenary Record 1859–1959*. Dublin, 1962, pp.79–84.

47. Ibid., pp.97–98.

48. *Catholic Press* (Sydney), 30 March 1922. These relatives were probably his father's sisters Honora, Mary Ellen, Nellie and Bridget, who lived in the neighbouring counties of Limerick and Clare. None of his mother's people remained in Barefield. Liston to Cleary, 19 March 1919, Cleary Papers, ACDA. Biographical material on the Liston family sent to Fr E. R. Simmons (archivist), 1 April 1985.

49. *Holy Cross College*, p.97.

50. *Tablet*, 7 September 1899.

51. Liston recalled his years at the Irish College in a contribution for an intended publication in 1972. The draft (entitled 'Pontificio Collegio Irlandese: Memories') remains among his papers.

52. Mosgiel's roll rose to around 25 students by 1904, requiring additions to be built. It had swollen to 30 in 1906, and doubled again within ten years. Verdon to Dwyer, 9 May 1902, 7 November 1916, Dwyer Papers, MCDA. *Manly*, 1, 1 (October 1916). B Mannes (ed.), *Golden Jubilee: Holy Cross College, Mosgiel, New Zealand 1900–1950*. Dunedin, 1950, p.35.

53. *Tablet*, 3 February 1904. Releasing Cecil Morkane for study in Rome, a favour the latter would return in 1920 by replacing the Auckland-bound Liston as Mosgiel rector.

54. Mannes, *Golden Jubilee*, p.37. The chapter on Liston as professor and rector was written by Fr Edmund Lynch, a nephew of Dean Burke.

55. Ibid., p.36.

56. Ibid., p.39.

57. *NZH*, 28 April 1970.

58. Mannes, *Golden Jubilee*, pp. 16–17. *NZH*, 28 April 1970.

59. *Zealandia*, 31 January 1964.

60. *Tablet*, 26 May 1921.

61. Separate schools were seen as the key to Catholic survival in a Protestant colony. Akenson, *Half the World from Home*, Ch. 6.

62. Liston to the Dominion Council of the Catholic Federation, 5 March 1919, 'Report of Proceedings of 13th Half-Yearly Meeting of the Dominion Council of the New Zealand Catholic Federation.' Auckland, 1919, p.4.

63. Sweetman, 'New Zealand Catholicism', Chs 6,7 and 8.

64. P. S. O'Connor, 'Storm over the clergy – New Zealand 1917', *Journal of Religious History*, 4, 2 (December 1966), pp.129–148.

65. Liston to Monsignor Mahoney, 15 March 1917, Cleary Papers, ACDA. Mahoney acted as administrator during Cleary's absence in Europe (1916–17).

66. In July 1917, Fr James McMenamin, one of the historic 1909 ordinands, was killed at the Battle of Messines. *Tablet*, 28 June 1917.

67. Sweetman, 'New Zealand Catholicism', Ch. 10.
68. *ODT*, 15 December 1917.
69. M. Satchell, 'Pulpit Politics: the Protestant Political Association in Dunedin from 1917 to 1922', BA research essay, University of Otago, 1983.
70. *Tablet*, 22 March 1917.
71. Sweetman, 'New Zealand Catholicism', Ch. 10.
72. Liston to Cleary, 12 November 1920, Cleary Papers, ACDA.
73. During the influenza epidemic of 1918–19 he was encouraged by the degree of co-operation between the various Christian denominations, later claiming this as the birth of ecumenism in New Zealand. *NZH*, 28 April 1970.
74. *Tablet*, 20 March 1919.
75. Sweetman, 'New Zealand Catholicism', Ch. 7.
76. Liston to Cleary, 25 November 1917, Cleary Papers, ACDA.
77. James Coffey (1866–1923) was Administrator of St Joseph's Cathedral, Dunedin, for the last fifteen years of his life. Coffey to Cleary, 21/24 November 1917, Cleary Papers, ACDA.
78. The bishops' report to Rome is included in the *Relazione circa la nomina del Vescovo di Dunedin, e di un Coadiutore con diritto successione del Vescovo di Auckland, nella Nuova Zelanda*. Sacra Congregazione de Propaganda Fide, Marzo 1920, Prot. N. 850/20, ff.116–37. [*Relazione*], APF. See also O'Shea to Redwood, 22 January 1919, Redwood Papers, WCAA.
79. *Relazione*, f. 8 (*'e più volte me lo indicò come suo successore'*).
80. *Tablet*, 1 March 1916. Liston to Brodie, 29 November 1920, Brodie Papers, CCDA.
81. *Relazione*, ff. 3–4. Coffey to Bishops and Archbishop, 19 January 1919, Redwood Papers, WCAA.
82. *Relazione*, ff. 3–4, 7, 12–15. Redwood to Cleary, 10 April 1919, Cleary Papers, ACDA.
83. *Relazione*, ff 4–5. Dated 3 July 1919, the petition was forwarded to Rome by Cattaneo on 11 July 1919.
84. *Relazione*, f. 7. Bishops' report on Dundedin clergy's terna, 17–18 January 1919, Redwood Papers, WCAA. Michael O'Farrell had conducted a retreat for the Dunedin clergy in January 1918. *Tablet*, 10 January 1918. On his splendid reputation as a missioner, see D. F. Bourke, *The History of the Vincentian Fathers in Australasia*. Melbourne, 1980. pp.141, 147. (My thanks to Fr Bourke for the gift of this book.) O'Farrell was consecrated as the fourth Bishop of Bathurst on 30 November 1920.
85. Kelly to Hagan, 4 and 31 December 1918, 18 March 1919, 3 August 1919, 3 January 1920, Hagan Papers, ICR. Many of these complaints would be heard again after Liston became a bishop. Perhaps the Dunedin clergy did not relish the prospect of feeling what Fr E. J. Lynch termed the 'reverential apprehension of doing aught that might displease him'. Some of them hoped they had left that behind when graduating from Holy Cross College. Mannes, *Golden Jubilee*, p.39.
86. After relations between the two men deteriorated some years later, the story spread that Cleary had been saddled with Liston much against his will; in fact the bishops had unanimously nominated Liston for this post should Rome find him unacceptable for Dunedin. Indeed, rather than Cleary being landed with Liston, the reverse was true. See Brodie to Propaganda Fide, undated [1929?], Brodie Papers, CCDA.
87. Mannes, *Golden Jubilee*, p.44. See also Liston to Cleary, 29 April 1920, Cleary Papers, ACDA.
88. *Tablet*, 26 May 1921.
89. Liston to Cleary, 29 April 1920, Cleary Papers, ACDA.
90. *Relazione*, ff. 10–13.
91. *Month*, 22 January 1921.
92. Liston to Brodie, 10 January 1921, Brodie Papers, CCDA.
93. Liston to Brodie, 10 January 1921, Brodie Papers, CCDA. Dean Jeremiah Cahill was particularly friendly. Named first on the Auckland clergy's terna, Cahill was terrified by the very thought of the mitre and greatly relieved when Liston was appointed.
94. Brodie to Cleary, 5 May 1921, Cleary Papers, ACDA.

95. Liston to Brodie, 10 January 1921, Brodie Papers, CCDA.
96. Liston to Brodie, 22 February 1921, Brodie Papers, CCDA.
97. Liston to Parr, 23 February 1922, Liston Papers, ACDA.
98. 'Report of Proceedings of 13th Half-Yearly Meeting' p.3–7. *Month*, 22 January 1921.
99. Ibid.
100. *Tablet*, 15 July 1920.
101. *Tablet*, 3 March 1921. The report continued: 'He recalled that typical Irish mother, who, in 1916, freely offered up her two fine sons for the cause of Ireland. This Irish mother took an American visitor to the spot where she had bade her two boys an earthly farewell, and averred that, bitter as the sacrifice was, she willingly endured it for Ireland. Here the Bishop recited in feeling terms the poem dedicated to Patrick Pearse and his brother.'
102. *Tablet*, 26 May 1921.
103. In August 1919, Bishop Cleary warned his clergy that 'an organised watch is being set upon our concerts and other such functions.' Circulars File, Cleary Papers, ACDA. See also Ch. 2, p.25.
104. The image of Ireland as martyr held a special attraction for the children of emigrants. Cardinal O'Connell touched on this in early 1920: 'The story of Ireland and her wrongs thrills me beyond anything I can say, next to the story of Christ and the Crucifixion. There is such a tragedy in Ireland's story that I, a son of the Gael, devoted and patriotic to my country America, am thrilled and overpowered by the wrongs of Ireland.' *Tablet*, 25 March 1920. Kelly agreed, 'The nostalgia of the Irish exile is no poet's fancy. It burns like a fever and it never dies.' *Tablet*, 21 February 1918.
105. *Tablet*, 10 May 1917.

9
Mr Massey is Much Concerned

1. *EP*, 2 October 1920.
2. *NZH*, 20 March 1922. Bell promptly sent the papers on to Solicitor-General MacGregor, along with a copy of his cautionary reply to Gunson. One wonders whether Bell consulted Massey before penning the latter, a clear attempt to minimise the bishop's offence. Police File 22/477, NA.
3. Massey to Bell, 21 March 1922, Police File 22/477, NA.
4. *Tablet*, 16 December 1920.
5. *NZS*, 1 March 1922.
6. W. J. Gardner, 'The Rise of W. F. Massey, 1891–1912', *Political Science*, 13, 1 (March 1961). pp.3–30.
7. In 1909 the opposition assumed the name of Reform. Gardner, 'The Rise of W. F. Massey', p.25.
8. *NZPD*, Vol. 157, pp.68–69. See Michael Bassett, *Sir Joseph Ward: A Political Biography*. Auckland, 1993.
9. *NZPD*, Vol. 173, p.56. W. J. Gardner, 'W. F. Massey in Power,' *Political Science*, 13, 2 (September 1961), p.26. *EP*, 5 November 1920.
10. M. Bassett, (*Ward*, pp.117, 200) absolves Ward, while R. P. Davis and H. M. Moores indict Massey. Davis, *Irish Issues in New Zealand Politics*, p.9. Moores, 'The Rise of the Protestant Political Association'.
11. Bishop Cleary later described the Massey government as 'the very best friends that New Zealand Catholics ever had in the matter of education'. Cleary to Liston, 2 September 1922, Liston Papers, ACDA.
12. A performance which earned him the soubriquet of 'Mr Facing-both-ways'. *NZPD*, Vol. 171, p.593.
13. Dean Regnault to Cleary, 31 August 1912, Cleary Papers, ACDA. See Sweetman, 'New Zealand Catholicism', p.65.
14. See *EP*, 17 February 1916. Also O'Shea to Cleary, 27 August 1914, Cleary Papers, ACDA.
15. Sweetman, 'New Zealand Catholicism', Chs 7 and 8.
16. *NZPD*, Vol. 189, p.620.
17. Sweetman, 'New Zealand Catholicism', Ch. 10.
18. *Tablet*, 25 March, 21 October 1920.
19. The Solicitor-General urged that this action be taken within two months of Kelly's arrival in the editor's chair. Salmond to Attorney-General, 9 May 1917; Salmond to Chief of General Staff, 24 July 1917, 1917

Opinion Book, CLO. Salmond gets little credit for his decisive action from his biographer. See Alex Frame, *Salmond: Southern Jurist*. Wellington, 1995.

20. *NZH*, 17 July, 10 August 1920. Sweetman, 'Daniel Mannix and his Biographers', *Australian Studies*, 1 (1988), pp.61–71.

21. By September 1919 the PPA boasted 200,000 members organised in 225 branches. *Nelson Colonist*, 11 October 1919. For Australia, see Patrick O'Farrell, *The Catholic Church and Community: An Australian History*. Kensington, 1985, Ch. 5. For the United States, see Edward Cuddy, 'The Irish Question and the Revival of Anti-Catholicism in the 1920's', *Catholic Historical Review*, Vol. lxvii, No 2, April 1981, pp.236–255.

22. For other reasons why Ward fell, see *Truth*, 17 January 1920, and P. S. O'Connor, 'Politics and Religion, 1911–1920', *Political Science*, 19, 1 (July 1967), p.14.

23. Sweetman, 'New Zealand Catholicism', pp.254–55.

24. *Tablet*, 16 and 30 September 1920.

25. *Tablet*, 21 October, 11 November 1920.

26. Even Bishop Brodie abandoned his moderation in response to the final vote: 'Massey and Co. have become persecutors but the tables will soon be turned and Massey will meet the fate he and his party deserve.' Brodie to Cleary, 17 November 1920, Cleary Papers, ACDA.

27. Sweetman, 'New Zealand Catholicism', pp.258–71. *NZPD*, Vol. 189, pp.223–39, 605–74. Again, if Elliott foisted his clause on the House, then the belligerent Catholic response ensured its passage into law.

28. Moores, 'Rise of the Protestant Political Association', p.317.

29. *NZPD*, Vol. 189, p.660. P. S. O'Connor, 'Some Political Preoccupations of Mr Massey, 1918–20,' *Political Science*, 18, 2 (September 1966), p.35. Moores, 'Rise of the Protestant Political Association', p.317. James Samuel Dickson was the member of parliament for Parnell from 1911 to 1928.

30. Cleary to O'Shea, 29 September 1920, Cleary Papers, ACDA. One parliamentarian (E. J. Howard) believed that the PPA leader was a member of the House after seeing him there so after. *NZPD*, Vol. 189, p.663.

31. *Tablet*, 23 October 1919. In 1920 Massey rejected the suggestion that the PPA's Auckland secretary be appointed as Reform Party organiser for the North Island. O'Connor, 'Some Political Preoccupations', pp.29–30.

32. A. Paape to Massey, 16 November 1920, Massey Papers, NA.

33. O'Connor, 'Some Political Preoccupations', p.30.

34. Sweetman, 'New Zealand Catholicism', pp.258–271. Massey's two interventions during the lengthy debate were in response to gibes from the Labour members; he would not have spoken otherwise. While nominally a member of the House committee considering the Bill he attended only once, and that for an inattentive half-hour. Even when the final vote was taken, some three months after the key clause was drafted, Massey still had not found time to read the minutes of evidence.

35. *NZPD*, Vol. 189, p.235. The clause made it an offence punishable by two years' imprisonment to allege that anyone legally married was not 'truly and sufficiently' married.

36. *NZPD*, Vol. 189, p.233. Bishop Cleary was prepared to absolve the Prime Minister from blame for the Marriage Amendment Act. Referring to Massey's assurance that it was not a party measure, Cleary later told the Apostolic Delegate, 'I personally believe, from a long acquaintance with Mr Massey and many evidences of his good-will towards Catholics, that this statement was made at the time in all sincerity.' Cleary to Cattaneo, 13 February 1921, Cleary Papers, ACDA. Cleary later claimed to have received assurances that the law was intended to be 'a dead letter', passed *in terrorem*. Cleary to Van Rossum, 25 March 1923, Cleary Papers, ACDA. Had Massey been motivated principally by anti-Catholicism, he could have acted against the supposed effect of the *Ne Temere* decree ten years earlier, during his first administration.

37. *Tablet*, 20 November 1920.

38. R. P. Davis, *Irish Issues in New*

Zealand Politics, 1868–1922, Dunedin, 1974, p.9.
39. Sweetman, 'New Zealand Catholicism', p.79. *NZT*, 14 February 1914.
40. *NZPD*, Vol. 176, pp.51–56.
41. *NZPD*, Vol. 176, p.56.
42. *EP*, 18 September 1919.
43. *EP*, 24 October 1919.
44. *NZFL*, 3 December 1919. The Industrial Workers of the World (IWW) was a revolutionary labour movement founded in the US, pledged to overthrow capitalism by strikes and sabotage.
45. *NZPD*, Vol. 190, p.170.
46. *EP*, 4 August 1920.
47. *NZPD*, Vol. 192, p.910.
48. The Orangemen urged Massey to 'oppose unequivocally any concession to the Irish rebels that would weaken and disintegrate the Empire'. *NZH*, 29 March 1921. Kelly organised similar pressure from the Sinn Fein side. It was widely anticipated that the British Commonwealth leaders would be consulted on how best to settle the Irish question. The new Colonial Secretary, Winston Churchill, had recently advocated a policy of wider consultation between the constituent parts of the Empire on the problems faced by the whole. *EP*, 20 June and 21 July 1921.
49. *EP*, 31 May 1921.
50. *EP*, 25 July 1921.
51. *EP*, 6 July 1921.
52. *EP*, 20 June 1921, 2 September 1921, 26 January 1922. *NZH*, 31 October 1922.
53. Cited in the *EP*, 19 October 1921.
54. Massey's New Zealand-born sons fought with the NZEF. His brogue was noted by the *Daily Mail* (London) on 6 January 1917, while Frank Morton described him as speaking 'the Mangarene dialect' (*NZFL*, 18 October 1913).
55. *NZPD*, Vol. 191, p.501.
56. *EP*, 6 May 1920, 1 October 1921.
57. *EP*, 6 May 1920, 1 January 1921.
58. *NZPD*, Vol. 206, p.14. Massey thought that the Empire had been specially protected by God so that it might fulfil its destiny of bringing peace to the world: 'The risks that we ran during the war were frightful. The escapes we had were most extraordinary. I honestly believe that nothing but a miracle saved us. Nothing but the intervention of Divine Providence saved us in March 1918. I believe that we have been specially protected, because we are being preserved for some great purpose which has not yet been revealed. Part of that purpose, I believe, will be to assist . . . in bringing about the day when men shall turn their swords into ploughshares and learn the arts of war no more.' *NZPD*, Vol. 196, p.485.
59. *EP*, 10 September 1921. 'The British Empire is the most important factor for peace in the world at the present time. I have no hesitation in saying that it is the greatest Empire the world has ever seen, that those great Empires of the past . . . have been unimportant compared to it.' *NZH*, 1 October 1921.
60. *EP*, 24 June 1921, 18 September 1922. 'It is almost too awful to think of,' Massey concluded. *NZPD*, Vol. 191, p.500.
61. *EP*, 28 September 1920. Massey held that the 17,000 troops who did not return home had sacrificed themselves 'to save freedom and civilisation'.
62. *EP*, 18–20 September 1922. K. O. Morgan, *Consensus and Disunity. The Lloyd George Coalition Government 1918–1922*. Oxford, 1986, p.323.
63. *EP*, 20 September 1922.
64. *EP*, 1 October 1921.
65. *EP*, 15 February, 17 and 26 August, 14 October 1921.
66. *EP*, 23 May 1922.
67. *EP*, 14 October 1921. 'No man would be allowed to give vent to seditious utterances in the country, no matter what his position was', Massey told Parliament. *NZPD*, Vol. 195, p.67.

10
Why Prosecute?

1. *EP*, 13 October 1919.
2. *EP*, 5 October 1921.
3. *EP*, 25 August 1920.
4. *EP*, 27 July 1921.
5. *NZPD*, Vol.183, p.187.
6. *NZH*, 16 April 1921. *EP*, 18 July 1921.
7. 'Recently the patriotism of Egypt has followed much the same course as that of Ireland.' *EP*, 4 March 1922.

8. *NZH*, 21 March 1922. The *EP* (14 February 1921) called the South African nationalists 'the avowed enemies of the Empire'.
9. A. Draper, *The Amritsar Massacre*. London, 1985.
10. *EP*, 12 July 1920. Winston Churchill preferred to describe Amritsar as 'a monstrous event, standing out in sinister isolation'. (*EP*, 13 July 1920).
11. J. M. Brown, *Gandhi*. London, 1989. *EP*, 1 January 1921.
12. *NZH*, 21 March 1922.
13. Ibid.
14. *EP*, 4 March 1922.
15. R. P. Davis, 'The New Zealand Labour Party's 'Irish Campaign', 1916–1921,' *Political Science*, 19, 2 (December 1967). pp.13–23. Sweetman, 'New Zealand Catholicism', pp.237–47, 302–4, 332–36.
16. Sweetman, 'New Zealand Catholicism', p.302. In September 1919 Holland questioned the Allied commitment to self-determination by citing the 200,000 British soldiers stationed in Ireland. *NZPD*, Vol.184, p.621. See also, Paul Baker, *King and Country Call*. Auckland, 1988. For Labour's wartime record, see B. Gustafson, *Labour's Path to Political Independence*. Auckland, 1980, Ch. 10.
17. Davis, *Irish Issues in New Zealand Politics*, p.207. At a Wellington meeting in August 1920 Holland 'explained and justified the NZLP's attitude towards the Irish question.' *Tablet*, 5 August 1920. One of Holland's meetings in Auckland was so crowded that 500 people had to be turned away.
18. *Maoriland Worker*, 14 July 1920.
19. *Maoriland Worker*, 10 August 1921.
20. *Maoriland Worker*, 16 November 1921; *Tablet*, 6 December 1918, 28 October 1920, 21 April 1921.
21. *Tablet*, 20 March 1919.
22. *Tablet*, 24 February 1921. Kelly also pronounced Holland 'that rare thing, an honest politician'. *Tablet*, 12 August 1920. Fraser's lecture, entitled 'The Crucifixion of Ireland,' was based on an imported pamphlet which the Crown Law Office felt was clearly seditious. W. C. MacGregor (Solicitor-General) to Comptroller of Customs, 27 May 1921, Opinion Book 1921, CLO.
23. *NZH*, 3 December 1919.
24. *AS*, 1 December 1920.
25. *NZPD*, Vol.184, pp.1154–55.
26. Whyte to Massey, 29 March 1921, Massey Papers, NA.
27. *Tablet*, 12 August 1921. Kelly claimed that Massey had 'tried to browbeat Holland with vague threats'.
28. Massey claimed that its effect would be to hand Ireland over 'to the enemies of Great Britain and the Empire and to those who wish to have a republic in Ireland'. *NZPD*, Vol.186, pp.684–86.
29. *NZPD*, Vol.190, p.193.
30. *NZPD*, Vol.192, p.190.
31. Holland rejoiced that the Irish would now 'be able to work out their destiny in the way they desire'. *NZT*, 12 December 1921.
32. *Tablet*, 15 December 1921.
33. *ODT*, 8 December 1921.
34. *Tablet*, 25 November 1920.
35. *AS*, 6 March 1920. In its advocacy of Dominion home rule for Ireland, *AS* went further than the *ODT* (2 February 1920) which declared the scheme 'impractical'.
36. *AS*, 22 July 1921.
37. *AS*, 15 August 1921.
38. *Tablet*, 15 March 1917.
39. *Tablet*, 29 May 1919, 8 and 22 September 1921.
40. O'Shea to Kelly, 25 May 1917, Cleary Papers, ACDA. This was one of many letters in which O'Shea urged moderation on the fiery *Tablet* editor.
41. *NZPD*, Vol.191, pp.928–63.
42. *NZPD*, Vol.185, p.832.
43. *NZS*, 1 February 1922, 1 May 1922.
44. Peter Fraser did nothing to contradict this charge by refusing to add his signature to the Wellington City Council's address of welcome to the Prince of Wales. *EP*, 17 May 1920.
45. *Tablet*, 9 June 1921.
46. Baker, *King and Country*, Ch. 6.
47. Despite the repeated advice of Solicitor-General J. W. Salmond (1862–1924). Salmond to Attorney-General, 9 May 1917, Salmond to Chief of General Staff, 24 July 1917, Opinion Book 1917; Salmond to Attorney-General, 20 August 1918, Opinion Book 1918, CLO.
48. Archbishop O'Shea complained about

'the continuance of regulations that may have been useful in time of actual warfare, but are an insult to free peoples now'. *Tablet*, 21 July 1921.

49. *EP*, 3 May 1921.

50. *Tablet*, 25 March 1920.

51. *Tablet*, 20 January 1920. The same thing happened to Esmonde in Australia, and he was later deported from Canada after being convicted of seditious utterances. On Katherine Hughes, see Sweetman, 'New Zealand Catholicism', p.300. *Tablet*, 2 June 1921. O'Regan to Pat O'Regan, 10 July 1921, O'Regan Papers, ATL.

52. Sweetman, 'New Zealand Catholicism', pp.204–206.

53. Salmond to Attorney-General, 9 May 1917, Opinion Book 1917, CLO. *Green Ray*, June 1918. *Truth*, 3 August 1918.

54. *Maoriland Worker*, 2 October 1918. In mid-1921 the *Maoriland Worker* suffered a similar fate for republishing a British pamphlet called 'The Irish Tragedy, Scotland's Disgrace'. *NZH*, 10 May 1921.

55. *Truth*, 10 July 1920.

56. 'Ideals of Empire', Dunedin, 1908, p.5.

57. Ibid., p.13.

58. MacGregor to Attorney-General, 27 June 1920, Opinion Book 1920, CLO.

59. MacGregor to Comptroller of Customs, 15 February 1921 (on the Irish *Weekly Independent*); MacGregor to Police Commissioner, 7 March 1921 (on 'The Irish Tragedy, Scotland's Disgrace'); MacGregor to Comptroller of Customs, 27 May 1921 (on 'The Crucifixion of Ireland'), Opinion Book 1921, CLO. Kelly rejoiced that 'the British press is at one with the *Tablet* in condemning the shameful and outrageous oppression of Ireland.' *Tablet*, 9 September 1920.

60. MacGregor to Massey, 23 March 1922, Police File 22/477, NA.

61. Ibid.

62. Ibid. He was the son of Rev. James MacGregor (1829–94), one of the pillars of New Zealand Presbyterianism, described as being 'deeply committed to the British Empire as a divinely appointed agent for Christian civilisation' (*Dictionary of New Zealand Biography, Volume Two, 1870–1900*. Wellington, 1993. pp.286–87).

63. *EP*, 24 March 1922.

64. 'For your *private* information, I may now tell you that M[assey] (like B[ell] was *strongly* opposed to your prosecution. It was the rabbit-brained section that got that through, by a very narrow majority.' Cleary to Liston, 27 February 1923, Liston Papers, ACDA. Cleary had spoken to Bell when the two men met in Italy. Cleary to Liston, 6 June 1922, Liston Papers, ACDA.

65. *EP*, 24 March 1922

66. *Tablet*, 5 January 1922, 2 March 1922. 'New Zealand is Masseyised rather than civilised.' *Tablet*, 16 March 1922.

67. *NZH*, 14 April 1919.

68. Cited in *Tablet*, 11 September 1919.

69. Kelly to O'Regan, 10 December 1922, O'Regan Papers, ATL. Lee was a solicitor, member for Oamaru 1911–22 and 1925–28, and Minister of Justice 1920–23.

70. *Tablet*, 9 February 1922.

71. *Tablet*, 10 November 1921, 9 February 1922. James Bryce, *Modern Democracies*. London, 1921, Vol.2, pp.291–364.

72. *NZPD*, Vol.183, p.716. Bell to Cleary, 25 May 1919, Cleary Papers, ACDA.

73. O'Shea to Cleary, 30 September 1920, Cleary Papers, ACDA.

74. This despite the close friendship and mutual respect the two men enjoyed, so much so that one historian has described the post-war administration as largely a Bell–Massey partnership. Gardner, 'Massey in Power', p.7–8. See also W. D. Stewart, *Sir Francis Bell*. Wellington, 1937.

75. Declaring the case *sub judice* blunted some editorial swords and gave others an excuse for excluding correspondence on the issue. Several editors couched their initial condemnation of Liston in terms drawn directly from the Crimes Act. *NZS*, 1 April, 1922.

76. *Dominion*, 21 March 1922.

77. *Dominion*, 27 March 1922.

78. *Tablet*, 7 November 1920.

79. *New Zealand Baptist*, June 1920.

80. *Tablet*, 30 June 1921

11
Not a Happy One

1. MacGregor to Wright, 27 March 1922, Police File 22/477, NA.

2. For A. H. Wright, see *NZH*, 9 November 1921.
3. Wright to Eales, 27 March 1922, Police File 22/477, NA.
4. Bell to MacGregor, 28 March 1922, Police File 22/477, NA.
5. *EP*, 18 December 1916.
6. Moores, 'Rise of the Protestant Political Association.'
7. *NZH*, 16 July 1901.
8. *Prohibitionist*, 22 February 1902.
9. Cleary's surveys appeared each week in the *Tablet* from 12 December 1901 to 15 May 1902.
10. 'The suggestion that the members of the Roman Catholic Church have been specially favoured appears to us to be unsupported by facts.' *Report and Evidence of the Royal Commission on the Police Force, AJHR*, 1898, H–2. p.viii.
11. *NZPD*, Vol 104, pp.69, 123.
12. *NZH*, 2 April 1904.
13. *EP*, 24 April 1918. *NZH*, 11 August 1922.
14. John Cullen was born in Ireland and served for six years in the Royal Irish Constabulary, before arriving in New Zealand in 1876. He was Police Commissioner from 1912 to 1916. See Richard Hill, *The Iron Hand in the Velvet Glove: the Modernisation of Policing in New Zealand 1886–1917*. Palmerston North, 1995.
15. Cleary to Ward, 4 April 1912; Grimes to Cleary, 8 April 1912, Cleary Papers, ACDA.
16. Helyar Wedderburn Bishop, born in England in 1851, was appointed a stipendiary magistrate in 1905.
17. Cleary to Ward, 4 April 1912, Cleary Papers, ACDA.
18. Cleary to Russell, 4 April 1912, Cleary Papers, ACDA.
19. Russell to Cleary, 16 April 1912, Cleary Papers, ACDA.
20. John O'Donovan, a qualified solicitor, was Police Commissioner from 1916 to 1921. *NZFL*, 11 October 1921.
21. *EP*, 18 December 1916.
22. *NZH*, 16 December 1916. McIlveney was the first New Zealand-born Police Commissioner (1926–30). Both his parents were Irish. He had become the youngest chief detective in the country in 1907. *NZFL*, 9 February 1907.
23. Attorney-General Herdman and Chief Justice Stout argued over police loyalty during the 1912–13 strikes. *EP*, 7 February 1914.
24. David McGill, *No Right to Strike: The History of the New Zealand Police Service Organisations*. Wellington, 1992. Ch. 2.
25. *EP*, 21 May 1918.
26. N. B. Fryday to Sir James Allen, 28 F ebruary 1917, Allen Papers, NA. P. J. O'Regan assisted many such objectors to evade the net by helping to organise a secret escape route to Australia. O'Regan to Fr Goodman, 15 February 1935, O'Regan Papers, ATL.
27. Statement by Thomas Wilford, Minister in charge of Police. *EP*, 21 May 1918.
28. By mid-1917 nearly all of the Labour leaders found themselves behind bars.
29. *1916 Sedition Trials*. Wellington, 1917.
30. Ward's brother Alfred was the long-serving chief detective in Wellington. *Truth*, 3 March 1917.
31. For his part in the case Ward has been immortalised as Detective Sergeant Wood in Maurice Gee's *Plumb*. On Ward's move to Auckland, see *NZH*, 26 July 1920.
32. Cleary to Fr Westeinde, 17 November 1915, Cleary Papers, ACDA.
33. Cleary to Fr Westeinde, 29 January 1916, Cleary Papers, ACDA.
34. Wilson to Police Commissioner [Cullen], 6 September 1916, Defence File 10/4/11, NA. Two years later Power was again reported to the authorities. 'I am informed that he waxes warm about Irish political matters', noted Commissioner O'Donovan. Subsequent inquiry revealed no one who had actually heard the Dean's supposed remarks. Police Commissioner [O'Donovan] to Inspector Hendrey, 2 March 1918, Defence File 10/4/11, NA.
35. Allen to Chief of General Staff, 26 February 1918; Superintendent [?] to Police Commissioner [O'Donovan], 1 April 1918, Defence File 17/5, NA.
36. *NZH*, 28 February 1917.
37. Ibid. Joseph Augustus Tole (1847–1920) was Auckland Crown Solicitor from 1892 until his death.
38. Both Inspector Keily and Minister of

Internal Affairs A. L. Herdman interviewed Elliott in early 1917. *NZH*, 12 July 1917. See Moores, 'Rise of the Protestant Political Association'.
39. Ibid., Ch. 8.
40. *NZH*, 16 February 1918, 24 October 1919. *Tablet*, 10 October 1918.
41. Cleary to Lee, 29 March 1921, Cleary Papers, ACDA.
42. *NZH*, 5 November 1917. His reference was to the *Auckland Free Press* (21 April 1918), which had warned its readers that the chief danger in conscripting Catholics was that they might bayonet their comrades in the back. Cleary sent a copy of the offending issue to Sir James Allen.
43. *NZH*, 15 September 1917.
44. *NZH*, 16 February 1918.
45. *EP*, 16 February 1918. Wilford had to face a second deputation in April 1918, this time led by Elliott. Evidently, the PPA leader had sources inside the force who fed him rumours of possible scandals. *EP*, 24 April 1918.
46. Ibid.
47. *Nation*, 10 December 1919.
48. *EP*, 3 December 1919. Elliott persisted in making this claim during the campaign, despite its refutation by government and Catholic authorities alike.
49. Meredith to MacGregor, 29 March 1922, File 732, CLO.
50. Hendrey to Eales, 20 March 1922, Police File 22/477, NA.
51. Police circular, 23 March 1922, Police File 22/477, NA.
52. The replies of Sgt. C. J. Halke, Sgt. J. Fitzgerald, Det. A. G. McHugh, and Constable Thomas Kelly are on Police File 22/477, NA.
53. Ward's original order was received on 23 March and repeated two days later. Police File 22/477, NA.
54. Report of Det. Sgt. Reginald Ward, 24 March 1922, Police File 22/477, NA.
55. Report of Det. M. Gourlay, 27 March 1922, Police File 22/477, NA.
56. Report of Constable J. R. Allen, 23 March 1922, Police File 22/477, NA.
57. Report of Constable Thomas Collins, 24 March 1922, Police File 22/477, NA.
58. Report of Constable J. Skinner, 24 March 1922, Police File 22/477, NA.
59. Report of Det. Sgt. Reginald Ward, 24 March 1922, Police File 22/477, NA.
60. Statement of Gordon Leith Stanbrook, 23 March 1922, Police File 22/477, NA.
61. Report of Det. Sgt. Reginald Ward, 24 March 1922, Police File 22/477, NA.
62. Statement of Francis Edward Carson, 24 March 1922, Police File 22/477, NA.
63. Ward noted optimistically: 'He is unwilling to have anything to say at present but I might be able to get him to corroborate any particular part of the speech if required.' Report of Det. Sgt. Reginald Ward, 24 March 1922, Police File 22/477, NA.
64. Statement of Francis Edward Carson, 24 March 1922, Police File 22/477, NA.
65. Statement of Stanley Albert Greenough, 23 March 1922, Police File 22/477, NA.
66. Statement of Francis Baller, 23 March 1922, Police File 22/477, NA.
67. Report of Det. Sgt. Reginald Ward, 24 March 1922, Police File 22/477, NA.
68. *NZH*, 19 January 1921. *NZFL*, 30 April 1915.
69. *NZH*, 24 April 1917.
70. Meredith to MacGregor, 29 March 1922, File 732, CLO.
71. Ibid.
72. Ibid.
73. Ibid.
74. Statement of Laurence Desmond O'Brien, 31 March 1922, Police File 22/477, NA.
75. Meredith to Under Secretary for Justice, 22 May 1922, File J1922/489, Justice Department Papers, NA.
76. Statement of John Thomas Todd, 7 April 1922, Police File 22/477, NA.
77. Statement of George Broadley, 3 April 1922, Police File 22/477, NA.
78. Statement of Gregory Ratcliffe Smith, 30 March 1922, Police File 22/477, NA.
79. Statement of Cecil Philip Gibson, 8 April 1922, Police File 22/477, NA.
80. Statement of Percy Stanley Nicholls, 6 April 1922, Police File 22/477, NA.
81. Statement of Robert Moffat Beswick, 4 April 1922, Police File 22/477, NA.
82. Ibid.
83. Statement of Graham Brook Bell, 1 April 1922, Police File 22/477, NA.

12
The Truth Shall make You Free

1. The building's magnificent interior, handsome stained-glass windows and statues soon earned it a reputation as 'the finest parish church in Australasia'. *Tablet*, 23/30 March 1922.
2. *NZFL*, 29 March 1922.
3. Fr J. R. Holley to Liston, 3 April 1922, Liston Papers, ACDA.
4. *Dominion*, 27 March 1922.
5. Ibid.
6. Ibid.
7. *NZS*, 1 May 1922. 'The flag remained in evidence for some days after the opening, no attempt being made to remove it until a correspondent of the *Dominion*, "an English Catholic", drew attention to the matter'.
8. O'Regan Diary, 25 March 1922, O'Regan Papers, ATL.
9. O'Regan Diary, 20 March 1922, O'Regan Papers, ATL.
10. Ibid.
11. O'Regan to Liston, 25 March 1922, Liston Papers, ACDA.
12. Ibid.
13. O'Regan Diary, 23 March 1922, O'Regan Papers, ATL.
14. O'Regan Diary, 25 March 1922, O'Regan Papers, ATL.
15. O'Regan Diary, 25–26 March 1922, O'Regan Papers, ATL.
16. John Callan (1882–1951) was born in Dunedin, qualified in law and practised there in his father's firm, Callan and Gallaway. He became a Supreme Court judge in 1935. In late 1919 he created a sensation by walking out during a sermon by a Sinn Fein priest at his North-East Valley church. See diary of T. J. Hussey (a *Tablet* director), 14 September 1919, Hocken Library, Dunedin.
17. This letter has not survived. Its contents can be inferred from Callan to Liston, 29 March 1922, Liston Papers, ACDA.
18. Liston to O'Regan, 2 April 1922, O'Regan Papers, ATL.
19. Dargaville Catholics to Liston, 27 March 1922, Liston Papers, ACDA.
20. Sr Mary Dominic to Liston, 27 March 1922, Liston Papers, ACDA.
21. Fr W. J. Forde to Liston, 28 March 1922, Liston Papers, ACDA.
22. Fr J. Riordan to Liston, 30 March 1922, Liston Papers, ACDA.
23. Liston to Whyte, 10 May 1922, Whyte Papers, Dunedin Catholic Diocesan Archives [DCDA].
24. Cleary to Liston, 6 April 1922, Liston Papers, ACDA.
25. Fr H. Holbrook to Cleary, 31 March 1922, Cleary Papers, ACDA.
26. *Month*, 15 June 1922.
27. Fr Farragher to Liston, 28 March 1922, Liston Papers, ACDA.
28. Fr M. Edge to Liston, 31 March 1922, Liston Papers, ACDA.
29. Ibid.
30. For John Conlan, see *Tablet*, 17 June 1907. Robert McVeagh (1866–1944) was a long-time member of Bishop Cleary's Diocesan Council.
31. *NZO*, 6 May 1922. Captain Conlan asked one Quaker appellant before the Auckland Military Service Board: 'Have you taken a greater interest in the Society of Friends since the outbreak of war than before?' *NZH*, 29 January 1917.
32. Callan to Liston, 29 March 1922, Liston Papers, ACDA.
33. Ibid. (See also *Tablet*, 11 July 1921.)
34. Ibid.
35. Ibid.
36. Holley to Liston, 3 April 1922, Liston Papers, ACDA.
37. O'Regan to Liston, 25 March 1922, Liston Papers, ACDA.
38. Fr W. J. Dunphy (Paeroa) to Liston, 27 March 1922, Liston Papers, ACDA.
39. 'I am always thinking of Ireland.' Sheahan to Dillon, 15 November 1918, Dillon Papers, TCD.
40. On the links between Sheahan, Davis and Nicholson, see E. R. Davis, *A Link with the Past*. Auckland, 1949. While Eliot Davis gave money to the Reform Party, his brother Ernest contributed to the Labour Party coffers. See Barry Gustafson, *From the Cradle to the Grave: A Biography of Michael Joseph Savage*. Auckland, 1986, p.276.
41. Liston to O'Regan, 2 April 1922, Liston Papers, ACDA. It seems unlikely that Liston met either Davis or Nicholson. The only surviving record of these

negotiations is in O'Regan's papers; as the Wellington lawyer had no patience with the apologetic politics of Sheahan and his ilk, one wonders whether Liston was telling him the whole story. If Davis and Nicholson did undertake to urge Massey to drop the case, they either broke their word or failed to make any impression on an obdurate Prime Minister. Perhaps Sheahan and Liston exaggerated the strength of the promise made by the local adherents of Masseydom. In any case, the outcome of the talks was remarkably consistent with the advice Liston was receiving from several other quarters; the Reform *démarche* merely hastened events rather than causing them. O'Regan Diary, 22 May 1922, O'Regan Papers, ATL.

42. Liston to O'Regan, 2 April 1922, O'Regan Papers, ATL.

43. O'Regan Diary, 22 May 1922, O'Regan Papers, ATL.

44. O'Regan Diary, 3 April 1922, O'Regan Papers, ATL. *AS*, 30 March 1922.

45. Callan to Liston, 5 April 1922, Liston Papers, ACDA. The drafts of Liston's letter to Massey are in Liston Defence Notes 6-1/29, ACDA.

46. Callan to Liston, 5 April 1922, Liston Papers, ACDA. See Ch. 14.

47. Ibid.

48. Liston to O'Regan, 12 April 1922, O'Regan Papers, ATL.

49. Liston Defence Notes 6-1/43, ACDA. Intended as an address from the dock, he was never to deliver it. It continued, 'I decided to write that letter for several reasons: (His W[orship] the Mayor & Newspapers) public feeling had been worked up to fever heat against me and grave and untruthful aspersions were cast upon my loyalty and upon the loyalty of the Catholic body. Under the circumstances I felt that it was due to myself and them to state our position clearly in this respect. (Real character & views).'

13
Loyal at Last?

1. *EP*, 6 April 1922.

2. Fr J. R. Holley to Liston, 7 April 1922, Liston Papers, ACDA. See Appendix 2 for the full text of Liston's letter to Massey.

3. Liston Defence Notes 6-1/29, Liston Papers, ACDA.

4. Liston to Massey, 5 April 1922, File 732, CLO.

5. Ibid.

6. See Appendix 1.

7. Liston to Massey, 5 April 1922, File 732, CLO.

8. Ibid.

9. The Auckland Catholic clergy cited Fogarty's support for the Treaty when arguing with the *AS* over their allegedly cool reception of the settlement. Cited in the *NZS*, 2 January 1922.

10. Liston to Massey, 5 April 1922, File 732, CLO.

11. *AS*, 6 April 1922,

12. Ibid. It was also prepared to accept O'Regan's recent declaration as proof of local Irish loyalty to the Empire.

13. *NZH*, 7 April 1922.

14. Ibid.

15. *ES*, 7 April 1922.

16. Ibid.

17. Ibid.

18. *Dominion*, 7 April 1922.

19. *WT*, 7 April 1922.

20. *Oamaru Mail*, 8 April 1922.

21. Ibid.

22. *Taranaki Daily News*, 8 April 1922.

23. Ibid.

24. *ODT*, 7 April 1922.

25. Ibid.

26. *ODT*, 8 April 1922.

27. Ibid.

28. Ibid.

29. Ibid.

30. *Tablet*, 23 March 1922.

31. Ibid.

32. Whyte to Liston, 6 April 1922, Liston Papers, ACDA

33. *Tablet*, 23 March 1922.

34. See Ch. 8.

35. Kelly to John Hagan, 30 January 1922, Hagan Papers, ICR.

36. Cleary came to believe that Kelly was extending to his young coadjutor the *Tablet* boycott applied against him for the past five years. Cleary to Liston, 23 November 1921, Liston Papers, ACDA.

37. Kelly to John Hagan, 7 August 1922, Hagan Papers, ICR.
38. Whyte to Liston, 6 April 1922, Liston Papers, ACDA.
39. Liston to Whyte, 8 April 1922, Whyte Papers, DCDA.
40. Whyte to Liston, 27 April 1922, Liston Papers, ACDA.
41. Fr J Kennedy to Liston, 5 May 1922, Liston Papers, ACDA.
42. Dean Regnault to Liston, 4 May 1922, Liston Papers, ACDA.
43. Callan to Liston, 6 April 1922, Liston Papers, ACDA.
44. Holley to Liston, 7 April 1922, Liston Papers, ACDA.
45. Liston to O'Regan, 12 April 1922, O'Regan Papers, ATL.
46. Liston to Whyte, 12 April 1922, Whyte Papers, DCDA.
47. Ryder to Liston, 7 April 1922, Liston Papers, ACDA. On the 'propaganda of hate' in the Auckland press see Ryder to Cleary, 24 August 1920, Cleary Papers, ACDA.
48. Callan to Liston, 6 April 1922, Liston Papers, ACDA.

14
A More or Less Trivial Incident

1. Cleary to Archbishop Cattaneo, 13 February 1921, Cleary Papers, ACDA.
2. *NZH*, 7 April 1922.
3. *NZH*, 8 April 1922.
4. See Ch. 12, note 41.
5. Liston to Massey, 5 April 1922, File 732, CLO.
6. MacGregor to Massey, 7 April 1922, P[rime] M[inister] File 9/72, NA.
7. Ibid.
8. O'Regan to Liston, 11 April 1922, Liston Papers, ACDA. O'Regan's letter appeared in the *AS*, 30 March 1922.
9. Liston to Whyte, 12 April 1922, Whyte Papers, DCDA.
10. *ODT*, 10 April 1922. *NZH*, 10 April 1922.
11. Sheahan to Massey, 8 April 1922, Liston Papers, ACDA. This is the only copy that has survived.
12. R. Dudley Edwards, *Patrick Pearse: the Triumph of Failure*. London, 1977. 'Christ's human heart had throbbed with passionate love for His own conquered Israel', according to Kelly. *Tablet*, 3 April 1919.
13. S. Lawlor, *Britain and Ireland 1914–23*. Dublin, 1983, Ch. 6.
14. *EP*, 1 February 1922. 'It can now be clearly seen that the much-maligned soldiers and police of Britain were protecting not merely Ireland against itself, but Sinn Fein against itself.' *EP*, 6 May 1922.
15. *NZH*, 23 January 1922. In Hackett's opinion de Valera was not even an Irishman. The *ODT* referred to him as a 'half-breed'.
16. *NZFL*, 22 February 1922.
17. *EP*, 23 March 1922.
18. De Valera's speeches at Dungarvan, Carrick, Cork and Killarney were briefly reported in the *NZH*, 18–22 March 1922. See M. Moynihan (1980), pp. 97–104.
19. *NZH*, 6 and 23 January 1922. De Valera was said to be 'fixed in his antipathy to everything English'.
20. *NZH*, 1 April 1922. *EP*, 3 April 1922.
21. *NZH*, 15 February, 24 March 1922.
22. Lawlor, *Britain and Ireland 1914–23*, p.152.
23. *NZH*, 9 April 1922.
24. Lawlor, *Britain and Ireland 1914–23*, p.172.
25. Ibid., pp.173, 188–194.
26. *EP*, 10 April 1922. *NZH*, 17 April 1922.
27. Olympus was the name of Liston's titular see. Fr Holbrook to Cleary, 31 March 1922, Cleary Papers, ACDA.
28. Cleary to Liston (cable), 6 April 1922, Liston Papers, ACDA.
29. Cleary to Liston, 5 April 1922, Liston Papers, ACDA.
30. Cleary wrote a number of letters from the Flanders trenches, where he was serving as a military chaplain. They were published as *Prussian Militarism at Work* (London, 1917). T. P. O'Connor wrote to Lord Robert Cecil on 28 May 1917: 'Bishop Cleary has the very best reputation of the Catholic clergymen at the front I have met – perfectly fearless, thoroughly loyal, thoroughly clear-headed.' Foreign Office Papers 395/129, News

Misc[ellaneous] (General) File 58, No 110943, PRO.
31. Collins to Churchill, 8 April 1922, CO Papers 209/312, File 18583, PRO.
32. Ibid.
33. *NZH*, 10 May 1921.
34. *EP*, 14 February 1921.
35. *EP*, 6 January 1922.
36. Cleary to Liston, 5 April 1922, Liston Papers, ACDA.
37. CO Papers, 209/312, File 18583, PRO.
38. *EP*, 17 April 1920.
39. *EP*, 20 December 1922.
40. *Tablet*, 15 January 1920. *NZH*, 23 February 1920.
41. *EP*, 28 September 1920.
42. Jellicoe to Massey, 13 April 1922; Massey to Jellicoe, 15 April 1922, PM File 9/72, NA.
43. Jellicoe to Churchill, 18 April 1922, CO Papers 209/312, File 23848, PRO.
44. Jellicoe to Churchill, 24 April 1922, CO Papers 209/312, File 25684, PRO.
45. Ibid.

15
An Easter Sacrifice

1. Sr Mary Gertrude to Liston, 12 April 1922, Liston Papers, ACDA.
2. O'Regan Diary, 7–8 April 1922, O'Regan Papers, ATL.
3. Liston to O'Regan, 12 April 1922, O'Regan Papers, ATL.
4. *Truth*, 3 May 1922.
5. Sheahan to Massey, 8 April 1922, Liston Papers, ACDA.
6. Liston to Whyte, 8 April 1922, Whyte Papers, DCDA.
7. Liston to Whyte, 12 April 1922, Whyte Papers, DCDA.
8. Sheahan to Massey, 8 April 1922, Liston Papers, ACDA.
9. Sr Mary Baptist to Liston, 2 April 1922, Liston Papers, ACDA.
10. Sr Mary Lynch to Liston, 10 April 1922, Liston Papers, ACDA.
11. O'Regan to H. McSherry, 14 June 1922, O'Regan Papers, ATL.
12. O'Regan Diary, 11 April 1922, O'Regan Papers, ATL.
13. O'Regan to Conlan, 17 April 1922, O'Regan Papers, ATL.
14. O'Regan Diary, 11 April 1922, O'Regan Papers, ATL.
15. O'Regan to Liston, 11 April 1922, Liston Papers, ACDA. See *Tablet*, 26 August 1915.
16. Ibid.
17. Liston to O'Regan, 12 April 1922, O'Regan Papers, ATL.
18. Whyte to Liston, 27 April 1922, Liston Papers, ACDA.
19. Conlan to O'Regan, 13 April 1922, O'Regan Papers, ATL.
20. *R.* v. *Burns* (1886), 16 Cox C.C. 355. *R.* v. *Holland* (1914) 33 NZLR 931. *EP*, 12 February 1914. P. J. O'Farrell, *Harry Holland*. Canberra, 1964. pp.58–59, 62–66.
21. Conlan to O'Regan, 13 April 1922, O'Regan Papers, ATL.
22. Ibid. Charles Skerrett and Michael Myers would both later be Chief Justices. Sir John Findlay, Ward's Attorney-General (1906–11), had experience of sedition law. See R. Cooke (ed.), *Portrait of a Profession*. Wellington, 1969, pp.219, 270.
23. O'Regan to Conlan, 17 April 1922, O'Regan Papers, ATL.
24. O'Regan had this in mind when writing to the *AS*, 30 March 1922. O'Regan Diary, 3 April 1922, O'Regan Papers, ATL.
25. O'Regan to Conlan, 17 April 1922, O'Regan Papers, ATL.
26. Liston to O'Regan, 22, 25 and 28 April 1922, O'Regan Papers, ATL.
27. Liston to O'Regan, 25 April 1922, O'Regan Papers, ATL. In 1904 Martin was quoted as saying 'the priests were his best friends'. *NZH*, 6 April 1904.
28. Liston to O'Regan, 25 April 1922, O'Regan Papers, ATL.
29. Callan to Liston, 19 and 26 April 1922, Liston Papers, ACDA.
30. Callan to Liston, 19 April 1922, Liston Papers, ACDA.
31. *EP*, 15 December 1919, 26 November 1920.
32. O'Regan Diary, 23 August 1922; O'Regan to Liston, 28 April 1922, O'Regan Papers, ATL.
33. O'Regan Diary, 8 September 1922, O'Regan Papers, ATL.
34. O'Regan to Liston, 28 April 1922; O'Regan Diary, 22 May 1922, O'Regan

Papers, ATL.

35. O'Regan to Liston, 28 April 1922, O'Regan Papers, ATL.

36. Whyte to Liston, 27 April 1922, Whyte Papers, DCDA.

37. Liston to Cleary, 24 April 1922, Brodie Papers, CCDA.

38. Howard Richmond and John Alexander were the President and Vice President of the Auckland Law Society in 1922. R. E. N. Russell was Robert McVeagh's partner at the Auckland law firm Russell Campbell & McVeagh. Richard Singer, Oliver Nicholson and Samuel Hesketh were well-known Auckland lawyers.

39. Liston to Cleary, 24 April 1922, Brodie Papers, CCDA.

40. Oliver Plunkett (1625–1681), Archbishop of Armagh, was found guilty of high treason in the aftermath of the 'Popish Plot'. He was hanged, drawn and quartered at Tyburn on 1 July 1681. Liston acquired a copy of Cardinal Moran's *Memoir of Oliver Plunkett* (Dublin, 1895) in June 1902, possibly as a gift from the author, for whom he was doing research in the Irish College library. James Kelly, yet another Irish College alumnus, wrote of 'the martyred patriot prelate . . . whom bigoted, persecuting, Protestant England killed and calumniated'. *Tablet*, 17 June 1920. Plunkett was beatified in 1920 and canonised in 1975.

41. Liston to Cleary, 24 April 1922, Brodie Papers, CCDA

16
Bishop in the Dock

1. *NZO*, 6 May 1922.
2. *AS*, 1 May 1922.
3. *NZO*, 6 May 1922.
4. Ibid.
5. Liston to Whyte, 3 May 1922, Whyte Papers, DCDA.
6. *NZO*, 6 May 1922.
7. Ibid.
8. Liston to Whyte, 3 May 1922, Whyte Papers, DCDA.
9. Meredith's evidence is taken from the reports *NZH* and *AS*, 1–3 May 1922.
10. *Rex* v. *Dr Liston*: copy of evidence on behalf of prosecution on 1 May 1922. Liston Papers 6-1/44, ACDA, [*Rex* v. *Dr Liston*], pp.1–4.
11. *Rex* v. *Dr Liston*, p.3.
12. *Rex* v. *Dr Liston* (p.11) has Greenough saying he 'had had enough', while *AS* (1 May 1922) quotes this as 'had heard enough'. For the full exchange see the *EP*, 2 May 1922.
13. *Rex* v. *Dr Liston*, pp.8, 10.
14. Liston to Whyte, 3 May 1922, Whyte Papers, DCDA.
15. Conlan to O'Regan, 2 May 1922, O'Regan Papers, ATL.
16. Ibid. L. P. Leary, *Not Entirely Legal*. Christchurch, 1977, p.11.
17. *NZO*, 6 May 1922.
18. *AS*, 2 May 1922.
19. *R.* v. *Burns* (1886), 16 Cox C.C. 355.
20. *EP*, 2 May 1922.
21. Hugh Martin, *Ireland in Insurrection*. London, 1921, p.11.
22. Meredith to MacGregor, 1 May 1922, File 732, CLO.
23. *NZH*, 2 May 1922. Cleary's difficulty in finding any trace of the speech tends to confirm this supposition.
24. Ibid.
25. *EP*, 2 May 1922.
26. Liston to Whyte, 3 May 1922, Whyte Papers, DCDA.
27. Conlan to O'Regan, 2 May 1922, O'Regan Papers, ATL.
28. Ibid.
29. Liston to Whyte, 3 May 1922, Whyte Papers, DCDA. See Ch. 17.
30. Conlan to O'Regan, 2 May 1922, O'Regan Papers, ATL.
31. Hall Skelton had just returned from representing New Zealand at the Irish Race Convention in Paris, where (to quote his own account) 'he was under the necessity of making it very plain to Mr de Valera that the Irish in the colonies were not to be dragged into anything that would disintegrate the Empire'. *AS*, 7 June 1922.
32. Conlan got this wrong; in fact, Liston saw Hall Skelton after the latter's Auckland speech but before he toured the North Island speaking on the same theme. *NZH*, 14 July 1921.

33. Conlan to O'Regan, 2 May 1922, O'Regan Papers, ATL.
34. See Cooke (ed.), *Portrait of a Profession*, p.171–72 for Alexander Gray, p.126 for A. H. Johnstone.
35. O'Regan to Conlan, 4 May 1922, O'Regan Papers, ATL.
36. O'Regan Diary, 4 May 1922, O'Regan Papers, ATL. For reasons why a jury might not respond to Myers, see Cooke (ed.), *Portrait of a Profession*, p.96: 'The elements of egotism, of self-assertion and of prejudice were sufficiently pronounced in him to make many in the profession doubt whether he would be suitable as Chief Justice.'
37. Callan to Liston, 19 April 1922, Liston Papers, ACDA.
38. Meredith to MacGregor, 6 May 1922, File 732, CLO.
39. H. H. Cornish to Liston, 10 May 1922, Liston Papers, ACDA.
40. F. Gill to Liston, 10 May 1922, Liston Papers, ACDA.
41. 'M.B.' to Liston, 6 May 1922, Liston Papers, ACDA.
42. Kelly to O'Regan, 23 May 1922, O'Regan Papers, ATL.
43. Regnault to Liston, 4 May 1922, Liston Papers, ACDA.
44. Kennedy to Liston, 5 May 1922, Liston Papers, ACDA.
45. Regnault to Liston, 4 May 1922, Liston Papers, ACDA.
46. O'Regan Diary, 22 May 1922, O'Regan Papers, ATL.
47. Nine Catholic lawyers, not including O'Regan. O'Regan Diary, 6 May 1922, O'Regan Papers, ATL.
48. O'Regan Diary, 6 May 1922, O'Regan Papers, ATL. Sullivan, an enthusiastic Irish nationalist, was to die in the Supreme Court of heart failure in 1944.
49. O'Regan Diary, 22 May 1922, O'Regan Papers, ATL.
50. O'Regan Diary, 7 May 1922, O'Regan Papers, ATL.
51. *NZH*, 10 May 1922.
52. Ibid.
53. Liston to Whyte, 10 May 1922, Whyte Papers, DCDA.
54. O'Regan Diary, 9 May 1922, O'Regan Papers, ATL. No one seems to have remembered that an identical memorial notice had appeared in the *Tablet*, 25 August 1921.
55. Ibid.

17
Let Me Carry Your Cross for Ireland, Lord!

1. Thomas Ashe (1885–1917), born in County Kerry, was active in the Easter Rising. Jailed in 1917 for making a seditious speech, he went on hunger strike and died while being forcibly fed. His poem, reprinted in the *Tablet* (10 January 1918), was classed as seditious literature in Ireland. *Tablet*, 27 March 1919. P. O'Farrell, *Who's Who in the Irish War of Independence 1916–1921*. Dublin, 1980, p.11.
2. O'Regan Diary, 9 May 1922, O'Regan Papers, ATL.
3. V. R. S. Meredith, *A Long Brief*. Auckland, 1966. R. M. Sweetman, 'Patrick Joseph O'Regan, 1869–1947: A Life of Advocacy', *Turnbull Library Record*, 21, 2 (October 1988). pp.93–7.
4. Meredith, *A Long Brief*, p.26.
5. According to L. P. Leary he felt embarrassed in raising his voice in comedy by night and tragedy by day. L. P. Leary, *Not Entirely Legal*. Christchurch, 1977, p.77.
6. *Truth*, 29 January 1921. Although despising Meredith's politics, O'Regan absolved him from any taint of religious bigotry. O'Regan to Liston, 28 April 1922, O'Regan Papers, ATL.
7. Meredith, *A Long Brief*, pp.22–3.
8. O'Regan Diary, 15 May 1922, O'Regan Papers, ATL.
9. Meredith to Under Secretary for Justice, 22 May 1922, File J1922/489, Justice Department Papers, NA.
10. Thomas Walter Stringer (1855–1944) was born in Christchurch, where he became Crown prosecutor in 1893. He was President of the Arbitration Court (1914–21) before his appointment to the bench.
11. O'Regan Diary, 15 May 1922, O'Regan Papers, ATL.

12. Ibid.
13. Ibid.
14. O'Regan Diary, 16 May 1922, O'Regan Papers, ATL.
15. Women were not permitted to serve on juries until the 1940s. K. Catran, *Hanlon: A Casebook*. Auckland, 1985, p.159.
16. This account of Meredith's performance is taken from *NZH* and *AS*, 16–18 May 1922.
17. This is the first time Meredith indicates which government he has in mind. O'Regan had already lost a battle to have the remaining sedition regulations limited to references to the New Zealand authorities. *NZH*, 10 May, 19 July 1921.
18. *NZH*, 17 May 1922.
19. Stanbrook's replies are taken from pp.5–9 of Notes of Evidence: *His Majesty the King* v. *James Michael Liston*, 16–17 May 1922. High Court, Auckland. [Notes of Evidence]. O'Regan's questions are in *NZH*, 17 May 1922.
20. *NZH*, 17 May 1922. *Tablet*, 27 January 1921.
21. Notes of Evidence, p.8. No one seems to have noticed that these categories amounted to 152 victims, not 155.
22. O'Regan Diary, 16 May 1922, O'Regan Papers, ATL.
23. Notes of Evidence, pp.10–13. O'Regan Diary, 16 May 1922, O'Regan Papers, ATL.
24. Notes of Evidence, pp.13–16.
25. O'Regan Diary, 16 May 1922, O'Regan Papers, ATL.
26. Notes of Evidence, p.15.
27. Ibid., pp.16–18.
28. Ibid., pp.17–18.
29. Ibid., pp.18–20. O'Regan Diary, 16 May 1922, O'Regan Papers, ATL.
30. O'Regan Diary, 16 May 1922, O'Regan Papers, ATL. Notes of Evidence, p.20.
31. *NZH*, 17 May 1922.
32. O'Regan Diary, 16 May 1922, O'Regan Papers, ATL.
33. *NZH*, 17 May 1922.
34. O'Regan Diary, 16 May 1922, O'Regan Papers, ATL.
35. *NZH*, 24 March 1922.
36. *AS*, 17 May 1922. As if to compensate for its bungling of Liston's Town Hall speech, *AS* published a very full report of proceedings in the Supreme Court.
37. Ibid.
38. *NZH*, 17 May 1922.

18

Rex v. *Liston*

1. *NZO*, 27 May 1922.
2. Notes of Evidence, p.22.
3. Ibid. Liston was echoing Bishop Fogarty and his own letter to Massey.
4. Lawlor, *Britain and Ireland 1914–23*. Dublin, 1983, Ch. 6.
5. Notes of Evidence, p.24.
6. Ibid., p.26.
7. O'Regan Diary, 16 May 1922, O'Regan Papers, ATL.
8. Meredith, *A Long Brief*, p.18.
9. Notes of Evidence, pp.28–29. See also *NZH*, 17 May 1922, and *AS*, 17 May 1922.
10. *NZH*, 17 May 1922. During 1920–21 the major dailies (especially the *EP* and the *NZH*) gave plenty of coverage to the Black and Tans and the semi-official reprisals they undertook as a form of counter-terrorism against the IRA. R. Bennett, *The Black and Tans*. London, 1970.
11. O'Regan Diary, 16 May 1922, O'Regan Papers, ATL.
12. Ibid.
13. Notes of Evidence, p.30-31.
14. *AS*, 17 May 1922.
15. See Ch. 16, note 31.
16. Notes of Evidence, p.32.
17. *NZH*, 18 May 1922.
18. *Month*, 15 June 1922.
19. *NZH*, 18 May 1922. Edmund Powell, *Powell's Principles and Practice of the Law of Evidence*. London, 1921.
20. *Month*, 15 June 1922.
21. J. J. O'Brien (1854–1933), born in Wellington, founder of the Kauri Timber Co, and Leyland and O'Brien. See *Month*, 1 September 1933. Notes of Evidence, pp.33–34. O'Regan Diary, 17 May 1922, O'Regan Papers, ATL.
22. *NZH*, 18 May 1922.
23. O'Regan Diary, 17 and 26 May 1922, O'Regan Papers, ATL.
24. O'Regan Diary, 17 May 1922, O'Regan Papers, ATL. O'Regan cited *R.* v. *Burns*

(1886) to show that a seditious intention was not necessarily to be inferred even when acts of violence followed the speech. He had his speech printed as a pamphlet, *Rex* v. *Liston*, (Dunedin, 1922).
25. *Month*, 15 June 1922. *Rex* v. *Liston*, pp.5–6.
26. *Month*, 15 June 1922.
27. *Ibid.* O'Regan could as easily have cited the *NZS* for furious denunciation of Lloyd George and questioning of his trustworthiness. He was described as 'a fit and proper person to betray his country', in the issue of 2 January 1922.
28. Ibid. See introduction (p.6) to Hugh Martin's *Ireland in Insurrection* (London, 1921).
29. *Month*, 15 June 1922.
30. Ibid.
31. Ibid.
32. O'Regan's diaries reveal his conviction that he had suffered politically for his Catholicism and radical sympathies.
33. *Month*, 15 June 1922.
34. Ibid.
35. O'Regan Diary, 17 May 1922, O'Regan Papers, ATL. *AS*, 17 May 1922.
36. The substitution of 'men and women' for 'many', and a dispute over the description of those who had been killed in Ireland.
37. *AS*, 17 May 1922.
38. *Month*, 15 June 1922.
39. *AS*, 17 May 1922.
40. O'Regan Diary, 17 May 1922, O'Regan Papers, ATL.
41. Notes of Evidence, p.34.
42. *NZH*, 18 May 1922.
43. Ibid.
44. Ibid.
45. See Appendix 3 for the words of 'A Nation Once Again' and 'God Save Ireland'.
46. *NZH*, 18 May 1922.
47. Ibid.
48. Ibid.
49. Ibid.
50. Ibid. The King's speech concluded: 'I appeal to all Irishmen to pause, to stretch out the hand of forbearance and conciliation, to forgive and forget and join in making for the land which they all love a new era of peace, contentment and goodwill.' Lyons, *Ireland Since the Famine*, p.426.
51. O'Regan Diary, 17 May 1922, O'Regan Papers, ATL.
52. Ibid.
53. Ibid. Notes of Evidence, p.34.

19
Verdict

1. O'Regan Diary, 17 May 1922, O'Regan Papers, ATL.
2. Ibid.
3. Ibid.
4. *AS*, 18 May 1922.
5. *NZH*, 18 May 1922.
6. Ibid.
7. *Star* (Christchurch), 18 May 1922.
8. *EP*, 18 May 1922.
9. *Dannevirke Evening News*, 18 May 1922.
10. *Evening Star* (Dunedin), 18 May 1922. In 1921 a Juries Act Amendment Bill providing for majority verdicts in criminal cases passed the Legislative Council for the fourth successive year, but went no further. The judges were said to favour it (especially Chief Justice Robert Stout). *Truth* (1 September 1917) saw only 'another British birthright threatened'. Of course, Irish Catholics had their own ancestral memories of jury packing. See *Tablet*, 24 January 1901.
11. *Northern Advocate* (Whangarei), 18 May 1922.
12. *NZT*, 20 May 1922.
13. *NZT* (20 May 1922) continued, 'which, as the Judge pointed out, were actually murders, and were so regarded by the British Government, and so spoken of freely in the House of Commons, without any tinge of disloyalty or sedition'.
14. *EP*, 18 May 1922.
15. *SDN*, 18 May 1922.
16. *EP*, 18 May 1922.
17. Ibid.
18. *Evening Star* (Dunedin), 18 May 1922.
19. *Balclutha Free Press*, 19 May 1922.
20. *Dominion*, 19 May 1922.
21. *ES* (Dunedin), 18 May 1922.
22. *NZT*, 20 May 1922.
23. *EP*, 18 May 1922.
24. *AS*, 18 May 1922. The *Balclutha Free*

Press (19 May 1922) correctly guessed that he had been piqued by the 'hot-headed' Mayor of Auckland, whose actions were 'enough to get any man's back up, especially when taken in conjunction with excited newspaper comments and denunciations which echoed through the land from Auckland to the Bluff'.
25. *Carterton Daily News*, 19 May 1922.
26. *Wairarapa Age*, 19 May 1922.
27. *Press* (Christchurch), 19 May 1922.
28. *Sun* (Christchurch), 18 May 1922.
29. *LT*, 18 May 1922.
30. *NZT*, 20 May 1922.
31. *Sun*, 18 May 1922. The case had also proved that the law was no respecter of persons – the bishop's rank had not protected him from the consequences of his actions. (Liston would have been amused to read in the *Oamaru Mail* that his co-religionists were 'given to accepting his utterances without challenge'.)
32. *NZT*, 20 May 1922.
33. *SDN*, 18 May 1922.
34. *ODT*, 18 May 1922.
35. *Tablet*, 25 May 1922.
36. Ibid.
37. A reference to the *Auckland Free Press*. See Cleary to Allen, 17 May 1918, Cleary Papers, ACDA.
38. *Tablet*, 25 May 1922.
39. Kelly to O'Regan, 23 March 1922, O'Regan Papers, ATL.
40. *Evening Star*, 19 May 1922. Robinson's argument had a disarming simplicity. If it was wrong to say certain things, then surely it was worse to repeat them, 'and if a newspaper is so loyal that it hates disloyal utterances, it ought to be loyal enough to refrain from repeating them, even if they do make good copy'. Kelly said exactly the same thing in the *Tablet*, 23 October 1919, 26 May 1921.
41. Mary McKeefry to Liston, 17 May 1922, Liston Papers, ACDA.
42. It seems that Liston wrote this himself. Liston Defence Notes, 6-5, ACDA.
43. Ibid.
44. After clearing heavy legal expenses, he was able to devote the surplus £600 to Catholic charitable institutions. Liston to Propaganda Fide, undated [1929?], Liston Papers 6-3, ACDA.
45. The slap to Catholic pride had stung. Maria McCarthy (Oamaru) told Liston: 'I feel so mad when I think of the cheek of them taking one of our bishops to court that I think I had better stop or I will be writing something queer.' Maria McCarthy to Liston, 17 May 1922, Liston Papers, ACDA.
46. 'Proposed letter to Mayor of Auckland (handed to him), 20 May [1922]', Liston Papers, ACDA.
47. Conlan to Liston, 23 May 1922, Liston Papers, ACDA. Gunson conveyed his reply through R. E. N. Russell, a prominent Auckland lawyer, then followed up with a letter on 24 May 1922 (Liston Papers, ACDA).
48. 'Memo on proposed letter to Mayor, 22 May [1922]', Liston Papers, ACDA.
49. Liston to Gunson, 26 June 1922; Gunson to Liston, 28 June 1922; Liston to Gunson, 29 June 1922, Liston Papers, ACDA.
50. Liston to Whyte, 3 July 1922, Whyte Papers, DCDA.
51. Gunson to Liston, 3 July 1922, Liston Papers, ACDA. *NZH*, 28 July 1922. Liston to Whyte, 1 August 1922, Whyte Papers, DCDA.
52. O'Regan to Liston, 2 August 1922, Liston Papers, ACDA.
53. Liston to Whyte, 3 July 1922, Whyte Papers, DCDA.
54. T. W. Leys was probably the mysterious 'mutual friend' referred to by Barry Gustafson in his life of M. J. Savage, *From the Cradle to the Grave*. Auckland, 1986, p.123.
55. *NZH*, 15 December 1922.
56. *NZO*, 1 April 1922.
57. Elliott was unable, as he put it, 'to be about'. *NZS*, 1 May 1922, 1 June 1922.
58. *Napier Daily Telegraph*, 19 July 1922, cited by *Month*, 15 September 1922. See also *NZS*, 1 June 1922.
59. Cleary to Liston, 2 September 1922, 17 February 1923, Liston Papers, ACDA. Cleary to Cardinal Van Rossum, 25 March 1923, Cleary Papers, ACDA.
60. *Month*, 15 September, 15 December 1922. *Tablet*, 30 November 1922.
61. *Month*, 15 September 1922.
62. Liston applauded O'Regan's efforts to

arrange a pact between Liberal and Labour parties (on the basis of proportional representation) to avoid vote splitting and the loss of seats to Reform. Liston to O'Regan, 9 December 1922, O'Regan Papers, ATL.
63. O'Regan to Kelly,19 November 1922, O'Regan Papers, ATL.
64. Dean Lane to Liston, 11 November 1922, Liston Papers, ACDA. Lysnar retained his seat.
65. O'Regan to Liston, 2 December 1922; O'Regan to Kelly, 9 November 1922, O'Regan Papers, ATL.
66. M. Bassett, *Three Party Politics in New Zealand 1911–1931*. Auckland, 1982, pp.32–3.
67. *Tablet*, 14 December 1922.
68. Liston to O'Regan, 8 December 1922; O'Regan to Liston, [undated], O'Regan Papers, ATL.
69. Liston to O'Regan, 9 December 1922, O'Regan Papers, ATL.
70. Sweetman, 'New Zealand Catholicism', p.336.
71. O'Regan Diary, 8 December 1922; O'Regan to Kelly, 13 December 1922, O'Regan Papers, ATL.
72. Sweetman, 'New Zealand Catholicism', pp.337–338.
73. *AS*, 13 December 1922. *Tablet* (19 June 1919) had already predicted that 'Labour is coming into its own'. For Cleary's hostile reaction, see Cleary to Liston, 17 February 1923, Liston Papers, ACDA.
74. *NZH*, 14-22 December 1922.
75. R. Weekes to O'Regan, 20 December 1922, O'Regan Papers, ATL.
76. Lee received special praise from Howard Elliott for his role in the case, *NZS*, 1 June 1922. On Massey and the second Oamaru poll, see *NZFL*, 9 May 1923. For Catholic gloating on Lee's fall, see Kelly to O'Regan, 10 December 1922, O'Regan Papers, ATL.

20
Aftermath

1. Cleary to Propaganda Fide, undated [1929?], Liston Papers 6-3, ACDA. Simmons, *In Cruce Salus: A History of the Diocese of Auckland 1848–1980*. Auckland, 1982. pp.229–30. N. J. Byrne, *Robert Dunne 1830–1917 Archbishop of Brisbane*. Queensland, 1991, Ch. 9.
2. Cleary to Propaganda Fide, undated [1929?], Liston Papers 6-3, ACDA.
3. The draft of the 1923 *Relatio* remains in the Liston Papers.
4. Cleary to Liston, 5 and 6 April, 22 and 23 May, 6 June, 25 August, 2 September 1922, Liston Papers, ACDA. (Also Cleary to Gunson, 3 August 1922, a copy of which survives in the Liston Papers, ACDA.)
5. Liston to Propaganda Fide, undated [1929?], Liston Papers 6-3, ACDA. The increase in attendances at Catholic services over the decade 1911–21 appears to support Liston's point. Hugh Jackson, 'Churchgoing in Nineteenth-Century New Zealand', *New Zealand Journal of History*, 17, 1, April 1983, pp.43–59.
6. Brodie to Propaganda Fide, [undated, 1929?], Brodie Papers, CCDA.
7. Brodie's dispute with the *Press* concerned what he described as its 'oppression of the poor', rather than any defence of the rebellion in Ireland. See Davis, *Irish Issues in New Zealand Politics*, p.195. *Tablet*, 2 November 1916. Brodie to O'Regan, 2 November 1916, O'Regan Papers, ATL.
8. Brodie to Canon Cotter, 30 July 1920, Brodie Papers, CCDA.
9. *Tablet*, 19 June 1919. While Kelly saw the Anglo–Irish conflict as 'a war on the Catholic Church', Howard Elliott described the Irish question as 'at bottom a fight between the Church of Rome and the British Empire.' *Tablet*, 23 December 1920, 4 July 1921.
10. See Sweetman, 'New Zealand Catholicism', Ch. 4.
11. Kelly to Hagan, 22 December 1917, Hagan Papers, ICR.
12. *Tablet*, 26 July 1917.
13. Cleary to Cattaneo, 31 May 1922, Cleary Papers, ACDA.
14. Kelly to William O'Brien, 18 December 1921, O'Brien Papers, University College Cork. The treaty removed a most potent weapon from the PPA's

armoury. It was denounced in *NZS* as a betrayal of Protestant Ulster and a shameful capitulation to Sinn Fein. As with home rule before the war, the anti-Catholics were marginalised by Irish events and left bitterly critical of the new dispensation.

15. *Tablet*, 15 December 1921.

16. *Month*, 15 August 1922.

17. *Month*, 15 September 1922.

18. *Month*, 16 October 1922. On the civil war violence, see Calton Younger, *Ireland's Civil War*. London, 1968.

19. Ibid., p.324. The rector of All Hallows College, Dublin, told Archbishop Mannix that Brodie 'has fled from Ireland having had some unpleasant experiences'. O'Donnell to Mannix, 13 August 1922, Mannix Papers, Melbourne Catholic Archdiocesan Archives. Fr Aylward to Brodie, 31 March 1923, Brodie Papers, CCDA.

20. Cleary to Liston, 29 September 1922, Liston Papers, ACDA. The *NZS* agreed with Cleary, 1 September 1922. The Irish hierarchy denounced as 'miscreants and murderers' those who would 'imbrue their hands in the blood of a fellow man'. *Month*, 15 September 1922.

21. Brodie to Cleary, 18 March 1925, Cleary Papers, ACDA.

22. Sweetman, 'Daniel Mannix and his Biographers,' pp.61–71.

23. Rex Taylor, *Assassination*. London, 1961. Lawlor, *Britain and Ireland 1914–21*. Dublin, 1983, pp.188–194. Massey said that Wilson (his 'personal friend') had 'died at the hands of a murderer.' *NZH*, 24 June 1922.

24. 'We are ready to act on your behalf when we know the proper moment has arrived . . .' St Patrick's Confraternity to Liston, 2 May 1922, Liston Papers, ACDA. Violence could easily have broken out in 1917 over the conscription issue, or if the Catholic community had seen its leaders thrown into jail, as was threatened in 1920. In 1922 James Gill was killed at Ashburton after proposing a toast to whoever shot Michael Collins. *EP*, 7 September 1922.

25. O'Regan Diary, 2 July 1922, O'Regan Papers, ATL. Michael Gilchrist, *Daniel Mannix: Priest and Patriot*. Melbourne, 1982, Ch. 3. It seems likely that an earlier division was prevented by Cleary's firm action towards the *Tablet* in 1917–18. Sweetman, 'New Zealand Catholicism', Ch. 8.

26. Cleary recognised this fact in 1918 by setting up the *Month* as a deliberate counter to the former sole Catholic organ. See Sweetman, 'New Zealand Catholicism', Ch. 8.

27. *Tablet*, 20 November 1919, 13 May 1921. Kelly declared that 'no true Irishman – no matter what his position or obligations – should have taken any part in the celebrations as long as England is carrying out systematic Prussianism in Ireland'. *Tablet*, 3 June 1920.

28. Fr Holbrook to Stan [?], 16 June 1921, Cleary Papers, ACDA. Five of Holbrook's cousins had served in the war, including Lieutenant Norman Douglas Holbrook RN, who earned a VC for taking his submarine through the Dardanelles. *NZFL*, 7 May 1915.

29. *Tablet*, 1 January, 27 May 1920, 8 December 1921. 'British Australians opted for monoculturalism, anxiously closing ranks to seek assurance under the familiar, protective umbrella of the empire, and, in the process, marginalising and discriminating against non-British Australian residents.' Gerhard Fischer, '"Negative Integration" and an Australian Road to Modernity: Interpreting the Australian Homefront Experience in World War 1', *Australian Historical Studies*, 26, 104, April 1995, pp.452–476.

30. *Tablet*, 29 December 1921. 'If any flag has to be saluted in our schools let it be the New Zealand flag; let loyalty be to our own country and let the anthem be the New Zealand national anthem, which at present is heard all too seldom', wrote Archbishop O'Shea to Bishop Whyte on 27 December 1921, Whyte Papers, DCDA.

31. *Tablet*, 2 and 23 September 1920.

32. Maureen Sharpe, 'Anzac Day in New Zealand: 1916 to 1939', *New Zealand Journal of History*, Vol 15, No 2, October 1981. pp.97–114.

33. *NZH*, 24 and 26 April 1922.

34. *NZH*, 26 April 1922.

35. *Tablet*, 4 October 1917.

36. *Tablet*, 12 July 1917. See Ch. 1.
37. *NZS*, 1 September 1922.
38. *Tablet*, 15 January 1920.
39. *NZFL*, 1 April 1911. *NZH*, 14 February 1922.
40. *NZH*, 7 May 1920. *EP*, 24 May 1920.
41. *NZH*, 14 December 1921.
42. *NZH*, 11 and 13 April 1922.
43. *Tablet*, 26 May 1921. To some degree this explains the subsequent estrangement between the two men.
44. As with his testimonial after the sedition case, it seems that Liston composed the message himself. A draft remains in the Liston Papers, ACDA. *Zealandia*, 5 March 1938.
45. *NZH*, 28 April 1970.
46. Ibid.
47. Liston to Propaganda Fide, undated [1929?], Liston Papers 6-3, ACDA. *NZH*, 28 April 1970. Gunson to Liston, 13 March 1941; Liston to Gunson, 15 March 1941, Liston Papers, ACDA.
48. Gunson stood unsuccessfully for Eden (1926) and Auckland Suburbs (1928). Liston to Propaganda Fide, undated [1929?], Liston Papers 6-3, ACDA.
49. *Truth*, 21 January 1922, 17 June 1922. *NZH*, 14 May 1965.
50. O'Brien's dismissal was reported in *NZS*, 1 July 1922. The Broadley lock-out appears in the *NZS*, 1 June 1922.
51. O'Regan Diary for June–July 1922, O'Regan Papers, ATL. See also *Rex* v. *Liston*. O'Regan's promotion can be seen as first fruits of the understanding between Labour and the Catholic Church forged in the heat of wartime controversies over sectarianism and conscription.
52. Meredith to Under Secretary of Justice, 22 May 1922, File J1922/489, Justice Department Papers, NA.
53. *NZS*, 1 July 1922.
54. File 732, CLO.
55. Hayden to Brodie, 6 January 1921, Brodie Papers, CCDA. Whyte to O'Shea, 26 August 1920, O'Shea Papers, WCAA. For Australian reaction to the case, see *Catholic Press* (Sydney), 9 April 1922; *Freeman's Journal* (Sydney), 25 May, 1 June 1922. O'Regan noted how differently *Truth* reported the case from its Australian counterpart. See his article in *Maoriland Worker*, 16 November 1922.
56. 'The Hon. Mr Justice O'Regan: His Interesting Career', *New Zealand Law Journal*, 13 (1937), pp.141–143, 147. Meredith, *A Long Brief*. Meredith was created a Knight Bachelor in 1952 and a Queen's Counsel five years later. He managed the 1910 All Blacks in Australia and the 1935–36 team in Britain. At a meeting of the Guild of Saints Cosmos and Damien in the early 1960s, Rolland O'Regan (Patrick's son) described Liston as one of New Zealand's most famous rebels. Far from appreciating the implied compliment, the bishop strongly disagreed with this description and privately reproved the speaker for recalling the incident.
57. *NZH*, 13 February 1995.
58. *NZH*, April-May 1995. The growing use of the Maori word 'tauiwi' has provoked a sharp debate over just who are the 'foreigners' in New Zealand today. In March 1919, Liston answered those who questioned the place of Irish Catholics in colonial society: 'We are no aliens in a land that has been built up by our brains and hands, tears and blood, as much as those of others.' See Ch.8, note 62.
59. Dr Morgan Grace, *A Sketch of the New Zealand War*. London, 1899. The Maori–Irish parallel was occasionally touched on by Kelly: 'The only laws affecting [both races] were framed for their extermination.' *Tablet*, 21 June 1921.
60. Akenson, *Half the World from Home*. Wellington, 1990, p.201. *NZH*, 24 March 1922.
61. *EP*, 23 March 1921.
62. *EP*, 23 March 1922.
63. O'Farrell, *Vanished Kingdoms*, p.7.

Bibliography

PRIMARY MATERIAL

(a) Official Publications

Appendices to the Journals of the House of Representatives
New Zealand Parliamentary Debates
New Zealand Census Returns

(b) Newspapers

Auckland Free Press
Auckland Star
Balclutha Free Press
Carterton Daily News
Catholic Press (Sydney)
Church Gazette (Auckland)
Coromandel County News
Evening Post (Wellington)
Evening Star (Dunedin)
Dannevirke Evening News
Dominion
Franklin Times
Freeman's Journal (Sydney)
Gisborne Times
Green Ray (Dunedin)
Grey River Argus
Hawke's Bay Tribune
King Country Chronicle
Lyttelton Times
Manawatu Daily Times
Maoriland Worker
Month (Auckland)

Napier Daily Telegraph
Nation (Wellington)
Nelson Colonist
New Zealand Baptist
New Zealand Free Lance
New Zealand Herald
New Zealand Methodist Times
New Zealand Observer
New Zealand Sentinel
New Zealand Tablet
New Zealand Times
New Zealand Truth
Northern Advocate (Whangarei)
Oamaru Mail
Otago Daily Times
Pahiatua Herald
Press (Christchurch)
Rotorua Chronicle
Southland Daily News
Star (Christchurch)
Sun (Christchurch)
Taranaki Daily News
Timaru Herald
Waikato Times
Wairarapa Times
Wairarapa Age
Wanganui Chronicle
Zealandia

(c) Archives

AUCKLAND
Auckland Catholic Diocesan Archives:
  Lenihan Papers
  Cleary Papers
  Liston Papers
Auckland City Council Archives:
  Minutes of Meetings 1922
  Liston Case File
Auckland High Court:

Notes of Evidence, *His Majesty the King* v *James Michael Liston*, 16-17 May 1922
Auckland Public Library:
J. A. Lee Papers

CHRISTCHURCH
Christchurch Catholic Diocesan Archives:
Brodie Papers

CORK
University College:
William O'Brien Papers

DUBLIN
State Paper Office
Trinity College:
Michael Davitt Papers
John Dillon Papers

DUNEDIN
Dunedin Catholic Diocesan Archives:
Moran Papers
Verdon Papers
Whyte Papers
Hocken Library:
T. J. Hussey Papers

LONDON
Public Record Office:
Colonial Office Papers
Foreign Office Papers

MELBOURNE
Melbourne Catholic Archdiocesan Archives:
Mannix Papers

NEWCASTLE (Australia)
Maitland Catholic Diocesan Archives:
Dwyer Papers

ROME
Irish College:
O'Riordan Papers
Hagan Papers

Archives of Propaganda Fide:
Oceania Files

SYDNEY
St Patrick's College, Manly:
Verdon Papers
Murphy Papers
Sydney Catholic Archdiocesan Archives:
Kelly Papers

WELLINGTON
Alexander Turnbull Library:
P. J. O'Regan Papers
Wellington Catholic Archdiocesan Archives:
Redwood Papers
O'Shea Papers
Crown Law Office:
Case File 732
Opinion Books 1914–22
National Archives:
Allen Papers
Defence Files
Justice Dept Files
Massey Papers
Police File 22/477
Prime Minister's File (1922) 9/72

SECONDARY MATERIAL

(d) Books and Articles

Akenson, D. H. *Half the World from Home: Perspectives on the Irish in New Zealand 1860–1950*. Wellington, 1990.
Amos, K. *The Fenians in Australia 1865–1880*. Sydney, 1988.

Baker, P. *King and Country Call*. Auckland, 1988.
Bassett, M. *Sir Joseph Ward: A Political Biography*. Auckland, 1993.
Bassett, M. *Three Party Politics in New Zealand 1911–1931*. Auckland, 1982.
Bennet, R. *The Black and Tans*. London, 1972.
Binney, J. *The Prophet Rua Kenana and His Community at Maungapohatu*. Wellington, 1979.
Boland, S. J. *Faith of Our Fathers*. Armidale, 1982.
Boland, T. *Archbishop Duhig*. Queensland, 1986.
Bourke, D. F. *The History of the Vincentian Fathers in Australasia*. Melbourne, 1980.
Boyce, D. G. *Englishmen and Irish Troubles: British Public Opinion and the Making of Irish Policy, 1918–1922*. Cambridge, Mass., 1972.
Bracken, T. *Musings in Maoriland*. Dunedin, 1890.
Brady, C. (ed.). *Interpreting Irish History: the Debate on Historical Revisionism 1938–1994*. Dublin, 1994.
Brosnahan, S. 'The "Battle of the Borough" and the "Saige O Timaru": Sectarian Riot in Colonial Canterbury', *New Zealand Journal of History* 28, 1 (April 1994), pp.41–59
Brown, J. M. *Ghandi*. London, 1989.
Bush, G. W. A. *Decently and in Order: the Centennial History of the Auckland City Council*. Auckland 1971.
Byrne, N. J. *Robert Dunne, 1830–1917: Archbishop of Brisbane*. Queensland, 1991.
Caughcy, A. *An Auckland Network*. Auckland, 1988.
Coogan, T. P. *Eamon de Valera*. London, 1993.
Cooke, R. (ed.) *Portrait of a Profession*. Wellington, 1969.
Cuddy, E. 'The Irish Question and the Revival of Anti-Catholicism in the 1920s,' *Catholic Historical Review*, lxvii, 2 (April 1981), pp.236–255.
Davis, E. R. *A Link with the Past*. Auckland, 1949.
Davis, R. P. *Irish Issues in New Zealand Politics 1868–1922*. Dunedin, 1974.
Davis, R. P. 'The New Zealand Labour Party's "Irish Campaign", 1916–1921', *Political Science*, 19, 2 (1967), pp.13–23.
Davis, R. P. 'Tasmania and the Irish Revolution, 1916–22', *Tasmanian Historical Research Association (Papers and Proceedings)*, 21, 2 (1974), pp.69–88.
Donnelly, J.S. 'The Irish Agricultural Depression of 1859–64', *Irish Economic and Social History*, III (1976), pp.33–54.
Draper, A. *The Amritsar Massacre*. London, 1985.

Edwards, R.D. *Patrick Pearse: the Triumph of Failure*. London, 1977.

Fischer, G. '"Negative Integration" and an Australian Road to Modernity: Interpreting the Australian Homefront Experience in World War 1', *Australian Historical Studies*, 26, 104 (April 1995), pp.452–476.

Fitzpatrick, D. *Irish Emigration 1801–1921*. Dundalk, 1984.

Foster, R. *Modern Ireland 1600–1972*. London, 1988.

Frame, A. *Salmond: Southern Jurist*. Wellington, 1995.

Galvin, P. *Irish Songs of Resistance*. London, 1962.

Gardner, W. J. 'The Rise of W. F. Massey, 1891–1912', *Political Science*, 13, 1 (March 1961), pp.3–30.

Gardner, W. J. 'W. F. Massey in Power', *Political Science*, 13, 2 (September 1961), pp.3–30.

Gearon, P. J. *The Truth About Ireland*. Adelaide, 1921.

Gee, M. *Plumb*. Auckland, 1978.

Gilchrist, M. *Daniel Mannix: Priest and Patriot*. Melbourne, 1982.

Gleeson, J. *Bloody Sunday*. London, 1962.

Gustafson, B. G. *From the Cradle to the Grave: a Biography of Michael Joseph Savage*. Auckland, 1986.

Gustafson, B. G. *Labour's Path to Political Independence*. Auckland, 1980.

Hill, R. *The Iron Hand in the Velvet Glove: the Modernisation of Policing in New Zealand 1886–1917*. Palmerston North, 1995.

Jackson, H. 'Churchgoing in Nineteenth-Century New Zealand', *New Zealand Journal of History*, 17, 1 (April 1983), pp.43–59.

Jones, T. *Whitehall Diary: III. Ireland 1919–1925*. London, 1971.

Lawlor, S. *Britain and Ireland 1914–1923*. Dublin, 1983.

Leary, L. P. *Not Entirely Legal*. Christchurch, 1977.

Lee, J. *The Modernisation of Irish Society 1848–1918*. Dublin, 1973.

Livingstone, K.T. *The Emergence of an Australian Catholic Priesthood 1835–1915*. Sydney, 1977.

Lyons, F. S. L. *Ireland Since the Famine*. London, 1982.

Lyons, F. S. L. *John Dillon. A Biography*. London, 1968.

Lyons, F. S. L. and R. A. J. Hawkins (eds). *Ireland under the Union*. Oxford, 1980.

MacDonagh, O. 'The Irish in Victoria, 1851–91: a Demographic Essay', *Historical Studies*, VIII, Dublin, 1971. pp.67–92.

McGill, D. *No Right to Strike: the History of the New Zealand Police Service Organisations*. Wellington, 1992.

McGill, D. *The Lion and the Wolfhound*. Wellington, 1990.

MacGregor, W. C. *Ideals of Empire*. Dunedin, 1908.

Mannes, B. (ed.). *Golden Jubilee: Holy Cross College, Mosgiel, New Zealand 1900–1950*. Dunedin, 1950.

Martin, H. *Ireland in Insurrection*. London, 1921.

May, P. R. *The West Coast Gold Rushes*. Christchurch, 1962.

Mecham, F. *'John O'Brien' and the Boree Log. A biography of Patrick Hartigan, 'John O'Brien'*. Sydney, 1981.

Meredith, V. R. S. *A Long Brief*. Auckland, 1966.

Mokyr, J. *Why Ireland Starved*. London, 1983.

Morgan, K.O. *Consensus and Disunity: the Lloyd George Coalition Government 1918–1922*. Oxford, 1986.

Mountain, J. *The Triumph of British-Israel*. London, 1930.

Moynihan, M. (ed.). *Speeches and Statements by Eamon de Valera 1917–1973*. Dublin, 1980.

North, J. J. *Roman Catholicism 'Roots and Fruits'*. Napier, 1922.

O'Brien, J. *Around the Boree Log*. Sydney, 1944.

O'Connor, P. S. 'Sectarian Conflict in New Zealand,1911–1920', *Political Science*, 19, 1 (July 1967), pp.3–16.

O'Connor, P. S. 'Some Political Preoccupations of Mr Massey, 1918–20,' *Political Science*, 18, 2 (September 1966), pp.16–38.

O'Connor, P. S. 'Storm over the clergy – New Zealand 1917', *Journal of Religious History*, 4, 2 (December 1966), pp.129–48.

O'Farrell, P. *Who's Who in the Irish War of Independence 1916–1921*. Dublin, 1980.

O'Farrell, P. J. 'Emigrant attitudes and behaviour as a source for Irish history', *Historical Studies*, X, Dublin, 1976, pp.109–131.

O'Farrell, P. J. *Harry Holland*. Canberra, 1964.

O'Farrell, P. J. *The Catholic Church and Community: an Australian History*. Sydney, 1985.

O'Farrell, P. J. *The Irish in Australia*. Sydney, 1986.

O'Farrell, P. J. *Vanished Kingdoms: Irish in Australia and New Zealand*. Sydney, 1990.

O'Kelly, J. J. *St Patrick as a World Figure*. Dublin, 1952.

O'Malley, E. *On Another Man's Wound*. Dublin, 1979.

Phelan, R. (ed.). *Irish-Australian Studies: Papers Delivered at the Seventh Irish-Australian Conference*. Sydney, 1994.

Quinlivan, P. and P. Rose. *The Fenians in England 1865–1972*. London, 1982.

Rice, G. *Black November. the 1918 Influenza Epidemic in New Zealand*. Wellington, 1988.

Sharpe, M. 'Anzac Day in New Zealand, 1916 to 1939', *New Zealand Journal of History*, 15, 2 (October 1981), pp.97–114.

Shiel, W. J. and D. Wood (eds). *The Churches, Ireland and the Irish.* Oxford, 1989.

Simmons, E. R. *In Cruce Salus: a History of the Diocese of Auckland 1848–1980.* Auckland, 1982.

Stewart, W. D. *Sir Francis Bell.* Wellington, 1922.

Sweetman, R. M. 'Daniel Mannix and his Biographers', *Australian Studies,* 1 (1988), pp.61–71.

Sweetman, R. M. 'New Zealand Catholicism and the Irish Issue, 1914–1922,' in W. J. Sheils and D. Woods (eds), *The Churches, Ireland and the Irish.* Oxford, 1989, pp.375–84.

Sweetman, R. M. 'Patrick Joseph O'Regan: A Life of Advocacy', *Turnbull Library Record,* 21 (2), October 1988, pp.93–97.

Taylor, R. *Assassination.* London, 1961.

Tod, F. *Pubs Galore: a History of Dunedin Hotels 1848–1984.* Dunedin, 1984.

Trembath, K. A. *Ad Augusta: A Centennial History of Auckland Grammar School 1869–1969.* Auckland, 1969.

Vaughan, W. E. *Landlords and Tenants in Ireland 1848–1904.* Dundalk, 1984.

Wood, G. A. and P. S. O'Connor (eds). *W. P. Morrell: a Tribute.* Dunedin, 1973.

Younger, C. *Ireland's Civil War.* London, 1968.

(e) Theses

Cadogan, B. F. 'Lace Curtain Catholics: the Catholic Bourgeoisie of the Diocese of Dunedin, 1900–1920', BA research essay, University of Otago, 1984.

Davis, R. P. 'The Irish-Catholic Question and New Zealand Society 1868–1922', PhD, University of Otago, 1968.

Laracy, H. 'The life and context of Bishop Patrick Moran', MA, Victoria University of Wellington, 1964.

Moores, H. M. 'The Rise of the Protestant Political Association: Sectarianism in New Zealand during World War One', MA, University of Auckland, 1966.

Satchell, M. 'Pulpit Politics: the Protestant Political Association in Dunedin from 1917 to 1922', BA research essay, University of Otago, 1983.

Sweetman, R. M. 'New Zealand Catholicism, War, Politics and the Irish Issue, 1912–1922'. PhD, University of Cambridge, 1991.

Index